The Making of the Tunisian Revolution

For Tunisian youth, the architects of the Revolution of Freedom and Dignity; for the men and women, young and old, who stood up against injustices when very few dared to do so; for those who fought, disappeared, or died in the process and for those who were exiled, imprisoned, and tortured, and had to live with the consequences; for those whom we remember and, more so, for those victims of authoritarianism whom we have forgotten and continue to forget; and for those new victims we no longer remember in this pressing transitional period of Tunisia's history: the martyrs, the survivors, and the injured!

The Making of the Tunisian Revolution

Contexts, Architects, Prospects

Edited by Nouri Gana

EDINBURGH
University Press

Edinburgh University Press Ltd
22 George Square, Edinburgh EH8 9LF
www.euppublishing.com

Typeset in 11 on 13 Baskerville by
Servis Filmsetting Ltd, Stockport, Cheshire
and printed and bound in the United States of America

A CIP record for this book is available from the British Library

ISBN 978 0 7486 9103 6 (hardback)
ISBN 978 0 7486 9104 3 (paperback)
ISBN 978 0 7486 9105 0 (webready PDF)
ISBN 978 0 7486 9106 7 (epub)

Published with the support of the Edinburgh University Scholarly
Publishing Initiatives Fund.

Contents

Part 3. Prospects: The Postrevolutionary Moment

Acknowledgments

The Making of the Tunisian Revolution: Contexts, Architects, Prospects grew out of a one-day conference, "Mapping and Remapping the Tunisian Revolution," held on Friday, May 20, 2011 at the University of California, Los Angeles. The conference would simply have been impossible without the financial and organizational support of the Center for Near Eastern Studies (CNES); I am particularly indebted to the generosity, enthusiasm, and encouragement of Susan Slyomovics, the director of CNES at the time, and to the patience and diligence of Johanna Romero, the program director, as well as to the help of Mona Ramezani, CNES administrator. I also thank Efrain Kristal, the chair of Comparative Literature, and William Schniedewind, the chair of Near Eastern Languages and Cultures, for sponsoring the conference. I am grateful to the Political Theory Workshop for its financial support and to my colleague Kirstie McClure with whom I have continually had fruitful conversations about the revolution in Tunisia and elsewhere. Ra'anan Boustan, the director of the Center for the Study of Religion at the time, and David N. Myers, the chair of the Department of History, have sponsored this conference from the beginning and for that I am thankful to both of them.

The Making of the Tunisian Revolution presents twelve original chapters on the most important topics relating to the Revolution of Freedom and Dignity. Particular thanks are due to the authors for graciously writing, revising, and then editing their chapters. Above all, I am grateful for their commitment to this project and their willingness to comment on each other's work in progress. Without their dedication, generosity, and collaborative engagement, this book would simply have been impossible. I owe special thanks to Amy Kallander who read and commented on several chapters. Special thanks also go to James Gelvin who read the introduction carefully and offered very helpful feedback. At Edinburgh University Press, I am grateful to Thom A. Brooks and especially Nicola Ramsey for their belief in the importance and urgency of this project. Many thanks also to all the EUP staff with whom I have been in touch: Michelle Houston, Jenny Peebles, Rebecca Mackenzie, and Eddie Clark. I am immensely thankful to the anonymous reviewers for their insightful critique of the manuscript.

Apart from the twelve contributors to this book, I have also been in conversation about the initial conference and the book project with numerous friends, scholars, colleagues and professionals, including Christopher Alexander, Arjun Appadurai, Alexis Arieff, Talal Asad, Rym Ayadi, Karim Azaiz, Etienne Balibar, Mohamad Bamyeh, Asef Bayat, Seyla Benhabib, Fethi Benslama, Imed Bouslama, Mounira M. Charrad, Juan Cole, Arif Dirlik, John Entelis, Steffen Erdle, Oguzhan Goksel, William Granara, Michael Hardt, Mansar Hedhili, Clement M. Henry, Béatrice Hibou, Rich Jankowsky, Hédi A. Jaouad, Noureddine Jebnoun, Nabiha Jerad, Ronald A. Judy, Muqtedar Khan, Stephen Juan King, Adnan Mansar, Alexander Martin, Moncef Marzouki, Susan Marie Ossman, Stefania Pandolfo, Larbi Sadiki, Sonia Shiri, Irene R. Siegel, Kenneth Surin, Mahmoud Tarchounaa, Mark Tessler, Susan Waltz, Sabra Webber, Rafika Zahrouni, Mohamed Zayani, and Malika Zghel.

Selected Abbreviations

AFL-CIO	American Federation of Labor and Congress of Industrial Organizations
AKP	Adalet ve Kalkınma Partisi (Justice and Development Party)
ANC	Assemblée Nationale Constituante (National Constituent Assembly)
AT	Afek Tounes (Tunisian Aspirations)
ATFD	Association Tunisienne des Femmes Démocrates (Tunisian Association of Democratic Women)
ATI	Agence Tunisienne d'Internet (Tunisian Internet Agency)
BOO	Build-Own and Operate
CAS	Country Assistance Strategy
CAWTAR	Center for Arab Women Training and Research
CEDAW	Convention to Eliminate All Forms of Discrimination Against Women
CNLT	Conseil National pour les Libertés en Tunisie (National Council for Liberties in Tunisia)
CPG	Compagnie des Phosphates de Gafsa (Gafsa Phosphate Company)
CPR	Congrès pour la République (Congress for the Republic)
CSP	Code du statut personnel (Personal Status Code)
Ennahda	Mouvement Ennahda (Ennahda Movement, or Renaissance Party)
ERTT	Établissement de la Radiodiffusion-Télévision Tunisienne (Tunisian Radio and Television)
Ettakatol	Forum Démocratique pour le Travail et les Libertés (Democratic Forum for Labour and Liberties)
EU	European Union
FDI	Foreign Direct Investment
FDTL	Forum Démocratique pour le Travail et les Libertés (Democratic Forum for Labor and Liberties)
FIS	Front Islamique du Salut (Islamic Salvation Front)
FLN	Front de Libération Nationale (National Liberation Front)
FNS	Fonds National de Solidarité (National Solidarity Fund)
GDP	Gross Domestic Product

GNP	Gross National Product
IBRD	International Bank for Reconstruction and Development
ICFTU	International Confederation of Free Trade Unions
IFC	International Finance Corporation
IFIs	International Financial Institutions
IMF	International Monetary Fund
INRIC	Instance Nationale pour la Réforme de l'Information et de la Communication (Higher Authority for Information and Communication Reform)
ISIE	Instance Supérieure Indépendante pour les Élections (Independent High Electoral Commission)
LPR	Ligue de Protection de la Révolution (League for the Protection of the Revolution)
LTDH	Ligue Tunisienne de Droits de l'Homme (Tunisian Human Rights League)
MDS	Mouvement des Démocrates Socialistes (Democratic and Social Movement)
MENA	Middle East and North Africa
MPD	Mouvement des Patriotes Démocrates (Movement of Patriotic Democrats)
MTI	Mouvement de la Tendance Islamique (Islamic Tendency Movement)
NATO	North Atlantic Treaty Organization
NDI	National Democratic Institute
NGO	Non-Governmental Organization
PDM	Pole Démocratique Moderniste (Modernist Democratic Pole)
PDP	Parti Démocrate Progressiste (Progressive Democratic Party)
PJD	Parti de la Justice et du Développement (Party of Justice and Development)
POCT	Parti des Ouvriers Communistes Tunisiens (Tunisian Communist Workers Party)
PR	Parti Républicain (Republican Party)
PSC	Personal Status Code
PSD	Parti Socialiste Destourien (Socialist Destourien Party)
PTT	Parti du Travail Tunisien (Tunisian Workers Party)
RCD	Rassemblement Constitutionnel Démocratique (Constitutional Democratic Rally)
SATPEC	Société Anonyme Tunisienne de Production et d'Expansion Cinématographique (Tunisian Production and Cinematographic Expansion Company)
SOE	State-Owned Enterprise

TAP	Tunis Afrique Presse (Tunisian news agency)
TIFA	Trade and Investment Framework Agreement
UGTT	Union Générale Tunisienne du Travail (Tunisian General Labor Union)
UNFT	Union Nationale des Femmes de Tunisie (National Union of Tunisian Women)
UNTT	Union National des Travailleurs Tunisiens (National Union of Tunisian Workers)
UPM	Union pour la Méditerranée or Euromed (Union for the Mediterranean)
US AFRICOM	US Africa Command
UTICA	Union Tunisienne de l'Industrie, du Commerce et de l'Artisanat (Tunisian Federation of Industry, Commerce, and Handicrafts)
WB	World Bank
WFP	World Food Programme

Introduction: Collaborative Revolutionism

Nouri Gana

> The eighteenth century is known as the century of the French and American revolutions, the twentieth century as the century of the Russian and Chinese revolutions, but the twenty-first century will be known by historians as the century of the Arab revolutions.
>
> Moncef Marzouki[1]

The Tunisian revolution took the world by surprise. Never before in the history of the modern Arab world had a grassroots revolt toppled an entrenched dictator of Zine El Abidine Ben Ali's caliber and longevity without recourse to any established ideology, organized social movement and political party, or foreign intervention, which until recently continued to be bandied about as the only midwife to real democracy in the Arab world. Never before had the will of the Tunisian people, for so long expropriated or trodden upon and denigrated, lived up to its latent potential of courting the impossible and led the way to revolutionary change not only in Tunisia but also across the entire region and beyond. Not that Tunisia was not meant to happen[2]—any more than was Egypt, Libya, Yemen or Syria—but much of what might have made it happen remained either invisible or inscrutable, not to say, in the end, negligible.[3] *The Making of the Tunisian Revolution: Contexts, Architects, Prospects* seeks to unmask and clarify what used to be invisible (that is, the roots of discontent) or inscrutable and therefore negligible (that is, the genealogies of dissent), as well as to develop a holistic and integrative analytical approach to the Tunisian revolution from a number of diverse but cohesive angles of inquiry.

The undeniable geotemporal differentials between living through an event and reconstructing it retrospectively as a possible object of knowledge are oftentimes complicated by the politics of remembering/amnesia, ideological constraints/concerns, and methodological limitations. The Tunisian revolution has not infrequently been approached through flower (Jasmine) and bird (Black Swan, Butterfly) metaphors as well as through the cognate technologies of social media (Twitter, Facebook, BlackBerry) and satellite TV (Al-Jazeera). More recently, and following the resurgence of Islamic parties in Tunisian and Egyptian elections, the obsolete orientalist lenses of political Islam have been put to popular use once again after decades of apprehensive scrutiny. While cognizant of the importance of each of these approaches, *The Making of the Tunisian*

Revolution steers clear of any unidirectional or omnidirectional methods of study, and approaches instead the Tunisian revolution from a multidirectional and multidimensional perspective.

There is no master narrative of the Tunisian revolution and certainly no theory of its origins that might explain adequately, let alone justifiably, what happened between December 17, 2010 and January 14, 2011. The sequence of events that immediately preceded Ben Ali's ouster would make little sense if presented separately from the longer histories of discontent and contentious politics across spaces, places, and generations, as well as political affiliations. Mixing political, historical, and economic analyses and approaches as well as interviews and field research, *The Making of the Tunisian Revolution* advances a cohesive and sustained set of arguments on the local, regional, and transnational dynamics as well as the long-term and short-term factors that combined to set in motion the Tunisian revolution and the Arab uprisings writ large. Above all, the book maps the intertwined genealogies of cultural and political dissent that contributed to the mobilization of protesters and to the continuation of protests between December 17 and January 14 and beyond. The final section of the book assesses the transitional period thus far, sheds light on the major challenges encountered by the successive interim governments, and offers insights into the prospects for consolidating democracy in postrevolutionary Tunisia.

The Tunisian revolution emerges as a complex chain of dispersed endeavors and micronarratives whose chapters have been (and are being) written in concert between different peoples in different times and locations. I call these discrete, fragmented, geotemporal, and transgenerational efforts collaborative revolutionism. There are, of course, local and transnational collaborative efforts that can be duly noted but, oftentimes, collaborative work emerges as an effect of endogenous, private, and non-organized activities—really, as the cumulative byproduct of "the collective actions of non-collective actors," to borrow Asef Bayat's felicitous expression.[4] Whether coordinated or uncoordinated, whether local or transnational, what I call collaborative revolutionism hinges significantly on the existence of everyday revolutionaries (without a revolution) chipping away at the system of authoritarian power with a variety of individuated, stylized, and transversal actions and tactics that may or may not eventually become part of an overarching strategy of subversion.[5] Fortunately, in the Tunisian case, they have become part of the popular upsurge that rallied across the country to shout the irrevocable verdict: "Ben Ali, *Dégage*/Ben Ali, Out." Rather than relying solely on a top-down and crisis-oriented approach to the breakdown of authoritarianism in Tunisia—and without falling back on the grand narrative of democracy[6]—collaborative revolutionism foregrounds the bottom-up, grassroots, and non-collective forms of political agency that have combined (with labor movements as well as other socioeconomic and political variables) to lead the way to insurrection and revolt.

While *The Making of the Tunisian Revolution* is divided into three separate parts (the first dealing with the roots of discontent, the second with the genealogies of dissent, and the third with democracy's prospects), the logic of the argument evolves organically in a continuum of interlinked and complementary reflections that shed light on the central paradox of the Tunisian revolution: the fact that it was simultaneously impossible and inevitable. In what follows, I will explain this paradox of impossibility and inevitability. In the process, I will map the contours of the book and expand the argument I charted sketchily above. I focus mainly on the genealogies of dissent and comment on the roots of discontent in an interactive and dialectical fashion as the argument unfolds. It might not be too contentious to say at the outset that part of the reason why the Tunisian revolution might have seemed impossible (at least, from a pre-revolutionary perspective) is the longevity of authoritarianism (especially insofar as it continues to be produced and reproduced by the hegemony of imperial designs in the entire region). Yet, as will become clear in due course, the longevity of authoritarianism was matched, and eventually exceeded, by the longevity of dissent, which made the revolt inevitable.

Dictatorial and imperial longevity

Before the revolt, Tunisia was lauded by the international community, the Western media, the World Bank (WB), and the International Monetary Fund (IMF) as a model of economic growth and political stability. Under the mask of stability and prosperity, however, there lurked the foreboding reality of mass youth unemployment, deepening poverty, unbridled corruption, rising fuel and energy prices, and, above all, authoritarian longevity. The complicity of the European Union, France, and the United States with the successive regimes of Bourguiba and Ben Ali bordered on cruel cynicism. In the very same period when the United States had no fewer than ten successive presidents, the Republic of Tunisia was headed by two presidents only. From 1956 to 1987, Tunisia was ruled by Habib Bourguiba, a self-professed nationalist and francophone secularist who sought to hitch the wagon of the young nation to the train of European modernity both socially and economically. While his era was marked by laudable developments in the areas of healthcare, education, and women's rights, unmatched by any other Arab nation, his reign was unbendingly autocratic. He established a strict one-party rule and gradually but steadily tightened his grip on power, becoming president for life in 1975, a position he held until he was suddenly deposed by his then prime minister Ben Ali in 1987. Rounding up a team of doctors who attested to Bourguiba's mental and physical inability to perform his duties, Ben Ali snatched power in what amounted to nothing less than a palace coup (backed up by a constitutional maneuver of Article 57, according to which the president of the Chamber of Deputies, not the prime minister, assumes the presidential role in case of vacancy at the top), thus illustrating the tenacity rather than the collapse of authoritarianism. Yet, by constantly ennobling his seizure of power as a watershed moment in Tunisia's postcolonial history (calling it *al-taḥawul al-mubārik* or "the blessed change"), Ben Ali manufactured its legitimacy and the legitimacy of his entire rule afterwards.

Since November 7, 1987, Ben Ali had amended and reamended the constitution in such a way as to remain in power, and this is partly why his twenty-three-year-rule over Tunisia was also referred to by some commentators as Bourguibism without Bourguiba or Benalisme *tout court.*[7] Although Ben Ali nullified the title of presidency for life and limited the position of the president to two five-year terms in the major constitutional reforms he initiated in 1988, he ironically sought and won the right to run for a third term in 1998 and then a fourth term following the widely successful 2002 referendum which abolished term limits altogether and raised the age limit to seventy-five (all of which amounted to nothing less than a veiled bid for presidency for life). Not only did Ben Ali outstay his constitutional welcome, but he also trampled under his feet the very constitutional reforms he had spearheaded and trumpeted again and again upon his assumption of power in 1989. It became clear that while Ben Ali had abolished the title of presidency for life, he would stop at nothing to stay in power: he sought and won a fifth term in 2009 and was already preparing the ground to run for a sixth term in 2014. In short, his authoritarian impulse seemed unlikely to be overturned at a time when his regime had perfected its coup-proof techniques.[8] As US Ambassador to Tunisia William J. Hudson reported in a cable that dated back to September 1, 2006, "One of the standard jokes about President Zine El Abidine Ben Ali (usually delivered only half in jest) is that he has three goals for his presidency: to stay in power; to stay in power; and to stay in power."[9]

The US embassy may have tried but failed to press Ben Ali to democratize; the 2006 cable suggests they were already considering other options, namely a suitable successor for the ailing and aging dictator. A more recent cable that dates back to July 17, 2009 shows, however, the extent to which the United States was indeed complicit with Ben Ali's dictatorial longevity. Time and again, the US Ambassador to Tunis, Robert F. Godec, cautions that "we cannot write off Tunisia. We have too much at stake. We have an interest in preventing al-Qaeda in the Islamic Maghreb and other extremist groups from establishing a foothold here." Ben Ali consistently told the United States exactly what the United States wanted to hear: that he would cooperate "without reservation" in the global effort to combat terrorism.[10] It was understood that for Ben Ali such a commitment implied that he would be let off the hook for human rights abuses, and he did not shy away from pointing that out to Assistant Secretary for Near Eastern Affairs David Welch. It was understood that for the United States the travesties of democracy were a price willingly (or reluctantly) paid in exchange for Ben Ali's aforementioned commitment even though the threat of al-Qaeda in the Maghreb and particularly in Tunisia had remained, and still remains, more of an exaggeration rather than an actual reality. In the wake of 9/11, with its police forces quadrupled since the presidency of Habib Bourguiba (1957–87), Tunisia became an Orwellian police state, a gigantic surveillance camp, and Ben Ali found in the War on Terror and the so-called Islamist (aka terrorist) threat a convenient ruse to recast allegations of human rights violations, along with various abuses of democracy and freedom of speech, as part of the global effort to fight terrorism.

Ben Ali's presidency for life might, as did that of his predecessor, have served well American strategic security purposes, but it weighed heavily on everyday Tunisians. In Chapter 2, Kenneth Perkins examines the ways in which Tunisian political elites have played upon the concept of Islam as a vehicle for creating fears that a polity that highly valued Islamic principles and practices would inevitably compromise many of the practical advantages of modernity and westernization that had become hallmarks of the country's development. Perkins focuses on the years from the end of World War II through the presidencies of Bourguiba and Ben Ali and contends that the use and abuse of Islam by these rulers "creat[ed] in the process a reservoir of ill will that guaranteed future problems." To say that Ben Ali's regime exaggerated the Islamist threat and exploited the fault lines of the global war on terror to entrench him in power is to be accused of the crassest understatement. Much of the credibility of Ben Ali's autocratic reign derived also from the swiftness and consistency with which it intimidated and punished its detractors, critics and opponents as well as from the politics of fear which it used to engineer the consent of the population.[11] Basically, the United States focused on its own geostrategic priorities and did not pressure Ben Ali to democratize.

When the United States Congress gave a standing ovation to the Tunisian revolution on January 25, 2011, it did so not so much as a gesture for a change of policy as an attempt to ride on the revolutionary wave it had deliberately missed before. In Chapter 3, Lotfi Ben Rejeb takes the supportive ovation and the accompanying declarations with a pinch of salt. Historically speaking, according to Ben Rejeb, the United States, as well as the other Western powers that had a stake in the region, did precious little to bring that democratic transformation about, although they consistently paid lip service to advancing democratic values. Ben Rejeb delves into the details of US–Tunisian relations since Tunisia's independence and how they evolved in the following decades into what has been routinely framed by both sides as a friendship, sometimes even as an alliance, while in actual fact amounting to nothing more than a working relationship that basically guaranteed US support for Tunisian governments, regardless of their systemic violations of human rights and democratic values. Not infrequently, Ben Rejeb concludes, Tunisia was on the expendable end of the relationship when a third party came into the picture. This was the case in October 1985 when Israel bombed the headquarters of the Palestinian Liberation Organization in Tunisia, killing sixty-eight Palestinians and Tunisians with impunity (that is, with Ronald Reagan vowing to veto any denunciatory resolution by the United Nations Security Council).

While Tunisia would not be as expendable to France as it had been to the US, France has, like the US, consistently supported the dictatorial regimes of Bourguiba and Ben Ali for strategic security as well as neocolonial and economic reasons. France has been one of Tunisia's most important trading partners and international advocates, a position that was consolidated with the formation of the European Union and the emergence of Euro-Med partnerships and free trade agreements. In Chapter 4, Amy Aisen Kallander argues that support for the Tunisian regime has become increasingly aligned with questions of national security and immigration. Beginning with Habib Bourguiba, Kallander locates the roots of the Franco-Tunisian alliance in the French desire to maintain an international profile and articulate what Charles de Gaulle called a specifically "Arab policy" that would contrast with Anglo-American diplomacy. Tunisia having received various forms of aid since independence, Bourguiba's relations with France improved during the 1970s and 1980s as he undertook a program of economic liberalization.

Appreciated for continuing economic liberalization and for his commitment to policing religious mobilization, Ben Ali's era signaled more continuity than rupture. At the same time, French initiatives in focusing the attention of the European Union on the Mediterranean as a region bore fruit in a series of bilateral accords following the 1995 Barcelona summit. Since 2001, Kallander concludes, Ben Ali's vision of political Islam as threatening, and his desire to eliminate activist Islamic currents within Tunisia, corresponded to French security interests of limiting immigration to France in the name of preventing terrorism. No wonder, then, that when Ben Ali was faced with the prospect of his own imminent demise, the French Minister for Foreign Affairs, Michèle Alliot-Marie, continued to cling to his dying regime, with its collapsing and openly despised circle of crony capitalists, and offered "to dispatch French security forces to Tunis to shore up the unpopular regime."[12]

On January 14, 2011, however, massive popular protests forced Ben Ali to flee to Saudi Arabia. At the same time that Ben Ali was in the air looking for asylum, his prime minister, Mohamed Ghannouchi, declared himself acting president according to Article 56 of the constitution, which stipulates that a sitting president may delegate his powers to his prime minister in the event of temporary disability. But because Ben Ali had never actually delegated his powers to Ghannouchi before his unceremonious exit, the Constitutional Assembly met on the following day, January 15, and adopted Article 57 of the constitution, which stipulates that the president of the Chamber of Deputies becomes president should there be a vacancy in the office of the president. Fouad Mebazaa then served as acting president and ordered Mohamed Ghannouchi and then Béji Caïd Essebsi to form successive interim governments.

There is no need here to go into more detail about a constitution that has now been nullified; it is depressingly ironic to note, though, that a country that had only two presidents in an entire fifty-five-year period should switch from one president to another in a matter of hours and from one prime minister to another in a month and a half. If this wasn't unprecedented enough, following the National Constituent Assembly (Assemblée Nationale Constituante, ANC) elections on October 23, 2011, Tunisia would have its third president and fourth prime minister. In the wake of the assassination of radical leftist and outspoken Popular Front opposition leader Chokri Belaïd on February 6, 2013, a new prime minister was appointed and yet another government was formed.

The question I would henceforth like to ask and then try to answer, however schematically, is as follows: If Tunisians were this impatient with the interim government of Mohamed Ghannouchi and then with that of Béji Caïd Essebsi, not to mention the current impatience with the Troika, how come they had waited for fifty-five years before they rose up against the successive authoritarian regimes of Bourguiba and Ben Ali? Was this impatience impossible at the time or was it rather subdued and inscrutable? At any rate, where does the popular uprising that forced Ben Ali to flee the country on January 14 come from? I respond to this question in a dialectical way, but rather than proceeding by the logic of sublation or elimination toward a single answer, I strive to create the effect of a cumulative, transactive, and multidirectional approach to an answer.

The longevity of dissent

The Tunisian revolution was called by several different names, each of which gained varying degrees of authority but failed to achieve full legitimacy. What happened in Tunisia remained—and still remains—beyond the many labels that were wheeled out to comprehend it, including those that approached the Tunisian revolution as the harbinger of new forms of revolutionism. The list of names expanded from such contiguous descriptors as the "Internet Revolution," the "Facebook Revolution," and the "Twitter Revolution" to a host of other monikers: the "Wikileaks Revolution," the "Al-Jazeera Revolution," the "Jasmine Revolution," the "Dignity Revolution," the "Sidi Bouzid Revolution," and the "Bouazizi Revolution." Obviously, there is no gainsaying the fact that social media and Al-Jazeera played a pivotal role in relaying reports of dispersed protests and agitation in the southwestern regions of Tunisia at a time when the state/regime media was deliberately oblivious to what was going on in Sidi Bouzid, Tala, and Kasserine. Moreover, the crucial importance of the combined efforts of social media and Al-Jazeera in finding and circulating the news lies in channeling—or actually *channelizing*—them toward a single affective disposition to civil disobedience. The emergent sense of discontent, in other words, has become—thanks to the mediating role of Facebook, Twitter and Al-Jazeera—nothing less than an incitement to revolt. What is more important by far is that once the sociopolitical grievances that sparked the revolt in Sidi Bouzid started to come to light and travel to neighboring cities and from there to major cities like Sfax and Sousse before reaching Tunis by the end of December 2010, the role of social media, cellphone technology, and Al-Jazeera became key to sustaining the intensity and continuation of the protests which led to Ben Ali's deposition from power. In the weeks that followed, Facebook became de facto the gathering space par excellence for *mobilizing* Tunisians and for organizing and coordinating sit-in protests in the Qasbah Government Square and elsewhere across the country.

In Chapter 6, Tarek Kahlaoui offers a firsthand witness account of the history of cyberactivism in Tunisia from the days of the syndicalist and student movements of the 1980s and 1990s to the 2000s and the emergence of a transnational and rhizomatic network of cyberactivists agitating (at times in concert and at others in isolation from each other) against internet censorship. Being involved himself in many of these microcontestatory efforts over the years, Kahlaoui disputes the allegations, popularized most notoriously by Tariq Ramadan, that cyberactivists received training from western NGOs and US government institutions.[13] Kahlaoui laudably inquires instead about the yet to be revealed history of internet censorship in Tunisia, namely about the "implication of Western governmental consultants and companies in building its structure."[14] Indisputably, these are crucial questions worthy of more inquisitive, archival research, especially at a time when field bloggers have received little, if any, attention while tech-elite pajama bloggers have achieved worldwide fame, including nods from *Time*'s annual list of the 100 most influential people in the world.

The Facebook community has become markedly divided and polarized, not to say stigmatized, in postrevolutionary Tunisia. While it continues to be the virtual gathering place of a fully fledged oppositional force to the status quo, exemplary at times in the ways its different members have tirelessly pointed out and critiqued the actions of the successive postrevolutionary interim governments and the opposition parties alike, many Tunisians feel increasingly dismayed and disenchanted with Facebook and social media, especially in view of the amount of false information, foul language, and baseless allegations these new media now circulate. The same can be said about Al-Jazeera, which has now become very much associated in the imagination of a large segment of Tunisians (especially from the opposition parties) with the role Qatar is unequivocally playing in Tunisia—and elsewhere in the Arab world—as a proxy for American hegemony. Be that as it may, the fact of the matter is that social media and Al-Jazeera, however important a role they might have played in the Tunisian revolution, could by no means have replaced the actors on the ground, the actual demonstrators and protesters who stormed the streets and braved live ammunition to rid themselves, and all Tunisians of Ben Ali and his Mafia ring. After all, both Facebook and Al-Jazeera had been around for quite some time by 2010 and must have had ample opportunities to start a revolution in Tunisia if they were indeed capable of doing so by themselves.

Other factors came into play, most notably Julian Assange's more recent whistle-blowing website, Wikileaks, which publicized diplomatic cables that exposed the opulent lifestyle and widespread web of corruption of Ben Ali and his wife and their extended family (the Trabelsis). For instance, one cable which dates back to November 17, 2007 chronicles Ben Ali's decision to revoke Suha Arafat's Tunisian citizenship after her fallout with his wife, Leila Trabelsi. The cable includes Suha Arafat's perspective on her ouster from Tunisia and details the criminal and illegal means whereby all her properties in the country had been confiscated by falsifying documents transferring ownership. The cable concludes with Mrs. Arafat pointing out to the US Ambassador, Robert F. Godec, that while Ben Ali was completely absorbed in battling cancer, his wife and her family were stealing everything of value in the country with impunity.

Notwithstanding the crucial importance of (the likes of) this leaked cable in stirring the outrage of Tunisians and their contempt for the Trabelsis, Wikileaks (or Tunileaks,[15] as the local Arabic version was called) can be said to have added in the end no more than mere details to what every Tunisian already knew about the president and his wife and the Trabelsi Mafiosi clans, in particular, who were the worst offenders. It becomes clear, then, that neither social media and Al-Jazeera nor Wikileaks could fully account for the Tunisian people's grassroots revolt. What else could have started this popular uprising? In Chapter 7, Rikke Hostrup Haugbølle pursues a more historically mined approach to the role of what she calls the "media ensemble" in the Tunisian revolution. In her view, the old media reforms (radio and television especially, as well as newspapers) under Bourguiba and Ben Ali, along with the advent of the new media, have cumulatively resulted in the improvement of the critical thinking skills of Tunisians, skills which they in turn redirected toward insurrectionary use. Haugbølle elaborates a counterintuitive approach to the role of state media, not to redeem it but to read it otherwise and attentively. In an attempt to upgrade authoritarianism, the regimes of both Bourguiba and Ben Ali, she concludes, carried media reforms to their own peril. The importance of these reforms in fostering debate and public literacy cannot be underestimated, especially given that critical thinking is capable of swerving seamlessly from the social to the political, which is what happened as soon as the wall of fear finally fell apart in the wake of Mohamed Bouazizi's self-immolation on December 17, 2010.

Little wonder that most retrospective narratives of the events that led to Ben Ali's deposition have stressed the catalyzing role of Bouazizi's self-immolation. There are conflicting reports of Bouazizi's story, but the majority of them agree now that he was a fruit and vegetable street vendor who had to drop out from high school to be able to provide for his family and siblings. He was constantly harassed by the local police because he did not have a vendor's permit and, allegedly, because he did not make enough money to offer bribes to the officers. On December 16, 2010, the police confiscated his cart and electronic scale, and, what is worse, they insulted and mistreated him. The following day, Bouazizi went to the governor's office to complain, but when the latter refused to see or listen to him, he bought a can of gasoline, doused himself in front of the municipal headquarters of Sidi Bouzid, and set himself ablaze. Initially, local activists and syndicalists in Sidi Bouzid deliberately promoted an adapted version of his story as an unemployed university graduate in an attempt to, first, capitalize on and mobilize a new disgruntled majority of unemployed university graduates (accounting for 250,000 of the 750,000 job-seekers in the country) and, second, to counter the disparaging campaign of pro-Ben Ali pundits who left no stone unturned to psychologize, privatize, and discredit the sociopolitical grievances at the origin of Bouazizi's act.[16] Besides, this tactical lie (in a stockpile of lies circulated during the revolution) proved of crucial importance for the early protesters as it helped them win the sympathy and solidarity both of Tunisians and simultaneously of the international public opinion at large.

In the wake of Bouazizi's self-immolation, protesters started gathering regularly in downtown Sidi Bouzid and in front of local government buildings. Family and tribal ties played an instrumental role in exciting the outrage of the dozens of protesters who stormed downtown Sidi Bouzid immediately after the news of the immolation had reached them. What is more, local syndicalists and political opponents had neither forgotten nor forgiven the brutality with which the riot police repressed the June 2010 protests of Régueb and Sidi Bouzid farmers against the abuses of the National Agricultural Bank; they immediately seized on the possibilities opened up by Bouazizi's action in order to resume their subdued protests and widen the protests that ensued. They started by experimenting with their message, switching cleverly from elitist to populist slogans. Note, for instance, that the initial slogans made social demands for "work, freedom, and national dignity" (*shughl, ḥurriya, karāma waṭaniyya*), but remained abstract and therefore incapable of appealing to the popular, let alone populist, imagination. Soon, however, the organizers of the protests discovered that the more concrete and direct the slogans, the better they could capture Tunisians' feelings and grievances. Hence, the slogans started to target specific individuals from the ruling family, especially the Trabelsis, symbols of corruption and cronyism. They called upon the "scruffy Trabelsis [to] spare some bread for the poor" (*yā Trabelsī yā ḥaqīr, khellī il-khubza lilfaqīr*) before they took on a more openly political bent and called for Ben Ali to be ousted altogether: "we can live on bread and water, but no more Ben Ali" (*khubz wa mā' wa Ben Ali lā*). The latter slogan echoes similar slogans used in the 1970s and the bread riots of 1984,[17] which broke out on a national scale in protest against the sudden rise of the price of semolina announced by the government on December 29, 1983. Even though Bourguiba announced on January 6, 1984 that the increase in bread prices would be rescinded, the episode de facto ushered in the agonizing demise of his regime.[18] What is interesting about this slogan is that it straddles both social and political demands even as it purports to move beyond the social need for bread and butter in favor of the political demand for Ben Ali's ouster. In short, the finite rhetorical economy of the slogan conjures up a sense of historical inevitability that far exceeds Ben Ali's ability to change it.

The gradual evolution of the slogans from generic ones about work, liberty, and dignity to more specific ones that not only target specific individuals such as the Trabelsis, but also point toward the way out (that is, the ouster of Ben Ali) has proven a key factor in inciting ordinary people to revolt, for bystanders tend to join protests against a specific individual (such as Leila Trabelsi, Ben Ali's wife, the most flagrant symbol of corruption) rather than protests against abstractions such as neoliberalism, authoritarianism, cronyism, and so on. Henceforth, the intelligibility of the slogans, their accessible content, and their clear target encouraged more and more people to take to the streets. Clearly, these protests testify to one of the exemplary moments in which public space was claimed back from the panoptic presence of Ben Ali's state apparatus, not to mention his foreboding Big Brother portraits, which convey his penetrating and conditioning influence. After decades in which Ben Ali used public spaces from mosques to soccer stadiums as instruments of propaganda, or as spaces for Tunisians to sublimate and channel the anger he excited in them,[19] Bouazizi's immolation in the most public of public spaces dramatizes the extent to which Tunisians lacked a forum and simultaneously what it takes to open one up.

When the news of Bouazizi's self-immolation and ensuing protests in Sidi Bouzid were downloaded on Facebook and YouTube by field bloggers, they went viral; they were picked up by globally dispersed bloggers and Facebookers and then by Al-Jazeera, and the wave of protests quickly reached the major cities in Tunisia and eventually hit the capital, Tunis. While Bouazizi could hardly have anticipated the full outcome of his action, he must have, at least momentarily, entertained the idea even as a remotely possible effect of his horrifying act. What Bouazizi committed was not so much a suicidal act as a suicidal protest: the difference cannot be overstressed since the former pertains to despair and resignation and the latter to defiance and hope—defiance of the police and government officers who treated him with utter contempt, and hope for a better future, free from injustice. Bouazizi's public act opened up new—even while it reclaimed old—spaces. On the soccer pitch, in the workplace, in educational venues, markets, places of worship, coffee houses, and in the streets, Tunisians from various walks of life found creative strategies to publicly draw upon their own expressive culture to recover their voices and their spaces in a creative combination of methods.

While both symbolic and tragic, even Bouazizi's self-immolation could not by itself have triggered a revolution of this magnitude which not only sent shockwaves throughout Tunisia, but also swiftly spread to other countries in the Arab world and beyond. The fact that the many copycat burnings that followed Bouazizi's in such countries as Algeria, Mauritania, and Morocco have not so far resulted in revolutions in those places makes it less likely that Bouazizi's act per se should be located retrospectively at the very origin of the Tunisian revolution.[20] Besides, Bouazizi's self-immolation could have been thrust into oblivion as was that of another street vendor before him, Abdesslem Trimech, who set himself on fire inside the city hall in Monastir on March 3, 2010, after his fruit cart was confiscated by the police and his demand to meet with the city mayor was rebuffed. This is not to say that Bouazizi's self-immolation was not inspiring and empowering, much less to say it was not an incitement to action, but rather to maintain that the protests that followed his self-immolation must have capitalized on longstanding rebellious instincts that Ben Ali's police state repressed but could not fully eradicate. Otherwise, how could Bouazizi's act have mobilized so many, so quickly?

I am driving here toward a genealogical and polydirectional approach to the Tunisian revolution, one that can take stock of both the long-term and short-term factors of its complex beginnings. The short-term factors would, of course, include such aforementioned immediate triggers as social media and Al-Jazeera as well as Wikileaks and Bouazizi's self-immolation. The long-term factors include not only the neoliberal economic restructuring of Tunisia in the mid-1990s and the culture of corruption it fostered, but also the longstanding US and French foreign policy and the countries' deliberate support for autocratic regimes for the sake of stability. Above all, if the Tunisian nonviolent revolution attests to anything, it is to the longevity of the traditions of political dissent and civil disobedience in decolonial and postcolonial Tunisia despite Ben Ali's transformation (or rather disfiguration) of the country into a gigantic surveillance camp. Perhaps nowhere else is this clearer than in the curious case of the Union Générale Tunisienne du Travail (UGTT), the Tunisian labor union whose leadership has gradually been coopted by the successive regimes of Bourguiba and Ben Ali but whose geographically dispersed militant bases (*qawāʿid*) have always persisted in their struggle for a classless society that guarantees equitable economic development for all Tunisians and not just for the lucky few at the helm of the government and their entourage.

In Chapter 5, Sami Zemni maps the trajectory of the labor movement from the colonial (the UGTT was created in 1946 under the leadership of Farhat

Hached) to the postcolonial period, focusing in particular on its ambivalent relationship with the governments of Bourguiba and Ben Ali, which alternated between alliance and alienation. Zemni emphasizes in particular the role of the local cells in keeping alive the foundational ideals of the UGTT, which have at various times led to internal dissension between the leadership and its dispersed members, especially in the 1980s and 1990s when the repressions of the radical left, Baathists, and trade unionists, and then the Islamists immediately afterward resulted in a number of human rights abuses, including incommunicado detentions, imprisonments without fair trials and, worst of all, torture, intimidation, blackmail, and harassment. The workers joined the Tunisian Human Rights League (Ligue Tunisienne de Droits de l'Homme, LTDH), founded in 1977,[21] in their contestation of the systematic repression of political dissidence, but they in turn came under fire and risked divisiveness and political paralysis, especially after the 1977 strikes of Ksar Hellal textile workers and Gafsa miners, which were followed by a general strike on January 26, 1978 (aka "Black Thursday," since it resulted in hundreds of dead, injured or arrested protesters). All of these strikes were, needless to say, brutally repressed by the riot police, the army, and the Neo-Destour party militias;[22] worse, the hard line adopted by Bourguiba against the UGTT had transformed it into a mere administrative entity with a "puppet" leadership by the time Ben Ali reached power. Zemni concludes, however, that at a time when the regimes of Bourguiba and Ben Ali showed no hesitation whatsoever in exterminating their political opponents or making them disappear, the UGTT "has always—in spite of myriad pressures, procrastinations, and doubts—rallied the cause of the workers movement in the end." True, the leadership almost always acts late, as was the case during the Tunisian revolution when it waited until January 11 to give the green light for its local sections to organize peaceful protests and solidarity actions, but, fortunately, the inaction of the leadership cannot override the fervent zeal and pioneering role of the grass roots. In the 2008 Gafsa uprising, the local militant cells initiated mass strikes before they were joined by numerous sections of society, including workers, the unemployed, civil servants, merchants, craftsmen, students, and other ordinary Tunisians.

The syndicalist and student involvement in the protest that followed December 17, 2010, and which proved crucial to the endurance of the revolution is informed by a long history of activist and political engagement that goes back to the 1970s at a time when leftist groups of various allegiances and lineages (Marxist, Trotskyist, Maoist, and Leninist) popped up like midnight mushrooms on university campuses across the country. In the 1980s, they were joined by Islamist student groups which, while adhering to a different worldview, shared their main discontent with Bourguiba's consolidation of power and clampdown on political dissidence. Student activists and syndicalists remained active during Ben Ali's era and agitated for democratization, human rights and freedom of expression, mostly in sync with the illegal Tunisian Communist Workers Party (Parti des Ouvriers Communistes Tunisiens, POCT). Leftists at times received support from the women's movement even though the latter needed support themselves after their application for official organizational status was refused. Indeed, women activists were denied any type of recognition from Bourguiba (who, ironically, presented himself as the champion of women's rights after the promulgation of the Personal Status Code in 1957). Acting in concert with the UGTT and the LTDH, the women's movement continued to press for recognition, for freedom of expression, and for a public forum which they were partially able to achieve through their club meetings at the Tahar al-Haddad Cultural Center in downtown Tunis and, above all, in their monthly magazine, *Nissa* (*Women*), which appeared in kiosks in April 1985; unfortunately, however, the magazine did not last and published its eighth and final issue in early 1987.[23]

Even while the umbrella organizations of the women's movement from the National Union of Tunisian Women (Union Nationale des Femmes de Tunisie, UNFT) to the Tunisian Association of Democratic Women (Association Tunisienne des Femmes Démocrates, ATFD) were coopted by the regimes of Bourguiba and Ben Ali respectively, they remained active, especially through their collective work with the LTDH to profile and expose human rights abuses, the political police (*al-būlīs al-siyāsī*), and the ring of corruption that prevailed in the country. I would be remiss not to mention here the laudable work at the crossroads of human rights, freedom of expression, and oppositional politics of three notable women, namely Sihem Ben Sedrine, who is both spokesperson for the National Council for Liberties in Tunisia (Conseil national pour les libertés en Tunisie, CNLT) and editor of the online magazine *Kalima* and radio station of the same name; Radhia Nasraoui, a leading human rights activist and the lawyer most in the line of fire; and Naziha Rjiba (aka Om Zied), an outspoken advocate of human rights and liberties and a daring journalist associated intermittently with the Congress for the Republic (Congrès pour la République, CPR). Borhane Bsaies (Ben Ali's mouthpiece, or devil's advocate as Tunisians call him) avowed after the revolution that out of all Ben Ali's detractors the one he dreaded debating the most was Om Zied.[24] These three women activists, along with many others such as Imen Triki of the Freedom and Equity Association, are exemplars of human resilience, intellectual integrity, and political dissidence.[25] They have inspired generations of young activists, journalists, lawyers, public figures, politicians, and justice-seekers who took part in the demonstrations that led to Ben Ali's deposition from power. For them, Bouazizi's self-immolation constitutes not so much the starting point of the Tunisian revolution as the crowning moment of decades of political engagement and collaborative revolutionism.

The question becomes gradually not so much how Bouazizi's suicide protest sparked a popular revolution (which has so far been the most travelled road of inquiry about the Tunisian and Arab revolutions), but how a popular revolution sparked by Bouazizi's suicide protest is indeed the materialization of a cultural and critical capital that has largely been determined by a collective tradition of collaborative revolutionism and dissenting political practices. Note, however, that critique and political dissidence have not always been manifest or explicit even though Bourguiba's and Ben Ali's regimes have always systematically tried to discredit political dissidence through smear campaigns against their critics and political opponents.[26] I am not speaking here only about labor unionists, human rights activists, syndicalists, historical political opponents, or opposition leaders such as Salah Ben Youssef (who was assassinated in 1961 and whose real or imputed supporters were persecuted and tried or removed from political life throughout the 1960s), Ahmed Ben Salah, Rachid Ghannouchi, Hamma al-Hammami, and Moncef Marzouki, among numerous others, who either disappeared or were killed under torture, imprisoned, exiled, or driven to submission, resignation, or silence. Rather, I am speaking about everyday Tunisians, journalists, novelists, playwrights, filmmakers, intellectuals, lawyers, high school teachers as well as university professors. Even soccer players, singers, and other popular figures have at times embraced and passed on the tradition of dissent in the Tunisian public sphere whether through explicit or encoded means and intents.[27]

Cultural dissent and neoliberal discontent

Cultural and artistic acts of dissidence are mostly characterized by their indirectness (if not rhetorical detours or outright abstractness) either because of stylistic choices or because of censorship (including self-censorship). They have protracted and intangible effects that may crystallize only years after the moment of their production on the cusp of watershed events. The tradition of cultural critique dates back at least to the struggle against French colonialism in the 1930s and 1940s and to the formation of the intellectual collective *Jamāʿit taḥta al-sūr* ("Against the wall group"), which brought together a heterogeneous number of intellectuals and helped raise awareness about the colonial condition through regular meetings and debates organized in popular cafés. By the time Bourguiba's Neo-Destour party emerged at the center of the broad-based Tunisian independence movement, several periodicals, newspapers, and magazines had been established and published translations of European fiction as well as the creative output of several early Tunisian novelists from Ali al-Douaji to al-Bashir Khrayyif. Among the most important intellectual figures of this pre-independence period, however, I should at least name Tunisia's foremost national poet, Abul-Qasim al-Shabbi, as well as Tunisia's foremost national playwright, Mahmoud al-Messadi. Both al-Shabbi and al-Messadi wrote about the human will to freedom and to a life worthy of its name. They are known for their ability to transform existential and political paralysis in their works into a basis for elaborating strategies of survival and defiance of French colonialism (euphemistically officiated as "protectorship").

It was not for nothing that the early protesters both in Tunisia and Egypt reiterated al-Shabbi's most compelling and influential couplet from his poem "The Will to Life" (ʾIrādit al-ḥayāt):

> *ʾIdhā al-shaʿbu yawman ʾarāda al-ḥayāt / fa-lā budda ʾan yastajība-l-qadar*
> *Wa-lā budda lil-layli ʾan yanjalī / wa-lā budda lil-qaidi ʾan yankasir*[28]
>
> Once a people assert their will to life / Destiny must answer their call
> Their darkness will have to vanish / and their chains to break and fall

The resurrection of al-Shabbi's memorable lines—and their reverberations across the Arab world during and after the Tunisian revolution—should not be understood as merely a form of facile sloganeering but as an evocation of the inextricable relationship between fighting both foreign and indigenous forms of oppression. The timelessness of al-Shabbi's couplet is matched only by its timeliness: not only has it inspired the one slogan—*Al-Shaʿb yurīd ʾisqāt al-niẓām* (The people want to topple the regime)—that would animate the entire Arab uprisings from Tunisia to Syria through Egypt, Libya, Bahrain, and Yemen, but it has also given rise to other forms of expression such as speeches, chants, and graffiti writing. If Jacques Rancière is right in his claim that poetry is always already political, always already implicated in a certain distribution or "partition of the sensible"—that is, in the very formation of "the cluster of perceptions and practices that shape this common world"[29]—it should be no exaggeration to suggest, then, that al-Shabbi's poetry has contributed to the emergence of new modes of intelligibility, new modes of creativity, and new modes of collaborative revolutionism—in short, a redistribution of the sensible through democratic and democratizing practices.

I believe there is a repository of critical dissent that has been sustained and consolidated by the insurgency of various cultural practices in postcolonial Tunisia, not to mention the robust educational system that was put in place after independence by Mahmoud al-Messadi himself, the playwright who served as Minister of National Education from 1958 to 1968 and Minister of Cultural Affairs from 1973 to 1976. Al-Messadi stopped writing plays when he became minister, but his most famous play, *Al-Sudd*, remains the first truly Tunisian play; produced in 1950 in the midst of anticolonial struggle, it dramatizes human will, creativity, and their transformational generative powers. Like all his other works which were not published and popularized until after independence, even though they were all written in the 1940s, *Al-Sudd* is a subtle allegory of human resilience and defiance in the face of colonial power and the colonial policies of *francisation* whose aim was to diminish Arabic literacy. Thanks to al-Messadi's educational vision, which survived even Ben Ali's onslaughts on public education, Tunisia has always boasted a high literacy rate, at times estimated at almost 90 percent, one of the highest and most envied in the region. Yet what bears mentioning here is that the level of literacy that most Tunisians acquired remained for decades at variance with the repressive policies of the successive regimes of Bourguiba and Ben Ali, a fact that made the popular uprising inevitable, if long overdue.

Sociopolitical and cultural critique is there in cinema, theater, poetry, and music. Whoever studies Tunisian literature and culture since independence would not miss the latent or indirect critique it carried and disseminated. Postcolonial Tunisian littérateurs engaged with the colonial legacy, its socioeconomic demarcations, and mental or psychological sedimentations, all the while exposing the sociocultural ills of Tunisian society and government and insisting on the link between decolonial and postcolonial critique. Of note here are three figures: Bashir Khrayyif, Mohamed Laroussi el-Metoui and Muhammad Salih al-Jabiri. While he wrote numerous short stories and novels and published to great acclaim his historical novel *Barq Al-Layal* (a knight's name that literally means "lightning of the night") in 1961, Khrayyif is more commonly known for *Al-digla fī ʿarājīnihā* (*Dates in their Branches*). Published more than a decade after Tunisia's independence, the novel takes place in the south of Tunisia in the 1920s and chronicles the beginnings of syndicalism and the nationalist movement by focusing on the multifaceted struggles of the mineworkers, inventing, in the process, a language that vacillates seamlessly between Arabic *fuṣḥā* (Modern Standard Arabic) in narration and Tunisian *dārija* (dialect) in dialogue. Similarly, al-Matwi's novels of this period—*Halīma* (1964) and, particularly, *Al-Tūt al-murr* (1967, *Bitter Blackberries*)—are mostly situated in the south and present both the struggle against colonialism and the misery of subaltern Tunisians. Al-Jabiri is an accomplished critic, novelist and playwright. In addition to *Al-Baḥru yanshuru al-wāḥahu* (1971, *The Sea Scatters its Driftwood*) and *Laylat al-sanawāt al-ʿashr* (1982, *The Night of the Decade*), his acclaimed debut novel *Yawm min ʾayyām Zamra* (1968, *One Day in Zamra*) sheds light on the popular uprisings against French rule while bringing into relief the treason of local collaborators..

The importance of this body of literature is two-fold: it constructs an alternative history of decolonialism, focused on downtrodden and ordinary Tunisians, and it juxtaposes it with the trajectory of postcolonial Tunisia whose leadership gradually internalized the practices of the colonizer. In Chapter 8, I address these very same issues from the perspective of film. The first part of the chapter focuses on the cinematic careers of Nouri Bouzid, Moufida Tlatli, and Mohamed Zran, among others, who in their films have been preoccupied with the staging of broken and defeated individuals. By showing defeat to Tunisian audiences, Bouzid, Tlatli, and Zran not only make it possible for viewers to identify with and distance themselves from the individuals on screen, but also—and simultaneously—offer them an opportunity to immunize themselves against the psychology of defeat and the state apparatuses that perpetuate it. In the final analysis, the cinematic tendency to grapple with and visualize the experience of defeat indirectly becomes the basis for fostering strategies of empowerment. Shakespeare's meta-dramatic injunction to his readers—"by indirections find directions out"[30]—became one of the tactics that artists made use of to evade censorship and simultaneously keep alive the culture of critique and dissidence. Tunisian cinema had gradually developed since independence a singular reputation for its audacious treatment of controversial and taboo subjects (even for an allegedly progressive Muslim country such as Tunisia). Yet the treatment of such wide-ranging and contentious topics as Islam, imperialism, and secular modernity or variations on them is almost always infused, directly or indirectly, by a penetrating critique of the postcolonial regimes of Bourguiba and Ben Ali, their medium- or long-term policies and their social, economic, and political ramifications.

The same can be said about theater, which, in addition to al-Messadi's pioneering work in playwriting, benefited from the emergence of such playwrights as Mustfa al-Farsi, Habib Boulares, and, above all, Ezzidine al-Madani whose historical plays *Thawrat Ṣāhib al-Ḥimār* (*The Revolt of the Donkey's Owner*, directed by Ali Ben Ayed in 1970) and *Dīwān al-Zinj* (*The Record of the Black Revolt*, directed by Moncef Souissi in 1972) had particular resonance in the neocolonial economic realities of Tunisia after independence. Because theater was the most closely watched cultural activity by the state and because it always faced censorship, there emerged theater practitioners who tried to survive in a climate of censorship through sparing flights into experimentation and allegorical detours. These include Triangular Theater (*Théâtre Triangulaire*), Theater of the Earth (*Théâtre de la Terre*) and especially New Theater (*Nouveau Théâtre*) with Jalila Baccar, Mohamed Idriss, Fadhel Jaïbi, Fadhel Jaziri, and Habib Masrouki. The works of New Theater produced a singular artistic vision with an avant-garde style and fresh approaches to the question of national disenchantment which is central to most of their plays, including Jaïbi's *Famīlia* (1993, *Family*) and Baccar's *Junūn* (2001, *Dementia*). Their most important and compelling play to date, however, is Baccar's *Khamsoun* (2006, *Captive Bodies*), which offers a biting critique of Ben Ali's regime. The starting point of *Khamsoun* is a suicidal act committed by Jouda, a young veiled physics and chemistry teacher, on November 11, 2005 in the courtyard of her own school, and, significantly enough, at the foot of a pole carrying the Tunisian flag. The play unfolds in a sequence of scenes organized along three major parts that move forward and simultaneously as far back as the early years of Bourguiba's presidency. *Khamsoun*, which means "fifty" in English, was produced in 2006, fifty years after Tunisia's independence from France. Baccar wants us therefore to understand her play literally, not metaphorically, as an allegory of postcolonial Tunisia. This is a play in which the many individual stories Baccar weaves together are situated firmly in the canvas of national history. As a female playwright, actress, and filmmaker, Baccar's work has consistently been interested in the margins of the rhetoric of nationhood from Bourguiba to Ben Ali. Her consistent reactivation of the unassimilated histories of injustice and victimhood in postindependence Tunisia bespeaks a pedagogical and methodological investment in the psychoaffective valences of artistic and creative reckoning, thus bearing deep similarities with Nouri Bouzid's and Moufida Tatli's early work in cinema. *Khamsoun*'s contestatory wherewithal is not the exception here but the exemplar.

Perhaps what theater evokes in the collective imagination of most Tunisians is the emergence of the one-man shows in the 1990s and 2000s with Lamine Nahdi and Raouf Ben Yaghlan, among several other talented stand-up comedians. Through a series of performances Nahdi and Ben Yaghlan managed to deliver devastating critiques of Tunisia's successive dictatorial regimes, couching them tactfully in a humorous register. Tunisians remember by heart many theatrical episodes from Nahdi's *Mekkī wa Zakiyya* (*Mekkī and Zakiyya*) and Ben Yaghlan's *En'abbar wella man'abbarshi* (*To Speak or not to Speak*). Nahdi and his troupe, Théâtre Maghreb Arabe, had been a usual suspect, the target of censorship commissions, harassment, arrests, and all types of threat. Ben Yaghlan courted similar risks; his abovementioned performance was censored for years under the pretext that it did not appeal to spectators (for once a poll in Ben Ali's Tunisia was accurate). As its title indicates, though, the show addresses the state of critique in mid-2000s Tunisia in which critical integrity and free expression had been compromised by both mainstream media and a large number of state intellectuals (aka "courtesans"). As Ben Yaghlan, in the middle of the show, sarcastically ponders the usefulness of critique at a time when there is nothing to critique, he strikes a chord with his audience who respond with relieved applause and bursts of passionate laughter.[31] Through these rare performances, Tunisians find room not only to channel their own malaise, but also to foster an affective and collective disposition toward civil disobedience. Far from mere cathartic spectacles, the performances become rehearsals of an implied or imagined commitment to collaborative revolutionism as a mode of relationality which might remain unlocalizable and free from the anxieties of direct action but not entirely oblivious to the promise of a popular eruption of mass solidarity and discontent.

In the months leading up to the revolution, cultural critique became, not surprisingly, more and more adventurous, vocal, and direct, particularly on YouTube and Facebook which circulated, among other things, explosive hip hop videos that had instantaneous effects. Indeed, and as I discuss in the second part of my chapter, the role of hip hop and rap music in particular as a vehicle of popular discontent against Ben Ali's regime before and after the revolution became so vital that many can no longer imagine the cultural scene in Tunisia without it (despite the very fact that this genre is novel in Tunisia and the Arab world in general). Take, for instance, the case of rapper El Général

(Hamada Ben Amor). He was hardly known before the autumn of 2010, not even in Tunisia's rap scene which was dominated by artists such as Psyco M, Balti, and Lak3y, among few others. On November 7, 2010 (the very same day that Tunisia was celebrating the twenty-third anniversary of Ben Ali's seizure of power), El Général uploaded a rap song called "Rais Lebled" ("Head of State") onto Facebook. The raw fury and politically combustible rhymes of the song cannot be overstated: "*Rais lebled, sha'bik met; barsha 'bed mizibla klet*"/"Mr. President, your people are dead; many, today, on garbage fed."[32]

El Général dares the president to come down to the streets and see for himself how people lead their everyday lives and how the political police clubs and harasses Tunisians wherever they show any resistance to their whims and wills. El Général dares the president to offer evidence of the stark contrast between the rhetoric of democracy he embraces and simulates and the culture of corruption he fosters and dissimulates but that prevails in the country and in Palace Carthage. Given that in his third and last speech, on January 13, 2011, the day before he fled to Saudi Arabia, Ben Ali avowed that he was "misled" ("*ghallṭūnī*") by his advisors who apparently kept him deliberately out of touch with the Tunisian people (out of a concern for his health, perhaps), El Général's plea becomes prophetic. Ben Ali was a dying man both physically and politically. At any rate, the song galvanized young men and women and sent shockwaves across the country before it was banned and El Général was arrested on January 6, 2011. By then, however, the revolution had reached the point of no return and Ben Ali was living on borrowed time. One of the reasons why the song resonated with almost every Tunisian is that it exposed the widespread governmental corruption, nepotism, and ineptitude—really, all the ills of Ben Ali's neoliberal restructuring of the country which started in the late 1980s and intensified in the wake of Tunisia's association with the European Union in the mid-1990s. The drastic process of privatizations that ensued spared nothing, not even the educational sector which was on the brink of being completely marginalized by the emphasis placed on the private sector of education, particularly since Leila Trabelsi, infamously nicknamed "the regent of Carthage," started her own private and for-profit school, called Carthage International School.[33]

Tunisia's economic reform program seemed to work quite well at first and, beginning in 1987, the country was able to privatize 140 state-owned enterprises. Georgie Anne Geyer wrote an article in the mid-1990s which was then turned into a book whose title needs no further clarification, *Tunisia: A Journey Through a Country that Works.*[34] During the period between 1970 and 2000, the WB was confident enough about Tunisia's success that it gave the country more loans than any other Arab or African country. Whoever was misled by statistics seemed to believe that Tunisia was a success story. That was not the case, however, much to the surprise and bewilderment of both Arab and non-Arab observers. In her wide-ranging contribution that forms Chapter 1, Emma

Murphy reviews the results of the economic reforms implemented under Ben Ali and the arguments of the IMF that Tunisia was a regional role model, a success story for neoliberal restructuring. Investigating the discrepancies between the international portrayal of the economy and the realities as they were lived by the Tunisian population, she unveils both the flaws in the way in which the international financial institutions measure success and the manner in which regimes can manipulate and disguise the data that informs their judgments. More crucially, Murphy sheds light on the hidden stories of economic liberalization under authoritarian regimes and the manner in which the instruments of reform translate into distortions and subversions of the very agendas they supposedly seek to promote.

As Murphy argues in a previous publication, what Ben Ali did was to create a "Tunisian entrepreneurial class eager to engage in globalized patterns of economic activity" and to "[locate] himself (and his family) firmly within that class."[35] In other words, while under Bourguiba the state controlled the bulk of the resources and the private sector assisted it in negotiating the rules of the game, under Ben Ali, by contrast, private operators acted as "catalysts of progress" and were assisted by the state in determining its political and economic priorities.[36] As a result, Ben Ali and his wife and their extended families got their hands on more than 40 percent of the economy at a time when the national unemployment rate had reached 13 percent and went as high as 40 percent in the southern and interior parts of the country.[37] Economic growth was mostly confined to Ben Ali's entrepreneurial class in the greater Tunis area and along the coastal urban areas to the detriment of the interior regions which trailed behind. While more than a third of the country's youth were unemployed, Ben Ali's entrepreneurial class continued to prosper by legal and illegal means.[38] The State Department cables released by Wikileaks exposed the extent to which the clan composed of the extended families of Ben Ali and Leila Trabelsi formed the nexus of corruption in the country. This "quasi-mafia" or "owning family" (as they are called by Tunisians) had no scruples whatsoever about coveting more assets and acquiring them through any form of shady dealings, be it cash, services, theft, money, property expropriation, extortion of bribes, money laundering or drug trafficking, illegal privatization of national assets and companies, and so on. Not even the National Solidarity Fund 26-26 (Fonds National de Solidarité, FNS), which was created in late 1992 and drew its income from annual, quasi-mandatory donations on December 8 (Tunisia's National Day of Solidarity), was spared. It suffered from a complete lack of transparency even though (or perhaps because) it was under the direct authority of Ben Ali himself.[39]

The US ambassador to Tunis, Robert F. Godec, is right to conclude that corruption was the elephant in the room in Tunisia—every Tunisian knew about it but no one dared to address it. Until the revolution started, this state of affairs seemed to beggar the imagination indeed because whoever visited, studied or learned about Tunisia could not fail to notice the striking disconnect between the will and dignity of its people and the corrupt and oppressive regime to which they almost readily submitted in a tacit social contract whereby they forsook politics for the sake of social benefits. Ben Ali's neoliberal adventure deliberately marginalized the southern and interior parts of the country where protests erupted in the mining area of Gafsa in 2008 and lasted for six months before they were brutally repressed by the security forces (who ended up killing a number of workers). The Tunisian revolution could very well have started in 2008 (in the manner in which the bread riots of 1984 against Bourguiba's economic policies prepared the ground for Ben Ali's constitutional coup in 1987), but neither Facebook nor Al-Jazeera saved the day then and the six-month-long demonstrations were contained within a media wall of silence, not attracting national and international attention until months afterwards when they completely died out. The consensus that (consciously or unconsciously, privately or publicly, willingly or unwillingly) compelled Tunisians to compromise political freedoms of various kinds in exchange for economic and social welfare became more and more volatile and untenable.[40]

El Général's song articulated the enormity of a people's discontent with Ben Ali's regime and inaugurated what would become an ever more vocalized and outspoken popular withdrawal of consent.[41] The carefully crafted video of "Rais Lebled," with its highly evocative opening segment, its black-and-white, crisply realist imagery and the underground location in which it was shot all combine to convey a sense of an uprising in the making. The underground is not only the musical genre of the song, but also its central conceit; it is an extended metaphor for going beyond Ben Ali's façade democracy and digging deeper into the regime's Mafioso-style gangsterism.[42] The slow, pulsating beat of the song, moreover, serves to focus attention on its highly explosive riff. Even though El Général's song and al-Shabbi's poetry have marked the Tunisian revolution—in a manner matched only by the chants, graffiti, and slogans that proliferated from December 17 onwards—it is necessary to highlight the critical importance of the cultural output between Al-Shabbi's 1934 poem and El Général's 2010 rap song and how it has contributed to the formation of the overall picture of collaborative revolutionism I have so far elaborated. The Tunisian revolution is a historic event and a historical process that has been years in the making and is not over yet. It is the crowning moment of decades of collective endeavors, fragmented engagements, transversal tactics, small-scale or micro-rebellions, and social, political, literary, and cultural practices of insurrection and revolt.

The postrevolutionary moment

Cultural, civic, and sociopolitical dissent has become synonymous to doing what comes naturally in postrevolutionary Tunisia. Note that since the deposition of

Ben Ali, there have been countless demonstrations, strikes, and sit-in protests across Tunisia but especially in the Qasbah Government Square and Avenue Habib Bourguiba in Tunis. The first Qasbah sit-in protest, for instance, came right after the formation of the first interim government and lasted for five days, from the January 23 to January 28, 2011. It forced a major cabinet reshuffle even though it was forcefully dispersed by riot police. The second Qasbah sit-in protest went on around the clock for twelve days and nights from February 20 to March 3 and achieved almost all its goals; unlike the first one, it ended peacefully with protesters rejoicing, singing, and cleaning the Qasbah Government Square, then preparing for their journey to the border with Libya where a humanitarian crisis was unfolding in the wake of the Libyan revolution and the flows of refugees who were seeking asylum in Tunisia.

What is worth mentioning here is that collective and civic action continued after the revolution, and in fact were it not for the successive sit-in protests in the Qasbah Government Square, Tunisians would not have had the National Constituent Assembly elections on October 23, 2011. It was the second sit-in protest in the Qasbah that called for the formulation of a new constitution and for elections. The sit-in protesters, mostly young and marginalized Tunisians, refused to become an organized social or political movement, or to endorse a specific party or ideology.[43] Eventually, however, some of these young activists were absorbed by the many political parties that multiplied overnight (some of which have since then dissolved, splintered or dispersed into small factions and entered into new alliances, fronts or blocs). The success of this sit-in protest has now achieved mythical proportions since—in addition to the fulfillment of its central demand for National Constituent Assembly elections—it forced not only the resignation of then Prime Minister Mohamed Ghannouchi and the appointment of Béji Caïd Essebsi as a new prime minister, but also the dissolution of Ben Ali's state security apparatus and former party, the Constitutional Democratic Rally (Rassemblement Constitutionnel Démocratique, RCD), on March 7 and 9 respectively.

The National Constituent Assembly elections took place on October 23, 2011 (they were initially set for July 24, 2011, as Fouad Mebazza announced on March 3 of that year). What is interesting about the results is that despite the more than 100 parties and dozens of independents who took part in the elections, Tunisians voted in great numbers for the parties and political leaders that had established credentials and a long history of resistance to Bourguiba and Ben Ali. This explains, for instance, why Ennahda, which was founded in the early 1980s in opposition to Bourguiba's Socialist Destourian party, was the biggest winner in these elections. It earned 89 out of the 217 available seats in the National Constituent Assembly. The runner-up party was the CPR with twenty-nine seats. Together with Ettakatol (the Democratic Forum for Labor and Liberties), Ennahda and the CPR formed the coalition government, arguably the first legitimate governing body in Tunisia after free and fair elections. Of note here is that Ettakatol, like the Democratic Progressive Party (Parti Démocrate Progressiste, PDP), was a legal opposition party to Ben Ali's RCD, but Ennahda and the CPR were illegal resistant parties. Moncef Marzouki, the leader of the CPR, believed that Ben Ali's regime was incorrigible and so normal political opposition to it would lead to nothing. Unlike the leader of Ettakatol, Mustapha Ben Jafar, and the leader of the PDP, Ahmed Najib Chebbi, Marzouki chose to struggle against Ben Ali. Hence he called his party Congress for the Republic out of a sense that the Republic of Tunisia was yet to come.

Tunisians dealt a heavy defeat to the remnants of Ben Ali's regime and to the old and new parties that based their entire electoral campaign on the denigration of the Islamic party, Ennahda. By voting for the three parties that now form the coalition government, it is as if Tunisians wanted, in part, to right the incalculable wrongs (the years of lead involving disappearance, exile, imprisonment, torture, and so on) that were inflicted on the militants of these parties under the reign of both Bourguiba and Ben Ali. Apart from writing a new constitution, instituting the second republic, the tripartite coalition government (aka the Troika) had been assigned the task of governing the country as well as holding new elections, either presidential, parliamentary or a mixture of both, depending on what the new constitution would stipulate.

Since they gained power, the Troika has been dogged by countless problems, many of which had to do not only with the lack of alternatives to the neoliberal economic system they inherited but also with their inexperience and their inability to transition seamlessly from the tactics of opposition and resistance to the mechanics and logistics of governance. No wonder they had been routinely attacked by opposition parties and a growing portion of the population for their incompetence and failure to fulfill the promises of the revolution. What is worse, Ennahda had been relentlessly accused of doublespeak and of conniving with Salafi groups to transform Tunisia gradually from a secular state into an Islamic one. As Nadia Marzouki argues in Chapter 9, Ennahda leaders had tirelessly reasserted their commitment to a non-theocratic, civic state that would respect religious freedom, women's rights, and the principle of democratic *alternance*, or alternation. Rather than being a mere form of doublespeak, as its detractors contend, Ennahda's discourse on the concept of civic state (*dawla madaniyya*) stems from a long tradition of reflections upon the compatibility of Islam and democracy.

The political thought developed by Rachid Ghannouchi since the early 1980s belies the exaggerated doublespeak accusations. Marzouki elaborates the genealogy of the concept of civic state in Tunisian Islamists' thought, all the while pointing out the pitfalls that are associated with it. Above all, she assesses how the notion of civility, which has for so long been conceptualized as a key category of resistance among Tunisian Islamists, can be transformed into a category of governance. This transformation might take time to materialize, especially with the widening secular-religious divide and the ongoing mobilization and polarization of society. Scaremongering media campaigns, which persistently misconstrued Ennahda as inimical to democracy and women's rights, had soured the political climate, all the while deflecting attention away from the real issues for which Bouazizi immolated himself and Tunisians took to the streets immediately after. In Chapter 10, Monica Marks deftly weaves together the ways in which the issue of women's rights has been used and abused by Bourguiba and Ben Ali to maintain their hold on power. Counter-revolutionary forces, along with a host of opposition parties, have similarly wheeled out the issue of women's rights in order to show how bad Ennahda would be for women despite Ennahda's endorsement of the Personal Status Codes of 1957 and of a new constitution that does not include Sharia law. What has muddied the waters even further, however, is the rise to prominence of Salafism, one of the most mediatized phenomena in postrevolutionary Tunisia, especially insofar as it directly affects women's rights.[44]

Chapter 11, written by Fabio Merone and Francesco Cavatorta, paints a genealogy of the formation and eruption of Salafism into the public sphere as a local micro-movement; contrary to popular belief, the authors argue that Tunisian Salafism is indigenous, not imported from Afghanistan, Iran or Saudi Arabia (even while it maintains ties to transnational Islamic movements). They also demonstrate that Salafism is not a monolithic entity but an amalgam of heterogeneous small groups, most of which preach a return to Islam and engage peacefully in *daʿwa*, or missionary, activities. Not infrequently, though, what has attracted media attention are the jihadi salafis, a minority within a minority. The potential challenges that this minority poses, however, could be catastrophic, especially if deemed capable of transforming Tunisia into jihad land or *Tunistan*. They have already been involved in several violent events ranging from the demonstrations against the screening of Nadia El Fani's documentary film, *Neither Allah, Nor Master*, in June 2011 to the attack on the US embassy in September 2012 in the regional outrage against *The Innocence of Muslims*, a California-made low-budget film denigrating Prophet Mohammad. To their credit the Troika, and Ennahda party in particular, have stressed time and again the necessity of devising imaginative and nuanced strategies to contain Salafism by, for instance, convincing salafis to participate in democratic politics and pursue their agendas more effectively through legal associations, organizations or political parties.

In this vein, the Troika had showcased scientific Salafism or what might be called a *salafi-lite* version of Salafism that partakes in political life and that may continue to advocate for an Islamic state but not try to impose it by violence. In the meanwhile, the psychological distress and socioeconomic malaise, both of which constitute the underlying impetus for Salafi activism, need to be addressed and redressed.[45] Because Salafism was for some the only means to cope with and channel the anger excited by decades of compulsory secularism, its resurgence is a vivid reminder that any renewed repression of salafis would be counterproductive in the long run. Merone and Cavatorta conclude that postrevolutionary Tunisia could very well find in the challenge of Salafism an opportunity to test and perfect the democratizing process as it unfolds. Moreover, in the context of Tunisians' efforts to forge a truly democratic polity, threats to women's rights, Marks maintains, are more likely to stem from deeply embedded social norms and weak institutions rather than from deliberate machinations of Islamist ideology.

Ennahda's detractors may continue to contend that Tunisian Islamists astutely adjust their official discourse and support for democracy to gain power and establish an Islamic state, but the real challenge for postrevolutionary Tunisia is rather to stay clear of these kinds of interest- and identity-based politics that continue to fuel debate and appropriate attention away from the more urgent questions of creating jobs, offering reparations to the families of the martyrs and bringing the members of the old regime to justice. Not only that, but much else will also depend on attaining unanimous consent for the final version of the new constitution, especially since the latest version (dated April 22, 2013) as well as the supposedly final version (dated June 1, 2013) had already raised eyebrows in the ANC. In the final chapter, Lise Storm delves into a set of related factors—besides Islamism, Salafism and the state of the economy—that could potentially stall the democratizing process and that have to do with the character of the country's party system, the nature of the political parties, and the level of maturity and/or democratic commitment of the chief politicians.

For Storm, the current Tunisian party system is populated by entities that can only at a stretch be classified as political parties—most are simply office-seeking, while neglecting policy-seeking and their representative functions. Given the centrality of political parties to the consolidation of democracy, it is not surprising that Tunisian democracy is thus far fragile. The fragmentation and internal multiplication of parties, their confusing similarities and personalistic nature—along with the absence of clear-cut policies and strong links to society at large—may hinder the electorate from distinguishing between parties at election time, which may in turn delegitimize the credibility of the electoral process. There is obviously still much to be desired in the Tunisian party system, but Tunisia is on the right path to the consolidation of democracy, provided the new system of governance (semi-presidential, semi-parliamentary or a mixture of both) institutes the decentralization of power and keeps a system of checks and balances in place, so as to pre-empt the return of Bourguiba or the return of Ben Ali, that is, the returns of the one-party autocracy. I will come back to this issue (aka the counterrevolution) and other related issues in the postscript, which will also provide an overview of the most important developments since the 2011 ANC elections and assessment of the challenges that lie ahead.

Notes

1. Moncef Marzouki, *'Innahā al-thawratu yā Mawlaya* [It's Revolution, My Lord] (Tunis: Mediterranean Publisher, 2011), 15.
2. Robert Fisk, "The Brutal Truth about Tunisia," *The Independent*, January, 17, 2011, accessed January 20, 2011, www.independent.co.uk/voices/commentators/fisk/the-brutal-truth-about-tunisia-2186287.html.
3. Not only were the forces of change in Tunisia invisible, but so was the Tunisian revolution itself up until the departure of Ben Ali and not long after the start of the Egyptian revolution. See Nouri Gana, "Let's Not Forget about Tunisia," *Jadaliyya*, January 30, 2011, accessed January 30, 2011, www.jadaliyya.com/pages/index/500/lets-not-forget-about-tunisia.
4. Asef Bayat, *Life as Politics: How Ordinary People Change the Middle East* (Stanford, CA: Stanford University Press, 2010), 14.
5. Michel de Certeau defines a tactic as "an art of the weak," operating in "isolated actions blow by blow," and "determined by the absence of power just as a strategy is organized by the postulation of power," *The Practice of Everyday Life*, trans. Steven Rendall (Berkeley, CA: University of California Press, 1984), 37–8.
6. For instance what Tom Nairn calls the "process of global democratic warming", or "the third wave" in the words of Samuel P. Huntington; see Nairn, "Nations Versus Imperial Unions in a Time of Globalization, 1707–2007," *Arena Journal* 28 (2007): 33–44, and Martin Shaw, "The Global Democratic Revolution: A New Stage," *Open Democracy*, March 7, 2011, accessed May 12, 2011, www.opendemocracy.net/martin-shaw/global-democratic-revolution-new-stage. See also Huntington, *The Third Wave: Democratization in the Late Twentieth Century* (Norman, OK: University of Oklahoma Press, 1991).
7. While instantiating more continuity with than rupture from Bourguiba, Ben Ali had a different style from his predecessor; as Christopher Alexander discerns: "Ben Ali's style has been very centralized, but much less personalized. While Bourguiba constructed a state corporatist façade over a highly personalized management style, Ben Ali constructed a liberal democratic façade over a centralized and insulated technocracy. He successfully hijacked most of the secular opposition's themes with rhetoric that emphasized human rights, individual liberty, and political competition," *Tunisia: Stability and Reform in the Modern Maghreb* (Abingdon: Routledge, 2010), 7.
8. See John P. Entelis, "The Democratic Imperative vs. the Authoritarian Impulse: The Maghrib State Between Transition and Terrorism," *Middle East Journal* 59.4 (2005): 537–58. For an overview of the historical contexts in which the syndrome of presidents for life emerged and took root in the Arab world, see Roger Owen, *The Rise and Fall of Presidents for Life* (Cambridge, MA: Harvard University Press, 2012); for an overview of the psychic and pathological contexts, see Muriel Mirak-Weissbach, *Madmen at the Helm: Pathology and Politics in the Arab Spring* (Reading: Ithaca Press, 2012).
9. "US Embassy Cables: Finding a successor to Ben Ali in Tunisia," *The Guardian*, January 17, 2011, accessed July 10, 2012, www.guardian.co.uk/world/us-embassy-cables-documents/49401.

10. "Imperial and Dictatorial Logics Remain Intertwined," indeed! See Perry Anderson, "On the Concatenation in the Arab World," *The New Left Review* 68 (2011): 9.
11. See Noam Chomsky, "The Manufacture of Consent," in *The Chomsky Reader*, ed. James Peck (New York: Pantheon Books, 1987), 121–36.
12. See "Tunisian Protests have Caught Nicolas Sarkozy Off Guard," *The Guardian*, January 17, 2011, accessed January 20, 2011, www.guardian.co.uk/world/2011/jan/17/tunisian-protests-sarkozy-off-guard.
13. Tariq Ramadan, *L'islam et le réveil arabe* (Paris: Presses du Châtelet, 2011), 21–5.
14. In a recent piece, Ben Wagner unmasks the history of internet censorship and the international institutions involved in it; see "Push-button-autocracy in Tunisia: Analysing the Role of the Internet Infrastructure, Institutions and International Markets in creating a Tunisian Censorship Regime," *Telecommunication Policy* 36 (2012): 484–92.
15. An introduction to Tunileaks by Sami Ben Gharbia, its founder, can be found online at www.youtube.com/watch?v=crjbw6ICi5M (accessed July 13, 2012).
16. Lamine Bouazizi's contribution to this radio show entitled "Les vrais blogueurs de la révolution" [The true bloggers of the Tunisian revolution] can be found online at www.radioexpressfm.com/podcast/show/les-vrais-blogueurs-de-la-revolution (accessed July 13, 2012).
17. The 1960s and 1970s slogans targeted Prime Minister Hedi Nouira: "we can live on bread and water, but no more Hedi Nouira" (*khubz wa mā' wa Nouira lā*). Nouira was responsible for liberalizing the economy, moving aggressively toward privatization, and dismantling most of the nation's cooperatives (initiated by Ahmed Ben Salah in the 1960s), all the while showing little concern for social grievances.
18. See Mark Tessler, "Tunisia's New Beginning," *Current History* 89 (April 1990): 169–84, and "Tunisia at the Crossroads," *Current History* 84 (May 1985): 217–23.
19. In this respect, soccer performs under authoritarianism what dance used to perform under colonialism; see Frantz Fanon, *The Wretched of the Earth*, preface by Jean-Paul Sartre, trans. Constance Farrington (New York: Grove Press, 1968).
20. As James Gelvin rightly suggests, the "human element" remains a key variable in determining whether or not an uprising takes place. Yet, it is also what makes uprisings utterly unpredictable. See James Gelvin, *The Arab Uprisings: What Everyone Needs to Know* (New York: Oxford University Press, 2012), 25.
21. For more on LTHR, see "The Politics of Human Rights in the Maghreb," in *Islam, Democracy and the State in North Africa*, ed. John P. Entelis (Bloomington, IN: Indiana University Press, 1997), 75–92.
22. At the time, the Neo-Destour Party was called the Destourian Socialist Party (PSD).
23. The demise of the magazine resulted from unresolvable internal intellectual and political differences between the women involved with *Nissa* about the scope and purpose of the magazine; for a good overview, see Kevin Dwyer, *Arab Voices: The Human Rights Debate in the Middle East* (Berkeley, CA: University of California Press, 1991), 143–210.
24. Mohamed Kilani pays tribute to other brave journalists like Om Zied in *La Révolution des Braves* (Tunis: Impression Simpact, 2011). *La Révolution des Braves* is the first book ever to be published on the Tunisian revolution, barely two weeks after January 14, 2011.

25. These female activists present a picture in stark contrast to the one presented by the Tunisian Association of Democratic Women (ATFD) who, in commemoration of the forty-seventh anniversary of the Personal Status Code sent a letter to Ben Ali in which they urged him to curb the resurgence of the veil in public spaces; see "The Tunisian Women's Movement Open Fire on Veiled Women," accessed July 10, 2012, www.alwasatnews.com/358/news/read/330150/1.html.
26. "The Tunisian government has a history of bringing claims against journalists and human rights activists of sexual assault, harassment, and indecency. In 1993, pornographic photographs that purported to depict Ben Sedrine began circulating in Tunis, an apparent effort to smear her reputation and discourage her from continuing her human rights work," see "Tunisia: President, Emboldened by Vote, Cracks Down on Critics," *Human Rights Watch*, December 23, 2009, accessed July 15, 2012, www.hrw.org/news/2009/12/23/tunisia-president-emboldened-vote-cracks-down-critics.
27. Since Ben Ali "eliminated any possibility for opposition movements willing to work within the system to operate legally and freely . . . Tunisia's disenfranchised masses," as Laryssa Chomiak and John P. Entelis rightly observe, "developed mechanisms for dodging the tentacles of the authoritarian state, including tax avoidance, illegal tapping of municipal water and electricity supplies, and illicit construction of houses." See "The Making of North Africa's Intifadas," *Middle East Report* 259 (2011): 13. For a good overview of the extra-institutional informal political activities, see Laryssa Chomiak, "The Making of a Revolution in Tunisia," *Middle East Law and Governance* 3 (2011): 68–83.
28. Abul-Qasim Al-Shabbi, *Aghani al-Hayat* [Songs of Life] (Tunis: al-Dar al-tunisiya li-l-Nashar, 1966), 5.
29. Jacques Rancière, "The Politics of Literature," *SubStance* 33.1 (2004): 10.
30. William Shakespeare, *Hamlet,* ed. Susanne L. Wofford (Boston, MA: Bedford Books, 1994), 2.2.66.
31. A sample from the performance can be found online at www.youtube.com/watch?v=H_GzsGmPhXU (accessed July 10, 2012).
32. El Général (Hamada Ben Amor), "Raies Lebled," online at www.youtube.com/watch?v=-jdE_LpmAIQ (accessed July 11, 2011). See also Nouri Gana, "Rap Rage Revolt," *Jadaliyya*, August 5, 2011. Online at www.jadaliyya.com/pages/index/2320/rap-rage-revolt (accessed July 10, 2012).
33. Nicolas Beau and Catherine Graciet, *La régente de Carthage: Main basse sur la Tunisie* (Paris: La Découverte, 2009).
34. Georgie Anne Geyer, *Tunisia: A Journey Through a Country that Works* (London: Stacey International, 2003).
35. Emma C. Murphy, "The Foreign Policy of Tunisia," in *The Foreign Policies of Middle Eastern States*, ed. Raymond Hinnebusch and Anoushiravan Ehteshami (Boulder, CO: Lynne Rienner, 2002), 255.
36. Steffen Erdle, *Ben Ali's "New Tunisia" (1987–2009): A Case Study of Authoritarian Modernization in the Arab World* (Berlin: Klaus Schwarz, 2010), 431–2.
37. According to Cyril Grislain Karray, the number of unemployed and excluded will increase exponentially in the next five years until it hits the two million mark by 2015. This might be somewhat exaggerated for one reason or another, but it should be noted that a third of Tunisians live on less than $3 a day while 1 percent

of Tunisians are drowning in wealth. See Cyril Grislain Karray, *La Prochaine Guerre en Tunisie: La Victoire en 5 batailles* (Tunis : Cérès Éditions, 2011).

38. See Stephen Juan King, *The New Authoritarianism in the Middle East and North Africa* (Bloomington, IN: Indiana University Press, 2009).
39. For the ways in which 26-26 was used as a form of power, see Béatrice Hibou, *The Force of Obedience: The Political Economy of Repression in Tunisia*, trans. Andrew Brown (London: Polity, 2011), 196–8.
40. Mahmoud Ben Romdhane, "Social Policy and Development in Tunisia Since Independence: A Political Perspective," in *Social Policy in the Middle East: Political, Economic and Gender Dynamics*, ed. Massoud Karshenas and Valentine M. Moghadam (London: Palgrave Macmillan, 2006).
41. Stathis Gourgouris, "Withdrawing Consent," *The Immanent Frame*, accessed July 16, 2011, http://blogs.ssrc.org/tif/2011/02/15/withdrawing-consent.
42. See Larbi Sadiki, "Bin Ali's Tunisia: Democracy by Non-Democratic Means," *British Journal of Middle Eastern Studies* 29.1 (2002): 57–78. See also Clement Henry, "Tunisia's 'Sweet Little' Regime," in *Worst of the Worst: Dealing with Repressive and Rogue Nations*, ed. Robert I. Rotberg (Washington, DC: Brookings Institution Press, 2007), 300–23.
43. Some observers characterize the revolution as "largely secular" and "essentially secular," and therefore totally unrelated to Islam; see, for instance, Peter J. Schraeder and Hamadi Redissi, "Ben Ali's Fall," *Journal of Democracy* 22.3 (2011): 5–19. I personally doubt that ordinary Tunisians know much about laicism or secularism, let alone identify with it. Lotfi Abdelli's most recent performance, *100% Halal*, invents the expression "*barra layek*" (literally, "go laicize"), but the power of the expression hinges on the fact that it is a pun on the vulgar expression "*barra nayek*" ("fuck off"). The expression is a jab at both self-professed secularists and Islamists alike, since no Islamist would appreciate the vulgarity of the form in which the attack on their opponents is couched. "*Barra layek*" is what every Tunisian caught in the crossfire between laicism and Islamism would feel tempted to utter. Generally, laicism may still be misunderstood in Tunisia, but so is the notion of Islam as cultural practice and practice of protest, for that matter. Nothing can be gained, I believe, by passing over in silence the mobilizing power of religion in the Tunisian revolution. Note, for instance, that the most decisive demonstrations and protests in Tunisia, including the one on January 14, 2011, took place after Friday prayers, which is evocative of the rallying force of prayer and the galvanizing valences of religion in the service of sociopolitical contention and civil disobedience. To characterize the Tunisian revolution as "essentially secular," as Schraeder and Redissi maintain, strikes one as a claim that may have some tenacity but no overall veracity.
44. Alarmist discourses about an Islamist takeover, the death of secularism and the myriad threats to women's rights have been vulgarized in social media as well as in the old media in Tunisia, which have become anti-state media at large, as well as in books and research articles by foreign observers and international media agencies (French in particular). See, for instance, John R. Bradley, *After the Arab Uprising: How Islamists Hijacked the Middle East Revolts* (New York: Palgrave Macmillan, 2012), and Jane D. Tchaicha and Khedija Arfaoui, "Tunisian Women in the Twenty-first Century: Past Achievements and Present Uncertainties in the Wake of the Jasmine Revolution," *The Journal of North African Studies* 17.2 (2012): 215–38.

45. For more on the precipitants of Islamic activism writ large, see Quintan Wiktorowicz, "Introduction: Islamic Activism and Social Movement Theory," in *Islamic Activism: A Social Movement Theory Approach*, ed. Quintan Wiktorowicz (Indianapolis, IN: Indiana University Press, 2004), 1–33.

PART 1

Contexts: Roots of Discontent

CHAPTER 1

Under the Emperor's Neoliberal Clothes! Why the International Financial Institutions Got it Wrong in Tunisia

Emma C. Murphy

As popular protests spread across Tunisia in January 2011, a narrative developed which attributed the profound and widespread discontent to the economic failures of the Ben Ali regime. Far from being the regional success story which had made the country a pin-up for the international financial institutions (IFIs), Tunisia was wracked by mass unemployment, deepening poverty, endemic corruption, and economic crises. For many, the IFIs were co-conspirators with Western governments (particularly the USA and France), the EU, and the Western-controlled media, all of whom were considered to have largely ignored the human rights abuses of the Ben Ali regime, its brutal authoritarianism, and its rampant self-enrichment in the interests of securing an important ally in the War on Terror, containing Islamic fundamentalism and securing their own borders from illegal immigration.[1] Tunisian compliance with the neoliberal economic agenda was applauded, while rising unemployment and poverty were barely noted.[2] More than that, the economic reforms pushed by the IFIs actually created the opportunities for ruling families and their cronies in Tunisia, Egypt and across the region to divert resources into their own pockets and to structure whole economies to their own private interests. The financial institutions were complicit then: they did not just endorse regimes, they helped to make them what they were.

There is room to dispute the proposition that the protests—in Tunisia or elsewhere in the Arab world—were specifically manifestations of resistance to neoliberal policies or their international instigators. The growing incidence of workers' strikes and food price protests in North Africa over recent years is indisputable, but the December–January protests were notable not least for the emphasis on less material demands such as dignity and freedom. Indeed, Mustapha Kamel Nabli, the now former Governor of the Tunisian Central Bank, cautioned against seeing what he termed "pocket-book factors" as overly deterministic.[3] But whatever the motivations of protesters, it is clear that the IFIs had failed to fully comprehend what was going on within the Tunisian economy and had instead endorsed a regime which was failing its people's economic needs.

This chapter seeks to understand the specific ways in which the International Monetary Fund (IMF) and World Bank (WB)—and by association other international actors— got it wrong.[4] I will seek first to establish the basis on which IFIs made their positive assessments of Tunisia's reform process, and to identify when and how they noted the evidence that all was not well. Second, I will discuss what may be considered the three key pressures upon the sustainability and distributive efficiency of the country's economic growth: rising prices (particularly of food and fuel), unemployment, and corruption. Together, these pressures contributed to the two major "missed stories" in IFIs' assessments. The first was rising and increasingly widespread poverty; the second was the growth of a deviant hybrid private sector, clustered around the president and his extended family, which drew on political resources to transfer state assets to itself and to squeeze the Tunisian economy for its own self-enrichment. In doing so, it undermined the entire strategy of the IFIs, which was premised on supporting a vibrant private sector as the engine for growth and employment creation. A final thread to the story is the IFIs' misplaced faith in sophisticated systems of data collection and presentation, which allowed the Tunisian regime to hide the evidence that reform outcomes were not all they seemed. The chapter concludes with the IMFs' own (limited) admission of mistakes made, asking whether the lessons learned have been sufficient given postuprising Tunisia's continuing relationship with these institutions.

A regional success story

Until recently, Tunisia under Ben Ali was widely acknowledged as something of a regional development success story, not least—it has to be admitted—by myself in previous publications.[5] The accolade was always relative: Tunisia was seen to do well given its very limited hydrocarbon resources and despite significant handicaps. The country is bedeviled by small market size, the constant interruptions of regional political instabilities and climatic unpredictabilities (which impact heavily on two of its main export sectors, tourism and agriculture). Ben Ali had inherited a stagnant economy in the wake of his constitutional coup in 1987. The early socialist experiments of the postindependence era had soon been abandoned by his pragmatic predecessor, Habib Bourguiba, but, after initial successes, the economy had become bogged down by excessive state intervention, declining and inefficient agricultural production, uncompetitive and unprofitable import-substituting industry, and spiraling national debt.[6] By 1986, the situation had reached crisis point and, to avoid bankruptcy, the government was forced to turn to the IMF and the WB for loans which were conditional upon structural adjustment.[7]

The liberal alternative was not entirely new to Tunisia: a series of investment laws in the 1970s constituted an early *Infitāḥ* to encourage export-led growth, but the measures were too little in the face of an ongoing political commitment to the state as the principal owner of capital, employer of labor, and distributor of resources. Thus Ben Ali inherited the economic crisis along with an unsteady and deeply unpopular policy direction. It has to be said that Ben Ali took the bull by the horns, and this has been the root of much of the praise which has since been lavished upon his economic policy making. He fully embraced the structural adjustment process, designing a Tunisia-specific, tailor-made, and government-led program of reforms in advance of the IFIs' impositions. A strategy was devised which would be implemented through five-yearly development plans. The seventh development plan (1987–91) would strive to achieve macroeconomic stability and initiate public-sector, trade, and financial reforms. The eighth development plan (1992–6) would consolidate these measures, introduce legislation to encourage foreign direct investment (FDI), accelerate privatization, develop the stock market, and deepen integration with overseas markets.[8] In fact, and mostly due to the determination of Ben Ali to push reforms through with top-down management and with only marginal tolerance of resistance, much was achieved during the period.

During the period of the eighth development plan, and by 1996, the economy was stabilized, public finances were balanced—with the budget deficit being held below 3 percent of gross national product (GNP)—inflation was brought down to around 5 percent per annum, and the international debt profile was rehabilitated. Nonetheless, structural change was slower than anticipated. The public sector continued to account for 40 percent of total added value, 54 percent of gross fixed investment, and 60 percent of bank assets. State-owned enterprises still accounted for 22 percent of gross domestic product (GDP), unemployment hovered at a depressing 15–17 percent, the trade profile remained unsteady and full convertibility of the dinar was delayed. The mixed picture can be attributed in part to continuing resistance within the bureaucracy and its corporatist allies—particularly the long-protected workers unions, which Ben Ali was at the time still courting in his efforts to establish a political consensus behind his own regime (and the by-now violent repression of Islamist opposition).[9] But one must also acknowledge the scale of the transformation being attempted, the weakness of domestic capital, and the fragility of a banking sector which was burdened with decades worth of underperforming loans. Add to this the complexities of a new partnership agreement with primary trading partners in Europe which held out on the one hand the long-term promise of open markets and on the other the short-term devastation of uncompetitive domestic production (not to mention closed agricultural markets). The program was thus incomplete and the ninth (1997–2001), tenth (2002–6), and eleventh (2007–11) development plans consequently sought to deepen structural reforms, more fully liberalize the economy, and integrate it more profoundly with global markets. A key component of this was the *programme de mise à niveau*, or industrial upgrading program, which was a centerpiece of the ninth development plan and provided financial and technical support for the upgrading of industrial firms to improve their international competitiveness through enhanced quality. Much of the support was focused on the important textile sector, which faced the prospect of the removal of import quotas and new competition from cheaper-labor countries as a global multifiber agreement came to an end in 2005.[10] The tenth development plan focused on the introduction of technology and innovation, while the eleventh development plan was geared towards deepening and widening the global integration of Tunisia such that higher-added value, technology-based production and exports could create the maximum number of jobs for new entrants to the labor market and lift per capita incomes. The language and the mode were very much in tune with those of the IMF, the WB, and the EU, all of whom provided substantial financial support to underpin the necessary structural reforms which the program entailed.

One only needs to look at the WB's International Bank for Reconstruction and Development (IBRD), Country Partnership Strategy for the Republic of Tunisia, produced in 2009, to see how IFIs were finding reasons to applaud the policies of Ben Ali's government. Topping the list of achievements was an average 5 percent per annum growth rate over the previous twenty years, with an accompanying steady growth in per capita incomes above those of mid-range development stars such as Taiwan, Turkey, Poland or Brazil,[11] amounting to a 37.6 percent increase from 2000 to 2005. Official poverty levels had declined over the same period from 4.2 percent of the population to 3.8 percent, although interestingly the report noted that the government threshold indicated only bare essentials needed for physical survival and that a higher standard poverty line would have set this at around 7 percent, which would still be the lowest in the Middle East and North Africa (MENA) region. The growth had been fuelled by increasing integration into the global economy, with exports having diversified significantly since the 1980s (when fuel exports accounted for half the total imports). The 1990s had seen new markets being developed for some sectors, such as electrical and mechanical engineering, although the domestic market still lagged significantly behind the growth in offshore trade.

Fiscal policy was rated as good and effective: fiscal deficits, public debt, and interest payments had fallen sufficiently for Tunisia to be awarded stable investment credit ratings of BBB/Baa2. Inflation had also largely been kept to below 3 percent per annum up until 2008 and the success in reducing interest payments on public debt had enabled a gradual raising of social transfers to offset the impact of rising fuel and energy prices. Overall, Tunisia was considered to "have made remarkable progress on equitable growth, fighting poverty, and achieving good social indicators," one of the most publicized of which was its promotion of women in all aspects of public life. As a result, Tunisia was considered to be on track to achieve its millennium development goals in key development arenas such as education, health, life expectancy, reduced infant mortality rates, and access to key socioeconomic services (water, electricity, sanitation).

The country earned particular praise for its "remarkable" results in developing potable water resources, increasing water efficiency—particularly in the key agricultural sector—and in investing early and effectively in energy efficiency and conservation programs. Also notable was the steady climb up the rankings on governance (in the form of legal and regulatory reform) and international competitiveness.

While these assessments were echoed by the IMF—which proclaimed in 2007 that "Effective economic management has helped achieve relatively strong growth while preserving macroeconomic stability, hereby positioning Tunisia among the leading economic performers in the region,"[12]—the organization was not entirely blind to a number of seriously problematic features of the Tunisian economy. The 2007 report specifically stated that, despite the relatively impressive economic performance in terms of growth, this was insufficient to absorb the large number of new entrants onto the job market every year, let alone make a dent in the existing stock of unemployed workers. Demographic changes also meant growing pressure on the social security system, which was teetering on the edge of an embedded deficit despite reforms to health insurance and the pension system. Finally, rising fuel costs meant that fuel subsidies were placing a substantial burden on public finances, and the report recommended moving away from general subsidies to more targeted assistance. In the 2010 report,[13] it was further noted that Tunisia remained overly dependent on the EU for exports, tourism receipts, remittances, and FDI. With between 75 and 90 percent of these coming from Europe in any given year, Tunisia was profoundly vulnerable to spillovers from Europe's own economic woes, with exports and tourism being the most volatile transmission channels.

The WB noted more directly the problematic nature of governance in Tunisia. As early as 2000, a country assistance strategy document was questioning whether the prevailing model could continue indefinitely despite the apparent macroeconomic successes thus far. Tunisian economic reform was a top-down affair, which relied on the competence of highly centralized officialdom under close supervision by the political structure. However, this left the private sector "hamstrung by complex incentives at the discretion of public officials, costly infrastructure, weak corporate governance, and lack of training and expertise."[14] The highly centralized decision-making process was "overly controlling and close-knit," political participation was stifled and there was a "worrisome," albeit still "minor," perception of corruption. The Tunisian government was therefore encouraged to develop a more transparent business environment, to broaden its dialogue with the private sector and to implement a progressive engagement with civil society. If the Bank's concerns with proliferating cronyism and repressive politics were couched in overly diplomatic terms, the reason was also clear: the report's authors attributed much of the Tunisian regime's success in reforming the economy to their having maintained social stability and continuity in decision making at a time when instability in neighboring countries was threatening to spill over. In other words, they had no desire to rock the boat at that point in time.

The next WB Country Assistance Strategy (CAS) in 2004 reiterated the areas for concern, including an erosion of economic performance: while progress had been made in poverty reduction overall, a significant proportion of the population was clustered above, but close to, the poverty lines, with poverty in rural areas sitting at twice the national average. Unemployment was rising, not only because of demographic growth but also as the economy was restructured away from labor-intensive activities like agriculture and textiles towards more competitive sectors. Moreover, a structural private investment gap existed with investors deterred by strong government interference in the economy, discretionary interventions, weak economic governance, low levels of public accountability, and the constant strengthening of the hand of "insiders" in the absence of strong competitive forces.[15] For the WB, private-sector growth was crucial, not only to absorb at least some of the new entrants on the labor market, but also to generate a stronger tax base so that social assistance could be maintained at the same time as international debt was serviced or reduced and health and education spending was set to grow. The report included a shot across the Tunisian regime's bows—"The full CAS envelope of $1.0 billion is unlikely to be committed unless there is an acceleration of reforms, including those addressing constraints to private investment"—leading the government to insist on its own sixteen-page rebuttal of the allegations being appended to the report.

Yet despite these concerns, the IFIs continued to express their support for the Tunisian regime's economic reform program. Their view of Tunisia was dependent on first, a reliance on selected macroeconomic indicators which painted a rosy national picture but which (as we shall see) obscured the imbalances, inequalities, and distortions that were evolving below the surface. Second, Tunisia's performance was considered relative to its regional context. This has two dimensions. In their direct dealings with the country, IFIs constantly measured Tunisia's achievements against its regional competitors as a comparator group (most of which suffered from similarly authoritarian regimes and weak domestic economies). In 2007, the IMF concluded that: "Effective economic management has helped achieve relatively strong growth while preserving macroeconomic stability, thereby positioning Tunisia among the leading economic performers in the region."[16] In 2009, the WB began its Country Partnership Strategy document thus: "Since independence, Tunisia has performed better than most countries in the region, successfully implementing a far-reaching and ambitious development strategy with strong results."[17] Compared to its regional neighbors, Tunisia scored highly in its apparent willingness and capacity to implement economic reforms, in its macroeconomic indicators, and in its ranking in key indexes like the Human Development Index and the Global Competitiveness Index. Even its economic growth rate looked good. But had it been compared to countries with comparable GDP and GNP per capita (PPP), like Peru and Thailand, which witnessed growth of up to 9 percent in some years, the distortions might have become clear and the picture more complex.

The other side of the coin of its regional context was that the discourse of Tunisia's development process was securitized. The IFIs and partners accepted the Tunisian regime's proposition that the economic reform process had to be protected from destabilizing political elements (Islamists). Some of the more desirable components of a reform process, specifically those that decentralized power or introduced real accountability and transparency, were effectively sacrificed in the short to medium term so that the economic policies that were intended to generate growth could be pushed through whilst stability was maintained. The reports of the WB and the IMF show that they were not unaware of the challenges that the Tunisian economy was facing, but they were complacent in their acceptance of government narratives of policies that sought to address them, hardly surprising given that the Tunisian regime was eager to demonstrate its conformity with the IFIs' own Washington consensus agenda. Moreover, by focusing on national pictures and macroeconomic data, they missed the detail of how those challenges were translating in the everyday lives of Tunisians themselves.

Poverty

Perhaps the single biggest "missed story" was poverty. In fact, the reduction of poverty in Tunisia under Ben Ali was touted as one of the key successes of his supposed balance between economic reform and targeted social assistance. However, in April 2011, the World Food Programme (WFP) conducted a rapid assessment of food security in Tunisia[18] and concluded that the available statistics—provided by the Tunisian regime—had seriously understated the breadth and scale of poverty in the country. IFIs had been reliant in their own assessments on figures provided by the Tunisian government which had used dubious criteria as to what constituted a reasonable poverty line, thereby keeping the poverty rate unrealistically low. When set at TD400 per person per year, only 3.8 percent of the population counted as poor. A more realistic rate of TD585 per person per year raised this to 11.5 percent of the population. The WFP found significant regional disparities, and indeed disparities within regions, with the rural southwest of the country being most clearly vulnerable.

Even at the lower rate, the WFP team estimated that poor households would be spending up to 50.4 percent of their household income on food.[19] Food prices in Tunisia have spiked sharply since 2008 as global food demand has risen. Eighty-seven percent of food prices are unregulated in Tunisia, a result of the government's efforts to get consumers to self-target when it comes to food subsidies. By maintaining subsidies and price controls only on those foods that are staple components for the poor, such as semolina, it is hoped to discourage wealthier Tunisians from drawing on the subsidies. However, this leaves the entire population vulnerable to fluctuations in global food prices. The Food and Agriculture Organization price index shows that between 2000 and 2011 the prices of oils and fats quadrupled, cereals and sugars prices tripled, dairy and meat prices doubled.[20]As those prices rose dramatically, and with Tunisia dependent on imports for over half its cereal needs, the impact on Tunisians was deeply felt. Fish and red meat became too expensive for most Tunisians, forcing more to turn to lower-calorie foods and particularly those products that are subsidized, in turn raising the food and domestic fuel subsidy bill in Tunisia from 4.1 percent of current government expenditures in 2002 to 11.6 percent in 2009 (or 0.8 percent of GDP).[21] Tunisia is also a net importer of energy and suffered badly from rising global energy prices. Domestic prices are regulated, entailing a subsidy regime, but ultimately the government had to introduce a price adjustment mechanism which meant that domestic fuel prices rose repeatedly from 2008. Even so, by 2009, fuel subsidies amounted to 1.6 percent of GDP, having been negligible only five years before. Not surprisingly, and with the government injecting a fiscal stimulus into the economy to offset the difficulties caused by the global recession, inflation as a whole rose in Tunisia from 2.7 percent per annum in 1999 to 4.5 percent per annum in 2010, even as Tunisians' capacity to pay higher prices was eroded.[22]

The picture painted here of widespread poverty in Tunisia is at odds with the traditional portrayal of a large middle class. Due to early postindependence investments in education, Tunisia does have the largest middle class in Africa. Indeed, the African Development Bank suggests that a whopping 89.5 percent of Tunisians can be categorized as middle class, living on more than $2pppd.[23] However, 45.6 percent of Tunisians are classed as "floating middle class," that is living on between $2 and $4 per day, and are liable to fall into poverty in the event of exogenous economic shocks (such as rising food and fuel prices). A prominent feature of these floating middle classes is their dependence on salaried employment—they are highly likely to be urban dwelling and remote from subsistence support. Thus, in countries like Tunisia where the floating middle class amount to over half the total middle class, secure employment environments are profoundly important to underpin an ability to offset exogenous shocks in the short term. This is even more true when households have low access to savings capital. The Tunisian middle classes had little or no access to savings. In 2010, a study released by the national Consumer Protection Agency stated that 85 percent of Tunisians were already in debt, with the Central Bank estimating that household debt averaged $2,000.[24] Much of this was the result of a credit card boom over the previous decade, but it left households ill-prepared to face the steep inflationary pressures, a problem compounded by the deep-rooted crisis of unemployment.

With their focus on macroeconomic indicators, and with a poor understanding of the nature and scale of poverty across the country (and not just in urban pockets), the IFIs were focused on the need to contain the budgetary implications of rising subsidy bills. Whilst constantly reasserting the importance of protecting the poorest in society, they were equally adamant that the Tunisian regime should "firmly control current expenditure, including subsidies, to make as much room as possible for public investment, which they see as most effective for supporting current and future growth."[25] Moreover, the Tunisian government was urged to embark on substantive reform of the social security system, including adjusting retirement ages and pension contribution rates, in order to prevent government expenditures escalating in line with demographic changes and to ensure it could meet its obligations for the coming two decades. As one critical observer put it, the IMF was recommending cuts in fuel and food subsidies, and a diminishment of the social security net for a middle-class population which was nonetheless "just hanging on to the edge, hardly able to make it from day to day."[26] With the margin for floating into poverty so small, the IFIs unwittingly became complicit in the middle classes' demise.

Youth unemployment and its remedy

It is perhaps unfair to label youth unemployment as a missed story: IMF and WB country strategy reports consistently highlighted the scale of the problem, although their reliance on statistics generated by the Tunisian government meant that they still underestimated it. In 2009, the creation of high-skilled jobs was cited as a priority by the WB since the export-oriented model thus far had generated largely low-skilled jobs for the textile, manufacturing, and agricultural sectors, whilst the Tunisian labor force was relatively highly educated (although not necessarily with the knowledge-intensive skills required by a globally competitive economy).[27] The public sector, which had traditionally employed young graduates, was under fiscal pressures, and an accelerating privatization program was reducing job opportunities further. Unemployment was officially recognized as having reached 14.2 percent in 2008, with the greatest burden falling on young people and amongst them on new graduates.[28] In 2000, the WB estimated that the Tunisian economy would need to grow by an annual average of 8.6 percent between 2005 and 2025, just to absorb new entrants on the labor market,[29] and since 57 percent of them had university degrees,[30] this clearly meant extraordinarily rapid growth in high added-value knowledge-economy sectors.[31] Furthermore, unemployment was heavily concentrated in some geographic regions. In Moularès, Mdhilla and Redeyef, the main towns of the Gafsa Mining Basin area, for example, unemployment in 2007 officially stood at 38.5 percent, 28.4 percent and 26.7 percent respectively (in large part due to the contraction of the workforce of the Gafsa Phosphate Company as it underwent modernization and restructuring).[32] What new jobs were created were heavily concentrated in the coastal cities, leaving rural and inland areas behind in the distribution of development benefits.

Ironically, given that there was a direct correlation between higher levels of educational qualification and higher levels of unemployment, the labor force suffered a deficit of suitable technical, engineering or business skilled labor, indicating profound weaknesses in the educational system despite the achievements towards meeting the Millennium Development Goals (which focused on literacy rates and free universal and compulsory primary school education). Again, these deficiencies were well known and documented in, for example, the Arab Human Development Reports[33] and the WB's own MENA Development Report: *The Road Not Travelled: Educational Reform in the Middle East and Africa.*[34]

If the IFIs recognized some of the structural determinants of unemployment, their remedy was premised on matching human resources development policies to private-sector growth. But by 2009, it was clear that Tunisia's private-sector growth—like that of its regional neighbors—was in trouble. Another MENA Development Report produced in 2009 argued that, while it has come to contribute between 70 and 90 percent of GDP in most MENA countries—representing a major shift in their economic structures as a result of the economic reform process—"the private sector still falls well short of transforming MENA countries into diversified, highly performing economies."[35] Private sectors were growing, but not fast enough, and not as fast as comparator countries in other developing regions. Private investment, both domestic and foreign, had not responded as well to reforms and this was due not to dilatory reform processes but to specific failings in the state-business-society relationships. More explicitly, the report identified the primary causes of low private-sector growth as being corruption, nepotism, bribery, lobbying, tax avoidance, and non-transparent governance. The lack of transparency, discretionary capacities, and rent-seeking activities of regime elites and public officials had eroded the relationship between public and private sectors such that it was described as a story of mutual mistrust.[36] The business environment, as it was termed, was inadequate.

The report made its way into the WB's *2009 Country Partnership Strategy*, which noted that

> there exists a business environment in most MENA countries, including Tunisia, that is perceived to be based on privilege and unequal application of the rules of the game and has resulted in less competition. In Tunisia, this environment has constrained the creation of jobs and is the likely reason why private domestic investment has remained intractably low.[37]

Given the unequivocal attribution of low private-sector growth—on which all the outcomes of reform processes depended—on the deeply entrenched malgovernance of the state and regime elites, the country strategy thereafter makes astonishingly little reference to the need for any kind of clean-up program. There is one brief statement under "Areas for future reform" which indicates that "the role of the state needs to become more selective and much lighter with a smoother and more equal implementation of policies"; acknowledges that "CSOs would like to see the Government encourage a more effective participatory dialogue and implicate it in aspects of the decentralization process"; and recommends the introduction of financial support for broad reforms in quality of service of the public administration. Nowhere in the strategy document does the bank identify any kind of program, project or conditionality that would address this most fundamental cause of insufficient economic growth and consequent structural unemployment.

A full third of the economy

Even the WB report on MENA private sectors did not fully uncover the scale of the cronyism and corruption in Tunisia. Indeed, Tunisia was often cited as having relatively low corruption compared to other developing countries. Transparency International's Corruption Perception Index, which ranked countries on a scale of 0–10 (from highly corrupt to very clean) saw Tunisia fall from thirty-third place to sixty-fifth out of 180 countries between 1998 and 2009, but in 2010 Tunisia still ranked well above a number of European countries (including Italy and Greece) and the faster developing BRIC countries.[38] According to the WB's Governance Indicators, Tunisia remained throughout the period from 1998 to 2009 in the 50th–75th percentile of countries in terms of corruption, and consistently scored better than the regional average. Its *Ease of Doing Business Index* also appeared to show Tunisia climbing the ranks, from seventy-third in 2008 to fifty-fifth in 2010. So what were all these indexes missing given the high profile of corruption in the list of protesters' grievances being aired in the January 2011 uprising?

Once again, by concentrating on the macroeconomic picture and failing to drill down into the reality beneath, the IFIs failed to see beyond the emperor's new clothes. The picture they missed was of a third sector, a relatively small, close-knit, family-connected group of individuals who amassed vast amounts of private wealth in the form of business empires on the basis that they pulled the political strings of the state itself. Technically this was indeed a growing private sector, but it was not capital independent of the state and subject only to the latter's appropriately calibrated regulation. Rather, it was a concentration of capital which was able to circumvent the regulations of the state, to privilege itself at the expense of the genuine private sector and to ultimately transfer wealth out of the country rather than generating the investment capital that would fuel the kind of economic growth and job creation that the economy needed.

It is instructive to look at the privatization process as an example of this. Tunisia took steps towards privatizing some state-owned enterprises (SOEs) in the 1980s but only launched a privatization program as such after 1987. Until 1994, the government focused on forty-five small, mostly unprofitable enterprises in the service sector, setting rigid conditions which prevented them from subsequently trimming their workforces, thereby escaping significant political costs. In 1994, under pressure from the IFIs (and with Ben Ali's avaricious new wife installed in the palace at Carthage), the program was expanded to include larger and more profitable firms and was accompanied by a reform of the stock exchange so that sales of blocks of shares could be initiated (rather than just outright sale of firms). From the late 1990s, the program appeared to accelerate with a growing number of whole or partial sales of SOEs, even in strategic sectors such as telecommunications, transport, and banking, and with more innovative mechanisms such as concessions and Build-Own and Operate (BOO) being brought into play. To external observers, including the IFIs, this "signalled a clear commitment to private ownership as a more efficient and dynamic method of generating growth and jobs."[39] By December 2009, 219 enterprises had been partially or wholly privatized, of which 116 had been wholly privatized and twenty-nine partially privatized. Ten of them had a sale of capital by public offer, and five represented concessions.[40] In fact, such was the "success" of the program, which had raised some $4.2 billion for the government over a twenty-year period that by 2011 the process was running out of steam simply because the state was running out of assets to sell.[41] The income from sales was not as high as might have been expected, but the firms sold in the latest spree seemed reassuringly secure and profitable after privatization.

Dig a bit deeper and it becomes clear why the program had been accelerated but also why the receipts to the treasury were not as high as anticipated. State assets were sold outright to members of the president's extended family[42] and their close friends at discounted prices, and usually without genuine competitive bidding. In other instances, holding companies owned by Family individuals partnered international investors in buying block shares in state-owned companies, and in other cases Family individuals "facilitated" privileged purchases and concessions for international partners in return for either cash or a stake in the business. Wikileaks famously "outed" the sale of a 17 percent stake in Banque du Sud even before its privatization to Ben Ali's son-in-law, Marouane Mabrouk, a stake which he subsequently sold at a substantial profit. Mabrouk, who was married to Ben Ali's daughter, Cyrine, also purchased a flagship company, La Société Le Moteur, again at a discounted price, which gave him control over all Mercedes and Fiat distribution in the country. Other infamous Family "purchases" include La Céramique and the National Society for Raising Chickens by Ben Ali's son-in law, Slim Zarrouk; the transfer of significant parts of Tunisair to brother-in-law Belhassan Trabelsi; and even the sale of the duty-free shops to a Ben Ali company. Belhassan Trabelsi also bought the state-owned company which held the licenses for distribution of Ford, Rover, Jaguar, and Hyundai vehicles, and grew a tourism empire through purchasing privatized hotels.

Privatized land was also ripe for Family picking. The state land agency sold premium land (such as Les Côtes de Carthages and the Baie des Anges) to the extended Family, usually nominally for agricultural purposes and therefore at discounted prices. The Family then "obtained" permits to alter the usage to real estate, dramatically inflating the value. Son-in-law Slim Chiboub partnered the French hypermarket chain Carrefour in building a branch on Soukra land bought from the state at only a nominal price and Leila Trabelsi's brother-in-law even leased such land back to the Ministry of Transport at advantageous rates. Sakhr El Materi was also provided with land from the Tunisian Water Company, SONEDE, to build palatial accommodation in Sidi Bou Said. Capital for Family purchases came from subverting the funds of state agencies such as the housing fund, and from the hijacking of the management of parts of the banking sector such as the Banque de Tunisie by Belhassan Trabelsi in 2008. For example, Trabelsi managed to secure cheap dinar loans to the Turkish company TAV, which he represented in Tunisia, to purchase the rights to run Enfida-Hammamet International Airport, a deal which controversially included running down the passenger transport side of state-owned Monastir Airport and which also received support from the WB's International Finance Corporation (IFC). Indeed, the IFC provided significant financial support for the very banks that were making the dubious loans to the Family, many of which were never paid back or were unsecured.

Sakhr El Materi used an unguaranteed loan to buy Ennakl Automobiles, which owned a concession to import Volkswagen, Audi, Porsche, Seat, and Kia cars, for, it was rumored, just one third of the concession's real price. He also purchased the national shipping company and soon after was granted land, without having to go through any consultation or bidding process, around the port of La Goulette on which his holding company built tourist facilities and commercial shops, which gradually squeezed the state-owned Office des Ports Aériens de la Tunisie out of the market. One of the most recent Materi scandals was the purchase, as a partner with Watania-Q-tel, of the Orascom holding in mobile telephone company Tunisiana. Q-tel sought to increase its own existing stake and to obtain a 3G license: the price was to share the deal with Materi. Orascom's initial purchase had been controversial enough—it was funded with a dinar loan provided by Tunisian banks at the president's bidding despite this meaning that the Tunisian public sector effectively bought the shares for an overseas private company.

The regime made much of its liberalization of the banking sector, claiming ambitious plans to turn the country into Africa's financial services hub. Foreign investment was encouraged and private banks proliferated. In reality, however, capital remained concentrated, with the three state-owned banks dominating over half the market and continuing to be burdened with substantial underperforming loans. The remainder of the sector was highly fragmented, heavily infiltrated by Family interests[43] and given little incentive by the regime to invest in micro or small enterprises, or business start-ups. The sector served to financially lubricate a system of capital concentration as much as to facilitate genuine private-sector growth.

Other areas in which profitable licenses were distributed were the media, the airline sector, and telecommunications. Licenses for private radio stations were sold first to Belhassan Trabelsi's majority-owned Radio Mosaïque and then to Sakhr El Materi (for Zitouna FM) and the Mabrouk family (for Shems FM). Trabelsi was later a partner in Express FM and then in Carthage TV. El Materi meanwhile purchased a 70 percent stake in Dar Assabah, one of Tunisia's largest printing, publishing, distributing, and advertising companies. In doing so, he assumed virtual ownership of the last two even remotely independent newspapers (*Le Temps* and *Al-Sabah*). When the private sector was "let in" to the airline sector, the two new private companies were Belhassan Trabelsi's Karthago Airlines, and Slim Chiboub's Nouvelair (later merged under Trabelsi's control). The concession for the third telephone operator, after Materi's capture of Tunisiana, was sold to Orange, who partnered the president's daughter, Cyrine Ben Ali, in Planet Tunisia, the largest internet service provider in Tunisia.

Once privatized, what were now Family firms were often allocated profitable monopolies. For example, Mourad Trabelsi, one of Leila's brothers, was granted the monopoly on tuna exports (to complement his monopoly on fishing in the Lac de Tunis). Thus what looked like an opening of state-controlled sectors to the private sector was actually a redistribution of state assets around the Family. In fact, a whole string of corrupt practices were enacted which undermined the very regulatory systems that the state had officially introduced and which the IFIs had so favorably endorsed. Favored import companies were unofficially exempted from paying customs duties, creating unfair competition with the legitimate private sector. Public procurement was directed specifically to Family-held companies and not subjected to competitive pricing. Family connections became vital for individuals and firms seeking to purchase licenses and concessions. For example, the superstores Géant and Monoprix were able to operate only with licenses obtained by the Mabrouk family. As a last resort, the Family simply forced a purchase upon a firm against its owner's will or seized public assets for their own private use (the most notorious examples being the airplanes used to carry Leila Trabelsi on shopping sprees).

With their political influence, the Ben Ali and Trabelsi clans came to dominate whole economic geographies. The economy of the Greater Tunis area was dominated by the extended business dealings of the Trabelsi clan, while Ben Ali's siblings and children spread their empires south along the coastal plains. The extent of their empires was hard to gauge since often their participation in ventures was hidden behind complex company fronts. Estimates of the Family wealth abound: $7 billion,[44] $10 billion,[45] $15 billion[46]—we will probably never know—but there is no doubt that the Family virtually controlled whole sectors such as the media, cement production, petroleum distribution, construction, car dealerships, telecommunications, insurance, shipping, and air transport, that they held large parts of the private banking sector and worked in partnerships of some form or other with most major international investors. Transparency International made a simple calculation that between them the Family controlled a full third of the national economy, between 30 and 40 percent.[47]

Not only did they disguise the scale of their holdings in a complex web of partnerships and front companies, but they also used illegal means to transfer much of their subsequent wealth out of the country for investment in Switzerland, France, Argentina, the UAE, and elsewhere. By June 2011, Tunisian investigators had tracked down Ben Ali and Trabelsi assets in twenty-five countries with an estimated value of €10bn.[48] Subsequent to the uprising, the new government has identified 110 Family members whose assets have been confiscated, pending investigation and possible renationalization or sale. It has also established a commission charged with investigating corruption, including tracing back the processes by which privatizations were implemented, licenses allocated, and loans secured. Within seven months, the committee had received nearly 9,000 cases for investigation.[49]

Whilst everyone inside Tunisia knew about the corruption,[50] it was impossible to do anything about it. The two state instruments for enforcing anti-corruption, the National Audit Office and the Disciplinary Financial Court, were rendered ineffective by the political power of the Family, by the reliance of the regime on an extensive and repressive security apparatus, by their control of the media, by the weakness of the judiciary, and by the placing of key political allies of the Family within the very instruments set up to call them to account.

The impact of this high-level corruption was profound. For a start, the famously Wikileaked US Embassy cable recounted how nepotism and corruption trickled down through the economy and everyday life in general.[51] With the right connections or a bribe, passports, school places, scholarships for children, and public-sector jobs could be secured, parking tickets could be made to disappear, and loans could be raised from banks. Indeed, one of the principal grievances that led the Gafsa-basin mine workers to protest in 2008 was the belief that the few jobs available were distributed according to connections and bribes. The picture of an ever more efficient and formalized economy which the government communicated to the IFIs and which was represented in legal and regulatory reforms veiled the reality of an increasingly informal and distorted economy.

The second major impact was on the growth of the economy itself. A report by Global Financial Integrity produced in January 2011 suggested: "The amount of illegal money lost from Tunisia due to corruption, bribery, kickbacks, trade mispricing, and criminal activity between 2000 and 2008 was, on average, over $1 billion a year."[52] Add to this the massive transfers of the Ben Ali and Trabelsi fortunes overseas, and it becomes clear that Tunisia's economy lost much of its capacity to grow and generate employment because of the corruption. Not only were resources sucked out of the economy, but the trust of the private sector in the rule of law and in the integrity of state operations and regulatory activity was profoundly eroded, deterring domestic investment in particular. Subsequent investigations have shown that many international investors often had few qualms about dealing with the Family in order to capture Tunisian markets (which were made profitable by the monopoly status of their investments and by the wage repression which the state pursued at the behest of the IFIs). Hence we can explain the predominance of FDI in privatization revenues—some $3.7 billion of the $4.2 billion was FDI.[53] This also explains the continuing failure of the domestic private sector to grow at rates comparable with other developing countries, and the continued over-reliance of the economy on public and speculative investments and investments in low-skilled subcontracting operations established by FDI.

This highly personalized, deeply subverted version of a liberal economy bore little resemblance to the role model which the IMF and WB understood Tunisia to be. In making their own assessments, the IFIs were overly reliant on, and confident in, the information provided to them by the Tunisian government, which was carefully packaged to disguise the reality—emperor's clothes indeed. Since 2001, Tunisia had subscribed to the IMF's Special Data Dissemination Standard which aimed to implement best practice when it came to economic and financial statistics, and in 2006 it was in the pilot group of countries to undergo a data module in the IMF Report on the Observance of Standards and Codes. The subsequent report concluded that the quality of macroeconomic statistics in Tunisia had improved over the previous decade, that it was now "largely adequate" and that the Tunisian authorities were committed to improving their quality further. The legal and institutional frameworks were considered to be broadly effective, and the culture within data collection and processing agencies to be in line with international standards. Some methodologies were outdated and—interestingly—some statistics relating to sensitive areas like employment/unemployment were not released in as regular, timely or consistent manner as others.[54] The report noted that benchmark years were now very out of date, that data collection was often not detailed enough and that information was not as accessible as it should be. Moreover, the presentation of national-level data obscured regional disparities of consequence, a problem that had actually been identified within the 2004 United Nations *Tunisia National Report on Millennium Development Goals*.[55]

These problems can all now be seen to have helped paper over the emerging disparities in wealth distribution and opportunity,[56] just as the manipulation of the official poverty line had created a false understanding of the breadth and scale of vulnerability. The problem was not falsification of data (Rob Prince concluded after much study of it that it was "not so bad"[57]), but that it was compiled and presented—albeit systematically—in ways that obscured rather than illuminated. When inequality in unemployment or income had regional dimensions, the worst figures could be hidden by aggregation at the national level. Massively inflated incomes of the few would balance out with the squeezing of the middle classes and the poor. Survey sample groups were too small to be truly statistically significant and definitions selective.[58]

The IFIs failed to pursue the gaps in the data, preferring in some instances to cross-check the data provided by the Tunisian regime itself with limited engagements with a very narrow section of the population, usually the wider elite. For example, in the 2006 report, the IMF indicated it had surveyed fourteen Tunisian data-user representatives including individuals from the banks, international and regional organizations, financial media, think tanks, employers' organizations, and public administration. It neglected to recognize that all of these were either themselves embedded in the crony-elite or politically "captured," and that in an environment where speaking out or criticizing the regime in any way brought intense personal and arbitrary punishment, there was little likelihood that those surveyed would draw attention to the data deficits that mattered.

Getting it right next time

In April 2011, the IMF's then managing director, Dominique Strauss-Kahn, acknowledged the weakness of the IMF approach thus far, stating that the IMF should have paid more attention to the distribution of income, not just aggregate results, and that henceforth it would incorporate data on unemployment and inequality into its analysis, working with other institutions that specialize in these areas.[59] However, the discussion above suggests that a more radical review of the IFIs' approach to country partnership strategies was needed, one that did not shy away from political sensitivities but rather acknowledged that non-democratic government acts as a fundamental obstruction to the very programs the IFIs are seeking to pursue. Indeed, good governance cannot be pursued effectively without good government. The various IMF and WB reports referred to in this chapter show that the IFIs were not unaware of the deficiencies within regime governance, although they may not have fully appreciated their extent or impact, and there was no doubting the deficiencies of the authoritarian government. But at no point did the IFIs' country partnership strategies include specific programs or projects to address this, and there was certainly no political conditionality. In the end, the IFIs stood by while their own neoliberal projects were converted into cash generators for the corrupt regime and Family elites.

To be fair to the IFIs, they are banks after all, not political agents. They have no mandate to act as global enforcers of liberal democracy and must ultimately work with whatever national political structure exists at a given point in time. Nonetheless, as a result of their complicity in Tunisia's authoritarian past, they have lost the confidence of large sections of the Tunisian population and are having to relaunch themselves as credible partners in the economic project. As the first deputy managing director of the IMF, David Lipton, explained:

> As we engage more closely in the region, we find we have to explain the role of the IMF and how we work with governments today. We know from experience that programs are much more likely to succeed if they are designed and owned by the national authorities and enjoy broad support within the country. We are also focusing much more explicitly on policies that ensure that the benefits of economic growth are shared much more broadly. And now we consult widely with civil society, labor, and parties across the broad political spectrum.[60]

The WB too has recast itself, working closely with the interim government to support transition principally through a new single multisector lending operation (the Governance and Opportunity Development Loan) which focuses on improving transparency and reform within government itself (the interim governments not having a mandate to partner in more long-term commitments). Following the 2011 Constituent Assembly elections, an interim strategy established three core pillars which reflected the goals of the uprising: sustainable growth and job creation; social and economic inclusion; and strengthening governance.[61] But pending more long-term political arrangements, and whilst further programs are being developed that tackle key Tunisian concerns such as poverty and youth unemployment, actual disbursement by the WB since has fallen dramatically.

The IMF also declares itself ready to support the country's reform program with a Precautionary Stand-by Arrangement worth $1.78 billion. Yet ultimately, while both IFIs have adjusted their approach—and their language—to be more inclusive of multiple stakeholders and more sensitive to the social conditions that accompany macroeconomic underperformance, their prescription for recovery remains much the same. The IMF has so far endorsed increased government spending, notably on job creation and subsidy support, as necessary to offset the temporary economic crises created by first Tunisia's own political instability and then the impact of the European downturn. But it insists that policy adjustments must soon be made to direct that spend into public investment for growth rather than consumption, and that in the medium term Tunisia must return to a path of greater openness to trade and FDI, less government intervention, and tighter targeting of subsidies.[62] With or without Ben Ali, economic liberalization must go on.

Tunisians are not so sure. Protracted political crises, labor strikes, and public protests continue to obstruct the stability that the economy needs. The revolution has not brought relief from unemployment or poverty and for most the crisis is deepening, not relenting. Few see the solution as lying in carefully crafted technical negotiations with the IFIs, which ultimately seem to promise more of the same. The country's borrowing needs may determine its dependence on these institutions, not least as its commercial credit ratings continue to slide, but, even if the IFIs have taken the political lessons of the past to heart, Tunisians are unlikely to love them more or blame them less.

Notes

1. This perception was fueled, for example, by the Wikileaked US cables. In Cable EO12958 of July 17, 2009, the US Ambassador to Tunis outlined the corrupt and repressive behavior of the Tunisian regime but said: "Not withstanding the frustrations of doing business here, we cannot write off Tunisia. We have too much at stake. We have an interest in preventing al-Qaeda in the Islamic Maghreb and other extremist groups from establishing a foothold here . . . Moreover we need to increase mutual understanding to help repair the image of the United States and secure greater cooperation on our many regional challenges." See "US Embassy Cables: Tunisia – a US Foreign Policy Conundrum," *The Guardian*, December 17, 2010, accessed October 7, 2011, www.guardian.co.uk/world/us-embassy-cables-documents/217138.
2. Mahdi Darius Nazemroaya, "Dictatorship, Neo-liberalism and IMF's Diktats: The Tunisian People's Uprising," accessed July 14, 2011, http://realisticbird.wordpress.com/2011/01/20/dictatorship-neo-liberalism-and-imfs-diktats-the-tunisian-peoples-uprising.
3. Carnegie Middle East Center. "A Conversation with Mustapha Nabli, Governor of Tunisia's Central Bank. The Economic Dimensions of Unrest in the Arab World," posted February 23, 2011, accessed July 20, 2011, http://carnegie-mec.org/events/?fa=3165.
4. This is not a discussion of the virtues or otherwise of neoliberalism per se, but rather of its actual implementation in Tunisia over the course of several decades (although admittedly one could argue that such a separation is artificial).
5. See, for example, Emma Murphy, *Economic and Political Change in Tunisia: From Bourguiba to Ben Ali* (London: Macmillan, 1999) and "The Tunisian Mise à Niveau Programme and the Political Economy of Reform," *New Political Economy* 11.4 (2006): 519–40.

6. For a competent and abbreviated economic history, see Christopher Alexander, *Tunisia: Stability and Reform in the Modern Maghreb* (Abingdon: Routledge, 2010), Chapter 2, 68–88.
7. Alexander, *Tunisia: Stability and Reform in the Modern Maghreb*, 79.
8. For details of these plans and their outcomes, see Murphy, *Economic and Political Change in Tunisia*, Chapters 4 and 5.
9. See Kenneth Perkins's chapter in this book.
10. For more details of this programme, see Murphy, "The Tunisian Mise à Niveau Programme."
11. World Bank, "International Bank for Reconstruction and Development Country Partnership Strategy for the Republic of Tunisia for the period FY10-13" (Washington, DC: World Bank, 2009).
12. IMF, "Tunisia: 2007 Article IV Consulting Mission Preliminary Conclusions." IMF Country Report No. 02/122, accessed July 28, 2011, www.imf.org/external/np/ms/2007/062907.html.
13. IMF, "Tunisia: Selected Issues." IMF Country Report No. 10/109, accessed July 28, 2011, www.imf.org/external/pubs/ft/scr/2010/cr10109.pdf.
14. World Bank, "Memorandum of the President of the International Bank for Reconstruction and Development to the Executive Directors on a Country Assistance Strategy of the World Bank Group for the Republic of Tunisia." Report No. 20161-TN (Washington, DC: World Bank, 2000).
15. World Bank, "Memorandum of the President of the International Bank for Reconstruction and Development to the Executive Directors on a Country Assistance Strategy for the Republic of Tunisia." Report No. 28791-TUN (Washington, DC: World Bank, 2004).
16. IMF, "2007 Article IV Consultation Mission Preliminary Conclusions," 1.
17. World Bank, "International Bank for Reconstruction and Development Country Partnership Strategy for the Republic of Tunisia for the period FY10-13," i.
18. Naouar Labidi and Erminio Sacco, "Food Security in Tunisia: Rapid Assessment Report" (Rome: World Food Programme, 2011), accessed July 17, 2011, http://home.wfp.org/stellent/groups/public/documents/ena/wfp235120.pdf.
19. Labidi and Sacco, "Food Security in Tunisia," 8.
20. Food and Agriculture Organization, "FAO Food Price Index," accessed September 27, 2011, www.fao.org/worldfoodsituation/wfs-home/foodpricesindex/en.
21. Ronald Albers and Maarga Peeters, *Food and Energy Prices; Government Subsidies and Fiscal Balances in South Mediterranean Countries*, European Economy Papers 431 (Brussels: European Commission, 2011).
22. "CIA Factbook, 2011," accessed July 10, 2011, www.cia.gov/library/publications/the-world-factobook/geos/ts.html.
23. Maurice Mubila and Mohamed Safouane Ben Aissa, *The Middle of the Pyramid: Dynamics of the Middle Class in Africa*, Chief Economist Complex Market Brief (Tunis: African Development Bank, 2011).
24. Bertelsmann Stiftung, 2011, "BTI 2010 Tunisia Country Report," accessed September 27, 2011, www.bertelsmann-transformation-index.de/145.0.html?L=1.
25. IMF, "Tunisia: 2010. Article IV Consultation – Staff Report; Public Information Notice on the Executive Board Discussion; and Statement by the Executive Director

for Tunisia," IMF Country Report No. 10/282, accessed July 28, 2011, www.imf.org/external/pubs/ft/scr/2010/cr10282.pdf.

26. James Pilant, "Did the International Monetary Fund Push Tunisia into Revolution? YES," Pilant's Business Ethics Blog, September 20, 2010, accessed July 20, 2011, http://pilantsbusinessethics.com/2011/01/29/did-the-international-monetary-fund-push-tunisia-into-revolution.
27. World Bank. "International Bank for Reconstruction and Development Country Partnership Strategy," 9.
28. According to the World Bank, in 2007 youth unemployment in Tunisia stood at 41 percent. See World Bank, "Economic Developments and Prospects: Job Creation in an Era of High Growth," accessed October 3, 2011, http://web.worldbank.org/WBSITE/EXTERNAL/COUNTRIES/MENAEXT/0,,contentMDK:21483969~pagePK:146736~piPK:226340~theSitePK:256299,00.html.
29. World Bank, "Republic of Tunisia: Social and Structural Review 2000." (Washington, DC: World Bank, 2000), 1.
30. World Bank, "International Bank for Reconstruction and Development Country Partnership Strategy," 12.
31. For more detail on youth unemployment in Tunisia, see Marco Stampini and Audrey Verdier-Chouchane, *Labour Market Dynamics in Tunisia: The Issue of Youth Unemployment*, African Development Bank Group Working Paper 123 (Tunis: African Development Bank, 2011).
32. Eric Gobe, "The Gafsa Mining Basin Between Riots and a Social Movement: Meaning and Significance of a Protest Movement in Ben Ali's Tunisia," accessed July 16, 2011, http://halshs.archives-ouvertes.fr/halshs-00557826. See also Sami Zemni's chapter in this book.
33. United Nations Development Programme/Arabic Fund for Economic and Social Development. *Arab Human Development Report 2003: Building a Knowledge Society* (New York: UNDP, 2003).
34. World Bank, "The Road Not Travelled: Educational Reform in the Middle East and Africa." MENA Development Report (Washington, DC: World Bank, 2008).
35. Najy Belhassine et al., *From Privilege to Competition: Unlocking Private-Led Growth in the Middle East and North Africa*, MENA Development Report (Washington, DC: World Bank, 2009), 4.
36. Benhassine et al., *From Privilege to Competition*, 3.
37. World Bank, "International Bank for Reconstruction and Development Country Partnership Strategy."
38. BRIC is a group acronym used to refer to the countries of Brazil, Russia, India, and China, all of which were deemed to be at a similar stage of advanced economic development by economist Jim O'Neill in "Building Better Global Economic BRICs," Global Economics Paper 66 (London and New York: Goldman Sachs, 2001). Since then it has been commonly accepted that South Africa has joined the group, constituting the BRICS.
39. Alexander, *Tunisia: Stability and Reform in the Modern Maghreb*, 81.
40. Government of Tunisia, "Privatisation in Tunisia: The Value of a Strategic Investment," 2007. "Privatisation in Tunisia: The Value of a Strategic Investment," accessed September 15, 2011, www.privatisation.gov.tn/www/en/doc.asp?mcat=1&mrub=50.

41. *Executive Magazine*, "Tunisia's Sell-off Slowdown," *Executive* 93 (April 2007), accessed September 15, 2011, http://robertjprince.wordpress.com/2011/08/07/the-world-bankimfs-strange-fuit-civil.
42. The Family, as it was known to Tunisians, comprised two main lineages: President Ben Ali's seven siblings and his three children and their partners through his first marriage, and the family of his second wife, Leila Trabelsi, which included her ten siblings, two daughters, and son (and the latter's respective spouses), and her nieces and nephews. The Family was linked by marriage to major business families such as the Jilanis, Mzabis, Mabrouks, and Materis.
43. As well as Materi's ownership of Zitouna, and Trabelsi's control over Banque de Tunisie, the Mabrouk family controlled the Banque Internationale de Tunisie (BIAT), the Ben Alis had interests in the Amen Bank, and Slim Zarrouk controlled Mediobank, for example.
44. Damien McElroy, "Tunisia Orders Investigation into £5bn Fortune of Ben Ali," *The Telegraph*, January 19, 2011, accessed April 26, 2011, www.telegraph.co.uk/news/worldnews/africaandindianocean/tunisia/8269734/Tunisia-orders-investigation-into-5bn-fortune-of-Ben-Ali.html.
45. Aidan Lewis,"Tracking Down the Ben Ali and Trabelsi Fortune," *BBC News Africa*, January 31, 2011, accessed October 4, 2011, www.bbc.co.uk/news/world-africa-12302659.
46. Rob Prince, "The World Bank/IMF's Strange Fruit: Uprising in Tunisia: Part One," August 7, 2011. *Colorado Progressive Jewish News*, accessed September 15, 2011, http://robertjprince.wordpress.com/2011/08/07/the-world-bankimfs-strange-fruit-civil-war-in-algeria-uprising-in-tunisia.
47. Aidan Lewis, "Tracking Down the Ben Ali and Trabelsi Fortune."
48. *Magharebia*,"Ben Ali, Trabelsi Assets Found in 25 Countries," *Magharebia*, June 23, 2011, accessed October 4, 2011, http://magharabia.com/en_GB/articles/awi/newsbriefs/general/2011/06/02.
49. Ahmed Lachheb, "Investigation Committee Against Corruption Will Embarrass Tunisian Lawyers," August 14, 2011, accessed October 4, 2011, www.tunisia-live.net/2011/08/14/investigation-committee-against-corruption-will-embarrass-tunisian-lawyers.
50. Details of the family corruption were widely circulated in two books which were originally published in French; they were banned from sale in Tunisia but available to Tunisians through the internet. See Nicolas Beau and Jean-Pierre Tuquoi, *Notre ami Ben Ali* (Paris, La Découverte, 1999), and Nicolas Beau and Catherine Graciet, *La régente de Carthage: Main basse sur la Tunisie* (Paris, La Découverte, 2009).
51. Wikileaks. "Corruption in Tunisia: What's Yours is Mine." Classified cable from Ambassador Robert F. Godec to Secretary of State Washington DC, Reference ID 08TUNIS679, EO 12958, June 23, 2008, accessed October 7, 2011, www.wikileaks.ch/cable/2008/06/08TUNIS679.html.
52. *The Economist*. "Ali Baba Gone, But What About the 40 Thieves?," *The Economist*, January 20, 2011, accessed October 7, 2011, www.economist.com/node/17959620?story_id=17959620
53. *Executive Magazine*, "Tunisia's Sell-off Slowdown."
54. International Monetary Fund. "Tunisia: Report on the Observance of Standards and Codes-Data Module; Response by the Authorities and Detailed Assessments Using

the Data Quality Assessment Framework." IMF Country Report No. 06/300. August 2006, accessed March 1, 2012, www.imf.org/external/pubs/ft/scr/2006/cr06300.pdf.

55. United Nations. *Tunisia: National Report on Millennium Development Goals* (Geneva: IMF, 2004).
56. The WFP's Food Security Rapid Assessment in April 2007 noted, for example, that poverty statistics had been overly aggregated at the macroregion level and poverty lines unclearly defined, allegedly to obscure poverty prevalence figures. See Labidi and Sacco, "Food Security in Tunisia."
57. Prince, "The World Bank/IMF's Strange Fruit," 5.
58. Stampini and Verdier-Chouchane, *Labour Market Dynamics in Tunisia*, 1.
59. IMF Survey Online "Mideast Unrest Shows Need to Consider Bigger Picture," IMF Survey Online, April 8, 2011, accessed October 4, 2011, www.imf.org/external/pubs/ft/survey/so/2011/car040811b.htm.
60. International Monetary Fund, "Enabling Economic Transformation in the Middle East and North Africa." Speech given by David Lipton at the London School of Economics, November 13, 2012, March 25, 2013, accessed www.imf.org/external/np/speeches/2012/111312.htm.
61. World Bank. "Implementation Completion and Results Report IBRD 80750. On a Loan in the Amount of US$250 Million and EUR 168.3 Million to the Republic of Tunisia for a Governance and Opportunity Development Policy Loan" (Washington, DC: World Bank, 2012).
62. International Monetary Fund, "Enabling Economic Transformation."

CHAPTER 2

Playing the Islamic Card: The Use and Abuse of Religion in Tunisian Politics

Kenneth Perkins

When Tunisia became independent in 1956 after seventy-five years of French colonial control, the country enjoyed a positive image in Europe and North America, where it was seen as a progressive, pro-Western, and secular, albeit almost totally Muslim, state. The contrast to the recently initiated and violently bitter struggle for independence in neighboring Algeria reinforced that image, as did the positive relationship many of Tunisia's leaders enjoyed with important European statesmen and diplomats. That much the same attitudes still prevailed half a century later was evident during the state visit to Washington in February 2004 of its president Zine El Abidine Ben Ali. George W. Bush praised Ben Ali's leadership and cited Tunisia as an ally in the global war against terrorism, once again contrasting Tunisia with its North African neighbors. Indeed, despite its many ties with Algeria and Libya, Tunisia had avoided the trauma inflicted on the former by a decade of strife following aborted elections of 1991 and the global opprobrium directed against the latter during the rule of its idiosyncratic and ultimately murderous leader. The government of Ben Ali, on the other hand, had virtually annihilated an Islamist movement in the 1990s, driving religion from the nation's political discourse—although Bush's appeal for improvements in Tunisia's human rights and civil liberties record served as a reminder of the enduring costs of that campaign which haunted the country in the years that followed, as manifestly revealed in the 2011 revolution. By the next occasion on which a high-ranking Tunisian official (Prime Minister Béji Caïd Essebsi) and President of the United States Barack Obama conferred, Tunisia had provided the launching pad for the "Arab Spring," Ben Ali had fled the country, and a new government was preparing to hold elections for a Constituent Assembly. While failing to secure a majority in that voting, Ennahda, Tunisia's best-organized and most active Islamic party, had rebounded from earlier efforts to eradicate it and was playing a critical part in shaping postrevolutionary Tunisia. Consequently, questions about the appropriate role of Islam in the state—and, indeed, about the very nature of Tunisian Islam—had come to the fore after years of government efforts to discourage such discussion or at least to cast it in frameworks of its own formulation. Islam was very much at center stage.

In fact, while decades of development had left some—though not, as the revolution dramatically emphasized, all—areas of Tunisia virtually indistinguishable from Mediterranean Europe and its urban population among the most westernized in the Arab world, Islam—with its concern for political, social, and economic organization, no less than for matters of worship—had remained an important component of Tunisian identity. But in the minds of many Tunisians, Islam has often been ill-served by their governments. For much of the time from 1956 to 2011, an appeal to Islamic ideals proved an effective tool for the mobilization of popular opinion on those occasions when political forces allowed Muslim leaders latitude to promote their views. During the 1980s and 1990s, some extreme proponents of political Islam resorted to violence, but their actions were often responses to the government's intransigent refusal to deal the Islamist movement into the political game, much less to allow it to win a hand. The authorities' unwillingness to acknowledge the Islamic movement as a participant in the political process fits a pattern in Tunisian history discernible for more than half a century. That Islam and the Islamists were not, at the outset, the driving force behind the broad, popular, electronically organized demonstrations that toppled the Ben Ali regime in 2011 is a fact worth noting. So too is the alacrity with which Islamists attained a position of greater prominence on the Tunisian political scene than either they or their opponents could have imagined only a short time before. Today, as the global community awaits the appearance of pluralism, tolerance, and representative government, along with the curbing of elements incompatible with democratic principles across the Middle East and North Africa as an outgrowth of the "Arab Spring," Tunisia's historical experience can be instructive as the country embarks on an overhaul of its political structures that has at least the potential for genuine change.

In the decade between the end of the Second World War and independence, two men stood out as key figures in the nationalist Neo-Destour (New Constitutional) party, which had been founded in 1934 and was built on a tradition of indigenous political organization dating back to the closing decades of the nineteenth century. Its president, Habib Bourguiba, was French educated (he held a law degree from the Sorbonne), secular, and deeply committed to reforming or, even better if possible, eliminating the French protectorate and replacing it with a modern, progressive state. His anticolonial activism had led to his arrest in 1938 and, with a few brief exceptions, he spent most of the time from then until 1955 either in prison or outside the country, seeking to generate international support for the party's goals. In his absence, Secretary-General Salah Ben Youssef presided over the party. Far less westernized than Bourguiba, Ben Youssef succeeded in attracting into the Neo-Destour many traditional and conservative Tunisians who had previously been inclined to hold the party at arm's length. Prominent among his recruits were reform-minded students and faculty at the Zitouna mosque's theological university, a bastion of traditional Islamic education that had been swept by the currents of the Islamic reform movement that flourished in Egypt and the eastern Arab world in the late nineteenth century and remained a powerful influence in Tunisia.[1] Together, these groups came to constitute an Arab- and Islamic-oriented wing of the party that the secular westernized nationalists who remained in the majority largely strove to subordinate, creating in the process a reservoir of ill will that guaranteed future problems.

The early 1950s witnessed a frustrating and inconclusive dialogue between Tunisian leaders and French officials, as the latter sought to mute the voices of influential Neo-Destourians. Not until 1954, when Paris acknowledged that only discussions with the previously sidelined Bourguiba could bear fruit, did progress towards altering Tunisia's protectorate status occur. Not all party members, however, approved of the ensuing dialogue. Ben Youssef criticized Bourguiba's willingness to discuss an agreement offering less than full independence, but the divergent worldviews of the two men created tensions that went beyond tactical disagreements. Ben Youssef had increasingly identified himself with an Arab and Islamic perspective just as his rival was laying the groundwork for preserving a strong, if decidedly altered, relationship between Tunisia and France that took the form of an agreement granting Tunisia control over its internal affairs in April 1955. When the secretary-general went on the offensive against what he termed "a step backward" the Neo-Destour political bureau ousted him from the party.[2]

Ben Youssef continued to rail against Bourguiba, drawing support from disenchanted quarters within the party, not least among them the men of Zitouna. The confrontation came to a head when he tried, but failed, to mount a boycott of a party congress in November 1955. With Bourguiba and his allies providing the orchestration, congress delegates endorsed the internal autonomy accords. Despite this setback, Ben Youssef and his followers—20,000 of whom came out into the streets of Tunis and other cities in protest—did not abandon their campaign. Some organized rival party cells; others resorted to violence against the mainstream Neo-Destour. As the country teetered on the brink of civil war, Ben Youssef fled to Cairo in January 1956 and Bourguiba was compelled to request French military and police assistance to curb the violence and stabilize the country. Two months later, internal autonomy gave way to complete independence; this was the result less of the efforts of the Tunisian nationalist leadership than of circumstances in Morocco, where the return from exile of the enormously popular Sultan Muhammad V all but guaranteed a rapid transition to independence, and in Algeria, which was engulfed by then in a full-scale rebellion that required French prudence elsewhere in the Maghreb if it were to have any prospect of salvaging what was left of its North African empire. But even after independence, Ben Youssef went on berating his former comrades from his Egyptian exile until his assassination in 1961, which many of his followers immediately laid at Bourguiba's doorstep—an accusation ultimately borne out, albeit not until decades later. With respect to Islam, the men symbolize what might be thought of as two discrete, enduring Tunisian publics, whose divergent views range across a broad spectrum from finely nuanced distinctions to diametrically opposed perspectives, with a considerable grey area between the black and white extremes. Within that grey area are the millions of citizens who admire aspects of the West and of "modernization," but also insist on the Arab and Islamic identity that lies at the core of their being. At the margins—the realm of the true believers—matters are clear-cut and appropriate policy decisions obvious; in the grey zone, considerable maneuvering room exists for exploring options. Bourguiba's presentation of himself as the personification of the latter inevitably cast Ben Youssef as the personification of the former in a process that enshrined the dichotomy in the country's political culture.

Bourguiba and Islam: the house makes the rules

In the spring and summer of 1956, Bourguiba took advantage of the nation's euphoria with independence and his power as the first head of an independent Tunisian government to bring certain aspects of religion under the control of the state. The Habus Administration, which managed land set aside to support mosques, Qur'anic schools, and other religious institutions, came under fire first. By confiscating its property, the government brought the religious, educational, and charitable institutions that were beneficiaries of its funds under state control. Shortly thereafter, the merger of Sharia law courts into the state judicial system cleared the way for the introduction of a Personal Status Code altering numerous practices sanctioned within Sharia but regarded by progressives as prejudicial to women. Women won the right to divorce and to approve marriages arranged on their behalf, as well as a broader range of entitlements in matters of child custody and inheritance. Other provisions outlawed polygyny, ended the male right of repudiation, and set minimum ages for marriages.

The most innovative legal reform in the Muslim world since Turkey's abolition of Sharia in the 1920s, the Personal Status Code clearly revealed the trajectory Bourguiba envisioned. He took pains, however, to portray himself not as sweeping aside Islam, as Ataturk had, but rather as using critical thinking skills (*ijtihad*) to reinterpret it—a process highly regarded by many nineteenth- and twentieth-century Muslim reformers. (Indeed, during the 2011 Constituent Assembly election campaign, the leading Islamist figure in the country cited the Code's grounding in *ijtihad* as reason enough for not advocating its annulment.) Bourguiba's careful explanation of his approach reflected his awareness of the importance of not being seen as anti-Islam. Aspects of his earlier political activism credited that image. In the 1930s, as an anticolonial journalist, he had endorsed actions rooted in traditional Islam rather than seemingly more contemporary options—for example, opposing the burial of Tunisians who had adopted French citizenship (and thus abandoned Islam) in Muslim cemeteries and again by urging women to ignore French importuning to abandon the practice of covering their faces because doing so proclaimed their Tunisian identity as distinct from the values and practices of the colonizers. Bourguiba understood the risks, rewards, and limits of the path on which he was embarking by injecting himself into the understanding of Islam in Tunisian society. The 1957 constitution, into which he had considerable input, specified, for example, that Islam was the country's religion (and Arabic its language), but he was determined to keep Islamic institutions subordinate to the state.

This early overhaul of the Sharia courts, which extended to reassigning or retiring many judges, appointing a moderately progressive rector at the Zitouna mosque theological university, and offering blandishments of various kinds to other prominent members of the religious establishment, overcame much opposition to the code. Many lower-ranking men of religion cast aspersions on both their seniors' timidity and Bourguiba's temerity, but they knew they were powerless to stop him. From Cairo, Ben Youssef thundered that Bourguiba had taken it upon himself to "prohibit what God has authorized and authorize what God has prohibited"[3]—an inversion of the traditional obligation of the just Muslim ruler.

For the Neo-Destour males who engineered the Personal Status Code—and it was not until 1955 that women entered the inner circle of the party, and then only in minuscule numbers—the full emancipation of Tunisia demanded eliminating antiquated social practices wherever they existed, including those once endorsed by Bourguiba himself as symbols of national identity in the colonial era. Relieved of the need to embellish further his anticolonial credentials, Bourguiba's liberal and progressive instincts came to the fore as he faced about on this issue and enthusiastically campaigned to discourage all forms of traditional dress. He asserted that old-fashioned clothing encouraged old-fashioned modes of thinking and acting; those who chose to wear it were, at least subconsciously, expressing their rejection of the modern world. In speech after speech during the first years after independence, he condemned the veil as an "odious rag" that demeaned women, had no practical value, and was not obligatory in order to conform to Islamic standards of modesty. But despite his strong personal convictions and his efforts to present these views as not merely his own, but those of all enlightened and thinking Muslims, Bourguiba understood the tenacity with which many Tunisians clung to customs they had followed since childhood and, except for banning the veil in classrooms, he did not attempt to proscribe traditional clothing.

The social revolution set in motion in the first years of independence by men, and a few women, whose backgrounds and education had rendered them far more westernized than the great majority of the Tunisian population brought Tunisia into the international spotlight. Devised by high-level Neo-Destour officials and imposed from above by a regime enjoying broad support but hardly mindful of democratic conventions, the reforms embodied the agenda of a leader determined to build a "modern" society that had the respect of the global community. At a time when colonial mentalities about the Afro-Asian masses' need for enlightened (that is, westernized) guidance remained prevalent, neither the arrogance of the reformer nor his often heavy-handed methods drew much criticism from abroad. Instead, the Bourguiba government won praise for its assault on "outmoded traditions," its expansion of education, and its enhancement of the status of women. These social policies, coupled with Bourguiba's unflinching Cold War alignment with the West, helped to secure the economic assistance of the United States, which touted Tunisia as a model for other developing countries, comparing it particularly favorably with Arab states that had sacrificed social progress to revolutionary politics. As decolonization hit full stride across Africa, Tunisia's social programs were taking root and leaders from across the continent acknowledged Bourguiba's credentials as an advocate of social change. The Tunisian example influenced many of them as they set their countries' postindependence courses.

But respect in the international arena meant little to resolute opponents at home, especially within the religious establishment. The many Zitouna students, faculty, and alumni who had broken with the mainstream Neo-Destour leadership in the last years of the independence struggle resented the changes Bourguiba had instituted, among them the placement of the mosque's university under the supervision of the Ministry of Education, which they regarded as a prelude to its coming under more stringent political control. But it was his public disparagement of the Muslim fast during the month of Ramadan that provided the proverbial straw that broke the camel's back.

In a 1960 speech, the president asserted that Tunisia's battle against underdevelopment constituted a jihad that absolved its citizens from fasting during the sacred month, just as warriors in a jihad in defense of Islam were exempted. Even among the party faithful, the argument won little support. When Bourguiba renewed the campaign in the following year, rioting erupted in Kairouan, the site of the country's oldest and most revered mosque. Its influential religious leaders denounced Bourguiba's views and despised his efforts to cast himself as a religious authority. The government's decision to reassign a popular and outspoken prayer leader sparked a day of street battles between demonstrators and the police in the most serious challenge to the political establishment since independence.

Bourguiba subsequently smeared the religious leaders with allegations that their loss of economic power, not spiritual concerns, lay behind their discontent. He once again made a point of urging Tunisians to ignore the fast, but then let the matter drop. Regardless of the extent to which new schools and new legal codes were transforming their society, the vast majority of Tunisians had no intention of breaking with core religious practices that defined them as

Muslims. The assault on Islamic institutions between 1956 and 1961 confirmed the religious leaders in their abhorrence of the Neo-Destour and its secular leader, but they knew they could not defy Bourguiba. As if to underscore that reality, the University of Tunis absorbed the Zitouna mosque's university as a faculty of theology in 1961, completing its subordination to the state. Since both Bourguiba and the religious leadership understood that the state had the power to hold the religious establishment in check, there was, for the moment, no merit in either continuing to antagonize the other.

There the matter rested while Tunisia pursued an ambitious program of development predicated, in the 1960s, on a heavy dosage of state management of the economy and, in the 1970s, following some spectacular disappointments, on a pendulum swing towards economic liberalism. These years witnessed considerable growth, but they were also a time of considerable social and economic dislocation, in response to which several religious organizations with their roots at the Zitouna cautiously emerged in the early 1970s. The most vocal, the Association for the Preservation of the Qur'an, bemoaned the weakening of Islamic values and morality in the country and urged its members to embed Islamic precepts at the core of their lives as a source of strength and comfort, but also as a necessary first step toward altering objectionable national policies. Since the organization skirted direct condemnation of the government, the authorities adopted an attitude of vigilance towards it but took no more forceful action.

By the end of the decade, however, an Islamic movement with a somewhat different perspective was taking shape. The Islamic Tendency Movement (Mouvement de la Tendance Islamique, MTI) advocated placing Islam more squarely at the center not just of private, but also of public, life. The example of the Islamic Revolution in Iran provided political inspiration to its co-founders Rachid Ghannouchi, a high school teacher, and Abdelfattah Mourou, a graduate of the Zitouna. While repeating its predecessors' calls regarding Islam, the MTI went further, demanding that the single-party state develop a more representative political structure and fairer and more just economic policies. The coupling of demands for economic and social justice with an explicit call for spiritual renewal particularly sparked the interest of Tunisians eager to find anchors as they drifted in a society changing faster and more thoroughly than they could easily grasp. This included those for whom piety and religiosity were not, as a rule, matters of profound daily concern. The MTI articulated proposals to which these citizens, and not the devout alone, could relate, thereby giving its message a broader appeal than would otherwise have been the case.

Tunisians who turned to religion, particularly in its most traditional forms, for comfort in these circumstances were far from alone. A similar turn to faith as a coping mechanism and as an anchor in a sea of turmoil was occurring in other Muslim countries across the Middle East around the same time (as shown, for example, by the growth of the Muslim Brotherhood and the Islamic revolution in Iran), but also in predominantly Christian countries in the Americas, not least among Protestants in the United States and in Israel. This was a plea to turn widely held theories of justice, respect for the "Golden Rule," and accountability into practice, often through very public demonstrations of faith and belief, in contexts where, more often than not, those ideals had come to receive little more than lip service. Even when these goals were not explicitly asserted, they were clear to those listeners with the most at stake, and it was obvious that their fulfillment was improbable under oppressive or dictatorial regimes whose primary purpose was maintaining themselves in power. Thus, religion became a potential tool in many anti-regime struggles, eventually including Tunisia.[4] Not surprisingly, the MTI gained followers in several, often overlapping, quarters: first, among the poor whom the World Bank (WB) defined as those Tunisians with annual incomes under roughly 700 Tunisian dinars, or $1,400, and who constituted a third of the population;[5] second, among young people who regarded the Socialist Destour (as the single party was known after 1964) not as the engine of independence (in most cases, before they were born) but rather as an anachronism with little to offer them; and finally, among middle-class men and women who valued their Islamic heritage (as they understood it) and had seen their lives disrupted by government experiments with socialism and capitalism, both of which failed to fulfill the expectations raised on their behalf.[6]

Bourguiba had steadfastly refused to countenance a multi-party political system even in the face of rising criticism within the party itself. But popular unrest, culminating in a general strike in 1978 marked by the most violent and bloodiest rioting since independence, induced him to allow more Tunisians into the political arena, although he was determined to do so without jeopardizing the tightly held control of the ruling establishment. In the 1981 parliamentary elections, political organizations were permitted, for the first time, to put forward lists of candidates provided they conformed to restrictive government-imposed criteria. Groups that secured 5 percent of the vote were to receive official recognition as political parties, but none crossed even that minimal threshold.

A disturbing feature for the aggressively secular Socialist Destour leaders in the run-up to these elections was the popular enthusiasm for the MTI. Often speaking in mosques, its spokesmen tested the limits of the regime's tolerance as they condemned twenty-five years of policies that had removed virtually any trace of an Islamic dimension from Tunisian public life. On the eve of the elections, Ghannouchi and Mourou were arrested and charged with defaming the "president for life"—an "honor" bestowed on Bourguiba in 1974 that spoke volumes about the nature of the political system. Scores of MTI adherents were also jailed, throwing the entire movement into disarray. Nevertheless, candidates known to be sympathetic to the MTI fared as well as, and often better than, their secular counterparts. Fearful that the secular opposition would join forces with the MTI, the government recognized two new political parties in 1983. When the MTI demanded that it be accorded similar status, the authorities refused, citing a legal prohibition against parties based on religion.

As this modest flurry of political activity was transpiring, the economy was declining precipitously. State subsidies on bread, semolina (the basic ingredient of couscous, the staple of the national diet), and other basic commodities, were creating an enormous budgetary strain. Late in 1983, the International Monetary Fund (IMF) and the WB demanded the termination of subsidies as a requisite for their continuing support. After the price of these staples doubled overnight, in January 1984 two weeks of anti-government demonstrations erupted throughout the country. The police and the army restored order, but only at the cost of hundreds of civilian casualties. Within the inner circles of the Socialist Destour, charges and countercharges assigning blame first for the cancellation of the subsidies and then for the methods employed to quell the disorders flew back and forth among rival factions, but the recently legalized parties, still uncertain of how far they could safely go, refrained from fanning the unrest.

To distance himself from this public outcry and polish his somewhat tarnished image, Bourguiba restored the subsidies, giving Tunisians the false impression that his prime minister had acted without authorization. Aware that future economic adjustments were imperative but would meet an equally hostile reception, the government's approach was to attempt to minimize the effectiveness of the opposition rather than seek a viable solution to the national dilemma. Among other measures, General Zine El Abidine Ben Ali was named director-general of national security, a post in which he had earlier achieved prominence by repressing the disturbances in 1978. Not long afterwards, Ben Ali was promoted to the powerful position of minister of the interior, giving him control of the Gendarmerie Nationale and the shadowy political police, who were to become ever more ubiquitous in the years ahead.[7] In both positions, he closely monitored the opposition parties' leaders and their newspapers. It was, however, the MTI that came under the most intense scrutiny. Convinced that the organization had masterminded the 1984 riots, the government arrested scores of its sympathizers, who joined Ghannouchi and Mourou in prison. Although MTI leaders, in contrast with their secular counterparts, had certainly encouraged their followers to participate in the protests, the authorities produced no evidence they had engineered them. Although many of those arrested in early 1984 were released within a few months, the government continued to deny the MTI recognition as a political party. What some Tunisians perceived as government persecution added to the movement's stature, enhancing its standing as an organization committed to championing equitable and culturally appropriate solutions to the country's problems.

The traumatic events of January 1984 were but a prelude to a period of economic calamity brought on by an unforeseeable confluence of circumstances. A fall in crude oil prices translated into a reduction in excess of 50 percent of the petroleum revenue that had become the life blood of the economy. The return to Tunisia of tens of thousands of workers from Libya and other oil states as a result of the recession in the petroleum industry posed a double liability, depriving the national economy of their remittances as it aggravated already high levels of unemployment. The Tunisian decision, taken at the prompting of the United States, to allow the Palestine Liberation Organization to establish its headquarters in Tunis following its 1982 eviction from Lebanon had the doubly damaging effect of hurting tourism by identifying Tunisia with the Palestine–Israel conflict, a link it had avoided in the past, and casting its government in a role of subservience to Washington. The 1985 Israeli air raid on a Palestinian compound in the Tunis suburb of Hammam Lif had a particularly devastating impact on tourism, with consequences that ripped through the entire nation.

Every Tunisian felt the pinch of the deteriorating economy. Although the MTI increasingly drew support from a wide cross-section of the population, many of its more impoverished constituents experienced acute misery and often suffered the indignity of lacking the resources needed to provide, even minimally, for their families—a state of affairs utterly antithetical to the concepts of community, justice, and human dignity that the Islamist movement advocated as the philosophical underpinning of national life. Consequently, the MTI vigorously and persistently criticized the government, sometimes focusing on fundamental deficiencies in Socialist Destour economic policies that had no direct connection with religion or culture, but were henceforth squarely embedded in its understanding of appropriate public policy. Rather than building an economy dependent on international tourism and manufacturing "things not for ourselves, but for the West, and with cheap labor at that,"[8] MTI leaders advocated greater economic independence through the modernization of agriculture and the development of industries geared to the domestic market. Other recommendations for dealing with the economic crisis derived more explicitly from Islamic contexts. In 1985, for example, the movement called for a national referendum on the Personal Status Code, contending that, by expediting women's entry into the public sphere, it encouraged them to take jobs once reserved for men, the traditional breadwinners. This aggravated the problem of male unemployment, but also undermined what the Islamists regarded as a basic societal and familial precept dictating distinct male and female realms of responsibility. In related issues that went beyond economic concerns, the MTI also advocated limiting contact between the sexes and reviving traditional forms of dress as a manifestation of the rejection of foreign influence. The Socialist Destour, the opposition parties, and women's advocacy groups all came to the defense of the code, thwarting any immediate prospect of its abolition, which the MTI continued to endorse.

Consistently denied legitimization as a party, the MTI risked less in attacking the government than did the pseudo opposition parties whose primarily middle-class adherents were, in any case, better equipped to survive the economic shocks the nation was undergoing. But, in reality, the very concept of pluralism—never very solidly implanted in the Bourguiba era—was foundering. Convinced that the prevailing political and economic climate militated against free elections that might empower opponents of the government, all the opposition parties boycotted National Assembly elections in 1986. Following this meaningless balloting, the government adopted a sweeping program of structural economic adjustment at the urging of the IMF and the WB. Those sponsors backed it with some $800 million in loans and guarantees. Whatever its economic merits, however, the success of such a strategy hinged on persuading Tunisians, in a time of considerable economic and political uncertainty, that cutbacks were unavoidable and citizens needed to rally behind belt-tightening demands—a condition unlikely to be met.

After a spate of demonstrations in 1987, Ghannouchi and other prominent MTI figures were again arrested, no doubt out of fear that the organization was charting a collision course with the authorities. Bourguiba and his closest associates thoroughly despised the Muslim activists, whose aspiration to center public life on Islam they saw as the antithesis of the modern, Western-oriented, secular outlook that the party and state had assiduously promoted since independence. Conversely, MTI members believed that their movement's exclusion from the political process represented only the most recent manifestation of a systematic campaign, begun before independence, to sideline Tunisian Islam. In their view, the rejection of Islamic values in favor of imported ideologies, all of which had failed to create a just society, had been a grave error. Reinvigorating the Tunisian polity required a leadership committed to encouraging and assisting its people to cultivate their deep, but long neglected, Islamic roots.

Acting under presidential orders, Ben Ali turned the extensive resources of the Interior Ministry against the movement. The ensuing spiral of violence came to a head in August 1987 with the bombing of tourist hotels in, among other places, Monastir, Bourguiba's native city, with which he had always retained close ties. Because the incidents occurred on the eve of the national holiday marking the president's birthday, they had the appearance of a personal vendetta. Whatever the motivation, outrages of this kind at beach resorts popular with international visitors put the tourism industry in jeopardy and created a highly charged atmosphere when the trials of the Islamists arrested earlier in the year convened a few weeks later amid a swirl of rumors concerning the attacks. Many implicated the Islamists, which the MTI vigorously denied. The trials produced death penalties for Ghannouchi and a few other key leaders and lengthy prison terms for scores of others. Bourguiba applauded the sentences, but Ben Ali persuaded the president that capital punishment would make martyrs of the prisoners and stoke an already virulent blaze. Bourguiba further indicated his respect for Ben Ali's judgment by elevating him to the post of prime minister in October 1987, only to revert within days to his insistence on the execution of the Islamist leaders. The elderly chief executive's physical deterioration and erratic behavior—he was a victim of dementia or possibly a more severe disorder—convinced the prime minister and his inner circle that the president no longer had the capacity to govern. A team of physicians assembled to assess the president's health reached the same judgment and, in accordance with provisions of the constitution, declared him unfit to remain in office. Still in accordance with the constitution, Ben Ali assumed the presidency on November 7, 1987, to a collective national sigh of relief. Street names honoring the former president were changed, often to mark the events of November 7, statues of him were taken down or relocated from city centers to less noticeable locations, and his image was removed from banknotes (although coins on which his bust appeared remained in circulation). No more systematic process of "de-Bourguibization" occurred, but he gradually receded from the national consciousness, retiring to Monastir where he died thirteen years later, at the age of ninety-seven.[9]

The early Ben Ali years: a new (but phony) deal

The new president had no more sympathy for the Islamist movement than had his predecessor, but he believed that it constituted a greater potential threat outside the political tent than within it. To demonstrate his willingness to deal with the MTI, Ben Ali released its jailed leaders and accommodated some of its more symbolic demands, such as authorizing Tunisian radio and television to broadcast the call to prayer. In the fall of 1988, MTI leaders were invited to join government and party officials, representatives of legally functioning political groups, and other prominent national figures from both within and outside public life, in articulating a political philosophy that enjoyed broad support in advance of the first elections of the post-Bourguiba era, scheduled for early in the following year. The government no doubt envisioned a best-case scenario in which it coopted the MTI into an alliance against the left-wing parties that both viewed as long-term threats.

Ben Ali unveiled this "National Pact" on the first anniversary of his accession to office. The document acknowledged the centrality of the Arabo-Islamic heritage of Tunisia, which many citizens believed had been deliberately disparaged in the Bourguiba years. The document also expressed an appreciation of the Personal Status Code, which it insisted should be viewed as unassailable. In becoming a signatory, the MTI made major concessions. The government also offered a significant concession—not specifically to the Islamists, but to the entire spectrum of the opposition—by vowing to remedy the political shortcomings of the past through pluralism, respect for human rights, and explicit guarantees of basic freedoms.

The National Pact appeared to offer the MTI its first opportunity to enter the political arena. To conform to electoral laws prohibiting religious terminology in political parties' names, the organization became Hizb Ennahda (Renaissance Party) and applied for formal recognition. But despite the rhetoric of the pact, suspicions that the Islamists' ultimate goal remained the dismantling of the postcolonial state led the authorities to temporize, a tactic not without some public support. Desperate for a mechanism to pressure the authorities without provoking a self-destructive backlash, Ghannouchi launched a drive to recruit new members for Ennahda, but when campaigning for the April 1989 legislative contests began, the party remained ineligible to present lists of candidates. Determined not to accept their exclusion from the electoral process, Ghannouchi and other members of Ennahda ran for National Assembly seats as independents in twenty-two of the country's twenty-five electoral districts. They accused the government of blocking the emergence of a democracy in Tunisia by excluding Islamists from its conceptualization of pluralism. These independent candidates reminded voters that pressure brought to bear by the Islamists earlier in the decade deserved much of the credit for precipitating political reform, however incomplete it might have proven. Occasionally, they explicitly asserted that without the Islamist movement, Bourguiba would have remained in power. Like all such speculation, this assertion is impossible either to prove or disprove. Clearly, however, the Islamists did make a valuable contribution to Bourguiba's fall, which they naturally sought to exploit even as their rivals downplayed it, each for their own purposes. The impasse between religious and secular Tunisians was, of course, rooted in decades not only of failing to make an effort to understand each other, but also of generally dismissing each other out of hand as either religious fanatics or godless atheists, and thus never feeling the need to pursue a genuine dialogue.[10]

Reneging leads to violence (1989–2009)

The essence of Tunisian politics under Ben Ali is clearly discernible in the national elections held between 1989 and 2009. In the first contest, the Constitutional Democratic Rally (Rassemblement Constitutionnel Démocratique, RCD) won almost 80 percent of the popular vote and swept all of the parliamentary seats. Slightly more than 15 percent of the overall vote, however, went to Ennahda "independents", while the secular opposition parties, taken together, garnered a mere 5 percent of the vote. The 1989 elections created a foundation for the new government in a manner reminiscent of the struggle between Bourguiba and Ben Youssef in 1956. On both occasions, a serious regime competitor appeared to lack adequate popular support to claim a role in shaping Tunisia's political future, but only because on both occasions the dominant party or faction had tilted the playing field to its own advantage.

Nevertheless, the elections established the Islamists as a political factor of greater significance than the secular parties and second in importance only to the RCD. When Ennahda's leaders used the results to press their case for official recognition as a party, they were again turned down. A disgusted Ghannouchi absented himself from Tunisia, turning over the management of Ennahda's day-to-day affairs to Mourou, who continued to proclaim his faith in promises of reform. Retaining his position as spiritual and political mentor of Ennahda, Ghannouchi's parting gesture was to throw down the gauntlet to the political establishment: "Until now," he warned ominously, "we sought only a shop and we did not get it. Now it's the whole souk (marketplace) we want."[11] This remark appeared to indicate that the most militant Tunisian Islamists were no longer content to secure seats in a multiparty parliament—even if such a body were to come into existence, which they now had reason to doubt—but rather sought to dominate the political realm. Whether they intended to do so by besting their rivals in electoral contests or by amassing enough power to run roughshod over them remained unelaborated, giving their national audience the latitude to interpret what it heard in accordance with its fondest hopes or deepest fears. Either way, the result was an intensification and aggravation of the atmosphere of suspicion and mistrust. Ben Ali skillfully turned the situation to his advantage by casting himself as the defender of a progressive, secular republic under threat from religious chauvinism and by melding his vision of constrained political pluralism with a modified version of his predecessor's authoritarianism. This role brought him the support of the many Tunisians who no more wanted an Islamist government than they had wanted the autocracy of Bourguiba. It also assured him of the sympathy of Tunisia's Western allies, who had viewed the political resurgence of Islam since the Iranian Revolution with a decidedly jaundiced eye.

The 1991 Gulf War split Ennahda. Most of its adherents lined up behind Ghannouchi, who opposed Operations Desert Shield and Desert Storm, in contrast with Mourou, whose endorsement of the coalition's actions reduced his influence within the movement virtually to nil. On this issue, Ben Ali walked a tightrope, not condoning the occupation of Kuwait, but also insisting that Arab problems required Arab, and not international interventionist, solutions, even dispatching a ministerial-level team to the Gulf in a failed attempt to move the parties towards common ground. Large anti-war demonstrations occurred in Tunis but were carefully monitored to limit any damage to the government, which many citizens saw as equivocating on the war. The upshot of this turmoil on the domestic political front was to leave Ennahda's more militant wing dominant, paving the way for a confrontation with the state of a ferocity not seen since the last days of the Bourguiba regime. Late in 1990, hundreds of Ennahda supporters were arrested and charged with planning terrorist acts, including the assassination of the president. In February 1991, a deadly act of arson at an RCD office in Tunis produced a wave of public revulsion at the extremists' adoption of such indiscriminate violence. Judging that the situation verged on spiraling out of control, Ben Ali ordered a rigorous crackdown on Ennahda.

Events unfolding at more or less the same time in neighboring Algeria horrified many Tunisians and inevitably influenced their assessment of matters in their own country. The Islamic Salvation Front performed exceedingly well in voting for the National Assembly in December 1991 and its unanticipated success set in motion a catastrophic chain of events: army officers forced the president to resign, took control of the government, cancelled the elections, and soon faced a vicious civil war as the Islamists attempted to gain the fruits of the victory snatched from them at the ballot boxes. Ghannouchi, who had close ties with the Algerian Islamists, later ruefully observed that the course of events in Algeria "[did the Tunisian movement a great disservice by giving] our adversaries the opportunity to appear threatened. It created the impression that the West needed them to face the danger . . . spreading from Algeria towards Europe."[12] Indeed, as millions of Tunisian citizens looked across their western border in horror, they did very little to oppose harsh measures designed to rein in Ennahda, lest its clash with the government unleash a nightmare scenario replicating the Algerian tragedy.

Earlier campaigns in Bourguiba's Tunisia against regime opponents—and particularly religiously inspired ones—had also played fast and loose with the constraints of the law. Ben Ali had disavowed such behavior, but this onslaught was revealing. The violence that erupted after the 1989 elections, combined with the descent of Algeria into chaos, convinced him of the need to pursue new and aggressive countermeasures. In 1992, 279 members of Ennahda stood trial on a variety of charges, the most serious of which alleged their involvement in planning a coup that would pave the way for an Islamic state. The movement's most prominent figures (including Ghannouchi, who was tried in absentia) received sentences of life imprisonment. In addition to these high-profile cases, the authorities detained thousands of known and suspected Ennahda sympathizers, some of whom were summarily shipped to prison camps in the Sahara. Countless others endured harassment in neighborhoods, workplaces, and schools, often based on nothing more than their appearance (the decision to wear Islamic clothing, for example) and sometimes simply as a way of settling personal scores. So indiscriminate an approach inevitably alienated those whom it victimized and helps to explain why, when the revolution finally erupted, the hatred of the regime and its leaders ran as strongly and deeply as it did. By then, an alarmingly large number of Tunisian citizens had friends or family members who had suffered indignities for their beliefs, with many having had accumulated painful experiences in Ben Ali's jails.

Defense lawyers accused the security forces of widespread human rights violations, including the use of torture, while also claiming that legal irregularities tainted the trials themselves. As it had since its founding in 1977, the Tunisian League of Human Rights boldly tracked, publicized, and condemned disparities between the law and its application in the government's dealings with its critics, doing its best to monitor the activities of the security forces. This work by the League cemented the status towards which it had been evolving since the 1989 elections: an unabashed adversary of the regime.[13] The situation had deteriorated to such a point that the government could see no way of coping with its Islamic opponents other than by crushing them, although it continued to make relatively meaningless bows in the direction of Islam and tradition such as the president visiting Mecca or making a public show of attending Friday prayers. For all intents and purposes, the Islamic card had disappeared from the deck.

A new set of rules (2001–9)

Few Tunisians outside the Islamist camp shared the League's reservations concerning the state's dealings with Ennahda. In exchange for protection from the "green threat" of Islamic radicalism, most secular Tunisians turned a blind eye on the authorities' excesses. Leaders of the opposition political parties contented themselves with the collapse of their formidable Ennahda rival and, anxious to shield their own organizations from a similar fate, subordinated whatever misgivings they may have harbored. Behind their "go along to get along" attitude was the knowledge that, even after years of recruiting and organizing, no opposition party—nor any combination of them—could survive a head-on confrontation with the government or hope to prevail in an electoral challenge against the RCD. Consequently, they raised no objections to a law guaranteeing opposition parties that crossed a relatively low threshold of votes in the 1994 elections a proportional share of nineteen set-aside seats in the National Assembly. In this way, Ben Ali cultivated the appearance of pluralism without providing any substance. The system pitted the opposition parties against each other, rather than against the RCD, for a prize of dubious worth: their meager 12 percent of the seats in the legislature assured them a presence but denied them the opportunity to have any impact. In the presidential election, not even the pretense of pluralism was advanced. The government rejected the candidacy of the human rights activist Moncef Marzouki, the one person who came forward as a challenger, and Ben Ali ran unopposed for a second term. Shortly thereafter, Marzouki was arrested—a blunder that burnished his credentials as a regime antagonist and worked to his advantage after the revolution when he himself became Tunisia's president.

With the Islamist opposition broken and the secular opposition cowed, the RCD had a free hand in the 1999 elections, and Ben Ali officially won 99.44 percent of the vote. As if this were not sufficient evidence of a return to presidential autocracy, tinkering with the constitution allowed Ben Ali to stand again in subsequent elections, which he won with similar margins in 2004 and 2009. At the time of his deposition in January 2011, he had been Tunisia's chief executive for almost a quarter of a century—a period still short of, but closing in on, Bourguiba's presidency for life—and was reportedly planning to alter the constitution again so he could have still another term. Throughout that decade from 1999 to 2009, the Ben Ali regime increasingly strove to undercut any and all opposition to its rule, through corrupt enticements—political appointments, bribes, and kickbacks in instances where venality was sufficient to mute dissenting voices and by harsher, more coercive measures applied by the police and especially by the extra-judicial agents whose job it was to spy on and intimidate citizens when it was not. All of this made it extremely difficult for Tunisians reluctant to play the regime's game—indeed, for any Tunisian unwilling to submit abjectly and completely to the power of the state—to endure, leaving a bitter choice of self-imposed exile or self-censorship as survival strategies and, by and large, rendering the legal opposition impotent. For any who continued to voice their disapproval, the regime held a trump card, which it did not hesitate to play: an inversion of the Islamic card that labeled its opponents as Islamists and terrorists or, at best, cat's-paws for those groups. Up to a point, such fear-mongering had the desired effect on a public still mindful of Tunisian (and Algerian) events of the 1990s and the crowning, if remote, blow of September 11, 2001, enabling the ruler to reverse earlier measures that reached out to the Islamic-minded, such as the seemingly petty decision, widely attributed to Madame Ben Ali, to regulate (and reduce) the volume of the call to prayer in the interest of curbing "noise pollution," but its utility dissipated in the decade-long environment of repression and corruption that, in conjunction with the regime's inability—or unwillingness—to address crying economic and social injustices laid the groundwork for the revolution of 2011. In the uprising's incipient stages, the president blamed every demonstration that challenged state authority on religiously motivated activists, an assertion that he and the dwindling number of his supporters insisted on until well after he had become irrelevant in the Tunisian political process.[14]

A new set of players at the table (2010 and beyond)

The preliminary history of the Tunisian revolution is admirably recounted elsewhere in this book. As should be apparent from this chapter, however, Tunisians' sentiments about Islam and its place in their society were intrinsic to the revolution (as they were to every facet of Tunisian life, whether verbalized or not). That said, however, it must be stressed emphatically that what occurred in Tunisia was not an "Islamic revolution" in any usual understanding of that phrase. In early 2011, Ennahda remained institutionally anemic, its internal leadership unable to speak or act freely, its exiles impeded at every turn from connecting with their base. Neither was in a position to either plan or organize the tidal wave of opposition to the regime, which was a genuinely populist and spontaneous outburst by a population whose economic, social, and political situations had persuaded them of the imperative to agitate for change, even at considerable personal risk and cost, until their goals were met. Many supporters of Ennahda participated in the protests, at first as individuals and later in small cohorts of like-minded neighbors and colleagues. Certainly, these protesters had an Islamist vision of the revolution's ultimate outcome, but for as long as Ben Ali clung to power, and afterwards, for as long as RCD loyalists still figured prominently in the interim government of Mohamed Ghannouchi, all the protesters recognized the priority of rooting out the remnants of the old regime. When the prime minister stepped down, and elections for a Constituent Assembly were scheduled, Rachid Ghannouchi was among the first wave of returning exiles. Like the heads of other parties, he began traveling throughout the country to articulate Ennahda's objectives which, he was at pains to emphasize, would be pursued through the electoral process. Simply saying so did not, of course, erase decades of suspicion and mistrust harbored by dedicated secularists, and for every Tunisian buoyed by the prospect of a future in which the government respected Islamic values and culture, there were others who feared the demise of liberalism, gender equality, and democracy which had been stated aspirations, if not always achievements, of the old regime. As political activism was reborn in Tunisia, mutual recriminations flew back and forth between these two major factions, with other points of view showing themselves as their interests dictated. The conversations were heated, with participants striving to nourish the still fresh and invigorating atmosphere of the "Arab Spring" in which they attributed to their activism pride of place. Neither did any of them wish to jeopardize the obvious and profound success of the revolution (for which a high and painful price in human lives has been paid).

Having never been given the chance to participate in the governing process, Ennahda had no record, but only its stated platform, on which to stand when it participated in the electoral campaign for the Constituent Assembly in the autumn following Ben Ali's ouster. Its opponents hypothesized worst-case scenarios likely to flow from an Ennahda victory—"one man, one vote, one time"; "rule by the ayatollahs." The party vigorously refuted these charges, but it could not definitively disprove them, especially not to those who believed the *Nahdawīs* would say anything to win but were determined to impose their vision of Islam on all Tunisians. Most of the party's candidates reassured their countrymen that they understood and accepted the concept of civility. In addition to pledging to uphold the Personal Status Code, party spokespersons also went on the offensive against television ads appearing as the Constituent Assembly elections drew near that warned of empty hotels, shuttered restaurants, and unemployed service-sector workers on the day after an Ennahda victory. They vowed not to harm the economically critical tourism sector, even as they acknowledged the distaste of many Tunisians for the skimpy apparel favored by visitors on the country's beaches or the ready availability of alcohol almost everywhere. They perceived banning such behavior as economically suicidal and bound to have serious repercussions, revealing an important measure of non-ideological pragmatism in Ennahda thinking, even on a highly charged issue on which resorting to pandering might have been a less controversial choice.[15]

The Islamic card was back in the political deck, now with variable meanings to different constituencies. Secular politicians deployed it to arouse the same fears that Ben Ali had cultivated in the last decade of his rule, while Ennahda sought to attach to it a more liberal, inclusive, and progressive meaning that reflected the revolutionary goals of dignity, justice, peace, and prosperity for all citizens. In the October 2011 Constituent Assembly elections, Ennahda won slightly more than 40 percent of the vote, a figure none of its secular opponents came close to matching as they disastrously split the support of voters united primarily in their opposition to Ennahda's perspectives on religion and statecraft. A trio of veteran politicians—Moncef Marzouki of the Congrès pour la République, Hammadi Jebali of Ennahda, and Mustapha Ben Jafar of Ettakatol—hammered out, with their parties' approval, a deal to assume the presidency, the prime ministry, and the speakership of the Constituent Assembly respectively. While not without critics in both the secular and Islamic camps, the arrangement was an essential step in the search for a path advancing the goals of the revolution. As that process unfolded over the ensuing year and a half, suspicion and mistrust, frequently linked to religious views, deepened—perhaps inevitably—and outbursts of violence multiplied as positions hardened in all quarters. Compounding the situation was the assertiveness of Hizb al-Tahrir, a Salafi party angered by its exclusion from the elections.[16] Its militants vociferously demonstrated against what they viewed as un- or anti-Islamic activities ranging from showing films deemed offensive (Marjane Satrapi's *Persepolis* was an early target) to university officials' refusal to enroll women in *niqab* (a style of female covering once uncommon in Tunisia and long banned at its universities owing to its associations with conservative Islamic cultures in the Middle East). The Salafis attacked not only secularists, but also Ennahda, which they accused of putting political opportunism before commitment to Islamic principles, in an attempt to push their rival further to the right. To the extent that Ennahda took the bait, it traumatized those moderates who still retained confidence in its ability to master the situation. One Islamic card was being trumped by another, allegedly more Islamic, one. Destructive protests roiled Tunisian cities beginning in spring 2012 and continuing periodically thereafter, sometimes accompanied by accusations that the security forces, now largely controlled by Ennahda as the most powerful component of the government, were reverting to the tactics of the Ben Ali years. Salafi gangs and other thuggish elements added to the dangers of the streets. Nor was the other side averse to violence, especially as tactical and strategic splits undermined its capacity to cooperate across factional lines. The February 2013 assassination of the outspoken liberal Chokri Belaïd left the country in perhaps its most alarming condition since the elections more than a year earlier, prompting *Le Monde Diplomatique* to observe in the following month that "almost everyone in Tunisia believes that the benefits of the revolution are in danger."[17]

Whether or not so pessimistic an outlook is warranted, the Tunisian experience in the slightly more than half a century from its independence to its revolution does have lessons to offer in today's world. A very significant one is that, for many Muslims, deep-seated core aspects of Islamic culture, including the conviction that the political process should not be walled off from matters of faith and practice, are stubbornly resistant to contradictory assertions, and that this remains the case regardless of how thoroughly the society appears to have been infused with Western values or how vigorously Westerners (or Westernizers within the culture) pursue the attempt to recast it in an image not seen as consonant with its heritage. This is not to say that Islamic societies inevitably and invariably reject external ideas—indeed, one of the greatest strengths of the Muslim community throughout its history has been its capacity to assimilate positive concepts embodied in non-Muslim cultures. These "imports" have co-existed, and continue to co-exist, with the traditions and practices of Islâm, but they cannot flourish at their expense.

The Tunisia of recent years was, in the eyes of many devout Muslims, repeating the situation that had prevailed after Bourguiba's systematic dismantling of Islamic institutions. The state, with its formidable array of powers, had subordinated religion. But for how long could such a situation prevail? For the secularists, the desired answer was "for the duration," but millions of Tunisian Muslims never abandoned their hope of seeing a polity built on principles that had received little more than lip service since independence. As an engine of mobilization, a vehicle of protest, and a cornerstone for the construction of such an entity, Islamic activism had been marginalized, but not, contrary to most secularists' expectations, eliminated. In the exhilarating postrevolutionary atmosphere of liberation and freedom, with all things seeming possible, such a prospect, tweaked somewhat to conform to Tunisia's newly altered circumstances, moved from the shadows into the light.

A second lesson comes in the form of point-counterpoint. Islamic ideals and values survived attempts by the Neo-Destour, Socialist Destour, and RCD regimes to downplay them in favor of "modern", "progressive" concepts because many ordinary Tunisians experienced an almost primordial attachment to them. Conversely, the liberal ideals embedded in millions of Tunisians exposed to the world beyond their country and culture by education, emigration, travel, or more incidental contact—or through the legacy of leaders of the nineteenth-century Islamic reform movement and their many Zitouna-based disciples—cannot, nor should they be, expunged. Those Tunisians cherish their understanding of civil and human rights, gender equality, and democratic governance no less fervently than the Islamists cleave to their ideals. But to see this as a zero sum game in which the accommodation of one point of view means the inevitable and utter alienation of the other is a perspective dangerously devoid of both nuance and imagination.

Everywhere in the twenty-first century world, religiosity and secularism, faith and science, politics and religion must make room for each other; this is a tall and challenging order, to be sure, but one that seemed more possible in Tunisia in the wake of the Revolution of Freedom and Dignity—still the most spontaneous and populist, and potentially the most successful iteration of the Arab Spring—than it did before. Finding the basis for such accommodation is one of the most formidable challenges of this young century, and not only in Tunisia. It is too soon to write *finis* to the Tunisian experiment, but it remains possible (if the better angels of Tunisians' nature can prevail) to envision the country modeling such an accommodation, based on its own sense of a "Tunisian people," that cuts across ideological, political, and class lines in once unimaginable ways, and with a new constitution and democratically elected parliament.[18] For the moment, such a vision rests on a conviction of guarded optimism and is dependent on the assumption that the government can alleviate the most egregious injustices that gave rise to the revolution—a huge and seldom met challenge thus far. The possibility is real and the forthcoming elections should provide clues, but the final judgment is for a more distant future. Only time will tell.

Notes

1. Indeed, perhaps the most famous and highly respected proponent of the reform movement, Muhammad Abduh, had visited Tunisia twice—in 1885 and 1903—preaching and teaching at the Zitouna on both occasions. On the early Tunisian Salafis, see Kenneth J. Perkins, *A History of Modern Tunisia* (New York: Cambridge University Press, 2004), 65–6. For accounts of the Zitouna environment in the wartime and immediate post-war era that puts the attitudes of students and faculty into perspective, see two articles by Mokhtar Ayachi, "Le mouvement zeitounien dans le contexte de la seconde guerre mondiale," in *La Tunisie de 1939 à 1945* (Tunis: Ministère de l'Education, de l'Enseignement Supérieur et de la Recherche Scientifique and Centre National Universitaire de Documentation Scientifique et Technique, 1989), 271–309, and "Le Neo-Destour et les étudiants zeytouniens: de l'alliance à l'affrontement," in *La Tunisie de l'après-guerre (1945–1950)* (Tunis: Faculté des Sciences Humaines et Sociales, 1991), 231–50.
2. Clement Henry Moore, *Tunisia since Independence. The Dynamics of One Party Government* (Berkeley, CA: University of California Press, 1965), 62.

3. Quoted in Mounira Charrad, *States and Women's Rights: The Making of Postcolonial Tunisia, Algeria, and Morocco* (Berkeley, CA: University of California Press, 2001), 223. For a general discussion of the code, see 219–31. When Hammadi Jebali, Ennahda's secretary-general and prime minister after the 2011 elections, cited this same quote to assure his audience that Ennahda would not do such a thing, he was rebuked, underscoring the continuing resonance of the quote decades after Ben Youssef had referred to it and, of course, centuries beyond its origin.
4. The phenomenon of "fundamentalism" is analyzed across a wide thematic, geographical, and topical spectrum in the groundbreaking work of Martin E. Marty and R. Scott Appleby, *The Fundamentalism Project*, 5 vols. (Chicago, IL: University of Chicago Press, 1991). For a comparative view by a scholar of Islam that takes in multiple religious experiences, see Bruce B. Lawrence, *Defenders of God: The Fundamentalist Revolt against the Modern Age* (New York: Harper and Row, 1989).
5. Lisa Anderson, *The State and Social Transformation in Tunisia and Libya, 1830–1980* (Princeton, NJ: Princeton University Press, 1986), 244, citing WB statistics. For more on these numbers, see United Nations Department for Social and Economic Affairs, "Realizing the Millennium Development Goals through Socially Inclusive Macroeconomic Policies," accessed June 3, 2012, www.un.org/en/development/desa/policy/capacity/output_studies/roa87_study_tun.pdf
6. The early history of the MTI is discussed in Patrick Bannerman, "The Mouvement de la Tendance Islamique in Tunisia," in *Islamic Fundamentalism*, ed. R. M. Burrell (London: Royal Asiatic Society, 1989), 67–74. Initial attempts to explain the movement and its supporters can be found in Abdelkader Zghal, "Le Retour du sacré et la nouvelle demande idéologique des jeunes scolarisés: le cas de Tunisie," *Annuaire de l'Afrique du Nord* 18 (1979), 41–64 and in Susan Waltz, "Islamist Appeal in Tunisia," *Middle East Journal* 40 (1986), 651–70. For an insider's account of the movement at a slightly later stage, see Mohamed Elhachmi Hamdi, *The Politicization of Islam: A Case Study of Tunisia* (Boulder, CO: Westview Press, 1998).
7. For a brief biographical sketch, see Kenneth J. Perkins, "Zine al-Abidine Ben Ali," in *Dictionary of African Biography*, ed. Professor Emmanuel K. Akyeampong and Professor Henry Louis Gates, Jr. (New York: Oxford University Press, 2011).
8. Lisa Anderson, "Democracy Frustrated: The Mzali Years in Tunisia," in *The Middle East and North Africa: Essays in Honor of J.C. Hurewitz*, ed. Reeva Simon (New York: Columbia University Press, 1990), 201, quoting an MTI spokesperson.
9. After the revolution, the return to the political scene as interim prime minister, of Béji Caïd Essebsi, whose history with Bourguiba and the Neo-Destour dated to the 1950s, stirred fears in some quarters of a revival of Bourguibism, but if the octogenarian Essebsi entertained such visions, the country as a whole surely did not. In the October 2011 Constituent Assembly elections, the few competitors who sought to associate themselves with the deceased leader had virtually no impact on the voting.
10. The deterioration of the relationship between Ben Ali and the Islamists can be seen in Michael Dunn, "The Al-Nahda Movement in Tunisia: From Renaissance to Revolution," in *Islam and Secularism in North Africa*, ed. John Ruedy (New York: St. Martin's Press, 1994), 149–65.
11. Abdelbaki Hermassi, "The Rise and Fall of the Islamist Movement in Tunisia," in Laura Guazzone, *The Islamist Dilemma: The Political Role of Islamist Movements in the Contemporary Arab World* (London: Ithaca Press, 1995), 120.

12. Hermassi, "The Rise and Fall of the Islamist Movement," 125.
13. On the League, see Susan Waltz, *Human Rights and Reform: Changing the Face of North African Politics* (Berkeley, CA: University of California Press, 1995).
14. The revolution would not end the scapegoating of Islam and Islamists, but Ennahda's revival in its wake did impose some restraint on the practice. By the time the new government put the Ben Alis on trial (in absentia) in the summer of 2011, for example, their defenders had abandoned the ploy of assigning blame for Tunisia's woes exclusively outside the presidential palace, but still denied the former first couple's culpability for the circumstances that triggered the revolution. In fact, Ben Ali insisted that he had not "fled" the country as charged, but had only seen his family to a safe haven before returning to bring the situation in Tunisia under control—a plan he claimed was foiled when his flight crew disobeyed orders and left Saudi Arabia without him. To the end, he faulted others for what had befallen the country, but never blamed himself.
15. See, for example, the comments of Ridha Saidi, an important Ennahda figure deeply engaged in economic planning, who noted in a public forum shortly after the elections that, with respect to tourism, the goal was to restore international confidence in the sector and to avoid radical departures from pre-revolutionary practices. His remarks are cited at length in Businessnews.com.tn, October 11, 2011.
16. On the Salafi movement in post-revolutionary Tunisia, see Chapter 11 in this volume.
17. *Le Monde Diplomatique*, March 2013, 1.
18. See the thought-provoking essay on the appearance of this notion and its potential transformative qualities by Nadia Marzouki, "From People to Citizens in Tunisia," *Middle East Report* 259 (Summer 2011): 16–19 and Chapter 9 in this volume.

CHAPTER 3

United States Policy towards Tunisia: What New Engagement after an Expendable "Friendship"?

Lotfi Ben Rejeb

The people of Tunisia received a standing ovation in the United States Congress on January 25, 2011. The applause came when President Barack Obama saluted their "desire to be free" in his State of the Union Address. "The will of the people proved more powerful than the writ of a dictator, and tonight, let us be clear: the United States of America stands with the people of Tunisia, and supports the democratic aspirations of all people," he declared solemnly. "Our success in this new and changing world," he went on, "will require us to approach that world with a new level of engagement in our foreign affairs."[1] Shortly thereafter, Secretary of State Hillary Clinton travelled to Tunis where she praised Tunisians for leading a "great awakening of freedom across North Africa and the Middle East . . . The revolution here has begun the democratic transformation. And it is my great hope that Tunisia will be the model democracy for the twenty-first century." But as she spoke, Tunisians protested against her visit with banners denouncing US hypocrisy.[2]

The US government's vibrant encouragement to the Tunisian people is welcome yet ironic considering its long-standing support of Tunisia's previous autocrats and its concomitant negligence of people's aspirations to democracy, freedom, the rule of law, and dignity. Since World War II and decolonization, the United States has supported civil and military autocrats across the Arab world within quasi-neocolonial relationships designed to maintain their stability in alignment with US security interests in regional as much as in global politics, at the cost of sacrificing people's rights.[3] One scholar rightly calls such arrangements—which are generally glorified with the concepts of "friendship" and "alliance"—the "stability syndrome."[4] Another scholar uses the term "unpeople" which adequately describes the people whose lives and deaths and human dignity are expendable in the pursuit of political, economic, and strategic power.[5] Tunisia was arguably a poster child for such arrangements. The United States has no vital interests and only minimal commerce in Tunisia,[6] but it has prized the consistent alignment of Tunisian leaders with American strategic objectives in global and regional politics. However, the Tunisian revolution and its emulators in the Arab world have succeeded in expelling some of the most entrenched despots in the region, and have thrown that autocratic order and its

US support system into disarray. These sudden and deep political transformations are not ones the US government has sought, but are instead new realities it now finds itself obliged to come to terms with. The question now is whether the United States is actually adjusting from the role of sponsor of Arab dictatorships to that of champion of Arab democracy as Obama proclaimed. What does that adjustment look like after two years of "new engagement" in the new Tunisia?

This chapter examines the historical genealogy of US–Tunisian relations since Tunisian independence in 1956. It appraises the quality of those relations across three major periods in Tunisian modern history and leads to a questioning of the new departure in bilateral relations announced by Obama on the advent of the Tunisian revolution. The first part of the chapter covers the era of Habib Bourguiba (1956–87), which coincided with the Cold War context. The second covers the era of Zine El Abidine Ben Ali (1987–2011) which coincided with the US government's opposition to the rise of political Islam and its War on Terror. The third and final part explores the new context of revolution as a trigger for policy re-evaluation and the emerging nature of Obama's "new level of engagement."

The stability syndrome against the background of the Cold War

The nature and historical record of US–Tunisian relations cannot be adequately understood in a strictly bilateral framework. Those relations are essentially a function of international politics and are best understood through triangulation involving a catalyst for convergence or divergence.[7] The pattern of triangulation in US–Tunisian relations was at work before 1956. Prior to independence, Bourguiba traveled to the United States to appeal to American anti-colonialism in support of the Tunisian cause, but the US government chose to honor its North Atlantic Treaty Organization (NATO) alliance with France. According to State Department officials, colonial aspiration to self-government was a "second-category" issue for the United States and the Tunisian case a French internal affair.[8] In 1952–3, the United States opposed a United Nations resolution to examine French repression in Tunisia (while the USSR supported it) and opposed another resolution urging France to accept Tunisian autonomy. The possibility, evoked by the American Federation of Labor and Congress of Industrial Organizations (AFL-CIO), for example, of losing the Tunisian nationalists to the Soviets was considered remote. As indeed it was.

Less than a week after Tunisian independence in 1956, *The New York Times* published an article in which Bourguiba identified unequivocally with the capitalist-liberal West and sought membership of NATO (while snubbing the Arab League, which he joined two years later). In addition, Bourguiba went against the grain in 1956 by publicly opposing the Non-Aligned Movement that had just emerged from the 1955 Bandung Conference. Bourguiba proclaimed loud and clear: "I am against neutralism and I think it is in our interest to join the North Atlantic Treaty Organization. We are an integral part of the Occident and the free world."[9] He went on to reaffirm this choice, which he defined as a mix of historical/cultural affinity and political realism, in two manifesto articles: "Nationalism: Antidote to Communism" (1957) and "We Choose the West" (1958), both published in prominent foreign policy journals in the United States. Distinguishing Tunisian nationalism from the left-leaning Arab nationalism, he stated that in the Cold War Tunisia "has chosen unequivocally to follow the free world of the West . . . Inasmuch as the free world and the Communist world are two opposite camps, Tunisia belongs to the former." He reproached the United States for supporting France in the Algerian war but also reaffirmed Tunisian friendship "particularly towards that nation which is helping us, the United States."[10] In 1958, he broke diplomatic relations with the United Arab Republic and told the Tunisian Assembly: "Yes, I am western, and I will remain so." Observers took note that Bourguiba had given the United States and the West in general "the strongest pledge of support yet made by any leader of an Arab state."[11]

Over the entire Cold War period, the United States enjoyed in Tunisia the partnership of a genuine and vocal pro-West leader who despised Communist ideology and resisted the appeal of Arab nationalism and Arab socialism coming from Egypt, Libya, and Algeria. Deeply Francophile, Bourguiba considered the Mediterranean a bridge that helped North Africa "touch Western Europe and reach out toward America." North Africans, he liked to theorize, had a special affinity with the principles of the French and American Revolutions and, in his words, "a natural attachment to the liberal civilization of the West [as well as] a latent tradition of democratic liberalism."[12] Though Bourguiba lived up to his liberal convictions in social policy —especially in women's rights and universal education—and in effect gave Tunisia its first social, cultural, and institutional revolution that literally invented a modern nation, he failed to energize and concretize that professed "latent tradition of democratic liberalism." This is his paradox. His approach to governance remained exceedingly paternalistic and megalomaniac and he ended up proclaiming himself president for life. His tenure eventually spanned no fewer than seven American administrations from Dwight Eisenhower to Ronald Reagan. He tried to justify his single-party regime as an "incarnation of the nation . . . the crucible where the vital forces of the country are fused, the center where basic choices are made"—terms which strangely echoed the Communist myth of democratic centralism. In the same vein he defended relations between his party and the state as "relations between two parts of a whole . . . their objectives and responsibilities are the same; and very often those responsible in Party and government are also the same individuals." He described his system as a "kind of democracy" and unabashedly called it "the Tunisian way," justifying it as the only possible system for his country's "difficult circumstances," though he confessed that it was "different from the classic form known in the West."[13]

During his thirty-year tenure, Bourguiba was praised by the successive US administrations as a moderate leader because he repressed the leftist opposition and consistently supported US strategic interests and objectives, at the risk of antagonizing his Soviet-leaning neighbors and of being slurred as a stooge of Western imperialism. Bourguiba pursued the most maverick of postcolonial foreign policies in the region. He accepted the United Nations plan for the partition of Palestine and urged Palestinians to do likewise, advocated a negotiated settlement with Israel, disparaged Egyptian president Gamal Abdel Nasser's Pan-Arabism, and defied his pretense to regional leadership in the Arab Cold War, welcomed US Peace Corps volunteers, refused to follow other Arab states in breaking relations with West Germany for establishing ties with Israel, refused to break relations with the United States after the Six-Day War, supported the United States in the Vietnam War, and opened Tunisian ports for the US Sixth Fleet.

Bourguiba was never rewarded with a place in NATO—Tunisia was not Turkey—but he was offered economic aid and security guarantees. Following the attempted coup of 1958, the United States and France rushed to treble Bourguiba's armed forces.[14] In January 1974, Libyan leader Muammar Gaddafi, who actively opposed US interests, baited the megalomaniac Bourguiba into a pact of union by offering the latter the top seat, but the Western powers frowned and Bourguiba quickly retracted.[15] In 1981, President Ronald Reagan's decision to expel Libyan diplomats from Washington was followed by an armed attack in southern Tunisia by Tunisian dissidents believed to have been trained and armed in Libya. That event pushed US military sales to Tunisia up from $18.8 million in 1981 to $125 million in 1982 and the sales were projected to reach $1 billion by the end of a military modernization plan in 1986.[16]

The military sales program did not exactly enhance the stability of Bourguiba's regime. Military spending, which for years had been remarkably limited, put a huge strain on a troubled economy and an impatient society during the 1980s. Bourguiba's opponents, secularists as well as Islamists, questioned the wisdom of such policy choices, considering it far more ruinous for Tunisia to follow the Reagan administration than to normalize with Gaddafi.[17] They also complained that American policy, by supporting the Tunisian government in using the Libyan threat to justify internal repression, favored "the forces of stability over those of democracy."[18] In August 1985, Gaddafi reacted to the US arms sales to Tunisia by summarily expelling thousands of Tunisian workers from Libya —a move designed to amplify the economic woes of the Tunisian government—and by reportedly violating Tunisian airspace. Reagan vowed once again to protect "the sanctity of Tunisia's territorial integrity" and the two countries upgraded their military collaboration further on Tunisian territory.[19] The Bourguiba government and the United States were then at the highest level of political convergence and military association, but not for long.

On October 1 of the same year, Israel bombed the headquarters of the Palestine Liberation Organization across the Bay of Tunis from Bourguiba's palace, killing sixty-eight Palestinians and Tunisians. Reagan approved of the raid as a "legitimate" action and threatened to veto any UN Security Council resolution denouncing Israel. Clearly, when Israel became the third party in the triangulation, the US pledge to protect "the sanctity of Tunisia's territorial integrity" became utterly worthless. Shaken by the raid and even more so by the attitude of the US government, Bourguiba summoned Ambassador Peter Sebastian to lodge a protest. He pathetically said he felt like a man who had never doubted the loyalty of his wife but was shocked to discover after fifty years that he had been cheated on, and now he wondered whether he had been cheated on since the very beginning.[20] The references to marriage and disloyalty reflected his strong disappointment at being so easily discarded.

The bitter sensation of failure of a leader whose personal foreign orientation had been largely respected, indeed admired, by his people quickly created an unusual consensus of anti-Americanism in Tunisia and fed into the political discontent, social malaise, and economic problems that marked Bourguiba's final years in office. A week after the raid, intelligence relayed by *The New York Times* estimated that Bourguiba might have to choose between breaking relations with the United States and running the risk of being overthrown.[21] Prime Minister Mohamed Mzali declared that trust in the American security pledge was "a mistake."[22] For the next two years, opposition leaders across party lines denounced American duplicity and their views were duly reported by *The New York Times* and *The Washington Post.* The Islamist leaders Rachid Ghannouchi and Abdelfattah Mourou declared that US behavior was "strengthening people's commitment for Islam" and that "the US has shown us what their friendship is and can never be our friend again."[23] Social Democrat leader Ahmed Mestiri expressed the same bitterness two years later: "Washington put friendship with Israel and Tunisia on the scales and chose Israel. The damage is irreparable."[24] Everybody learned the lesson of expendability and spoke of the point of no return. In a move that was completely out of character, Bourguiba dispatched his foreign minister and his party chief to the Soviet Union in late 1985, received top Soviet military officials, and invited Mikhail Gorbatchev for a state visit.[25] Although Reagan rushed Vice President George Bush Snr. to mend relations with the Tunisian government, one American diplomat in Tunis said privately: "Tunisia and the United States are no longer friends, just countries which may have common interests."[26]

The stability syndrome against the background of the War on Terror

Bourguiba was removed in a palace coup in 1987. His successor Ben Ali solemnly announced a "national pact" for democracy and a revision of Tunisian foreign relations. The new government published a sort of charter, *Le Consensus National*, which claimed that "Tunisia can now present itself abroad as strongly anchored in the surrounding Maghreb, at peace with her Arab-Muslim identity, and yet resolutely open to the rest of the world."[27] What sounded like a radically new, horizontal prioritization based on geography and culture translated more modestly into a good-neighbor policy with Libya (trade, investment, migrant work, and tourism improved quickly) and increased investment from the Gulf countries.[28] Eighty percent of Tunisian trade, however, remained with the European Community,[29] while the estrangement with the United States, Tunisia's main military supplier, did not last long.[30]

In the new, post-Cold War context, the notion of US–Tunisian friendship was back on track as the two governments started collaborating against the rise of radical Islam, which was designated in the West as the new global enemy after Communism.[31] In Ben Ali, the United States had a successor who, by containing the Islamist surge in his area, was rather useful to US strategic objectives. At the same time, however, Ben Ali used the menace of Islamism and of civil war contagion from neighboring Algeria as a pretext to bury the national pact for democracy and to affix his personal authority on the country. Shocked by the atrocities in Algeria, Tunisian society by and large acquiesced to Ben Ali's form of stability as the lesser of two evils. Nonetheless, his authoritarianism grew to such a noxious degree by the late 1990s that Tunisia became in desperate need of a "re-contracting" between state and society.[32]

Following the attacks on the World Trade Center in September 2001, Ben Ali became a partner in George W. Bush's War on Terror and an associate of NATO's counterterrorism surveillance in the Mediterranean.[33] The partnership intensified following a deadly attack claimed by Al-Qaeda in 2002 on the Ghriba synagogue in southern Tunisia.[34] The Tunisian Assembly, largely obedient to Ben Ali, adopted a sweeping anti-terrorism law—patently inspired by the USA PATRIOT Act— which the US State Department welcomed as "a comprehensive law to support the international effort to combat terrorism."[35] The law, however, was mainly utilized to submit an entire society to a regimen of autocracy and fear under the pretext of security. In the reports of human rights groups and journalists' organizations, the Ben Ali government became synonymous with police state, large-scale abuse of human rights, systemic violation of freedoms, and the death of the press.[36] Yet this alarming picture did not bother the US government overly or reduce its support for Ben Ali.

The Bush administration could not ignore the excesses of its useful partner, but its criticism was routinely mild and tempered with praise for Tunisia's moderation and accomplishments in women's rights and economic growth. When Ben Ali visited Washington on February 18, 2004, he wanted to show his zeal in handling Islamic radicals and probably expected to be congratulated for it.[37] But for human rights advocates, Ben Ali's official visit was an opportunity to highlight his autocratic rule and to test Bush's commitment to democratic reform for a "new Middle East." Bush evidently had no intention of sacrificing his embarrassing yet useful collaborator, so to silence his critics he resorted to rebuking Ben Ali briefly about the press situation in Tunisia.[38] The public humiliation did give Ben Ali a taste of the expendable friendship, but it was not combined with any further pressure and it did not discourage him from seeking a fifth term in office and from tightening his grip on his country even more.

Not long after George W. Bush's 2005 re-election, Secretary of State Condoleezza Rice gave a startling foreign policy speech at the American University in Cairo in which she appeared to make a confession:

> For sixty years, my country, the United States, pursued stability at the expense of democracy in this region, here in the Middle East, and we achieved neither. Now, we are taking a different course. We are supporting the democratic aspirations of all people.

Rice went on to criticize the governments of Egypt and Saudi Arabia directly. Stunned observers were left wondering whether this was "a complete departure" for US foreign policy.[39] Was the Bush administration really abandoning realism and embracing a hazardous promotion of democracy in this sensitive and vital region? In practice, Rice's rhetoric had no more effect than Bush's reprimand of Ben Ali at the White House and her talk about "taking a different course" did not entail any policy change vis-à-vis the usual partners, including Tunisia. The US government did not engage the region's autocrats into a serious contract of reforms. There was simply no substance beyond the rhetoric. US concerns about Middle Eastern stability and Israel's security militated against introducing or helping democratic change. US credibility in democracy promotion was practically nil. The usual autocratic suspects remained ensconced in power. Anti-Americanism in the Islamic world, however, was on the rise.[40]

The Wikileaks cables offer an invaluable insight into the US perception of, and policy towards, the Ben Ali regime during its last three years. One of two particularly noteworthy cables from the US embassy, dated June 23, 2008, deals with the Mafia-style appropriation of the Tunisian economy by the reigning families of Ben Ali and his wife. Bourguiba was an autocrat but not a kleptocrat; Ben Ali had no such saving grace. In this fascinating cable, US Ambassador Robert F. Godec detailed the nexus of corruption and its modus operandi in Tunisia, and the orgy of greed of the first families. The ambassador leisurely crafted his largely descriptive cable—an exceptional specimen in the annals of diplomatic communication—with sarcastic headlines straight out of American popular culture: "The Sky's the Limit"; "Show Me Your Money"; "This Land is Your Land, This Land is My Land"; "Mob Rule?" and "All in the Family."[41]

One year later, however, Ambassador Godec was no longer in a mood for joking about the situation in Tunisia, as if it had dawned on him that the big Tunisian circus was not really funny after all. Time had come to consider the next move, so he switched to a prescriptive mode in a cable entitled "Troubled Tunisia: What Should We Do?" (July 17, 2009). He now described the Tunisian regime not only as a sclerotic police state in trouble but also as a liability to the United States: "Tunisia is in trouble, and our relations are too." He signaled that the end of Ben Ali's regime was fast approaching. He did not predict a popular uprising but he did advise his government to engage directly with "the Tunisian people" through the social media: "We need to engage directly with the Tunisian people, especially youth. The Embassy is already using Facebook as a communication tool."[42]

Monitoring the political pulse of countries through the social media has become widespread of late.[43] The US government, through the State Department and organizations such as Freedom House, the International Republican Institute, the National Democratic Institute and the National Endowment for Democracy, has also been training human rights activists and bloggers from Tunisia and other Arab countries and testing cyber dissidence as an instrument of political communication, organization, mobilization, and destabilization. Sami Ben Gharbia, a Tunisian dissident blogger and co-founder of nawat.org ("core" in Arabic), writes that "the number of workshops and conferences organized by US and Western NGOs targeting Arab bloggers and activists has dramatically increased over the last few years."[44] He also indicates that the map of the Arab blogosphere produced by his friends Bruce Etling, John Kelly, Robert Faris, and John Palfrey at Harvard University's Berkman Center for Internet & Society, was sponsored by a State Department grant of $1.5 million.[45] American companies such as Microsoft and McAfee/Intel, on the other hand, enrolled the Tunisian Internet Agency (Agence Tunisienne d'Internet, ATI) to test software they had designed for spying on political dissidents and for censorship, although such software is "said to be closely regulated under US law to prevent abuse by repressive governments."[46]

Activists and bloggers who were recruited for "democracy training programs" did not miss the cruel irony that the United States was also supporting the governments that oppressed them. "Some members of the activist groups," wrote a journalist in *The New York Times*, "complained in interviews that the United States was hypocritical for helping them at the same time that it was supporting the governments they sought to change."[47] Sami Ben Gharbia also described his disillusionment when he discovered that "the Internet Freedom mantra emanating from Washington DC is just a cover for strategic geopolitical agendas." "The most alarming development" was his discovery that American NGOs, researchers, and companies such as Facebook and Microsoft routinely shared "the knowledge that is being generated by bloggers, volunteer authors and activists" with "US policy makers, military commanders, intelligence community and the like." He denounced the "hypocritical policy" of manipulation by American officials and organizations using "them [Arab activists] and their causes for the sake of their own agenda." The crude double-dealing of the Tunisian opposition and the Tunisian government made his personal political engagement "difficult and uncomfortable":

> If the US government is really interested in democracy in the Arab world, it should stop sending aid to the dictatorships . . . If the US and other Western governments want to support Internet Freedom they should start by prohibiting the export of censor wares and other filtering software to our countries. After all, most of the tools used to muzzle our online free expression and monitor our activities on the Internet are being engineered and sold by American and Western corporations.[48]

US policy toward the Tunisian revolution: persistence of the stability syndrome

The Tunisian revolution came as a bad surprise not only to the Tunisian regime but to its foreign patrons as well, simply because, as British journalist Robert Fisk dryly observed, "The brutal truth about Tunisia" was that "Tunisia wasn't meant to happen."[49] Tiny Tunisia, the well-behaved poster child in a rough neighborhood, suddenly turned up at the forefront of a revolutionary tsunami that has only just begun to transform the entire North Africa/Middle East region. While protests and repression mounted quickly throughout the country in December 2010 and January 2011, the United States (and Europe) observed a heavy silence.[50] Coverage in mainstream American media was minimal and government reactions were prudent. One day before President Ben Ali's flight, political scientist Marc Lynch complained on foreignpolicy.com about the invisibility of Tunisia and of "the democracy promoters" in major US newspapers:

> Tunisia has erupted as the story of the year for Arab reformers . . . but the *Washington Post*'s op-ed page has been strikingly silent about the Tunisian protests. Thus far, a month into the massive demonstrations rocking Tunisia, the *Washington Post* editorial page has published exactly zero editorials about Tunisia.[51]

The day following Ben Ali's flight, British journalist and activist Yvonne Ridley accused the White House of "a show of cowardice." While peaceful demonstrators in Tunisia were being gunned down, she wrote, "Not one word of condemnation, not one word of criticism, not one word urging restraint came from

Barack Obama or Hillary Clinton as live ammunition was fired into crowds of unarmed men, women, and children in recent weeks."[52] The US government, much like its French counterpart, was extraordinarily slow to side with the protesters and Obama's formal statement in support of the revolution was not issued until after Ben Ali's departure. An analyst in the US Congressional Research Service later sheepishly admitted to this delayed reaction while striving to gloss over it: "US criticism of the [Tunisian] government's response to the December-January demonstrations, although initially muted, mounted as the protests grew."[53] The attitude of the US and European governments during the early stages of the Tunisian revolution is a sign that what happens in Tunisia is more than a domestic event.

Reactions to the Tunisian revolution from American journalists, scholars, and congressmen have been mixed, ranging from utter pessimism to cautious optimism. Some have asserted that Arab peoples are simply unfit for democracy and freedom because they have a tradition of despotism and of military rather than liberal revolutions.[54] Others have argued that the main threat to the promising nationalistic and democratic processes underway in some Arab countries will likely come from the United States and its allies, who would rather substitute old client autocrats with new ones in order to preserve imperial hegemony.[55] Members of the US Senate Foreign Relations Committee have expressed concern that secular autocrats would be supplanted by Israel-hating Islamist autocrats.[56]

Optimists, on the other hand, have contended that Tunisia has a rather exceptional chance of achieving positive change. Middle East expert and former State Department official J. Scott Carpenter put it squarely: "If Tunisia doesn't succeed, no other country in the region can."[57] "Of all the North African countries," wrote Professors Augustus Richard Norton and Ashraf El-Sherif, "Tunisia would seem to enjoy the best chance for a democratic transformation."[58] Tunisia offers "prospects for a clean, efficient, and technocratic government to replace Ben Ali," believed Lisa Anderson, Professor and President of the American University in Cairo.[59] These professional analysts generally agreed that Tunisia may qualify as a test case of how much democratic progress can be made in the most favorable conditions in the Arab world. These conditions are: a small, educated, and homogeneous population, a broad middle class, an active civil society, a resolute commitment to women's rights, a strong secular tradition, an Islamist Party—Ennahda [Renaissance]—that has pledged to respect the rules of democracy and the liberal institutions of society, and a small army that has kept out of politics and has not infiltrated the economy. Some, like Carpenter, have argued forcefully that the United States should give Tunisia priority help, not because it was the first Arab country in revolt but because those favorable conditions make it a good place to start making a positive difference in the region after years of faulty policy.

US policy makers scrambled to readjust their foreign policy to the new realities emerging in Tunisia and elsewhere in the region. Secretary of State Clinton spoke in an interview about how much US officials have had to jostle to adjust their approach: "We're facing an Arab awakening that nobody could have imagined and few predicted just a few years ago. And it's sweeping aside a lot of the old preconceptions."[60] Two key preconceptions in US policy towards the Arab world seem to have been swept aside. The first one is the macro, one-size-fits-all policy of supporting dictatorships and taking advantage of the stability they can secure. That policy has now been supplanted with a two-tier policy of accommodating change in one part of the Arab world and continuing to support the stability of repression in another part. The first tier concerns the Arab countries where the United States has decided to go along with the Arab Spring; these may be old "allies" like Tunisia and Egypt where the revolutionary current was simply unstoppable, or old foes like Libya and Syria where change might serve US interests and is therefore vigorously assisted with force of arms. The second tier concerns the Arab Gulf countries that produce most of the oil the United States and the West need and that are contiguous to the Islamic Republic of Iran. Autocracy in this second tier is still precious and will be even more so in the future as the United States is planning to bolster its military presence in the Gulf countries after withdrawing from Iraq.[61] Hence the quiet acquiescence of American officials to the ruthless crackdown on the protest movements in Bahrain, although they realize that the survival of friendly autocracies will depend on a dosed measure of reform (such as the right to vote that was hurriedly granted to Saudi women or the reforms promised by the Bahraini government).

The second old preconception that has been changed is the policy of non-engagement with the Islamist movements of the region. In the past, US policy makers found the Islamists useful only as instruments to oppose or topple defiant leaders like Nasser of Egypt and Mohammad Mossadegh of Iran, or to fight the Soviets in Afghanistan, and in using them in that manner they contributed significantly to building radical Islamist activism.[62] Otherwise, in concert with their autocratic allies, they excluded the Islamists as illegitimate political actors and as anti-democratic radicals who were inimical to US interests and policies in the Middle East. Thus, in the 1990s they acquiesced as the Algerian military annulled, at the price of a long and bloody civil war, the results of the elections that the Islamic Salvation Front (Front Islamique du Salut, FIS) had won. In the words of former Secretary of State James A. Baker III:

> we pursued a policy of excluding the radical fundamentalists in Algeria, even as we recognized that this was somewhat at odds with our support of democracy. Generally speaking, when you support democracy, you take what democracy gives you . . . If it gives you a radical Islamic fundamentalist, you're supposed to live with it. We didn't live with it in Algeria because we felt that the radical

> fundamentalists' views were so adverse to what we believe in and what we support, and to what we understood the national interests of the United States to be.[63]

In stark contrast with that traditional policy, the Obama administration has adopted a new strategic engagement with popular movements in the Arab Spring countries and with the Islamist groups that have emerged as unavoidable political forces after the revolutions. Testifying before the Senate Committee on Foreign Relations about the new American strategy in the Arab Spring countries, Under Secretary for Political Affairs William J. Burns said the United States was ready to modify the long-held approach that there were "only two political choices—the autocrats you know or the Islamic extremists you fear." The policy shift is warranted by the revolutionary transitions, and "helping to get [those transitions] right is as important a challenge for American foreign policy as any we have faced since the end of the Cold War."[64] The Obama administration now considers it a matter of national interest to engage with the Islamists because they are the new incontrovertible interlocutors. In the words of Secretary of State Clinton, "It is in the interests of the United States to engage with all parties that are peaceful and committed to nonviolence."[65] And so, as President Obama was outlining his new engagement in the Arab world in his key, long-awaited Mideast Speech of May 19, 2011, the leaders of the Tunisian Islamist party Ennahda were being hosted in Washington and introduced to US officials and congressmen.[66] US policy makers expected them to become the new leaders of Tunisia, and rightly so.

In his Mideast Speech, Obama named specifically Tunisia and Egypt, "where the stakes are high," as the places where the "new engagement" in US policy will first be applied. Tunisia is "at the vanguard of this democratic wave" and presents a fair possibility of success. Egypt, the largest Arab nation, is an essential player in the Arab–Israeli problem. The United States, Europe, and the other G8 countries have promised $20 billion worth of support for the "democratic transition" of the two countries. The fund targets governance reforms (transparency and accountability) and economic growth (job creation and economic stability).[67] On a bilateral level, the United States has multiplied fifteen times its assistance budget to Tunisia to reach $30 million, and has relaunched its 2002 bilateral trade and investment framework agreement (TIFA).[68] The United States has no interest in seeing Tunisia and Egypt become chaotic failed states.

A new position of Special Coordinator for Middle East Transitions developed in the State Department in September 2011, in which Ambassador William Taylor was tasked with following developments in Tunisia, Egypt, and Libya. Mr. Taylor explained what his government was trying to accomplish in his first media briefing on November 3, 2011. His briefing is worth quoting at length:

> There's no individual party out there in Egypt or in Tunisia, for that matter or in Libya that we are supporting. We don't do party support. What we do is party training. So we provide training for political parties to help them use polling, for example, or help them do constituent services or election preparations, these kinds of things. And we do it to whoever comes . . . So NDI, for example, the National Democratic Institute, they have trainings, and they will invite a range of parties . . . Sometimes, Islamist parties show up; sometimes they don't. It has been provided on a nonpartisan basis, not to individual parties. We are not interfering with the political processes there, but engaging, talking with, having discussions with all of the parties . . . what we don't want to do is wait until those governments are in place, (a) because that may take years, and (b) because we want to influence where they end up . . . our overall strategy is clearly to support them going in the direction that we would want them to go in. Now, if they are not, if they are going the wrong way, we still engage. We have to—because we want to try to bend them in the right—encourage them in the right direction. But that was—that—our—interference is not what we're after. We're not trying to interfere.[69]

His disclaimer notwithstanding, Mr. Taylor's language does reveal an intention to interfere. Secretary of State Clinton had used similar language earlier on. Immediately following the Islamist victory in Tunisia's Constituent Assembly elections, Representative Dan Burton, in a House Foreign Affairs Committee hearing, expressed concern about the hijacking of the Arab Spring by radical Islamists and asked Secretary of State Clinton what the Obama administration "plans to do to make sure that we don't have a radical government taking over those places." Her answer was: "We're going to do all that we can within our power to basically try to influence outcomes."[70]

The pithy, vague phrases essentially mean that, although the United States pragmatically has to adjust its policy to engage with new political players, the adjustment does not involve any change in US strategic priorities and objectives, and that the United States intends to make sure the new leaders understand clearly what those priorities and objectives are. They mean that the US government's new engagement will strive to accommodate change in the Arab Spring countries only to the extent that change does not threaten its core interests. The forms of engagement may change but the rules of engagement will remain unchanged. Under Secretary Burns reassured the Senate Committee on Foreign Relations that the new US agenda was "optimistic but not naïve": support for peaceful democratic change; support for economic modernization and job creation; pursuit of a comprehensive Arab–Israeli peace based on a negotiated two-state solution; and a fight against Iranian designs and terrorism.[71] Soft power and economic assistance may be required more now than in the past, but the security of Israel, the fight against terrorism, and the containment of Iran remain paramount. Victoria Nuland, spokesperson from the State

Department, said the Obama administration will not judge Tunisia's Islamists "by what they're called. We're going to judge them by what they do."[72]

Ennahda's leader, Rachid Ghannouchi, was in Washington, DC in late November and early December 2011, spreading a reassuring message of moderation and liberal intentions at the Woodrow Wilson Center, the Washington Institute for Near East Policy, the Carnegie Endowment for International Peace, and the Council on Foreign Relations. The Americans had their own message for him and it was not so much about domestic policy as it was about foreign policy. Ghannouchi was reminded that in the 1990s he had called the United States "the enemy of Islam" and had preached to "burn and destroy all [American] interests across the entire Islamic world." He tried to deflect those issues as best he could by saying that his comments were "not probably accurately reported" and that they were made twenty years ago "and only stones do not change in twenty years."[73] The Washington Institute for Near East Policy released a recording of him predicting the fall of Arab monarchies in 2012; he denied the comments as a Zionist fabrication aimed at hurting Ennahda's relations with the Gulf monarchies and the United States.[74] All think tanks questioned him about his attitude towards Israel. A *PBS Newshour* program about his visit provided a link to an interview he gave in May 2011 to a Qatari publication in which he predicted that the elimination of Israel could come as soon as 2027 or even earlier.[75]

Despite such misgivings about Ghannouchi's past attitudes and intentions, however, the United States government is displaying a familiar combination of pragmatism and opportunism by engaging with him, taking advantage of his open snubbing of France (as far as he is concerned, the real decolonization of Tunisia has only just started with his access to power) and of his preference for the English-speaking powers (England allowed him to stay for twenty years as an exile and the Royal Institute of International Affairs awarded him the Chatham House Prize for 2012). The picture emerging after two years of engagement with the new Tunisian leaders is that the United States is treating the Tunisian revolution essentially as an opportunity for closer security and military partnership with a new regime in need of recognition and support. The Obama administration has jumped in to build up its influence in the region by securing the cooperation of the new regime in its regional security strategy. Defense Secretary Leon Panetta undertook a high-profile trip to Tunisia in late July 2012; en route to Tunis, he declared that "the United States and Tunisia have started to forge a new chapter in our defense relationship, and we're prepared to partner more closely with them on a range of common regional security challenges."[76] The Pentagon chief urged Tunisian President Moncef Marzouki, Prime Minister Hamadi Jebali, and Defense Minister Gen. Abdelkarim Zbidi to develop a counterterrorism structure, assuring them of Washington's full support; Agence France Presse spoke of "unlimited support." "Our militaries have long been partners," Panetta said, "and the revolution provides an opportunity for us to partner even more closely."[77] During the same visit, Gen. Carter F. Ham, Commander of the US Africa Command (US AFRICOM), declared that US military assistance to Tunisia had doubled.[78] Prodded by Republican Senator John McCain and former Democratic Senator Joseph Lieberman, both staunch supporters of Israel, Congress was giving a bipartisan stamp of approval as it "pressed the administration to do more to build up the US–Tunisia security relationship."[79]

The new security relationship had its first test on September 14, 2012. Less than two months after Panetta's visit, a crowd of jihadist salafis attacked the American embassy and the adjacent American School in the suburbs of Tunis. The attack horrified Americans and Tunisians alike. The salafis looted both places and partially torched the school. They took down and burned the American flag and raised their own black flag on the embassy flagpole. jihadist salafis are notorious for their rejection of democracy and for their enmity to the West. In the same month, they also assaulted American diplomatic missions in Egypt and Libya, leaving four American diplomats dead in Benghazi, including the ambassador. The attacks in Tunis and Benghazi were carried out by the Ansar al-Sharia group, one of whose leaders in Tunisia, Seifallah Ben Hassine (alias Abou Iyadh), had fought in Afghanistan and been jailed by the Ben Ali government until he was set free by the general amnesty that followed the revolution. There is a widespread belief in Tunisia that Ennahda's leadership coddles the salafis and turns a blind eye to their unacceptable tactics as they attempt to terrify people into submission to their vision of societal life. Ghannouchi defended the formal existence of a salafi party in Tunisia as a logical counterweight to the extreme left. A video that went viral on the internet shows Ghannouchi advising salafis to be patient so as not to derail his long-term objectives:

> In this country the secularists control everything: the media, the economy, the army . . . I tell our young salafis: be patient. Why the hurry? Take your time to consolidate the gains. Today, more than a mosque we have a Ministry of Religious Affairs, more than a shop we have a State. The Islamists must fill the country with their organizations.

Responding to the accusation of double talk, Ghannouchi said that his words had been taken of context, but the explanation is hardly convincing.[80]

The US government reacted to the embassy attack in a measured manner. It ordered inessential staff out of the country (but allowed them to return six months later) and requested that the Tunisian government should bring the attackers to trial (one salafi leader was sentenced to a year in prison for inciting the attack).[81] The attack on the embassy did not alter US policy towards Tunisia; on the contrary, it vindicated the US government's prioritization of security and stability. The US government counts on the cooperation of the Tunisian government in order to face a widening circle of crisis not only in Tunisia but also in Egypt, Libya, Algeria (where salafi fighters of al-Qaeda in the Islamic Maghreb recently attacked a gas installation in In Amenas, resulting in a bloodbath), and the Sahel region (where a salafi offensive in northern Mali has prompted a French intervention).

In December 2012, William Burns, now Deputy Secretary of State, outlined "four inter-connected elements to effective American policy" in the region. Regional security is the primary element, while respect for the rule of law and for the fundamental rights of all people, including women and minorities, comes second.[82] Before 2012 was over, the US government had given the Tunisian government a gift of sixteen vehicles—the first portion of forty-four vehicles worth $1.5 million—to patrol the Tunisian–Libyan border and fight terrorism.[83] In 2013, it delivered two Lockheed Martin Super Hercules C-130J to the Tunisian Air Force, which will boost the country's ability to take part in airlift operations.[84] The Pentagon is also preparing to establish a drone base in North Africa, a move that indicates how significant the region has become for American strategists.[85]

On the other hand, for the last two years the US government has either ignored or downplayed American media reports that the new Tunisia is in turmoil, that journalists and professors are being intimidated, that women are harassed and even raped by policemen, that Ennahda has a record of selectively ignoring Islamist violence, that the justice system cannot be trusted, that the salafis are threatening and even murdering their opponents, that the Tunisian revolution is failing, and that the young Tunisian democracy is in mortal danger.[86] US officials keep repeating ad nauseam the familiar and by now clearly disingenuous rhetoric that "the United States remains a friend of the Tunisian people and will continue to support the transition to an enduring democracy in which the rights of all Tunisians are respected and protected."[87] The murder of Chokri Belaïd, a vocal enemy of Ennahda, has shocked Tunisians beyond belief, yet the State Department spokesperson managed to downplay the assassination after condemning it: "Despite today's tragic events, as a general matter, we're encouraged by the overall trajectory within Tunisia . . . There are obviously going to be setbacks. But as a general matter, we think Tunisia is beginning to make some progress."[88] The fate of the people is not yet a factor in policy making and the US government should not be expected to change its security and stability-first policy even though Defense Minister Gen. Abdelkarim Zbidi, its main partner in the security apparatus in Tunisia, sent a clear warning signal when he suddenly resigned in March 2013. Ex-Minister Zbidi washed his hands of the government dominated by Ennahda when he declared his disapproval of Tunisia's "political uncertainty" and revealed that he had submitted his resignation as early as September 15,

2012—the day after the embassy attack—because he had thought the attack was "just intolerable."[89]

Conclusion

Historically, the United States has structured its relations with Tunisia around autocracy and its interests and objectives there have been geopolitical. There is no real sign that this is changing with the proclaimed "new engagement." The syndrome of geopolitical stability and security in US–Tunisian relations which has trumped the domestic aspirations and needs of Tunisians for more than fifty years is alive and well after the Tunisian revolution. The US government is calculating that it could live with an Islamist-dominated government in Tunisia so long as the new Tunisian leaders respect US strategic interests and do not attempt to challenge US hegemony. This scenario translates as a revamped version of the old arrangement that used to be agreeable to both the United States and the old Tunisian regimes, with a few key differences. One difference is the removal of the stigma of dictatorship since Tunisians now have a freely elected, though not a majority, government. Another important difference is the removal of the stigma of supporting dictatorships since the United States can now project a new, positive image as a supporter of popular democratic change in the Arab world. This scenario, however, suffers from a challenging uncertainty about the genuine and long-term intentions of Ennahda leaders. If pursued, it would make the domestic situation in Tunisia yet again a secondary and expendable matter. Enabling the Tunisian government to fight terrorism locally and regionally may be sound policy, but it does not necessarily protect citizens' rights and freedoms or the democratic aspirations that gave birth to the Tunisian revolution in the first place. The Tunisian revolution gave the United States an opportunity—indeed a reason—to chart a genuinely new engagement for emancipation and development and to avoid treating people as "unpeople." If it missed this momentous chance, the United States would make yet another grave mistake that would come back to haunt it.

Notes

1. Barack Obama, "State of the Union Address," January 25, 2011. The author wishes to thank the editor and anonymous reviewers for their comments on the first draft. Citations from sources in Arabic and French have been translated by the author. A French version of this chapter is forthcoming in *Politique Américaine* (Spring 2013).
2. Secretary of State Hillary Clinton, "Town Hall Meeting in Tunis, Tunisia," US Department of State, March 17, 2011, accessed May 4, 2012, http://iipdigital.usembassy.gov/st/english/texttrans/2011/03/20110318093629su2.725947e-02.html#axzz2UvmntqlM.

3. See Saïd K. Aburish, *A Brutal Friendship: the West and the Arab Elite* (New York: St. Martin's Press, 1997); Daniel Mockli and Victor Mauer, eds., *European-American Relations and the Middle East* (London and New York: Routledge, 2011).
4. Brieg Tomos Powel, "The Stability Syndrome: US and EU Democracy Promotion in Tunisia," *The Journal of North African Studies* 14.1 (March 2009): 57–73.
5. Mark Curtis, *The Ambiguities of Power: British Foreign Policy since 1945* (London: Zed Books, 1995); see especially Chapter 5, entitled "Unpeople." See also his more recent *Unpeople: Britain's Secret Human Rights Abuses* (London: Vintage, 2004).
6. In 1985, an average year, US export-import trade with Tunisia amounted, respectively, to a paltry 2.3 percent ($253 million) and 0.2 percent ($12.6 million) of the value of US export-import trade with Arab countries. See United States Department of Commerce, Bureau of the Census: US Exports and Imports. See also US-Arab Chamber of Commerce, *US-Arab Trade in 1985* (New York: US-Arab Chamber of Commerce, December 1986), 3.
7. I explained "triangulation" and "friendship" in more detail in a previous article, "Tunisian-American Relations from 1942 to 1990: A 'Special Friendship,'" *American-Arab Affairs* 33 (Summer 1990): 115–25.
8. *Department of State Bulletin* 27 (1952): 987. See also Arthur L. Funk, "The United States and Tunisia during World War II," in Ahmed Khaled, *Documents Secrets du 2e Bureau* (Tunis: Société Tunisienne de Diffusion, 1983), 110–18.
9. *The New York Times*, March 24, 1956.
10. Habib Bourguiba, "Nationalism: Antidote to Communism," *Foreign Affairs* 35.4 (1957): 646–53; the quotation from this article is on pp. 650–1. Habib Bourguiba, "We Choose the West," *Orbis* 2.3 (1958): 315–19; the quotation from this article is on p. 315.
11. "Tunisians Split with Nasser," *Associated Press*, October 16, 1958. The quotation is from "Tunisia Boss Vows Loyalty to the West," *Associated Press*, October 17, 1958.
12. Bourguiba, "Nationalism: Antidote," 648–9.
13. Habib Bourguiba, "The Tunisian Way," *Foreign Affairs* 44.3 (1966): 482.
14. *The New York Times*, August 16, 1958; "Tunisia Supplied with US Arms," *Associated Press*, August 15, 1958.
15. Tahar Belkhodja, *Les trois décennies Bourguiba: témoignage* (Paris: Publisud, 1998), 145.
16. Claudia Wright, "Tunisia: Next Friend to Fall?" *Foreign Policy* 46 (1982): 121.
17. Wright, "Tunisia," 132–3.
18. Lisa Anderson, "Friends and Foes: American Policy in North Africa," in *Africa in the 1990s and Beyond: US Policy Opportunities and Choices*, ed. Robert I. Rotberg (Algonac, MI: Reference Publications, 1988), 177–8.
19. "Tunisia," *Facts on File Weekly World News Digest* (1985): 724.
20. *Le Quotidien de Paris*, October 4, 1985.
21. *The New York Times*, October 7, 1985.
22. *Le Monde*, November 6, 1985.
23. *The New York Times*, November 7, 1985.
24. *The Washington Post*, March 5, 1987.
25. *La Presse de Tunisie*, December 19, 1985; February 21, 1986; February 26, 1986; April 19, 1986.
26. *The Washington Post*, March 5, 1987.
27. *Le Consensus National* (Tunis: Ministère de l'Information, 1988), 19. See also *Le Pacte National* (Tunis: Rassemblement Constitutionnel Démocratique, 1988).

28. *Dhamen Al-Istithmar* [*Investment Guarantee*] 41 (June 1989): 4–5.
29. Banque Centrale de Tunisie, *Rapport Annuel* (1988), 100.
30. The Ben Ali government did not support the 1991 Gulf War, but it did not oppose the United States either. Ditto for the 2003 invasion of Iraq.
31. Margaret Thatcher, "Islamism is the New Bolshevism," *The Guardian*, February 12, 2002.
32. I. William Zartman, "Introduction: Re-Writing the Future in the Maghrib," in *Economic Crisis and Political Change in North Africa*, ed. Azzedine Layachi (Westport, CT and London: Praeger, 1998), 1–5.
33. Alexis Arieff, "Political Transition in Tunisia," Report RS21666. Washington, DC: Congressional Research Service, February 2, 2011.
34. "Al-Qaeda Deputy Leader Signals Involvement in Attacks," *Financial Times*, October 10, 2002.
35. US Department of State, "Patterns of Global Terrorism," April 29, 2004, accessed March 1, 2012, www.state.gov/j/ct/rls/crt/2003/c12153.htm.
36. Amnesty International, "In the Name of Security: Routine Abuses in Tunisia," June 2008; Committee to Protect Journalists, "10 Most Censored Countries," May 2006.
37. "Tunisian President Says He Wants to Share Experience in Handling Islamic Extremism with Bush," *Associated Press*, February 13, 2004.
38. Human Rights Watch, "Tunisia: Bush Should Call for End to Repression. Tunisian President's US Visit Will Test Bush's Commitment to Mideast Democracy," February 14, 2004; "Tunisia: Democracy Deferred," *Africa Focus Bulletin*, February 22, 2004.
39. "Rice Calls for Mid-East Democracy," *BBC News*, June 20, 2005.
40. Sigrid Faath, *Anti-Americanism in the Islamic World* (London: Hurst & Co., 2006).
41. See www.guardian.co.uk/wikileakscablesdatabase.
42. See www.guardian.co.uk/wikileakscablesdatabase.
43. See, for example, Evgeny Morozov, *The Net Delusion: The Dark Side of Internet Freedom* (New York: Public Affairs, 2011).
44. Ron Nixon, "US Groups Helped Nurture Arab Uprisings," *The New York Times*, April 14, 2011; Sami Ben Gharbia, "The Internet Freedom Fallacy and Arab Digital Activism," Futurechallenges.org, June 20, 2011.
45. Ben Gharbia, "The Internet Freedom Fallacy."
46. Tom Burghardt, "Secret Diplomatic Cables Reveal Microsoft's 'Win-Win' Deal with Tunisian Police State," *Dissident Voice*, September 12, 2011; Kristina Chew, "Ben Ali's Tunisia Tested Censorship Software For Western Companies," Care2.com, October 5, 2011, accessed May 4, 2012, www.care2.com/causes/tunisia-tested-censorship-software-for-western-companies.html.
47. Nixon, "US Groups Helped Nurture Arab Uprisings."
48. Ben Gharbia, "The Internet Freedom Fallacy."
49. Robert Fisk, "The Brutal Truth about Tunisia," *The Independent*, January 17, 2011.
50. Four days before President Ben Ali fled Tunisia, the French newspaper *Le Monde* deplored the guilty silence of France and the rest of Europe regarding the Tunisian tragedy: "Neither France nor Europe had anything to say!" Two days later, Michèle Alliot-Marie, French Minister for Foreign Affairs, broke that silence before the National Assembly, not to denounce the tragedy but to offer France's riot control expertise to the Tunisian government. Scores of scandalized Tunisian internet users "thanked" France scathingly for showing its true colors. See the editorial "Le silence

de Paris sur la tragédie tunisienne," *Le Monde*, January 10, 2011; "Tunisie: les propos 'effrayants' d'Alliot-Marie suscitent la polémique," *Le Monde*, January 13, 2011.

51. Marc Lynch, "Where are the Democracy Promoters on Tunisia?" *Foreign Policy*, January 13, 2011, accessed June 7, 2012, http://lynch.foreignpolicy.com/posts/2011/01/12/where_are_the_democracy_promoters_on_tunisia.
52. Yvonne Ridley, "Tonight we are all Tunisians," *Foreign Policy Journal*, January 15, 2011, accessed March 30, 2012, www.foreignpolicyjournal.com/2011/01/15/tonight-we-are-all-tunisians.
53. Arieff, *Political Transition in Tunisia.*
54. See, for example, Ty McCormick, "The Arc of Revolution: Egypt and Tunisia's Uphill Battle to Democracy," *Huffpostworld*, January 27, 2011, accessed April 1, 2013, www.huffingtonpost.com/ty-mccormick/the-arc-of-revolution-egy_b_814748.html.
55. Richard Falk, "Welcoming the Tunisian Revolution: Hopes and Fears," *Foreign Policy Journal*, January 24, 2011, accessed March 12, 2013, www.foreignpolicyjournal.com/2011/01/24/welcoming-the-tunisian-revolution-hopes-and-fears; Noam Chomsky, "The US and its Allies will do Anything to Prevent Democracy in the Arab World," accessed May 11, 2011, www.democracynow.org/2011/5/11/noam_chomsky_the_us_and_its
56. Michael Collins, "Mideast Revolts Spur Unease; Lawmakers Fear Extremism Could Prevail in Region," *News Sentinel* (Knoxville, TN), February 26, 2011.
57. J. Scott Carpenter, "Help Tunisia First," February 24, 2011, accessed May 11, 2011, www.foreignpolicy.com/articles/2011/02/24/help_tunisia_first.
58. Augustus Richard Norton and Ashraf El-Sherif, "North Africa's Epochal Year of Freedom," *Current History* 110.736 (May 2011): 202.
59. Lisa Anderson, "Demystifying the Arab Spring: Parsing the Differences between Tunisia, Egypt, and Libya," *Foreign Affairs* 90.3 (May/June 2011): 2–7.
60. Steven Lee Myers, "Tumult of Arab Spring Prompts Worries in Washington," *The New York Times*, September 17, 2011.
61. Thom Shanker and Steven Lee Myers, "US Planning Troop Build up in Gulf after Exit from Iraq," *The New York Times*, October 29, 2011.
62. Robert Dreyfuss, *Devil's Game: How the United States Helped Unleash Fundamentalist Islam* (New York: Metropolitan Books, 2005); Eric S. Margolis, *American Raj: America and the Muslim World* (Toronto: Key Porter Books, 2009).
63. "Interview with James A. Baker III," *Middle East Quarterly* 1.3 (September 1994).
64. William J. Burns, "American Strategy in a New Middle East. Statement before the Senate Committee on Foreign Relations," March 17, 2011.
65. Matt Bradley and Adam Entous, "US Reaches Out to Islamist Parties — Public, Private Warming Seen Toward Egypt and Tunisia Groups," *The Wall Street Journal*, July 1, 2001.
66. Bradley and Entous, "US Reaches Out to Islamist Parties."
67. G8 Summit, "Declaration of G8 on the Arab Spring," Deauville, France, May 26–7, 2011; Jose W. Fernandez, Assistant Secretary, Bureau of Economic, Energy and Business Affairs, "Opening Ceremony of the Tunisia Investment Forum," June 16, 2011.
68. "W. J. Burns: 'The USA Multiplied Fifteen Times Assistance to Tunisia, Since the Revolution,'" Agence Tunis Afrique Presse (Tunisia), June 28, 2011; "Tunisia, United States Re-launch Trade Talks," iipdigital.usembassy.gov, October 5, 2011. According

to the latter US government document, the United States was Tunisia's fifth-largest trading partner in 2010 with a trade value of $976 million (US exports to Tunisia were $570 million, and US imports from Tunisia were $406 million). Leading US exports to Tunisia include miscellaneous grain seed and fruit, cereals, machinery, and fats and oils. Tunisia predominantly exports mineral fuel, woven apparel, electrical machinery, and precious stones. US foreign direct investment in Tunisia was $220 million in 2009.

69. US Department of State. "US Support for Democratic Transitions in Egypt, Libya, Tunisia." Special Briefing by Ambassador William Taylor, Department of State, November 3, 2011, accessed March 1, 2012, http://london.usembassy.gov/midest110.html.
70. US Congress, "Burton Angry Obama Administration Has No Plan for Stemming the Rising Tide of Radical Islam in the Middle East," October 28, 2011; Ramzy Baroud, "Islamists on Probation," *Al-Ahram Weekly* (Egypt), November 3–9, 2011.
71. Burns, "American Strategy in a New Middle East."
72. Stephen Kaufman, "After Election, 'Real Politics' for Tunisian Coalition-Building," *IIP Digital*, October 28, 2011, accessed July 23, 2012, http://iipdigital.usembassy.gov/st/english/article/2011/10/20111028154144nehpets0.7106134.html#axzz2UsQaEpdZ.
73. Rachid Ghannouchi, "Tunisia's Challenge: A Conversation with Rachid al-Ghan nouchi" (Washington, DC: Council on Foreign Relations, November 30, 2011).
74. Nadia al-Turki, "Tunisian Islamist Leader: Zionist Parties Fabricated Anti-Arab Monarchies Comment," *Al-Sharq al-Awsat*, December 17, 2011; Wiem Melki, "Washington Institute for Near East Policy Releases Recording of Rachid Ghannouchi," *Tunisia Live*, December 22, 2011, accessed May 3, 2012, www.tunisia-live.net/2011/12/22/washington-institute-for-near-east-policy-releases-recording-of-rachid-ghannouchi.
75. P. J. Tobia, "Tunisian Leader Comes to Washington, Preaches Moderate Political Islam," *PBS Newshour*, December 2, 2011. The link is to ""Rachid Ghannouchi's Interview with *Al-Arab*" (Qatar), Alarab.com.qa, May 2, 2011.
76. Leon Panetta, "Remarks by Secretary of Defense Leon Panetta en Route to Tunisia," news transcript, US Department of Defense, July 29, 2012, accessed May 2, 2013, www.defense.gov/transcripts/transcript.aspx?transcriptid=5090.
77. Stephen Kaufman, "Panetta Sees Closer US Security Partnership with Tunisia," *IIP Digital*, July 31, 2012, accessed July 23, 2012, http://iipdigital.usembassy.gov/st/english/article/2012/07/20120731142561.html#axzz2UsQaEpdZ.; "Tunisie: Panetta assure Marzouki du 'soutien illimité' de Washington," *Agence France Presse*, July 30, 2012.
78. "US Willing to Give Tunisia any Military Help Needed," *Al-Jazeera TV*, July 30, 2012.
79. Josh Rogin, "Washington Prepares to Ramp up Military Cooperation with Tunisia," *Foreign Policy*, July 30, 2012, accessed March 1, 2013, http://thecable.foreignpolicy.com/posts/2012/07/30/washington_prepares_to_ramp_up_military_cooperation_with_tunisia. "According to the Congressional Research Service," writes Rogin, "Tunisia is set to receive $29.5 million in foreign military financing in fiscal 2012 and $1.9 million in military education . . . The administration has requested $15 million and $2.3 million, respectively, for fiscal year 2013. The administration allocated $13

million in Defense department-administered funding for a maritime and border security package in fiscal 2011."

80. Leela Jacinto, "'Secret' Video Stirs Islamist Fears in Tunisia," *France 24*, October 12, 2012, accessed December 1, 2012, www.france24.com/en/20121011-tunisia-secret-video-stirs-salafist-islamist-radicalism-fears-ghannouchi-ennahda.
81. Tarek Amara, "Tunisia Jails Salafist Leader in US Embassy Attack for One Year," *Reuters*, October 24, 2012, accessed January 12, 2013, www.reuters.com/article/2012/10/24/us-tunisia-us-embassy-idUSBRE89N1QV20121024; "US Returning Staff to Embassy in Tunis," *Agence France Presse*, March 13, 2013.
82. William J. Burns, "State's Burns on US Middle East Policy," iipdigital.usembassy.gov, December 8, 2012.
83. "Washington Supports the Tunisian Government with a Fleet of Vehicles to Combat Terrorism" (in Arabic), www.middle-east-online.com, December 14, 2012.
84. "Tunisia Gets First C-130J in Africa," *Defenceweb*, March 15, 2013, accessed March 27, 2013, www.defenceweb.co.za/index.php?option=com_content&view=article&id=29882:tunisia-gets-first-c-130j-in-africa&catid=35:Aerospace&Itemid=107.
85. Michael R. Gordon, "North Africa is a New Test," *The New York Times*, January 20, 2013; Eric Schmitt, "US Weighs Base for Spy Drones in North Africa," *The New York Times*, January 28, 2013.
86. Suzanne Daley, "Tensions on a Campus Mirror Turbulence in a New Tunisia," *The New York Times*, June 11, 2012; "Violence Plagues Tunisia's Politics 2 Years Later," *Associated Press*, January 14, 2013; "An Assassination in Tunisia" (editorial), *The New York Times*, February 8, 2013; Aida Alami, "Tunisia Sinks Back into Turmoil," *The New York Times*, February 13, 2013; Henry Ridgwell, "Fears Grow of Islamic Extremism in Tunisia," voanews.com, February 18, 2013; Henry Ridgwell, "Opposition Leader's Murder Tests Tunisia's Judiciary," *Voice of America*, February 22, 2013, accessed May 1, 2013, www.voanews.com/content/opposition-leader-murder-tests-tunisia-judiciary/1609011.html; Joshua Kurlantzick, "One Step Forward, Two Steps Back," *Foreign Policy*, March 4, 2013, accessed May 12, 2013, www.foreignpolicy.com/articles/2013/03/04/one_step_forward_two_steps_back; "Turmoil in Tunisia," *The Wall Street Journal*, March 5, 2013.
87. "Secretary Kerry on Formation of New Tunisian Government," iipdigital.usembassy.gov, March 13, 2013, accessed May 4, 2013, http://iipdigital.usembassy.gov/st/english/texttrans/2013/03/20130313144070.html#axzz2VAlB1VPW.
88. Victoria Nuland, "Daily Press Briefing," February 6, 2013, accessed May 27, 2013. http://www.state.gov/r/pa/prs/dpb/2013/02/203838.htm.
89. "Tunisian Defense Minister Washes his Hands of the Ennahda Government" (in Arabic), middle-east-online.com, March 6, 2013; "Tunisie: l'armée devrait se concentrer sur la menace islamiste, selon un ministre sortant," *20 Minutes* with *Reuters*, March 6, 2013.

CHAPTER 4

"Friends of Tunisia": French Economic and Diplomatic Support of Tunisian Authoritarianism

Amy Aisen Kallander

As revolutionary protests escalated in January 2011, French political elites demonstrated their willingness to stand behind the Tunisian regime despite its apparent faults. For instance, Minister of Culture Frédéric Mitterrand scoffed at descriptions of Tunisia as a dictatorship, dismissing them as "entirely exaggerated."[1] Perhaps more tellingly, Minister of Foreign Affairs Michèle Alliot-Marie minimized the impact of regime-led violence against unarmed demonstrators, defended the Tunisian government's imperative to maintain order, and even offered "the knowledge and experience of [French] security forces" towards these ends.[2] It was subsequently revealed that Alliot-Marie's support of the political status quo and her relations with prominent economic figures close to the Tunisian government went beyond the exigencies of her official role. *Le canard enchaîné* detailed how Tunisian tycoon Aziz Miled had escorted Alliot-Marie and her family around the country on his private jet during a late December vacation as the protests spread across the Tunisian interior.[3]

Though scandals made headlines, the collaboration between the French government and Tunisia's first two presidents consisted of more than bribery or beachside vacations. As the former colonial power (1881–1956), France maintained a privileged position within Tunisian affairs after independence, becoming one of Tunisia's most important trading partners and international advocates. Presidents Habib Bourguiba (1956–87) and Zine El Abidine Ben Ali (1987–2011) had both solicited Western approval and French partnerships, cultivating the reputation of moderate Arab Muslim rulers in terms that resonated with the Cold War and later the US-led War on Terror. This relationship was mutually beneficial. France funded and facilitated Tunisian access to development loans and financial assistance via supranational bodies such as the International Monetary Fund (IMF), the World Bank, and the European Union (EU), while Tunisia was a loyal ally and cheap source of labor. Though foreign policy and regional interests were articulated differently by each French president, this collaboration became particularly tenacious under Nicolas Sarkozy (2007–12) thanks to a shared criminalization of political Islam. As France and the EU restricted immigration as a counterterrorism strategy, Ben Ali's desire to eliminate activist Islamic currents within Tunisia and police national frontiers was well appreciated. The French Ambassador to Tunisia, Pierre Ménat (2009–11) aptly summarized this approach in his final telegram in office on January 13, 2011; he hoped that the president could "reassert control of the situation" otherwise it "could be exploited by Islamist movements and extremists."[4]

The proximity between the French and Tunisian governments was a function of the international and regional political climate, geostrategic calculations, and the perception of shared values. Appreciation for Tunisia's presidents coexisted with an awareness of their authoritarian practices, human rights abuses, and the climate of corruption. Diplomats complained that "the political stance regarding Tunisia . . . was determined by the president without any consideration of the analyses of our embassies," disavowing responsibility for choosing Ben Ali as a reliable partner within the Mediterranean.[5] This chapter situates French policies toward Tunisia up until the 2011 revolution within the context of Middle East, Arab, Muslim, and Third World politics to explain how it served broader foreign policy goals and the exigencies of national security. It traces the Franco-Tunisian alliance from the years following independence and locates its roots in French efforts to articulate a specifically "Arab policy." Focusing on the Ben Ali era, it argues that despite a lukewarm debut, security imperatives soon brought Tunisia back into the French embrace, signaling more continuity than rupture. Tunisia's relations with the EU offer further illustration of the economic benefits of French backing and demonstrate Tunisia's utility to EU policy. Finally, by considering Tunisian immigration to France, I suggest how the entanglement of foreign and domestic concerns underscored this security agenda.

Amicable foundations

Bourguiba, Tunisia's first president and the iconic figure of the nationalist movement, was a Parisian-educated lawyer with Francophone sympathies. Though he had also spent years in French prisons, he oriented the anticolonial nationalist movement around a strategy that emphasized negotiation and future cooperation with France. In a plea he penned to the French left in 1952, he stressed that if France would consent to ushering Tunisia toward independence, this would "prolong cooperation and preserve the fundamental interests of France and the free world."[6] Although Bourguiba's approach to state-building was ultimately less driven by ideology (he alternately invoked Islam, socialism, and liberalism) than by the desire to consolidate personal power, this reference to the "free world" was suggestive of how he molded his international image in terms of Cold War binaries.[7]

After the declaration of internal sovereignty marked the path toward Tunisian independence, Bourguiba further developed his reputation as a moderate, liberal, and pro-Western leader, in contrast to the revolutionaries of Algeria, the pan-Arab nationalists of Egypt, and, above all, his immediate rival within Tunisia, Salah Ben Youssef. As he declared in *Foreign Affairs*, Tunisia "has chosen unequivocally to follow the free world of the West" and not the Soviet bloc; "Tunisia's natural sympathies are with the democratic and liberal nations." He continued, "Tunisia has inherited ties of interdependence with France" and stood "to gain by maintaining close economic relations with a country which is in a position to extend considerable financial aid."[8] While his motivations included a complex array of domestic considerations, including the desire to secure economic support and attract foreign investments, Bourguiba explicitly framed them within the recognizable language of global superpower rivalries and geostrategic competition.

As the French colonial empire that had also included Morocco, Lebanon, and Syria was dismantled, President Charles de Gaulle (1958–69) hoped to maintain influence in what was becoming an Anglo-American sphere by articulating a *politique arabe.* This policy was based on presenting France as friendly to Arab countries to salvage a reputation severely tarnished by war with Algeria and the disastrous Suez invasion of 1956, in order to make a claim for France's global leadership as distinct from that of the United States. France subsequently renewed diplomatic relations with the majority of Arab countries and was careful to suggest support for the Palestinian nationalist cause. Still, relations with Arab states were more often conducted on a bilateral as opposed to a regional basis, and were driven more by economic and strategic concerns than ideology, as demonstrated by alliances with the Iranian monarchy and Saddam Hussein in Iraq in the 1970s and 1980s.[9]

Initial strife stemming from French disapproval of Bourguiba's support for the National Liberation Front (Front de Libération Nationale, FLN) in Algeria and French refusal to evacuate a naval base in Binzart or clarify Saharan borders briefly dissipated in 1961 when Bourguiba was invited to Paris to facilitate negotiations between France and the FLN. Later crises included the 1964 decision to nationalize land previously held by French settlers as part of an experiment with state-socialism and the suspension of French aid (which was in part replaced by the diversification of Tunisia's economic partnerships and increasing US aid).[10] Diplomatic relations improved when Habib Bourguiba Jr. began a series of mutual visits with his counterpart in the French Foreign Ministry in 1969, leading to accords reinforcing military cooperation and continued technical and cultural exchanges.

The economic component of Franco-Tunisian relations and preferential terms of exchange via a customs union was not entirely distinct from political relations. In the first decade after independence, France's three former North African colonies constituted its primary commercial partner. Tunisia received considerable amounts of public aid, and hundreds of French teachers and administrative personnel remained in the country. In fact, the first diplomatic exchanges on the presidential level in 1970 and 1972 corresponded to a period of economic transition within Tunisia. Bourguiba dropped his socialist gestures, reoriented the country on a path of economic liberalization, and invested in state efforts to market Tunisian beaches as a Mediterranean tourist destination. This succeeded in bringing in foreign currency and international investments, drawing about 80 percent of its tourists from Europe.[11] At a lunch in his honor, President Georges Pompidou (1969–74) commended Bourguiba's "solidarity with France and its culture" and his decision to "steer the country on a path of close collaboration" with the former colonial power, facilitating the concluding of an association accord with the EEC.[12] When Valéry Giscard d'Estaing (1974–81) became the first French president to visit Tunisia in 1975, he was treated to a tour of the country and its Roman ruins. For his part, Bourguiba proved conciliatory in negotiating the property claims of departed French settlers, and declared his intention to protect Tunisia's Jewish community, much to the relief of Paris.

Even as the tourism sector doubled during the 1970s, the limitations of Bourguiba's economic orientation were already evident. The development of full-service resort enclaves along the country's abundant coastline, around Hammamet and the island of Jerba, had only bolstered the socioeconomic power of the northern and coastal regions to the detriment of much of the south and the interior. The sector was severely impacted by the 1973 oil crisis, proving that despite its Mediterranean image, the country was vulnerable to Arab politics. As a development strategy, Tunisia faced common problems of overtaxing environmental resources such as water and neglecting agriculture, in exchange for the questionable benefit of expansion of unskilled and undereducated workers.[13] Overall, the export-driven economy furthered Tunisian dependence on Europe and engendered a regular trade deficit toward France.

Bourguiba's economic policies were profitable for the Tunisian middle class while widening the gap between rich and poor, causing increasing domestic strife in the 1970s and 1980s. There were major strikes in 1973 and 1976, and in the fall of 1977 textile and agricultural workers and phosphate miners across the country pushed the leadership of the Tunisian general labor union (Union Générale Tunisienne du Travail, UGTT) to reassess its conciliatory stance with the regime. The UGTT backed a general strike on January 26, 1978 targeting national economic policy. The government response was excessively violent and revealed the existence of a vast private militia affiliated with the ruling party. Thousands were arrested including the union leaders (who were immediately replaced with party loyalists), and while the government recognized over 100 deaths, others placed the toll closer to 500.[14] In the aftermath, the president sought to counter any nascent leftist opposition by courting intellectual allies in founding an Association for the Promotion of the Qur'an under the Ministry of Religious Affairs. As the association gained a broader following, including support from university students, it coalesced as a religiously based political party, the Islamic Tendency Movement (Mouvement de la Tendance Islamique, MTI).[15] Refusing to legalize the party, Bourguiba lashed out against the MTI who were pinpointed as leading a series of student strikes in 1981. Further student agitation in 1987 led to another crackdown: hundreds were arrested, many tortured, and most were tried at a special State Security Court whose convictions included public execution.

Bourguiba took hasty, drastic, and at times erratic steps to crush secular and religious critics, as seen in the reaction to a widespread uprising in December 1983 focused on popular economic grievances and frustration with political stagnation. Protests in the south and southwest were triggered in part by IMF-inspired austerity measures that would reduce subsidies and double the price of bread. Attempts to contain protests by isolating these regions failed, and within days people took to the streets in major cities and the capital targeting symbols of the state and middle-class consumerism. The response by the army and national guard left as many as 150 dead and thousands wounded before Bourguiba's January 6, 1984 announcement restoring subsidies, firing the minister of the interior, and blaming foreign elements for the disturbances.

In contrast to the facile binaries within which Bourguiba constructed his international image, his domestic policies could hardly be considered liberal. It was evident to scholars in the 1960s that the state controlled not only the ruling party, but legislative assemblies, the judiciary, the press, and party-affiliated civil society organizations. From his first decade of rule, Bourguiba silenced all forms of political opposition, routinized the use of torture, and even authorized assassination.[16] Economic and political power was concentrated in the capital, and in a typical postcolonial style, Bourguiba proclaimed national unity as a form of combat that solidified the power of the one-party state. Though he ran for elections, his lowest score was 99.78 in 1969, and he abandoned any pretense of electoral democracy with a constitutional amendment in 1975 that named him president for life. At the same time, Bourguiba cultivated his domestic and international reputation as indispensable; he was the founder of the nation, a national hero, and an embodiment of Tunisia itself.[17]

Economic grievances and the climate of impending political instability coexisted with continued French support for Bourguiba along the terms laid out in the 1960s whereby financial aid was exchanged for a moderate stance on regional politics. By 1980, Tunisia received the largest amount of French public aid per capita of any country in the world.[18] Subsequently, the socialist program of President François Mitterrand (1981–95) linked economic development to questions of peace in the Middle East wherein Bourguiba's views on Israel and Palestine were appreciated "for their moderation and realism, giving Bourguiba a distinct place among Arab leaders."[19] Bourguiba and Mitterrand exchanged visits in 1983 and 1985, and their relations were without major disagreements. Though the 1984 crisis hinted at the instability of the regime, as Bourguiba controlled the reins of succession the political parties, the UGTT, and even the Tunisian Human Rights League (Ligue Tunisienne de Droits de l'Homme, LTDH) rallied in his support.[20] Paris followed suit, with the Minister for Cooperation Christian Nucci traveling to Tunis in February to conclude three agreements of emergency financial aid to bolster the regime and stave off further crisis.[21] French confidence in "the founder of modern Tunisia" caused surprise at the Quai d'Orsay when, after serving as prime minister for roughly five weeks, Ben Ali forced the Supreme Combatant out of office in a medico-legal coup, though it did not dramatically alter bilateral relations.[22]

Ben Ali and the primacy of security

Whereas Bourguiba initially deferred to Cold War paradigms to indicate his Western sympathies and liberal gloss, Ben Ali shifted the rhetorical frame to the clash of civilizations, positing his version of democracy as the last rampart against anti-Western theocracy. For both, simplistic binaries justified the consolidation of power at the expense of more representative government while criminalizing the opposition. Ben Ali's emphasis on security corresponded to French domestic and foreign policy in a manner that contributed to his longevity, weathering the occasionally rough climate. The proximity between the official narrative of Tunisian success and the accolades of various French presidents reflected this convergence of views and at times the personal ties between the political elite of the two countries.

From his first speech as president, Ben Ali sought to garner domestic approval while reassuring foreign allies about the liberal aspects of government, promising to respect women's rights as defined by Bourguiba and to inaugurate political pluralism.[23] He declared his intention to continue traditional ties with the West, France in particular, as well as with the economic reforms suggested by the World Bank and IMF. Within an hour of announcing Bourguiba's destitution, the new prime minister phoned his French counterpart to discuss the situation and placate initial hesitation. Ben Ali further justified seizing power as preventing an attempt on the president's life by Islamic fundamentalists planned for the following day. Following Bourguiba's clamping down on the MTI earlier that year, this accusation set the stage for the narrative that Ben Ali was protecting the country from antidemocratic religious forces.

Ben Ali was eager to court French approval, making Paris the destination of his first journey outside the Arab world in September 1988 with an agenda focused on economic, cultural, and military cooperation. Summarizing his visit, the major public television channel, France 3, presented the new president as installing pluralism and reducing the power of Islamists. By the following year, when Mitterrand returned the favor, he qualified Franco-Tunisian relations as "excellent," describing his arrival as a way to reinforce a "personal relationship" with Ben Ali, and an extension of the "intimate connections" between the two countries.[24] The main objective was the conclusion of an agreement to broadcast the satellite channel France 2. In a speech he gave at the presidential palace, Mitterrand legitimized Ben Ali's coup, by depicting him as the "author of a peaceful transition and democratic renovation."[25]

Mitterrand also praised the "reinvestment of democracy, civil liberties, and human rights," though Ben Ali's reluctance to inaugurate multi-party politics signaled continuity with Bourguiba's autocratic legacy.[26] Despite Ben Ali's negotiations with the MTI, he did not release Rachid Ghannouchi from prison until May 1988, and efforts to legalize the party as Hizb Ennahda (the Renaissance Party) were fruitless. He constructed a pluralist façade by allowing Ennahda candidates to run as independents in the April 1989 legislative elections, but prevented them from entering parliament and secured a triumphant electoral victory of 99 percent.[27] If Ennahda candidates scored 30 percent in some cities, this bolstered the presidential position of defending secularism from the Islamization of the state. Ben Ali deployed women's rights as a consensus-building strategy to secure the support of middle-class secular women whom he claimed to protect.[28]

The Ennahda party was officially depicted as a threat and linked to violent activities.[29] Student protests in the fall of 1990, in which Ennahda-affiliated student groups played a visible role, inaugurated a cycle of demonstrations, police violence, arrests, and more demonstrations. The torching of a Constitutional Democratic Rally (Rassemblement Constitutionnel Démocratique, RCD) office in a working-class neighborhood of the capital in February 1991, which was attributed to Ennahda, was used as further justification for repression, even though Ennahda leaders repeatedly condemned the use of violence. In May 1991, the regime claimed to have unmasked a terrorist plot; an attack on a frontier post on November 29, 1991 by forty armed gunmen, supposedly affiliated with an Algerian Islamist party, confirmed the hypothesis that Algerian problems might spill into Tunisia. These accusations provided the basis for the arrest of approximately 8,000 suspects between 1990 and 1992, hundreds of whom were tried in military courts and subjected to torture.[30]

As this suggests, the binary opposition between Ben Ali's police tactics of ensuring secular democracy and the theocratic threat were amplified, if not legitimized, by a comparable framing of events in Algeria. There too, a ruling party monopoly was challenged by a vast cross-section of the Algerian population with the main opposition stemming from the Islamic Salvation Front (Front Islamique du Salut, FIS). A community-based pious organization providing educational and social services, it formed an official political party in 1989 for the first multiparty elections. After winning close to 55 percent of votes in municipal elections in June 1991, the state postponed further elections, and associated the FIS with a violent threat to democratic and liberal values. Much of its leadership was arrested as well as thousands of sympathizers. The FIS still gained a near majority of votes in legislative elections that December before the party was banned, further elections canceled, and the government and its military backers undertook increasingly dirty techniques of framing and criminalizing the Islamist opposition as they massacred civilians in their name. The depiction of the FIS to the international public as Islamic terrorists provided an alibi for suspending the democratic process and inaugurating almost a decade of civil war.[31]

Since the 1979 Iranian revolution and the deposition of the shah, concern that theocratic regimes would spread across the region encouraged French diplomatic and financial support for secular governments in the Middle East.[32] The war in Algeria built upon this with French media repeating the official mantra that the FIS was a terrorist group, a threat to democracy, and responsible for assassinations and attacks on civilians, thus simplifying the conflict as one between a secular modern state and religious fanatics.[33] Confrontations between the secular nationalist monopoly on political power and the FIS in Algeria set the context for Mitterrand's return to Tunisia in 1991 to sign accords promoting cultural cooperation and financial aid. During the press conference on July 11, he stated confidently that the two countries had re-embarked on a "path of active cooperation." Queried about regional politics, such as the state of martial law in Algeria, and the rise of fundamentalism in Tunisia, Mitterrand avoided taking a stance on what he deemed Algerian and Tunisian "domestic" affairs. On the contrary, he asserted that while his government would "prevent any violent or terrorist" acts within France, it was not taking other actions against foreign citizens of France who were legally guaranteed the right to free expression. He denied any knowledge of the fact that Ennahda's Rachid Ghannouchi had recently been refused refugee status in France and had instead sought exile in England. Regardless, the questions made explicit the perceived connection between terrorism in the Middle East, immigration, and domestic security.

Ben Ali too considered his elimination of terrorism as part of a broader regional and international struggle for which he hoped to elicit foreign support. He later chastised:

> If there are still a few fundamentalists abroad, that is primarily a problem for the countries that continue to give them asylum despite the evidence that they are continuing there [sic] terrorist activities, from the countries that house them and against their own homelands.[34]

He found an ally in Minister of the Interior Charles Pasqua (1986–8, 1993–5), who treated the exiled members of Tunisian (and Algerian) Islamist groups as a threat. For instance, in 1993 Pasqua attempted to deport Ennahda cadre Salah Karkar, though he obtained political refugee status and a ten-year residency permit after his arrival in 1987. When this failed, Pasqua placed him under house arrest, though he had not been accused or convicted of any illegal acts in France.[35] Further surveillance of Tunisians in France was coordinated by an RCD office in Paris, disguised as a Tunisian cultural center, presumably with the approval of French authorities.[36] Pasqua's collaboration with Ben Ali was also personal. When the French fiscal administration requested an interview with Pasqua's son Pierre early in 2002, the latter departed for an extended vacation in Tunisia. Until 2007, he stayed in the Sidi Bou Said villa of Youssef Zarrouk, himself part of Ben Ali's circle and a close friend of Ben Ali's son-in-law Slim Chiboub.[37]

Jacques Chirac's (1995–2007) favorable views of Ben Ali were evident from his first visit to Tunisia only five months after the beginning of his first term, as was the contrast with facts on the ground. In a lengthy speech he gave at the official reception, Chirac declared that his arrival was intended to signal "friendship and French support" for Tunisia. He praised how Ben Ali had placed Tunisia "on the path of modernity, democratization, and social harmony" while strengthening the economy through privatization. Though Ben Ali had again received over 99 percent of the vote in 1994, Chirac lauded the "political pluralism" inaugurated by the National Pact and attributed the re-election to Ben Ali's "intellectual and cultural reputation." As Ben Ali enforced Law 108, which banned women from wearing headscarves in public offices and educational institutions, the French president ironically pronounced his appreciation for how this plurality allowed Tunisians to "reconnect with the roots of their religious beliefs."[38] Showing his approval for Ben Ali's tactics, he touted how his conversations with the latter revealed the similarities of their positions on affairs such as "preventing the increase in religious fundamentalism."[39] The reason to overlook Ben Ali's authoritarian tendencies and repressive record was repeated in broadcasts on France 2 and France 3, framing the visit as reinforcing a joint commitment to fight Islamic fundamentalism.

In his public speeches Chirac praised Tunisian economic growth and the expansion of the middle class, which he referred to as the "Tunisian miracle." (This image endured the financial crisis so that even on a 2008 visit former president of the IMF Dominique Strauss-Kahn still maintained that the "assessment of the IMF regarding Tunisian politics is very positive," and its economy constituted a "good model" for other developing countries to follow.[40] Yet figures attesting to the minimal deficit, the decline in poverty, and unemployment rates were false or misleading.[41] The banking system was compromised by the president and his family, and poverty rates and unemployment were much higher than government numbers suggested. National averages glossed over the variation between regions, the increasing gap between different socioprofessional groups, and the existence of a vulnerable population that included the employed.[42] Regardless of their foundation, the narrative of economic success held a significant place in the legitimation of Ben Ali's rule. Improving the standard of living was attributed political significance based on the presumption that radical Islamic groups recruited from among the poor and unemployed.[43]

With the war in Algeria contained within national borders and terrorist threats on the wane, there was increasing discussion of Ben Ali's paltry human rights record by his second visit to Paris in 1997. At the state dinner held in his honor, Chirac praised Ben Ali's personal engagement in ensuring the success of his country, addressed him as "a friend of France, and a personal friend," and mentioned France's commitment to ending violence and inaugurating the rule of law. On the one hand venturing modest political critiques, on the other, the visit still resulted in an accord reinforcing their economic and financial partnership.[44] Concerns were raised again when Tunisian journalist Taoufik Ben Brik launched a hunger strike in 2000 to protest against constant surveillance, harassment, and the confiscation of his passport. An international awareness campaign on his behalf led to consistent criticism in the French press of Tunisia's human rights violations. After a phone call from Chirac, Ben Ali returned Ben Brik's passport, and France offered the journalist a tourist visa to defuse tensions.[45] This cooling of Franco-Tunisian relations followed a European Parliament resolution condemning the human rights situation in 1996, signaled French awareness of human rights abuses, and demonstrated its potential to exert pressure upon the regime.

Whether French politicians were willing to take a position on Tunisia's domestic affairs was tied to geostrategic calculations. Ben Ali responded to the September 2001 terrorist attacks on New York and Washington, DC as an occasion to resuscitate his tarnished reputation and gain foreign assistance for his domestic battle against the Islamic political opposition. When Chirac returned to Tunisia within months of the attacks, his concerns for personal liberties that had surfaced the previous year had vanished. Directly questioned about the poor situation of human rights in Tunisia, he responded evasively. For Chirac, Ben Ali was "a man of peace," and what mattered was the Tunisian "rejection of intolerance and religious fundamentalism," and its "exemplary" participation in the struggle against terrorism.[46]

Chirac returned two years later, lauding the success of Tunisian modernization thanks to Ben Ali's personal initiative and "the state of law and the consolidation of democracy."[47] At a press conference, faced mainly with French journalists, he qualified Franco-Tunisian relations as "excellent," and defined the economic situation as "especially brilliant" for a developing nation. In response to questions about human rights, Chirac denied any problems by claiming that "the primary human right is the right to eat, to get healthcare, to have a shelter," suggesting that "from this perspective, it must be recognized that Tunisia is very far ahead of many, many countries." He further insisted that in Tunisia, "the creation of wealth, economic growth, the distribution of wealth, occurred in a way that meets all the exigencies of human rights." This was sadly ironic, as the Tunisian human rights activist Radhia Nasraoui was engaged on a hunger strike the political relevance of which Chirac dismissed, saying: "There are also people in France who are on hunger strikes, have gone on hunger strikes, or probably will in the future, one day or another, for one reason or another."[48]

Tunisia's liberal reputation was further propagated by partisans and expatriots in France. Philippe Séguin, president of the national assembly (1993–7), who was born among the settler populations of Tunisia, accompanied Chirac on his first presidential visit to Tunis in 1995. Ben Ali later offered him the apartment of his childhood after evicting its occupants, and both Séguin and Pasqua were guests at the Carthage palace for a France–Tunisia soccer match in 2002.[49] The entrepreneur Hosni Jemmali cultivated personal ties among business and political elite of the two countries through his Franco-Tunisian Exchange group which had scheduled Frédéric Mitterrand as its guest of honor for a twentieth anniversary celebration in January 2011. He solicited the participation of well-connected and influential women in his Mediterranean women's group by offering all-expenses-paid vacations to his resort, the hotel Sangho. Guests included the owner of *Le Parisien*, a columnist from *Le Figaro*, and Sarkozy's sister-in-law.[50] These gifts were decried by journalists who posited that such personal ties superseded official responsibilities, leading to impartiality and a lack of transparency.[51]

While political liberalization proved ephemeral under Ben Ali and the judicial system was severely comprised, Chirac's reversal points to the renewed reliance on Ben Ali's cooperation and Tunisia's place as a regional ally which merited overlooking his authoritarian tendencies. The French president was willing to gently reference the rule of law, support EU resolutions, and champion human rights when these entailed few risks. Within Tunisia, the routine harassment of Tunisians who practiced their religion or expressed political views through religious language continued, as did the persecution of human rights activists and cyberdissidents. As these modes of contestation were subsumed under the label of terrorism, Ben Ali upheld his reputation as a liberal, modern ruler and a friend of the West, a cooperative ally committed to eliminating terrorism.

From France's "Arab policy" to EU–Mediterranean partnerships

Chirac's relations with Ben Ali represented a departure from the "Arab policy," as did French participation alongside the US in the 1991 Gulf War. Beginning in the 1970s, France took a leading role in focusing EU attention on the Mediterranean as a distinct region, through its influence over its former colonial territories in North Africa.[52] At the European level, this was concretely iterated in the 1995 Barcelona Accords, a series of bilateral agreements to create a free-trade zone, later reformulated as the European Neighborhood Policy and then the Union for the Mediterranean (Union pour la Méditerranée, UPM). Initiated by France, Spain, and Italy, the Barcelona process was intended to create economic and cultural partnerships, encourage democratization, the rule of law, and human rights, while allowing the EU to contribute to the Israeli-Palestinian peace process. France generally set the tone for relations with North African partners focusing on containing the war in Algeria, and supporting the regimes in place because of their ability to control extremist groups.[53] Despite the EU's domestic commitment to political pluralism and respect for human rights, in the case of Tunisia, subsequent accords legitimized Ben Ali as head of state offering economic and technical assistance in exchange for border surveillance.

In 1995, Tunisia became the first country to sign an association agreement, ratified in 1998, centering on the progressive abandoning of protective tariffs on EU-originated goods. In theory, the concomitant loss of state revenue would be compensated for by technology transfer, job creation, and foreign direct investment. Aid programs would support Tunisian industries to improve their ability to compete with European firms. In practice, subsidies for upgrading involved a lengthy state-controlled application process. Grants were often awarded to individuals connected to the regime, including Aziz Miled, a wealthy businessman involved in tourism, banking, and import-export (who later hosted Alliot-Marie and her family).[54] By creating closer ties between government and large entrepreneurs, the line between the public and private sectors was blurred. Far from a neat plan of economic liberalization, EU funds reinforced the predominance of the ruling party, facilitated state interference in the economy, and mainly benefited large businesses and multinational corporations.[55]

At best, the economic impact was uneven. It failed to increase exports which were already exported to the EU without tariffs, slowed the growth rate of imports, and "does not create trade but in fact reduces trade."[56] Various quotas continued to protect EU markets and the enormous subsidies of its agricultural program put Tunisian products at a disadvantage. The agreement privileged industrial development to the detriment of agriculture, perpetuating north–south inequalities and the underdevelopment of Tunisia's interior. A 2003 report by Oxfam worried that the agreements would produce a loss in employment and only "modest or negligible gains" for its Arab partners.[57] Harsher critics see the relationship as little more than "controlling immigrations in exchange for free-trade and financial aid."[58]

The association agreement included clauses whereby the allocation of funds depended upon Tunisia's respect for human rights. However, even when aid to Tunisia was reduced by 13.5 percent in 2004 for punitive reasons, Tunisia continued to receive more aid per capita than any other partner.[59] Ben Ali was not openly criticized and democratic reform was rarely addressed.[60] Discussing the elaboration of a joint defense program among different national militaries in her capacity as minister of defense, Alliot-Marie reduced the human rights situation to "an image problem." She summarized the French stance that "certain restrictions on freedom have to be considered from the perspective of their relevance for the war on terrorism," thus subordinating respect for human rights to matters of security.[61]

Sarkozy shared similar priorities and accommodated incomplete liberalization. He travelled to Tunisia less than two months after beginning his term in office to promote a new iteration of the Euro-Med partnership, the UPM. He depicted it idyllically in an interview with the Tunisian daily *Al-Sabah* as "a space of cooperation and solidarity" that would "promote exchanges instead of widening the gap between rich and poor." At the same time, he stressed the importance of bilateral relations and boasted of the "very strong friendship" between Tunisia and France.[62] Returning the following year, he told *Al-Chourouk* that the second visit signaled his "respect and support for President Ben Ali," taking pride in the fact that France remained Tunisia's first economic partner and supplier of aid.[63] Sarkozy glorified how French businesses were expanding or relocating to Tunisia at the rate of one every five days. Yet more lucrative French businesses arrived only with the collaboration of Ben Ali's extended family, who were part-owners of at least twenty French businesses according to the investigative work of Arnaud Muller. For instance, Imed Trabelsi controlled the home-improvements store Bricorama, and Halima Ben Ali was the intermediary for Peugeot, contributing to the nepotism and corruption of the ruling family and their omnipresent role in the national economy.[64]

Encouraging political reform was not a priority. While Sarkozy extolled the country's engagement in "promoting human rights" so that the "scope of freedoms is expanding," he accepted Ben Ali's assessment that democratization could only be achieved at a slow pace, quoting Bourguiba as saying that modest reforms were preferable to impossible miracles.[65] During a lengthy talk at the National Institute of Applied Sciences and Technology, he repeated the idea that education and development were the keys to fighting "barbarity" and "fundamentalism." In this respect, Tunisia offered a successful case of modernization within the Arab-Muslim world, an example "for all people who are threatened by fundamentalism." If Tunisians could succeed at westernizing, this might mean that "the war of civilizations and the clash of religions" could be avoided. He reiterated:

> If you fail, then those caricatures and stereotypes of Islam and the Arab world will be true, and no one can prevent the mortal confrontation between the East and the West. If you fail, then the clash of civilizations and the war of religions will be inevitable.

Sarkozy's analysis returned numerous times to this East–West binary, insisting that for Tunisia to remain on the side of democracy, it must exclude Islam.

With religion positioned as a threat to Tunisia's modernization, he placed an existential significance on Tunisia's international role to explain why the French president considered himself "in the camp of the friends of Tunisia."[66]

The UPM's inaugural summit in July 2008 coincided with the beginning of France's presidency of the EU. Held at Paris's Grand Palace, a structure built for the Universal Exposition of 1900 and its celebration of the French colonial empire, the location itself was an ironic symbol of the limitations of a union between unequal partners.[67] Sarkozy's program reiterated the emphasis on cooperation on security matters and in the prevention of terrorism, including migration under this umbrella. While the 2008 version allowed for increasing representation of the southern Mediterranean partners and joint presidency, it remained dominated by the EU and organized according to its foreign policy goals.[68] According to diplomats, very little was accomplished after its inauguration due to conflicts of interest among EU partners.[69] No summits were held in 2009 or 2010, as following the Israeli invasion of Gaza in January 2009 the majority of Arab leaders refused to participate in projects that involved Israel, and it stalled in the immediate wake of the Arab revolutions of 2011.

Agreements between Tunisia and the EU provided financial backing for the regime under the premise that development would dissuade potential terrorists and reduce emigration. As Chirac phrased it at a dinner honoring Ben Ali in Paris, Ben Ali's commitment to economic reforms had weakened fundamentalism because "when the standard of living improves, when unemployment, poverty, and marginality are on the decline, the temptation towards violence also disappears."[70] There were few structural mechanisms to encourage political pluralism and the EU prioritized political stability to stave off the potentially negative consequences of regime change, such as limiting European access to natural gas. Though Tunisia's EU accords included a clause ensuring respect for human rights, it was not enforced "not least because of French reluctance to engage in activities which Paris believed might endanger regional stability."[71] Especially after the European Council formulated a plan of action against terrorism in September 2001, the emphasis on a common security agenda further marginalized the liberal and humanitarian components of the Euro-Med discourse. As critics have caustically pointed out, these accords constitute a softer approach to EU interests in limiting illegal immigration as they are geared "to stabilize the sending countries and pacify Europe's own xenophobic reaction to the arrivals."[72]

Immigration, security, and national identity

As EU-Mediterranean programs demonstrate, foreign developmental aid was calculated to secure Europe's borders from illegal immigration and its perceived link with terrorism and drug trafficking. These prerogatives have been rephrased by a range of political parties to present all Arab and Muslim immigrants, residents, and citizens as potential security threats. Although there have been visible Arab communities in France since the nineteenth century, and immigrants formed an integral part of France's social fabric throughout the twentieth century, national identity and collective memory have tended to conceptualize the nation territorially and as culturally homogenous: Christian and white.[73] What was initially the monopoly of the extreme right—the view of North African, Arab, and Muslim immigrants as the cause of a host of demographic, social, and economic problems—was adopted by political parties across the spectrum by the 1980s.

Tunisians have been present in France since at least World War I working in factories and serving in the military, though many of these men later returned to Tunisia. It was not until after independence that significant numbers of Tunisian men and women made France their home, with a trend of family settlement around the 1970s. An economic crisis in 1973 coincided with attempts at restricting non-European immigration the following year and contributed to the popular correlation between immigrant labor and national unemployment. Though the number of Tunisians in France remained small, public and parliamentary debates over immigration became a consistent feature of French politics during a period that roughly corresponded to Ben Ali's presidency. In speeches accompanying diplomatic visits French presidents frequently referenced the resident Tunisian community as a symbol of ties between the two countries. In almost every press conference occasioned by a visit to Tunisia, journalists pressed the president on the issue of immigration. Would educated Tunisians emigrate to France? Were terrorism and immigration really a problem? What did Ben Ali think of the French debate over illegal immigration? By 2010, the estimated 600,000 Tunisians in France amounted to only about 1 percent of the total population, but they formed part of a larger North African community which was seen as synonymous with Arabs and Islam.

The increasing stigmatization of immigration (and immigrant communities within France) resulted from factors such as decolonization, increasing unemployment, and the electoral success of the right-wing National Front (Front National, FN) from the mid-1980s. At the same time, a series of initiatives by the Ministry of the Interior sought to organize France's Muslim populations in ways similar to Catholics, Protestants, and Jews with representatives providing an intermediary to the French state, while limiting the number of trained personnel and funds from their countries of origin and the Gulf.[74] Still, some foreign governments were involved in the affairs of their nationals; Algeria and its generals formed close alliances with leading figures such as the imam of Paris's Great Mosque. The Tunisian regime also closely collaborated with its French counterparts in matters of security and the surveillance of Tunisian nationals in France, increasing the significance of immigration to Franco-Tunisian relations.[75]

Both the minister of foreign affairs and the minister of the interior contributed to defining French relations with Tunisia, suggesting the close connection between foreign policy and domestic security. In controversies over Muslim girls covering their hair at school in 1989, and legislation banning the wearing of headscarves in public schools in 2004, personal religiosity has been conflated with proselytism, terrorism and women's oppression, and seen as a threat to French national values.[76] Because Muslims are believed to pose a potential problem, development loans and public aid have been justified as discouraging emigration.

The political correlation of immigration to questions of security was perhaps most explicitly identified in Sarkozy's 2007 formation of a Ministry of Immigration, Integration, National Identity, and Co-development that combined functions from a number of ministries, primarily the Ministry of the Interior and the Ministry of Foreign Affairs. While its inauguration spurred a heated polemic in the press about its distinction between immigration and national identity indicating that immigrants were not part of the nation, its statutes confirmed the goals of controlling and reducing immigration.[77] An agreement signed during Sarkozy's April 2008 trip to Tunisia was similarly intended towards limiting migrations through technical and financial support such as training for Tunisian personnel and equipment to be used in border surveillance. This offered financial incentives and material means for Ben Ali to police his own borders, and his willingness to do so improved his standing as a valuable ally.

Conclusion

Economic liberalization under Bourguiba and Ben Ali perpetuated neocolonial relations and financial dependence on Europe and its financial institutions. The concomitant development of service industries and marketing of an unskilled labor force contributed to regional disparities and uneven development. French diplomatic alliances with the two presidents fluctuated depending on their role in regional politics, and ultimately encouraged political stagnation to the detriment of pluralism and democracy. These factors contributed to popular resentment against both regimes as demonstrated in periodic strikes and the broader mobilizations beginning in December 1983 and December 2010. Successive French government officials adopted a policy of non-interference in domestic political affairs, facilitating loans, foreign aid, and free-trade agreements thereby proposing economic solutions to problems that were essentially political and social.

Despite the efforts of French presidents such as de Gaulle or Chirac to demarcate a particularly French approach to the Arab world and the Middle East, they reiterated the faults of their American counterparts. As they privileged narrow definitions of national security and domestic interests, French presidents consistently sidelined ideals of democracy promotion, respect for human rights, and the importance of the rule of law. Even when extensive reports detailing the practice of torture, the lack of an independent judiciary, and the silencing of dissent were published by French human rights groups such as Reporters without Borders (Reporters Sans Frontières, RSF) and the International Federation of Human Rights (Fédération Internationale de Droits de l'Homme, FIDH), circulated in the French media, and led to criticism by the European Parliament, they did little more than place a temporary strain on relations with Ben Ali. While bothersome, the increasingly vocal objections of scholars, journalists, and activists did not weaken official relations or alter the pace of ministerial exchanges, nor were they backed by economic sanctions or political pressure, despite the considerable leverage granted by France's position as Tunisia's main trading partner. As the French Minister of Foreign Affairs Bernard Kouchner synthesized it bluntly, human rights were a matter of concern, but not a priority:

> It is true that there are human rights violations [. . .] It is also true that we are more attentive due to the high economic and social status of Tunisia, and because its commitment to women's rights and secularism is unique within the region. But a minister of foreign affairs, I repeat, can not only be a human rights advocate.[78]

Collaboration with Bourguiba and Ben Ali was opportunistic, subordinated to shifting perceptions of domestic priorities, and generally defined at the highest official level. Public opinion factored in when successive presidents adopted a tough stance on immigration in accord with the security agenda that underscored Franco-Tunisian partnerships. Particularly evident during Ben Ali's presidency, his willingness to accommodate Western economic interests and contributions to patrolling international borders routinely trumped concerns over the local ramifications of his decisions or the methods utilized to carry them out.

Notes

1. This was during a January 10, 2011 interview on Canal+ for which he later apologized, "Frédéric Mitterrand exprime ses 'regrets' aux Tunisiens," *Libération*, January 23, 2011, accessed May 4, 2013, www.liberation.fr/monde/01012315388-frederic-mitterrand-exprime-ses-regrets-aux-tunisiens.
2. See the full text of her statements under the heading "Violences en Tunisie et en Algérie. Réponses du Ministre d'État, Ministre des Affaires Étrangères et Européennes, Michèle Alliot-Marie, à des Questions d'actualité à l'Assemblée Nationale," Paris, January 11, 2011, accessed May 4, 2013, http://basedoc.diplomatie.gouv.fr.
3. Combined with rumors that she met with the Tunisian Minister of the Interior Rafiq Belhajj Kacem, the mounting public outcry at Alliot-Marie's public support of Ben Ali's regime and his treatment of demonstrations as a security threat contributed to

her resignation on February 27. Nicolas Beau and Arnaud Muller, *Tunis et Paris: les liaisons dangereuses* (Paris: Jean-Claude Gawsewitch, 2011).

4. This was quoted in a number of news articles. See, for instance, Isabelle Mandraud's "Tunisie: l'ambassadeur de France pensait que le régime de Ben Ali tiendrait," *Le Monde*, January 27, 2011, accessed May 4, 2013, www.lemonde.fr/tunisie/article/2011/01/27/tunisie-l-ambassadeur-de-france-pensait-que-le-regime-de-ben-ali-tiendrait_1471201_1466522.html.
5. Marly, "La voix de la France a disparu dans le monde," *Le Monde*, February 22, 2011, accessed May 4, 2013, www.lemonde.fr/idees/article/2011/02/22/on-ne-s-improvise-pas-diplomate_1483517_3232.html#ens_id=1245377.
6. Habib Bourguiba, "Le problème franco-tunisien est un problème de souveraínté," *Les Temps Modernes* 77 (1952): 1567–71.
7. For instance, he alternated between strategic alliance and distanced skepticism toward labor and the Communists before and after independence. Abdesselem Ben Hamida, *Le Syndicalisme tunisien de la deuxième guerre mondiale à l'autonomie interne* (Tunis: Publications de l'Université de Tunis, 1989); Hassine Raouf Hamza, *Communisme et nationalisme en Tunisie: de la libération jusqu'à l'indépendance (1943–1956)* (Tunis: Université de Tunis, 1994).
8. Habib Bourguiba, "Nationalism: Antidote to Communism," *Foreign Affairs* 35.4 (1957): 646–53.
9. André Nouschi, *La France et le monde arabe depuis 1962: mythes et réalités d'une ambition* (Paris: Vuibert, 1994).
10. The nationalization of land was destined for agricultural production cooperatives formed in an attempt to counter the trend of land concentration resulting from French colonial rule. On agricultural reform more broadly, see Stephen J. King, *Liberalization against Democracy: The Local Politics of Economic Reform in Tunisia* (Bloomington, IN: Indiana University Press, 2003).
11. Robert A. Poirier and Stephen Wright, "The Political Economy of Tourism in Tunisia," *The Journal of Modern African Studies* 31.1 (1993): 149–62.
12. "Discours prononcé par le Président Pompidou au déjeuner offert en l'honneur de M. Bourguiba, Président de la République tunisienne," June 29, 1972, accessed May 4, 2013, http://basedoc.diplomatie.gouv.fr.
13. Waleed Hazbun, *Beaches, Ruins, Resorts: The Politics of Tourism in the Arab World* (Minneapolis, MN: University of Minnesota Press, 2008).
14. Nigel Disney, "The Working Class Revolt in Tunisia," *MERIP Reports* 67 (1978): 12–14.
15. Christopher Alexander, "Opportunities, Organizations, and Ideas: Islamists and Workers in Tunisia and Algeria," *International Journal of Middle East Studies* 32.4 (2000): 465–90.
16. Clement Henry Moore, *Tunisia since Independence: The Dynamic of One-Party Government* (Berkeley, CA: University of California Press, 1969).
17. On the crafting of this reputation see Aziz Krichen, *Le syndrome Bourguiba* (Tunis: Cérès Productions, 1993); Michel Camau and Vincent Geisser, *Habib Bourguiba: La trace et l'héritage* (Paris: Karthala; Institut d'études politiques, 2004).
18. Michel Treutenaere, "La coopération culturelle, scientifique et technique entre la Tunisie et la France: évolution et perspectives," *Annuaire de l'Afrique du Nord* 20 (1982): 489–507.
19. Nouschi, *La France et le monde arabe*, 162. Mitterrand hoped to maintain strong relations

with all Arab leaders as well as Israel and became the first French president to visit Israel in an official capacity in 1958 (he went there five times), Paul Balta, "Mitterrand et les Arabes," *Politique internationale* 13 (1981): 31–46.

20. David Seddon, "Winter of Discontent: Economic Crisis in Tunisia and Morocco," *MERIP Reports* 127 (1984): 7–16; Jim Paul, "States of Emergency in Tunisia and Morocco," *MERIP Reports* 127 (1984): 3–6; Jean-Philippe Bras, "Chronique Tunisie (chronologie et documents en annexe)," in *Annuaire de l'Afrique du nord,* ed. André Raymond and Hubert Michel (Paris: Éditions du CNRS, 1986), 957–1009.
21. The Minister of Foreign Affairs, Claude Cheysson, traveled to Tunis that August, Jean-Robert Henry, "Chronique international," in *Annuaire de l'Afrique du nord,* ed. André Raymond and Hubert Michel (Paris: Éditions du CNRS, 1986), 957–1009.
22. "La France 'prend acte' des changements en Tunisie," *Le Monde,* November 8, 1987.
23. Laurie Brand, *Women, the State and Political Liberalization: Middle Eastern and North African Experiences* (New York: Columbia University Press, 1998).
24. "Interview accordée par M. le Président de la République à la télévision tunisienne," June 4, 1989, http://basedoc.diplomatie.gouv.fr.
25. "Allocution prononcée par le Président de la République au cours du dîner d'état offert par Son Excellence M. Zine El Abidine Ben Ali, Président de la République tunisienne au Palais de Carthage," June 5, 1989, http://basedoc.diplomatie.gouv.fr.
26. Souhayr Belhassen, "Le legs Bourguibiens de la repression," in *Habib Bourguiba: la trace et l'héritage,* ed. Michel Camau and Vincent Geisser (Paris: Éditions Karthala, 2004), 391–404.
27. On electoral politics, see Vincent Geisser, "Tunisie: des élections pour quoi faire? Enjeux et 'sens' du fait electoral de Bourguiba à Ben Ali," *Maghreb/Machreq* 168 (2000): 14–28; Olfa Lamloum and Bernard Ravenel, "La fiction pluraliste," *Confluences Méditerranée* 32 (1999–2000): 173–82.
28. See, for instance, Agence Tunisienne de Communications Extérieures, "La Femme Dans Le Projet Nahdhaoui" and "Femme Et Famille: Extraits De Discours Du Président Zine El Abidine Ben Ali," 1991. Ben Ali did oversee legislative changes in 1993, 1996, and 1997, though feminists identify additional inequalities that were not addressed and deplore how women were used to justify the repression of the MTI. Olfa Lamloum and Luiza Toscane, "Les femmes, alibi du pouvoir tunisien," *Le Monde Diplomatique,* June 1998, 3.
29. Authorities tried "to provide evidence that Ennahda [sic] was an organization involved in attempts to overthrow the government by violence;" these were "without success" due to "insufficient evidence of a plot." Amnesty International, *Tunisia: The Cycle of Injustice* (London: International Secretariat, 2003).
30. Amnesty International, *Tunisia: Rhetoric Versus Reality: The Failure of a Human Rights Bureaucracy* (New York: Amnesty International USA, 1994).
31. This is not the place to elaborate on the cruelties of Algeria's dirty wars which have been detailed by scholars such as Hugh Roberts and Jeremy Keenan.
32. Olivier Roy, "Sur la politique arabe de la France," *Monde arabe Maghreb-Machrek* 132 (1991): 15–20.
33. Hugh Roberts, "Algeria's ruinous impasse and the honourable way out," *International Affairs* 71.2 (1995): 247–67.
34. Georgie Anne Geyer, "Interview: Zine El Abidine Ben Ali," *Middle East Policy* 6.2 (1998): 183–7.

35. Nicolas Beau and Jean-Pierre Tuquoi, *Notre ami Ben Ali: l'envers du "miracle Tunisien"* (Paris: La Découverte, 1999); Olfa Lamloum, "L'indéfectible soutien français à l'exclusion de l'islamisme tunisien," in *La Tunisie de Ben Ali: la société contre le régime*, ed. Olfa Lamloum and Bernard Ravenel (Paris: L'Harmattan, 2002).
36. Yasmine Ryan, "Tunisians Discover Secret Archive in Paris," *Al-Jazeera English*, June 27, 2011.
37. Beau and Muller, *Tunis et Paris.*
38. "Visite en Tunisie: Allocution prononcée par le Président de la République, M. Jacques Chirac, lors du dîner d'état offert par le Président de la République tunisienne, M. Zine El Abidine Ben Ali, au Palais de Carthage," October 5, 1995, accessed May 4, 2013, http://basedoc.diplomatie.gouv.fr. The law was adopted by Bourguiba in 1981 and expanded in 1985, effectively barring pious women from state employment and university education.
39. "Visite en Tunisie: Discours du Président de la République, M. Jacques Chirac, devant l'Assemblée Nationale tunisienne," October 6, 1995, accessed May 4, 2011, http://basedoc.diplomatie.gouv.fr.
40. See the video of parts of this speech dated November 18, 2008, Blandine Grosjean, "Raoult, Sarkozy et DSK sur la Tunisie: Les vidéos qui font mal," January 17, 2011. Online at www.rue89.com/2011/01/17/raoult-sarkozy-et-dsk-sur-la-tunisie-les-videos-qui-font-mal-186100
41. Béatrice Hibou, "Tunisie: le coût d'un 'miracle'," *Critique internationale* 4 (1999): 48–56; Béatrice Hibou, *The Force of Obedience, the Political Economy of Repression in Tunisia* (Cambridge: Polity, 2011); King, *Liberalization against Democracy*, especially Chapter 2.
42. The cost of a basic diet that was used in government calculations was based only on a minimal number of calories and did not include vitamins or iron which would increase the costs and consequently the poverty rate, see Raouf Saïdi, "La pauvreté en Tunisie: présentation critique," in *La Tunisie de Ben Ali: la société contre le régime*, ed. Olfa Lamloum and Bernard Ravenel (Paris: L'Harmattan, 2002).
43. For a cogent discussion of the shortcomings of Ben Ali's commitment to social welfare via the National Solidarity Fund (26-26), see Eric Gobe, "Politiques sociales et registres de légitimation d'un état néo-patrimonial: Le cas tunisien," in *Solidarités et Compétences: Idéologies et Pratiques*, ed. Monique Selim and Bernard Hours (Paris: L'Harmattan, 2003); Béatrice Hibou, "Les marges de manœuvre d'un 'bon élève' économique: la Tunisie de Ben Ali," *Les Études du CERI* 60 (1999): 1–33.
44. "Toast du Président de la République, M. Jacques Chirac, lors du dîner d'état offert en l'"honneur du Président de la République tunisienne, M. Zine El Abidine Ben Ali," October 20, 1997, accessed May 4, 2013, http://basedoc.diplomatie.gouv.fr.
45. Larbi Sadiki, "Bin Ali's Tunisia: Democracy by Non-Democratic Means," *British Journal of Middle Eastern Studies* 29.1 (2002): 57–78.
46. "Visite en Tunisie: Conférence de presse du Président de la République, M. Jacques Chirac," December 1, 2001, accessed May 4, 2011, http://basedoc.diplomatie.gouv.fr.
47. "Visite d'état en Tunisie: Allocution du Président de la République, M. Jacques Chirac, à l'occasion du dîner d'état offert en son honneur par le Président de la République tunisienne, M. Zine El Abidine Ben Ali," December 3, 2003, accessed May 4, 2013, http://basedoc.diplomatie.gouv.fr.
48. Though members of Chirac's delegation met with Radhia Nasraoui's

supporters. "Visite d'état en Tunisie point de presse du Président de la République, M. Jacques Chirac," December 3, 2003, accessed May 4, 2013, http://basedoc.diplomatie.gouv.fr.

49. Beau and Muller, *Tunis et Paris.*
50. The event was cancelled after Ben Ali's departure, see Matthieu Deslanes, "Des femmes d'influence pour vendre la Tunisie de Ben Ali," January 19, 2011, accessed May 4, 2013, www.rue89.com/2011/01/19/des-femmes-dinfluence-pour-vendre-la-tunisie-de-ben-ali-186304.
51. For instance, Olivier Tesquet, "France-Tunisie: Un roman d'amitiés," March 3, 2011, accessed May 4, 2013, http://owni.fr/2011/03/03/visu-france-tunisie-un-roman-damities. These relationships are not limited to Tunisia but are often part of a broader critique of the political class. The Sarkozys have vacationed free of charge in the palaces of Morocco's Muhammad VI, Jordan's King Abdullah, and at the expense of Egypt's former president Hosni Mubarak. Whereas Mitterrand's preference was Egypt and Chirac's Morocco, the latter also resides in a spacious Parisian apartment owned by the family of Rafiq Hariri. See Britta Sandberg, "Les ministres vont enfin payer leur notes," *Courrier International,* February 17, 2011.
52. Pia Christina Wood, "Chirac's 'New Arab Policy' and Middle East Challenges: The Arab-Israeli Conflict, Iraq and Iran," *Middle East Journal* 52.4 (1998): 563–80.
53. Olfa Lamloum, "L'enjeu de l'islamisme au cœur du processus de Barcelone," *Critique internationale* 18 (2003): 129–42.
54. Jean-Pierre Cassarino, "The EU-Tunisian Association Agreement and Tunisia's Structural Reform Program," *Middle East Journal* 53.1 (1999): 59–74.
55. Béatrice Hibou, "Domination and Control in Tunisia: Economic Levers for the Exercise of Authoritarian Power," *Review of African Political Economy* 33.108 (2006): 185–206; Brieg Powel and Larbi Sadiki, *Europe and Tunisia: Democratisation Via Association* (New York: Routledge, 2010).
56. Mohamed Hedi Bchir, Mohamed Abdelbasset Chemingui, and Hakim Ben Hammouda, "Ten Years after Implementing the Barcelona Process: What can be Learned from the Tunisian Experience?" *Journal of North African Studies* 14.2 (2009): 123–44.
57. Yara Abdul-Hamid, "The Euro-Mediterranean Agreements: Partnership or Penury?" Oxfam International, 2003.
58. Béatrice Hibou, "Le partenariat en réanimation bureaucratique," *Critique internationale* 18 (2003): 117–28.
59. Patrick Holden, "Development through Integration? EU Aid Reform and the Evolution of Mediterranean Aid Policy," *Journal of International Development* 20 (2008): 230–44.
60. Powel and Sadiki, *Europe and Tunisia*; Pia Christina Wood, "French Foreign Policy and Tunisia: Do Human Rights Matter?," *Middle East Policy* 9.2 (2002): 92–110.
61. "Déplacement en Tunisie: Conférence de presse du Ministre de la Défense, Mme Michèle Alliot-Marie," June 2, 2006, accessed May 4, 2013, http://basedoc.diplomatie.gouv.fr.
62. "Déplacement au Maghreb, entretien du Président de la République, M. Nicolas Sarkozy, accordée au quotidien tunisien 'As Sabah,'" July 10, 2007, accessed May 4, 2013, http://basedoc.diplomatie.gouv.fr.
63. "Visite d'état en Tunisie: Entretien du Président de la République, M. Nicolas

Sarkozy, avec le quotidien tunisien 'Ach-Chourouk,'" April 27, 2008, accessed May 4, 2013, http://basedoc.diplomatie.gouv.fr.

64. Beau and Muller, *Tunis et Paris.*
65. "Visite d'état en Tunisie: allocution du Président de la République, M. Nicolas Sarkozy, lors du dîner d'état offert par le Président de la République tunisienne, M. Zine El Abidine Ben Ali," April 28, 2008, accessed May 4, 2013, http://basedoc.diplomatie.gouv.fr.
66. "Visite d'état en Tunisie: discours du Président de la République, M. Nicolas Sarkozy, devant les étudiants de l'Institut National des Sciences Appliquées et de Technologie," April 30, 2008, accessed May 4, 2013, http://basedoc.diplomatie.gouv.fr.
67. On the civilizing connotations of EU programs and the projection of European norms as universal, see Federica Bicchi, "'Our Size Fits All': Normative Power Europe and the Mediterranean," *Journal of European Public Policy* 13.2 (2006): 286–303.
68. Paul James Cardwell, "Euromed, European Neighbourhood Policy and the Union for the Mediterranean: Overlapping Policy Frames in the EU's Governance of the Mediterranean," *Journal of Common Market Studies* 49.2 (2011): 219–41.
69. Pierre Alonso, "Union pour la Méditerranée (UpM): le naufrage?," February 23, 2011, accessed May 5, 2013, http://owni.fr/2011/02/23/union-pour-la-mediterranee-upm-le-naufrage.
70. "Toast du Président de la République," October 20, 1997. In many respects this equation echoes the official narrative behind the National Solidarity Fund more commonly known as the 26-26; see the relevant discussions in Gobe, "Politiques sociales et registres de légitimation d'un état néo-patrimonial: le cas tunisien"; Hibou, *The Force of Obedience.*
71. George Joffé, "The European Union, Democracy and Counter-Terrorism in the Maghreb," *Journal of Common Market Studies* 46.1 (2008): 156.
72. Greg Feldman, "Europe's Border Control with a Humanitarian Face," *Middle East Report* 261 (2011): 14–17. See also Sihem Bensedrine and Omar Mestiri, *L'Europe et ses despotes: quand le soutien au "modèle tunisien" dans le monde arabe fait le jeu du terrorisme islamiste* (Paris: La Découverte, 2004); Gregory Feldman, *The Migration Apparatus: Security, Labor, and Policymaking in the European Union* (Stanford, CA: Stanford University Press, 2012).
73. Ian Coller, *Arab France: Islam and the Making of Modern Europe, 1798–1831* (Berkeley, CA: University of California Press, 2010); Gérard Noiriel, "Histoire, Mémoire, Engagement Civique," *Hommes et Migrations,* 1247 (2004): 17–26.
74. Alec G. Hargreaves, *Immigration, "Race" and Ethnicity in Contemporary France* (London and New York: Routledge, 1995).
75. Vincent Geisser and Aziz Zemouri, *Marianne et Allah: les politiques français face à la "question musulmane"* (Paris: La Découverte, 2007).
76. Joan Wallach Scott, *The Politics of the Veil* (Princeton, NJ: Princeton University Press, 2007).
77. It was dismantled in 2010, Jérôme Valluy, "Quelles sont les origines du ministère de l'identité nationale et de l'immigration?," *Cultures & Conflits* 69 (2008): 7–18.
78. "Entretien du ministre des affaires étrangeres et européennes, Bernard Kouchner, avec l'hebdomadaire *Jeune Afrique,*" March 22, 2009, accessed May 5, 2013, http://basedoc.diplomatie.gouv.fr.

PART 2

Architects: Genealogies of Dissent

CHAPTER 5

From Socio-Economic Protest to National Revolt: The Labor Origins of the Tunisian Revolution

Sami Zemni

On February 8, 2013, a general strike, called for by the Union Générale Tunisienne du Travail (UGTT), the powerful labor union, brought thousands of Tunisians into the streets as a sign of protest against the murder of the leftist politician and lawyer Chokri Belaïd. The political murder of a leader of the Popular Front—a coalition of leftist parties—was one of the last culminating points in a series of confrontations between the union and the government led by Ennahda that have become recurrent in post-Ben Ali Tunisia. Since Ben Ali fled the country, Tunisia has witnessed many cycles of protest—organized or spontaneous—that combine political grievances and economic claims as well as social and cultural demands. In the post-Ben Ali period, the UGTT has come to play a central political role that stretches beyond its syndical mission. Union leaders have stated unambiguously that they defend not only the workers' interests, but also, in conjunction with civil society institutions and political allies, the institutions of the Republic. The two transitional governments (respectively led by Mohamed Ghannouchi and Béji Caïd Essebsi) and the government established by the Constituent Assembly have had the greatest difficulty to tame the revolutionary aspirations of the union with its many strikes, sit-ins, petitions, and lobbying. This preponderant political role of the union can only be understood against the backdrop of its historical role in postindependent Tunisia as well as its crucial role during the revolutionary period that led to Ben Ali's getaway.

Taken by the speed and the breadth of the popular revolt, the protests, culminating in the manifestations on the Avenue Habib Bourguiba, that led to Ben Ali's departure on January 14, were quickly framed as some sort of "pure" event, a unique occurrence where an almost mythical and homogeneous "Tunisian people" confronted and fought its "dictator". In such a depoliticized symbolic order, as Daniel Bensaïd states, the causes and consequences of the revolt were blurred and historical intelligibility was abandoned for a simplistic account of the present in which a good but repressed people—the so-called Facebook youths using new social media—was fighting a bad corrupt leader, his family, and his regime, only echoing a sort of biblical fight between good and evil. With a majority of academics focusing on explaining the persistence of Arab authoritarian structures and systems—and with an international media having reduced Arab political life since 9/11 to a question of Islamist politics and jihad—many observers missed out on the forces of change that had been taking shape over the last decade. While the Tunisian revolution drew on the participation of nearly every social stratum—thus warranting to a certain extent the temporary use of the collective noun "the people"—observers failed to seize the different dynamics at work, let alone understand the different types of mobilization of collective actors involved in the uprisings and framing the complex forces driving these historical events.[1]

The self-immolation of the young man Mohammed Bouazizi was not so much the starting point of the Tunisian revolution but rather the rallying point for different types and forms of protest to converge into a national uprising. In other words, the Tunisian revolution did not come out of nowhere but instead has a history. There is a genealogy of the protests and oppositions that can be mapped. The forces that coalesced in late December 2010 and early January 2011 that brought the revolution in a decisive phase can be traced back to the beginning of the 1990s. The Tunisian revolution, not coincidentally, as I will discuss later, started in the smaller cities of the center and southwestern parts of the country, that is the regions benefiting the least from economic development and redistribution of wealth.[2] Guided by militants of the workers' movement, well-educated but unemployed youth, and some of the urban poor, the unorganized protest movement gradually evolved from localized socioeconomic demands into a national popular movement encompassing—besides the workers, the urban poor, and the middle classes—a large proportion of the civil servants, members of professional associations (lawyers, engineers, and so on), and sectors of the economic elite.

In this chapter, I will focus on the workers' movement which played a significant role in the upheaval. In the Tunisian case, the workers' movement does not solely refer to the working class, defined as those who do not own the means of production and therefore have to sell their labor. The Tunisian workers' movement rather refers to the syndical movement containing, besides the working class, also civil servants, white collar workers, teachers, and so on.[3] In order to better understand the importance of the workers' movement, I will map the changing role of labor in Tunisia from independence to the downfall of Ben Ali. It is my hypothesis that while the major representative institution of the Tunisian workers' movement, the UGTT, had been coopted by Ben Ali, the struggles of the workers and local union militants was decisive in the January 2011 revolution.

The Tunisian revolution was (and is) a "cumulative process of learning and resistance"[4] that can only be understood as the interpenetration of past and present political and economic struggles. Placing the labor movement in a historical framework will help highlight the importance of the labor origins of the revolution. At the same time this will also show how the convergence of interests of nearly the whole population to topple the dictator was simultaneously concealing class divides and political differentiations that deeply affect the post-Ben Ali political cleavages within the country. I end, therefore, with a brief reflection on the role of the union in present-day Tunisia.

Labor and popular uprisings (2008–11)

The immediate history of the present period of struggles begins in early January 2008 when the Gafsa Phosphate Company (Compagnie des Phosphates de Gafsa, CPG) announced the results of a recruitment competition. The region of Gafsa, a small town in the southwest of Tunisia, has been, since colonial times, dependent on the exploitation of the richness of its soil, the mining industry accounting for most of the economic life of the region. Like many third world countries, Tunisia had to implement a Structural Adjustment Plan throughout the 1980s when it became clear that the financial situation of the country had become untenable.[5] As the CPG was one of the factories that had met with a lot of difficulties, largely due to mismanagement, the ensuing "restructuring" led to a heavy loss of jobs. From over 14,000 workers in the 1980s, the CPG employed only around 5,500 workers in the years 2007–8.[6]

The provision and quality of public services (healthcare, social security, education, and so on), hitherto a showpiece of the Tunisian state, declined as a consequence of unemployment, rising prices, inflation, and privatization. To that, one must add the mounting and blatantly visible forms of corruption. The January 2008 recruitment results of the CPG were seen by the local population as further proof that even the few jobs that remained were not really open to meritocratic competition but were being sold to the highest bidder or given to the individuals most loyal to the ruling party through nepotism or clientelism. The result was a five-month-long popular protest movement that was eventually crushed by police brutality: after aborted attempts in April and May, special police and army units raided the city of Redeyef in June and arrested numerous militants.[7]

The announcement of the competition results by the CPG triggered a revolt throughout the whole region. Today, in the light of its consequences, this event can be seen as a trivial incident but it nevertheless lies at the basis of a movement with a broad popular character.[8] Despite the fact that the uprising had a relatively limited regional aspect, the movement was still a popular uprising in the true sense of the word. In the towns of the region, workers, the unemployed, civil servants, women, merchants, craftsmen, students and so on joined the protests. There are several reasons why this mass strike in 2008 failed to become a nationwide movement. The uprising remained local not only because of the repression of Ben Ali's regime, which made it very difficult for the local activists to organize their struggle in other cities, but also because of the weakness of the (official) opposition parties and the silence of the intellectuals as well as the union's failure to openly support the movement.[9] Two years later, however, the popular revolt started in the same region. Before the self-immolation of Mohammed Bouazizi on December 17, protests were already simmering for months as "undercover" journalist Olivier Piot convincingly described how, from November 2010 onwards, the western and southwestern regions of Tunisia were in a state of unrest.[10]

Nevertheless, Mohammed Bouazizi's act of despair triggered a new phase in the protests. The same day, the family of the victim and militants from the union marched to the prefecture to express their anger. Riots ensued and for several days clashes erupted between the police and a growing number of youths identifying with Bouazizi's plight. The repression did not exhaust the demonstrations and resistance spread throughout the region to neighboring towns and communes. The response of the regime was two-fold. On the one hand, it stepped up the repression by using lethal force, killing two youngsters by gunfire on December 24; on the other, Ben Ali remained silent as he delayed any official statement (until December 28), thus trying to minimize and downplay the insurrection. His visit to Bouazizi in the hospital and the promises to meet the protesters' demands he made during the televised speech could not preempt the further politicization of the movement. The local union cells played, from then on, a decisive and crucial role.[11] Local syndical militants provided the diffuse popular uprising with a more efficient organizational structure, thus securing its sustainability over time.[12] After Mohammed Bouazizi succumbed to his wounds on January 4, 2011, the union's activities spread over the whole of the Centre region.

The response of the national UGTT was anything but homogeneous. Having grown accustomed under Ben Ali to playing an intermediary role between the state's institutions and the workers' demands, the UGTT was caught by surprise. On December 18, the Executive Bureau dispatched a mission to the city of Sidi Bouzid to meet with the governor and to listen to the grievances of the people, thus making obvious what Larbi Chouikha and Vincent Geisser have called "the two UGTTs," i.e. the syndical dissonance as a paradoxical vehicle of the dynamics of protest.[13] The ambivalence of the national leadership stood in stark contrast to the local sections that clearly chose the side of the protesters, thus revealing the complex and multifaceted relations between the national leadership of the UGTT and its local sections and federations. This ambivalence is not new, however, and constitutes one of the recurrent features of the labor movement since Tunisia's independence.

As the protest spread throughout the countryside, lawyers played an important role in attracting attention to the uprising in Tunis and in gradually mobilizing the urban lower and middle classes. Since 2000, the National Organization of Lawyers has functioned as one of the few strongholds of opposition to Ben

Ali.[14] Members of the bar organized a series of demonstrations on December 31, in cities such as Tunis, Sousse, Monastir, Jendouba, and Gafsa. A week later, on January 6, they went on strike. Meanwhile, the start of the new school semester after the New Year holidays amplified the protests as students and pupils also went on strike. The protests grew further in intensity when in cities such as Kasserine, Thala, and Feriana, state symbols of power, such as police stations and buildings of the ruling Constitutional Democratic Rally (Rassemblement Constitutionnel Démocratique, RCD), were attacked and ransacked, prompting ruthless retaliation and repression by the authorities. Police repression in Kasserine and Thala resulted in several casualties, and witnesses reported that snipers were firing randomly on the crowd.[15] On January 10, it became obvious to Ben Ali and his entourage that the situation had escalated from a local uprising to a national revolt. As the police withdrew from many cities, it was replaced by the army, which was welcomed as a liberator.

It was only on the eve of January 10 that the president appeared for a second time on national television. In his speech, Ben Ali promised to create 300,000 jobs but also denounced the "terrorist acts instigated from abroad," comparing the revolting youth with al-Qaeda operatives from abroad. These preposterous words brought the protests into a decisive phase as neither Ben Ali nor the government seemed willing or able to offer any credible solution to the situation. This pushed the protest movement into a direct and total confrontation with Ben Ali's regime.[16]

It is only from then on that the national leadership of the UGTT started to fully support the protest movement. The wait-and-see attitude seemed to become untenable while the pressure of local militants—mostly with a Communist or Arab nationalist background—grew stronger. This late about-turn of the UGTT proved to be decisive. On January 11, the National Administrative Committee of the Union recognized the right of local sections to organize peaceful protests and solidarity actions.[17] The section of Sfax organized a demonstration on January 12 that, according to union estimates, brought more than 30,000 people to the streets. The demonstration was backed not only by the union but also by the local businessmen and capitalists who were fed up with their marginalization in comparison to the entrepreneurial class of Sousse and Monastir (where the ruling families were well established). The demonstrators not only called for Ben Ali's departure but also introduced a slogan that became, from then on and until today, the rallying cry of the Arab revolt: *al-sha'b yurīd 'isqāt al- nizām* ("the people want to topple the regime"). A day later, demonstrations in Kasserine, Monastir, Kairouan, and Sousse repeated the slogan while in the capital more and more people from both the popular neighborhoods and the more middle-class districts all converged towards the Avenue Habib Bourguiba.

In this revolutionary atmosphere, Ben Ali addressed the nation once more, on Thursday January 13, in a historical televised speech—his last, as would become clear a day later. The speech showed a tired and doubting president. Speaking in the colloquial Tunisian dialect, he vowed that he had "understood" the Tunisians (*fhimtkum*) and promised jobs, food, oil, freedom, and free internet access. But these promises came too late: the general strike called by the UGTT a day later, on Friday 14, mobilized a whole country united in its desire for change. By 4 o'clock in the afternoon, Ben Ali and his family had fled to Saudi Arabia.[18]

To sum up the argument so far, the origin of the January 2011 revolution is to be found in the economically and politically marginalized areas of the country. Social protest had been recurrent and vital in the mining region of Gafsa over previous years and it is from there that the protest movement spread. The protests started out as spontaneous happenings and did not come together from a preconceived plan. The economic claims of the excluded and marginalized were gradually politicized because of the attitude of the government and the unwillingness of the union's regional and national leadership to fully back the protesters. As the social movement grew in numbers and power, it became more diverse in composition. In the end the Tunisian revolution was supported by a very broad alliance of different social classes of Tunisian society. The combined force of the workers, the urban poor and marginalized, the civil servants, the middle classes, and a part of the economic elites, as well as the gradual disintegration of a part of the regime, a "rupture in the oligarchy of power" as Pierre-Robert Baduel[19] observed, was strong enough to trigger Ben Ali's downfall but it also became obvious that this alliance would face internal confrontations once the common enemy disappeared.

The role of the UGTT in Tunisian politics

The hesitation of the national leaders of the UGTT to fully support the opposition against Ben Ali early on is partly the consequence of the gradual stifling of the only Tunisian political institution that, for a long time, was a strong competitor to the ruling party and partly the result of the unions' political culture, imbued as it is with a history of more than sixty years of struggle. One cannot understand the political history of Tunisia without taking into account the role of the Tunisian working class and its syndical organizations.

The Tunisian workers' movement was born in the 1920s under the French Protectorate with the growth of an autochthonous working class, different from (but not necessarily opposed to) a foreign (mainly French and Italian) working class and its organizations.[20] Until 1946, when the UGTT was officially established, the Tunisian workers' movement seemed torn between two different logics of action and mobilization. Small in numbers and without enough political leverage, it could not sever its ties with the French and Italian workers if it wanted to make any gains on the social level. On the political level, however, the Tunisian workers understood that the fight for a national identity was something that concerned all Tunisians, irrespective of their class affiliations. While the workers felt the social and political oppression all together, it remained a very precarious undertaking to simultaneously resist on both levels. Social protest and demands, on the one hand, necessitated an autonomous national workers' movement, independent of the political nationalist formations which in their bid to create a united front against colonialism neglected (or even refused) class demands and favored a consensual, homogeneous national identity. The anticolonial fight, on the other hand, required the severing of ties with the European unions and workers' organizations and an alignment—if not an alliance— with the nationalist movement. This fundamental question characterized the dynamics of the Tunisian workers' movement for more than three decades, that is at least until the country gained independence in 1956: either the workers' movement restricted itself to economic issues and classic trade unionism, thus remaining marginal vis-à-vis the nationalist movement, or it became "nationalist" and relinquished the class struggle.[21]

With the creation of the UGTT in 1946 under the leadership of Farhat Hached, the collaboration between unionists and nationalists was legitimized on the grounds of a subtle differentiation between "antagonistic contradictions" (between nationalism and imperialism) and "non-antagonistic contradictions" (between workers and autochthonous patrons).[22] The UGTT allied itself with Habib Bourguiba's Neo-Destour, the nationalist party created in 1934 and all in all sole representative of the nationalist aspirations.[23] The UGTT took on a national dimension and played a decisive role in the national struggle while simultaneously engaging in conflicts over wages in confrontation with employers. Habib Bourguiba's self-imposed exile in Egypt from 1945 to 1949 allowed Farhat Hached to assert himself as a nationalist and workers' leader. Upon his return to Tunis, Bourguiba and Hached were the two figureheads of the nationalist movement.[24] As the links between the UGTT and the Neo-Destour grew stronger, Hached's anti-Communist feelings[25] became more pronounced and the UGTT joined the International Confederation of Free Trade Unions (ICFTU) in 1950.[26] Hached's assassination on December 5, 1952[27] decapitated the workers' movement as the direction of the movement was mainly taken over by members of the Neo-Destour. The participation of the masses in the struggle was still very important but the workers had ceased to fight for their own objectives.

Tunisia gained internal autonomy in 1954 with little bloodshed, and independence followed in 1956. Between 1954 and 1958, political divergences, and social and territorial divisions appeared between supporters of Bourguiba and Ben Youssef. In March 1956, a Constituent Assembly was elected that consisted solely of members of the Neo-Destour, the UGTT, and the Tunisian Union of Industry and Handicrafts (Union Tunisienne de l'Industrie, du Commerce et de l'Artisanat, UTICA)[28] united in a national front. At first the government opted for a liberal economic policy but gradually it recovered and applied the economic program that the UGTT approved at its sixth national conference in September 1956. This program, masterminded by the union's leader, Ahmed Ben Salah, included *inter alia* the creation of cooperatives, the "collectivization" of land, and the introduction of ambitious land reforms and very strong state intervention in nearly all sectors of the economy. The adoption of this socializing development model by Bourguiba proved the strength of the union and its impact on the country. Ben Salah was first appointed as minister of social affairs[29] but became a sort of super-minister a couple of years later, combining the functions of minister of economy, health, finance and, most importantly, the Ministry of Planning, a crucial ministry that organized economic life. As it became an unavoidable partner in the creation of the new state, the union developed a bureaucratic apparatus that constituted (and constitutes) the backbone of its power.

The unfolding relationship between the UGTT and Bourguiba's Neo-Destour was not so much a symbiotic affair—as the entanglement of state, party, and union bureaucracies suggest—but rather a relation of permanent conflict, negotiation, and rivalry as Khiari asserts.[30] The entanglement of the structures and personnel of the union, the party, and the state's administration and their growing mutual interdependence turned the UGTT into a "quasi-partisan workers' movement" or, as Hamzaoui states, a "contradictory totality,"[31] referring to the union's simultaneous political role as partner of the state and oppositional role in countering some of the government's economic and social policies. The threat of creating a "workers' party" was, at least until Ben Ali took over power in 1987, a constant fear for Bourguiba's party.

In the decade of socialist-inspired economic development policies, the autonomy of the UGTT was threatened by Bourguiba's decision to change his Neo-Destour party into the Socialist Destour Party (Parti Socialiste Destourien, PSD) and to create national organizations (of women, farmers, young people, and so on) to control the population. In this context, Habib Achour, the union's secretary-general but also an influential member of the Political Bureau of the party, stepped up his opposition to Bourguiba, leading to years of conflict which resulted in Achour's imprisonment in 1966.[32] In a way, Bourguiba tried to control social groups by using the union's mobilization capacities in a larger project of national development that used socialist rhetoric.

The complex relationship of mutual interdependence between the UGTT and the state's institutions led by Bourguiba and his party became very evident a few years later when Ben Salah's socialist experiment failed and led the country to economic catastrophe. Ben Salah was arrested and within a few days the socialist experiment was completely pushed aside and replaced by a very liberal orientation. Amid the crisis that the country was going through and which threatened his legitimacy, Bourguiba personally asked Habib Achour to lead the union once again. In this turbulent period, the UGTT became completely immersed in the internecine conflicts raging within the party.[33]

Habib Achour's strategy to support Bourguiba's line (against the liberals) was not so much a sign of his or the union's complete allegiance or subservience to Bourguiba's rule. Rather, it showed, as Khiari rightly argues,[34] his conviction that the autonomy of the union was best served through the enlargement of the syndical bureaucracy's positions of power within the Destourien political system, more than through the liberty of syndical actions, mobilizing the workers to solve economic and/or social problems. This logic of action worked only for a few years, as long as the Destourian system was not nearing its limits, i.e. as long as the Destourian policies were keeping up with the aspirations of a growing population demanding social justice, economic development, jobs, and more freedom. Strikes started as early as 1973 but became widespread from 1976 onwards.[35] Many of these strikes were organized without the support of the union's central bodies, putting the leadership in a difficult situation. Achour, defending his "deal" with Bourguiba and the Destour, was also aware that the growing discontent felt by large numbers of workers was warranted in the face of deteriorating social conditions. As such, the union's leadership tried to support the strikers without going outside the accepted boundaries of their maneuvering space.

The union followed this ambivalent strategy until late 1977, when a larger confrontation between the state and the workers' movement became unavoidable. In October 1977, Ksar Hellal textile workers, striking against the appointment of a new manager, were ejected by the police. When the workers were joined by their spouses and children in a spontaneous march through the center of the town, the army brutally suppressed the action and the government started to follow a more hardline course. In November of the same year 13,000 workers from the mining region of Gafsa went on strike to demand the implementation of a law that stipulated that at least 20 percent of the mines' profits should return to the region. Already, then, the geographical disparities between the coastal towns, attracting the bulk of development investment, and a marginalized "interior" were apparent.

These strikes were pushing the union's political strategy to its limits. The "social contract"[36] that was signed in January 1977 between the government, UTICA, and the UGTT that wanted to ensure the union's help in keeping social stability was further put under pressure. By the end of the year, it seemed that a major confrontation between the party and the union was unavoidable. In its meeting in early January 1978, the union stated that the country, under the current policy choices, was "oriented towards the consolidation by all possible means of a capitalist class which is contrary to the national interest, especially because this class links its interests to exploitative foreign capital."[37] A general national strike was decided for January 26 and Habib Achour resigned from his position in the Political Bureau of the party. The strike revealed the extent to which a large part of the Tunisian population were disgruntled. The decline in the popularity of Bourguiba and his party ultimately led to the most important political crisis since Tunisia had become independent. The strike was harshly repressed by army, police, and party militias, leaving hundreds of protesters dead. For the first time since independence, a curfew was put in place that lasted for over a month.

At first, the government decided to decapitate the union: a so-called "puppet leadership" took over, while the legitimate leaders were, with few exceptions, all thrown in jail. This confrontational strategy, however, did not deliver the expected outcome of pacifying the workers' movement or bringing more social stability to the country. On the contrary, a younger and more militant syndical generation emerged, while during that same period, the first signs of a growing Islamist movement became visible (partly because of the opposition to leftist movements by Islamic movements that were supported by the government).[38] After a small armed group took over the control of the city of Gafsa in January 1980, the government reacted furiously, leaving numerous people dead or injured and pronouncing harsh verdicts for those arrested.[39] The social crisis that erupted in 1978 was joined in 1980 by a severe political crisis of the state's legitimacy after Gafsa. In this situation Bourguiba nominated a new prime minister, Mohammed Mzali, who was asked to put together a more appeasing policy, especially towards the union.

Amidst this deep systemic crisis, Habib Achour once more returned to the head of the UGTT after conciliatory steps towards the "puppet leadership" proved to be unsatisfactory for a large number of militant workers. It was Bourguiba himself who had asked Achour again to reclaim the leadership of the union and to reorganize it. Achour reverted to his policy of trying to accommodate simultaneously the interests of the party and those of his militant base. What was remarkably different from the pre-1978 situation was that Achour chose a more autonomous path for the UGTT and declined any fundamental role for union members in the state's institutions.[40] This does not mean, however, that Achour was able to rally the whole workers' movement as social inequalities and political injustice in the country grew. As Tunisia (just like many of its neighbors) was facing mounting financial problems and economic crisis (soaring inflation rates, overvalued currency, stagnating exports, and worsening public finances), some reform measures seemed unavoidable. In January 1984, Prime Minister Mzali announced major cuts to the state's food subsidies, leading to an immediate rise in the prices of basic commodities (bread became 100 percent more expensive overnight). Consequently, major riots erupted all over the country, with all parts of Tunisian society opposing the government.

This happened at a time when different political tensions were becoming increasingly visible: the rise of leftist organizations, the growing popularity of the Islamist movements, and internal strife between different parts of the ruling elite in the race to succeed Bourguiba. As Tunis was burgeoning with rumors about the president's health, Bourguiba reacted by immediately canceling the price increases. As Bourguiba put the blame for the failure on the government, he nevertheless reinstalled Mzali in his function as prime minister.

Amid the worsening political crisis—rumors of a civil war or an imminent coup d'état were common between 1984 and 1987—Mzali launched a head-on attack on the union and its leadership. Against and within the UGTT, he supported a group of disgruntled syndical militants who a year earlier had formed the National Union of Tunisian Workers (Union National des Travailleurs Tunisiens, UNTT)[41] while using any possible means to imprison Habib Achour and his allies. By the end of 1985, the UGTT was effectively paralyzed and its leadership given serious convictions.[42]

With a worsening economic crisis in a very unstable political situation, the Tunisian government decided to knock on the door of the International Monetary Fund (IMF) for help. With the power of the union broken, there was no opposition to what was considered the "only" alternative for the country. In fact, all attention was now focused on, first, the deterioration of Bourguiba's health, leading to an insidious race for succession,[43] and, second, on the Islamist question. Islamists who had become very popular seemed the only viable form of political opposition as the legal opposition parties had no real impact beyond the economic and/or intellectual and cultural elites of the capital. In this context, General Ben Ali became the strong man of the government. Bourguiba, who despised the Islamist movement, trusted this army man who seemed to share his aversion to Islamists. Furthermore, Ben Ali seemed to play no particular role in the political games between the many factions within the party. Faster than anybody had foreseen, Ben Ali climbed all levels of power until he finally took over the presidency of the country on November 7, 1987.[44]

The UGTT under Ben Ali's reign

The weakness of the UGTT in the last years of Bourguiba's presidency has, of course, impacted on its position under Ben Ali's rule. As Ben Ali set out to rally the Tunisian body politic behind him in a bid to legitimize his "constitutional coup," the union had to reorganize itself and renegotiate its position in relation to the political system. Habib Achour's definitive retirement and his replacement by Ismaïl Sahbani marked not only a change of leadership but also the end of a specific relationship between state, party, and union.[45] The short-lived moment of enthusiasm surrounding Ben Ali's takeover of power quickly disappeared from the late 1980s onwards. With the outcome of the second Gulf War, the coup d'état in Algeria, and the subsequent quasi civil war there, together with the mass hysteria about a possible Islamist takeover in Tunis, Ben Ali gradually put in place a new authoritarian political system.[46]

In this context, union leader Sahbani reorganized the union to normalize its relations with Ben Ali's authoritarian regime: he restructured syndical bureaucracy, pushed aside numerous collaborators and allies of the old leader Achour, and integrated a younger and less militant generation of syndical militants in the central structures of the organization. Under this more cooperative leadership strikes and violent protests became rare and the UGTT, as part of its so-called "policy of neutrality," backed nearly all major governmental decisions. The consequence of making the UGTT's central bodies toe the line paradoxically led to a more autonomous union but it paid a heavy price for it: the abandonment of its political role. As Béatrice Hibou writes: "Today, the union's central institution is an essential transmission belt for the political authorities, even if this function is not always executed with the docility and effectiveness that the authorities wish."[47]

The main task of the union was to safeguard, in consultation and collaboration with the employers' organization (UTICA), social peace in a rapidly changing economic environment, characterized by the effects of neoliberal policies. As a consequence, the UGTT became a "managerial"[48] or "administrative"[49] union; it compromised its militant potential such that key demands were conceded in favor of continuing to collaborate with the government in order to maintain its objectives in terms of competitiveness. A 2006 internal UGTT report admitted that the union's legitimacy was now based less on its ability to represent the workers and their interests than on its ability to be accepted as a major social partner for the government without being able to call power relations into question.[50]

The normalization and subjugation of the union was certainly not uniform, as some federations (especially those of education, the banking sector, or the postal services) and some regional unions (such as Sfax) were able to hold on to a certain autonomy in their relationship with central bureaucracy. This is partly why Geisser and Camau describe the UGTT as "le maillon faible des agences de pouvoir" (the weakest link of the agencies of power).[51] By the end of the 1990s, internal opposition to Sahbani's leadership had grown and crystallized around three issues, summarized by former militant Zeghidi: the excessive bureaucratization of the union's work that led numerous militants and adherents to be more preoccupied by their material interests than those of the workers; the uncritical alignment of the union with the government's liberal social and economic policies; and the unconditional support of Ben Ali that meant, among other things, complete silence on the issue of human rights and democracy.[52]

In September 2000, Ismaïl Sahbani was indicted for corruption and embezzlement of money belonging to the UGTT and replaced by Abdessalem

Jrad, the number two in the organization.[53] The scandal was causing a lot of damage to the reputation of the already weakened union but also managed to create some new possibilities for internal opposition.[54] While the team around the new leader set out on a program of "rectification" (*taṣḥīḥ*) which mainly focused on administrative restructuring, technical operations, and personnel reshuffling, other syndical militants seized the opportunity to address more general problems. A "syndical platform for the rehabilitation of the UGTT" was published in October 2001 to put pressure on the national leadership.[55] The promoters of the platform criticized the loss of the UGTT's historical role and maintained that "no real rehabilitation can take place without a total and radical break with the conceptions and practices that have distorted trade unionism since the Congress of Sousse (1989), and have seriously undermined the union's autonomy, its functioning, and social and national positioning."[56] The platform did not go unnoticed and became the central issue of the union's national conference held in Djerba in February 2002. As the conference[57] could not tackle the demands from the militants, from then on the UGTT leadership seemed to be confronted with more and more internal protest movements as well as with local cells operating more autonomously. The anti-war movement was the first area of mobilization where the union reclaimed its critical role, albeit very cautiously and within the confines of what was possible within Ben Ali's system. Just as in Morocco or Egypt, the Iraqi crisis and the plight of the Palestinians—while based on strong feelings of solidarity—were also used by local organizations to test the limits of political possibilities and as such to reveal a wider disgruntlement within the population.

An indication of the internal tensions within the UGTT (and a sign of its growing autonomy) is the way the organization approached the national presidential elections. The union backed Ben Ali's candidacy without any critique in the electoral charades of 1994 and 1999, but the 2004 and 2009 elections at least triggered heated debates within the union's commissions. Eventually, motions of support for Ben Ali in the presidential elections were approved, but not without leaving the local militants the freedom to support candidates of their choice in the legislative elections. In the 2000s, the UGTT also became more critical of certain governmental decisions, such as the invitation sent to Israeli Prime Minister Ariel Sharon to attend the World Summit on the Information Society in Tunis in November 2005, or the ban on the organization of the congress of the Tunisian League for Human Rights. Besides labor-based activism, the last years of Ben Ali's rule also saw a resurgence of citizens' activism primarily driven by students. Not necessarily influenced by any political party or ideology, students have organized strikes and sit-ins to complain about the poor quality of university training and the lack of adequate infrastructure. This has prompted the government to devote major efforts to restricting independent political activity and to suppressing any type of activism on campus (besides the RCD-led student union). As discussed above, these students (or ex-students) have played an important role in the revolutionary process.

While the successive regimes of Bourguiba and Ben Ali have tried to coopt the UGTT, the history of the institution has shown us that local militants have always kept the practice of dissent alive, thus creating opportunities to break away from governmental strictures. An enduring feature of the "normal" functioning of the UGTT has been a sort of original division of labor between a leadership trying to maximize its political influence (something that on occasion brought it under control of the regime) and a more militant base demanding more justice and freedom. The UGTT's independence has always been relative, oscillating between periods of alliance and estrangement with the regime.[58] Within the union, tensions have risen during the last decade as Ben Ali's attempts to coopt the leadership could not prevent internal dissension as well as social protest. The less the leadership was able to leave its mark in the definition of social and economic policies, the more a dissatisfied base began voicing its opposition. As such, while the UGTT had been partly disciplined, it nevertheless was one of the very few places where a minimum of contestation, protest, and opposition remained possible.

Labor, workers, and the UGTT in post-Ben Ali Tunisia

Demands for liberal-democratic freedom as well as economic justice and equality coalesced during the episode at the barricades against Ben Ali as a consequence of the momentous alliance between the lower, middle, and parts of the upper classes. However, in the months after Ben Ali's getaway, "the people" who stood as one against the regime in its categorical refusal of the status quo (*Dégage*), started to show their internal fragmentation and diversity. After Ben Ali had fled Tunisia, and the attention of the world shifted from Tunis to the ongoing battle on Tahrir Square in Cairo, the revolutionary movement did not falter. Quite the contrary. The period between January 14 and March 3, the day Interim President Fouad Mebazaa revoked the 1959 constitution, was marked by continuous tension and conflict between the legality of the government and the revolutionary legitimacy of "the people."

The union was quick to join the different protest movements (including the Qasbah I and II episodes, as well as numerous strikes and sit-ins) against the seated transitional governments while at the same time being subject to criticism from within (with rank and file members passing judgment on the national leadership) and from without. Mainly middle- and upper-class groups wanted a quick return to political normalcy (some sort of transition brokered and managed "from above") and asked the union to be more moderate in its demands. While the union, with its partners (leftist political parties, the marginalized youth from the interior, and even Islamists) wanted to get rid of every relic of the old regime, the middle-class mobilizations feared instability and lack of governance. While the former wanted a clean break with the past, including the neoliberal developmental policies, the latter wanted to keep the free market economy without the corruption, nepotism, and cronyism of Ben Ali's reign. Criticism of the union has not been only vocal and virtual: UGTT offices have been ransacked, demonstrations violently repressed, and strikes broken on numerous occasions. This mainly middle-class mobilization feared continuing pressure from the union leading—according to them—to a mounting instability that would further ruin the economy.

Gradually the union has become one of the major mouthpieces of the continuing mobilization of different social movements throughout the country and as such has become a vital political player in the post-Ben Ali era. While tensions erupted between the transitional government of Béji Caïd Essebsi and the union over economic policies (culminating in different forms of protest being harshly put down), this was only a prelude to a more deep-seated conflict with the government that was formed after the elections for a Constituent Assembly in October 2011. During this time, the UGTT had begun its own internal reform by appointing Houcine Abassi as its new secretary-general.

As the government, led by the Islamist party Ennahda, renewed the same neoliberal economic policies that were a significant trigger of the revolution, the UGTT became more politicized, reconnecting with its past. For the UGTT, safeguarding the revolution means that not only political issues (elections, political institutions, freedoms, and so on) should prevail but just as crucial are demands for economic and social reform in the spirit of dignity, justice, and equality. For the union, political and economic demands are indivisible. The government, however, is critical of the political demands of the union and tries to confine its work to syndical matters. Numerous clashes ensued: in February 2012 the union demonstrated in protest at the discharge of waste in front of many of its offices; during the May 1 demonstrations Ennahda militants organized a counter-demonstration to support the government clashing with union militants; during several protests and strikes in the summer (Sidi Bouzid) and the fall (uprising of Siliana) police retaliated with brutal force, injuring many protesters.[59] This tension culminated in late December 2012 when union members were attacked by members of the League for the Protection of the Revolution—considered by many to be a kind of militia acting on behalf of Ennahda—when trying to commemorate the assassination of Farhat Hached. In the wake of this incident, the UGTT threatened a massive national general strike that was only called off a couple of hours before it was due to start after firm pressure from the government as well as from influential national political figures. The respite in the tensions between the government (mainly Ennahda) and the UGTT was short lived as Chokri Belaïd's murder led to a massive strike on the day of his funeral. It is obvious that the political conflict between Ennahda and the UGTT is one of the important aspects of post-Ben Ali political life. The UGTT remains one of the few mass organizations that is able to mobilize its constituency against what many see as the derailment of revolutionary aspirations.

This condensed overview of the role of the workers' movement in the Tunisian revolution and the account of its historical trajectory has contributed to the questioning of a number of assumptions about the nature of the Tunisian revolution. Based on an analysis of the Tunisian workers' movement's different modes of contestation before the events of December 2010–January 2011, this chapter has presented a portrait of the labor-related origins of the revolution. By situating the movement that culminated in the departure of President Ben Ali within the longer history of Tunisian politics, I have charted the role of the workers' movement in the popular uprising and reframed it in a politicized and historicized account that goes beyond the simple dichotomy of "the people versus the dictator" and delves into class conflict. Furthermore, I have shown that the union has been involved in a complex relationship with the regimes of Bourguiba and Ben Ali, alternating periods of close collaboration and cooptation with periods of opposition and dissent. In the end, it is the practices of dissent within the ranks of the union that account for the abrupt changes in position and policy. From the 1970s until the January revolution for freedom and dignity, the UGTT has always—in spite of myriad pressures, procrastinations, and doubts—rallied the cause of the workers' movement in the end, putting it at odds with the powers that be. Undoubtedly, more could have been done, but nothing less.

Notes

1. See Daniel Bensaïd's analysis of depoliticization: Daniel Bensaïd, "Bêtisier impérial, les intellectuels 'moraux'. Operation 'Bullshit Unlimited,'" April 2002, accessed May 4, 2011, www.europe-solidaire.org/spip.php?article2381.
2. Habib Ayeb, "Social and Political Geography of the Tunisian Revolution: The Alfa Grass Revolution," *Review of African Political Economy* 38.129 (2011): 467–79.
3. It is the union that has had the most impact on post-colonial Tunisian politics, more than any political party or movement that represented the working class (such as the Tunisian Communist Party). Within the union, the so-called "petite-bourgeoisie" (teachers, civil servants, etc.) have always played a preponderant role.
4. Ayeb, "Social and Political Geography," 475.
5. Emma Murphy, *Economic and Political Change in Tunisia: From Bourguiba to Ben Ali* (London: Macmillan, 1999) and Gregory White, *A Comparative Political Economy of Tunisia and Morocco: On the Outside of Europe Looking in* (New York: State University of New York Press, 2001).
6. Ammar Amroussia, "Tunesië: een eerste balans van de opstand in het mijnbekken van Gafsa in 2008," *Marxistische Studies* 93 (2011): 61–75.
7. Amin Allal, "Réformes néolibérales, clientélismes et protestations en situation

autoritaire. Les mouvements contestataires dans le bassin minier de Gafsa en Tunisie (2008)," *Politique africaine* 117 (2010): 107–25.

8. For an in-depth analysis based on first-hand information, see Amin Allal, "Réformes néoliberales."
9. Amroussia, "Tunesië: een eerste balans," 61–75.
10. Olivier Piot, *La révolution tunisienne. Dix jours qui ébranlèrent le monde arabe* (Paris: Les Petits Matins, 2011).
11. International Crisis Group. "Soulèvements populaires en Afrique du nord et au Moyen-Orient (IV): la voie tunisienne." Rapport Moyen-Orient/Afrique du Nord 106, April 28, 2011, accessed July 3, 2011, www.crisisgroup.org/en/regions/middle-east-north-africa/north-africa/tunisia/106-popular-protests-in-north-africa-and-the-middle-east-iv-tunisias-way.aspx.
12. The teachers' union (dominated by leftists and Arab nationalists) played a crucial role in politicizing the movement and confronting the regime.
13. Larbi Chouikha and Vincent Geisser, "Retour sur la révolte du bassin minier. Les cinq leçons politiques d'un conflit social inédit," *L'Année du Maghreb* (2010): 415–26.
14. Eric Gobe and Michael B. Ayari, "Les avocats dans la Tunisie de Ben Ali: une profession politisée," *L'Année du Maghreb Édition* (2007): 105–32.
15. According to the authorities, twenty-one people were killed between January 8 and 10. Trade unionists and hospital personnel put the number at "nearly fifty."
16. It can be argued that this speech symbolized the end of Ben Ali's political formula. Even in Belgium, where I live (and more so in Tunisia), for many people, especially older people, the speech seemed so outlandish that the wall of fear—meticulously created and sustained by the regime—fell, as no one could remain silent anymore.
17. The official declaration can be found on the UGTT website and is dated January 11 (see www.ugtt.org.tn/userfiles/file/D%C3%A9claration%20CAN%2011-01-2011.pdf). However, Sofiene Belhadj, a young Tunisian blogger and one of the cyberactivists responsible for the translation and dissemination of the Wikileaks on Tunisia told the author that the UGTT leadership was pushed to rally the popular revolt as militants had issued numerous "false" declarations and made Facebook pages showing the UGTT's support for the protests (interview, Brussels, September 14, 2011).
18. For a comparative reading of the Arab revolts see Sami Zemni, Brecht De Smet, and Koenraad Bogaert, "Luxemburg on Tahrir Square. Reading the Arab Revolutions with Rosa Luxemburg's *The Mass Strike*," *Antipode* (2012), accessed May 1, 2013, http://onlinelibrary.wiley.com/doi/10.1111/j.1467-8330.2012.01014.x/abstract.doi: 10.1111/j.1467-8330.2012.01014.x.
19. Pierre-Robert Baduel, "Tunisie: le rôle complexe et déterminant de l'armée," *Le Monde*, February 10, 2010, accessed May 4, 2011, www.lemonde.fr/idees/article/2011/02/10/tunisie-le-role-determinant-de-l-armee_1477640_3232.html.
20. For an account of the historical roots of the Tunisian workers' movement see Tahar Haddad, *Les Travailleurs tunisiens et l'émergence du mouvement syndical* (Tunis: Maison Arabe du Livre, 1985 [1927]).
21. Juliette Bessis, "Le mouvement ouvrier tunisien: de ses origines à l'indépendance," *Le Mouvement Social* 89 (1974): 85–108.
22. Elbaki Hermassi. *État et société au Maghreb. Étude comparative* (Paris: Anthropos, 1975), 126–7.
23. We should mention that in 1946 another Tunisian union, the Union Syndicale

des Travailleurs Tunisiens (USTT), was even more influential. Being a part of the Communist movement, the USTT was gradually bypassed by the more nationalist UGTT. In 1956, the USTT merged with the UGTT.

24. This does not mean, of course that within the Neo-Destour there were no differences or internal conflicts. Early on, it became clear that Bourguiba and Salah Ben Youssef were on a collision course. With the two protagonists of the party holding opposite views, it was only a question of time before the conflict erupted. In the end, Bourguiba's secret services killed Ben Youssef in the streets of Frankfurt (Germany) in 1961.
25. A major difference between Hached and Bourguiba is that the latter rejected any idea of class struggle, negating any difference of interest among all Tunisians, while the former remained very sensible to the plight of the workers and social problems.
26. The International Confederation of Free Trade Unions (ICFTU) was created on December 7, 1949, following a split within the World Federation of Trade Unions (WFTU), dominated by the Communist movement.
27. This assassination has been confirmed but no one has so far been held responsible for the murder.
28. Habib Bourguiba became prime minister, chairman of the new constitutional monarchy, and combined the functions of minister of foreign affairs and minister of defense. The Constituent Assembly abolished the monarchy a year later and replaced it with a republican presidential form of government with Habib Bourguiba as its first president.
29. The subterranean struggles between Bourguiba and the union's leadership became a constant feature of Tunisian politics. Bourguiba feared the rising power of Ben Salah, so he backed two other popular union leaders, Ahmed Tlili and Habib Achour, to take over the reins of the organization (using ruse, subterfuge, and administrative tactics). Being removed from the UGTT, Bourguiba could not but offer Ben Salah a post in the government.
30. Sadri Khiari, "Reclassements et recompositions au sein de la bureaucratie syndicale depuis l'indépendance. La place de l'UGTT dans le système politique tunisien," Centres d'Études et de Recherches Internationales, Le Kiosque, 2000, accessed May 3, 2011, www.ceri-sciencespo.com/archive/dec00/khiari.pdf (note that the page in question is no longer on the website).
31. Salah Hamzaoui, "Champ politique et syndicalisme en Tunisie," *Annuaire de l'Afrique du Nord* 38 (1999): 369–80.
32. A fire on a boat owned by the UGTT is used as a pretext to imprison the union leader.
33. Two cleavages, partly overlapping, divided the party. The first opposed the union against the business-led wing of the party (the UTICA becoming more assertive in the wake of Ben Salah's departure); the second opposed within the party itself a more "liberal" wing (led by Ahmed Mestiri) and a more Bourguibist wing, favoring a big role for the state in the economic order.
34. Sadri Khiari, "Reclassements."
35. For an overview of the many strikes and conflicts in the 1970s see Al-Amin Al-Yousfi, *Al-Haraka Annaqabiyya bi Tounis* (Tunis: Dar Mohammed Ali lil-nashr, 2011).
36. The social contract foresaw a raise of 33 percent in the minimum wage and a stabilization of the prices of certain basic commodities. In return, the UGTT pledged to start a campaign to increase workers' production.

37. UGTT cited in Nigel Disney. "The Working Class Revolt in Tunisia," *MERIP Reports* 67 (1978): 12–14.
38. The growth in strength of the union but also the growing success of leftist ideologies (Trotskyism, Maoism, Leninism) during the 1970s prompted the government to back and promote what seemed to be conservative non-political associations spreading the call to Islam and advocating the reading of the Qur'an.
39. While all insurgents were Tunisians, it has never been fully clear what exactly their demands were, nor how they were funded or recruited. In fact, it seems that Algerian and Libyan secret services played a crucial role in the events, leaving the hypothesis that Gafsa was mainly intended to destabilize Bourguiba. For a more detailed account of the events see Mohsen Toumi, *La Tunisie de Bourguiba à Ben Ali* (Paris: PUF, 1989).
40. Issa Ben Dhiaf, "Chronique tunisienne 1982," *Annuaire de l'Afrique du Nord* 21 (1984), 655–97.
41. They had left the UGTT in 1981 when Habib Achour took over the leadership of the union and "purged" it of "collaborators."
42. For a detailed account of the political crisis between 1984 and 1987 and the policies of Mzali and his successor, Rachid Sfar, see Toumi, *La Tunisie de Bourguiba à Ben Ali.*
43. Of course, the issue of succession had already been present since the late 1980s but it nevertheless moved to center stage of the political agenda when it became obvious that the president was not physically able to lead the country effectively.
44. After serving as military attaché in several embassies (including Morocco and Poland), he was called back to Tunis after the January 1984 riots. He was appointed head of National Security in 1984, became minister of the interior in 1986, and a member of the Bureau of the Party. In October 1987, he was promoted to prime minister, using his office to take power in November 1987 by removing President Bourguiba.
45. Sahbani was a young syndical militant in the metallurgy sector. He was imprisoned after the 1978 strike and severely tortured. A long-time ally of Achour, he chose a conciliatory stance towards Ben Ali. He was officially elected secretary-general at the UGTT Sousse conference in 1989.
46. Many (especially Anglo-Saxon) observers focused on "naming" the type of regime (authoritarian state, neo-authoritarian state, police state, semi-liberal state, and so on) which, in the end, did not provide any information on how the system functioned on a daily basis. Beatrice Hibou's analysis (2006) remains one of the strongest and most interesting on the concrete functioning of Ben Ali's Tunisia.
47. Béatrice Hibou, *La force de l'obéissance: économie politique de la répression en Tunisie* (Paris: La Découverte, 2006), 147.
48. Riadh Zghal, "Nouvelles orientations du syndicalisme tunisien," *Monde Arabe, Maghreb-Machrek*, 162 (1998): 6–17.
49. Zeghidi, Salah. "L'UGTT, pôle central de la contestation sociale et politique," in *Tunisie: mouvements sociaux et modernité*, ed. Mohammed Ben Romdhane (Dakar: CODESRIA, 1997), 13–61.
50. Union Générale Tunisienne du Travail, "Vers un renouveau syndical: diagnostic quantitatif de l'U.G.T.T. par ses cadres," November 2006, accessed March 21, 2012, http://library.fes.de/pdf-files/bueros/tunesien/04797.pdf.
51. Michel Camau and Vincent Geisser, *Le syndrome autoritaire. Politique en Tunisie de Bourguiba à Ben Ali* (Paris: Presses de Sciences Politiques, 2003), 222.
52. Zeghidi, Salah. "UGTT: à quand le véritable renouveau?," *Alternative Citoyennes* 1

(2001), accessed May 12, 2012, www.alternatives-citoyennes.sgdg.org/num1/actu-syndicalisme-w.html.

53. While it is certainly true that corruption had become part of the UGTT's functioning, there still remain a lot of questions regarding the fall of Sahbani. One of the most striking features of the scandal was that the whole affair was handled by the union itself, without any interference from Ben Ali, the RCD, or the government. Obviously, it is only when he fell out of favor with president Ben Ali—presumably because he was cautiously talking about nominating union members as candidates for the parliamentary elections of 1999—that the union's internal procedures against him were set in motion.
54. There are no official numbers but out of the presumed 500,000 members in the 1970s, there remained around 250,000 in the mid-1980s while, according to numbers whispered in Tunisia, by the mid-1990s only a maximum of 100,000 people belonged to the UGTT.
55. Among the initiators of the platform are Mohamed Chakroun, former secretary-general of the Regional Union of Tunis; Salah Zeghidi, former secretary-general of the Federation of Banks and Insurances; Ali Ben Romdhane, former member of the Executive Bureau; Habib Guiza, former secretary-general of the Regional Union of Gabes; and many others. Tens of syndical militants rally behind the platform, a lot of them anonymously.
56. See www.alternatives-citoyennes.sgdg.org/num5/synd-pf-w.html.
57. The conference reinstalled Jrad as secretary-general. The platform movement seemed divided over the course to follow, as one group made a compromise with Jrad while another remained oppositional. See www.alternatives-citoyennes.sgdg.org/num7/dos-djerba-w.html.
58. This was also stressed by Abdellatif Hamrouni, secretary-general of the federation of public works employees. See Chris Toensing, "Tunisian Leaders Reflect Upon Revolt," *MERIP Report* 258 (2011): 31.
59. For an account of social protests in the post-Ben Ali era see Hèla Yousfi, "Les luttes sociales en Tunisie: malédiction ou opportunité révolutionnaire?," accessed March 7, 2013, http://nawaat.org/portail/2013/02/19/les-luttes-sociales-en-tunisie-malediction-ou-opportunite-revolutionnaire.

CHAPTER 6

The Powers of Social Media

Tarek Kahlaoui

The Tunisian revolution constitutes an unprecedented, non-violent mass movement calling for democratization. Like prior mass movements, it initially focused on social issues but, unlike them, it quickly changed from a timid political movement into a radically non-violent movement to overthrow first the head of the regime and second its intractable system. While the revolution reached its first goal fairly quickly, and is still struggling with the second, it is noteworthy that it was accompanied by two failures. First, there is the failure of the international monetary institutions to assess the worsening situation in Tunisia before December 17, 2010; Ben Ali's Tunisia was the International Monetary Fund's (IMF) and the World Bank's (WB) "model" in the Middle East of a country supposedly delivering economic growth to its people.[1] Second, there is the failure of the Western political establishment (notably in France as well as, although perhaps less so, in the United States) to grasp at an early stage the significance of the revolt. These two failures, however, were left mostly unaccounted for as Western media braced themselves to claim a Euro-American hand in supplying the tools of the revolt, namely the technological gadgets and all the techniques of social media.

No wonder, then, that the role of the internet and social media, in particular, in the Tunisian revolution has been exaggerated by Western media, especially in France and the United States. Mainstream US media, for instance, focused on the Tunisian situation only after the fall from power of Ben Ali. The coverage changed quickly from very limited to wide yet poorly informed. Many of the first major reports in widely read websites and on TV popularized early on the concept of a "Facebook Revolution" or a "Twitter Revolution".[2] The internet did not create the revolution, however; it mainly overthrew the regime's media. The major players demanding basic political and social changes were not limited to internet activists, but included a larger cross-section of the middle and working class, large numbers of unemployed and highly educated youth. In addition, student groups and union activists, especially from the Tunisian general labor union (Union Générale Tunisienne du Travail, UGTT) and the lawyers' Bar, were the major "political" transmitters and protectors of the revolt.

Two of the most pressing issues regarding the role of the media in the Tunisian revolution are, first, how influential the role of social media was and, second, the kind of relationship the "old media" (satellite TV) had with the "new media" (the internet). I discuss these two issues below but I will start by making a few remarks on the revolution as I see it, from the perspective of someone who was actually involved in the cybernetwork collective and can testify to what transpired from a personal, insider perspective.

The revolt

By mid-January 2011, the Tunisian wave of protests had reached its fourth week, during which it was growing slowly but surely and spreading across the country. With its political radicalization and overwhelming geographical presence the protests were by then taking the form of a genuine national revolt. Initially, the protests were the result of a deep social malaise affecting not only unemployed young men, with or without university diplomas, but also impoverished students, young employees, and families around the country, especially in the poorest provinces away from the major coastal cities. Yet, only a week after the protests had begun on December 17 in the province of Sidi Bouzid, the protesters started to express a very clear political message explicitly targeting former president Ben Ali and his family, with an emphasis on the growing popular perception of a corrupt ruling family. By that time a huge red line had been crossed by the protesters; slogans were more or less unified throughout the country and showed an insistence on the political message to the point that it sometimes seemed to surpass any kind of strictly social demands. In other words, from the very beginning the protests had been targeting consistently and without any ambiguity the very existence of the regime.

Sidi Bouzid, the poorest province in Tunisia, was the center of the protests for at least a week and saw widening clashes with the police throughout its small urban and rural centers, culminating in the first deaths under firepower in Menzel Bouzaiane. By the second week, the last week of December 2010, it was the turn of the neighboring and equally poor province of Kasserine to see popular street demonstrations as the protests in Sidi Bouzid seemed to wind down. Meanwhile the lawyers' and the workers' unions highlighted the protests with their visible demonstrations (within the purviews of legality) in the main urban centers, including the capital, Tunis. After the end of the winter break, the return of students back to their high schools and universities opened up more pockets of protest within the main cities. When, by the end of the third week of the revolt, the continuing protests in Kasserine turned unprecedentedly deadly with more than twenty deaths from live bullets (according to very well documented human rights sources), the leadership of the large trade union decided to give the green light to its regional branches to announce general strikes. The night of January 11 was marked by the first public demonstrations and confrontations in the large popular quarters of Tunis, for the first time since the beginning of the protests in the southern parts of the country. On the night of January 12, hardly any place in the whole country escaped violent clashes (including the escalating use of live bullets by the riot police and professional snipers). Ben Ali's third speech on January 13, which was seen as his last attempt to recast and rescue his collapsing regime, was quickly undermined by the continuous use of live ammunition the same night. Finally, on January 14, the people in the streets responded to the speech with more protests, bursting out this time into the capital's main street, Avenue Habib Bourguiba. Later in the afternoon, Ben Ali fled in ambiguous circumstances with many questions still remaining unanswered many months afterwards.

Between December 17 and January 14, the revolt was remarkable in terms of its very explicit political nature and its wide geographic spread, especially in the main urban centers. It was non-violent, other than the occasional use of firearms by security forces to repress the demonstrators, and, more importantly, it was without any clear ideological leadership. The revolt was in essence independent of any political movements in spite of all the attempts by the Ben Ali regime to link it via its media outlets to "extremist elements." The revolt, however, was the first phase of a revolutionary process that continued through various means, including the first free elections in Tunisian history on October 23, 2011, bringing into power some of the major political opponents of the old regime.

The roots of Tunisian cyberactivism

When Mohamed Bouazizi set himself on fire on December 17, 2010, no one thought that his act, which was immediately belittled by the national media, would start a revolt. Yet, a few internet activists who had been particularly attentive to social problems had already seized on the incident to press forth their human rights agenda. Many of these bloggers were part of the Tunisian anti-censorship movement, which dated back to the end of the 1990s, when the regime decided to start a well-organized campaign of censorship.[3] One story of the Tunisian history of internet censorship, yet to be fully revealed, is the involvement of Western governmental consultants and companies in creating the structure of the censorship apparatus. One of the key elements of this story is probably found in a masters thesis completed in 1999 by a marine captain in the Postgraduate Naval School that remains for the most part classified, as it "comprises part of a Defense Requirements Study conducted for the Republic of Tunisia." In the abstract, we read what seems to be an invitation to censor ("control") the growing use of the internet to prevent imminent political unrest by "subversive" groups:

> The political climate is sensitive to increases in unemployment, downturns in the economy, or crisis in Iraq or Israel. If the regime loses control of the information flow over the internet, the political opposition will gain an increased ability to

> organize its supporters, and subversive groups will gain an increased ability to operate underground.[4]

The ideas of the internet activists were first vocalized around websites hosted and administered largely outside the country, such as Takriz, Tunezine, and Nawaat, which were both censored and hacked.[5] After 2007, blogging led to a gradual transformation of cyberactivism, in which the balance was shifted from expatriate websites to mainstream blogs largely administered by bloggers based in Tunisia. Though many bloggers were not politically active, one community within the blogosphere was dedicated to combating censorship via digital group actions on certain days of the year (such as July 24 and November 4). As one of these bloggers, I actively took part in these protests.[6]

In the spring of 2010, the bloggers undertook the first serious attempt to create an organized group pushing to turn this movement from one of active digital resistance based mainly in expatriate networks to a grassroots movement inside Tunisia. The heavy escalation of censorship from early 2010, targeting a wide range of blogs that were not necessarily very politically active as well as certain video-sharing websites, sparked an increasingly wider desire not only to strengthen cyberresistance but also to move the battle to the streets from May 2010 onwards. With the Egyptian model in mind (notably the "April 6th Movement"), a nucleus of organized cyberactivists was slowly taking shape. The experimental organization happened spontaneously after the November 2009 presidential elections when the police arrested the blogger Fatma Riahi (who writes under the pseudonym Fatma Arabica) for questioning about a cartoon-oriented blog administered by the anonymous blogger "z" (debatunisie.com). In order to pressure the government to free Fatma, a group of cyberactivists based in Tunisia and other parts of the world came together in a concerted effort to reach the "old media" and propagate the news of the arrest through Skype.[7] A Facebook page was created and quickly became an outlet for support that also came from mainstream internet users, not necessarily those who were traditionally politicized. Fatma was freed after a week and the incident created a feeling of empowerment among internet activists.

It was from this nucleus that a more organized and dedicated group of people decided to continue their protests when the regime escalated its censorship campaign the following spring. My blog ("Nocturnal Thoughts"/"Afkār Layliyya") was censored in February 2010, marking the beginning of a wave targeting the Tunisian blogosphere on an unprecedented scale, and creating the feeling that everyone might be censored.[8] During the same period, Facebook became the refuge for outspoken bloggers. It was on Facebook in April 2010 that I posted two texts proposing the establishment of a platform to widen the anti-censorship movement and move it towards the real world.[9] These texts were shared and commented on by cyberactivists, which in May led to the formation of the group that attempted the first street demonstration not only specifically targeting censorship but also relying heavily on social media to achieve its goals. This group would be recognized through two Facebook pages "Sayyib Saleḥ" (aka "Sayeb Sale7")[10] and "Nhar ʿAla ʿAmmar" (aka "Nhar 3la 3ammar").[11] "Sayeb Sale7" literally means "leave Saleḥ alone," the name "Saleḥ" being used to refer to any Tunisian. By asking all Tunisian internet users to post photographs featuring them protesting against censorship, this page created a lot of buzz in late April (more than 20,000 members in a few days and thousands of pictures). "Nhar 3la 3ammar" literally means "a bad day for ʿAmmar". The name "ʿAmmar" stands for the censor-in-chief and ultimately for Ben Ali himself. The page was the main Facebook platform to organize the first solely anti-censorship demonstration using social media for that purpose (acquiring more than 20,000 members in few days).

The latter group was more organized and began planning events spanning May to August 2010. The first major event, which took place on May 22, was a demonstration in Tunis in front of the Ministry of Technologies and Communication coordinated in concert with demonstrations among the Tunisian diaspora in major global cities such as Paris, Montreal, Bonn and New York. The demonstration in Tunis was obstructed after the arrest of two of its representatives but it was the first major attempt to use the internet as a means of political protest centered on the issue of censorship.[12] The group remained motivated and continued its actions throughout the summer, writing open letters to members of parliament, and then attempted another small flashmob demonstration on August 4, 2010.[13] Even though the group faded away from the public radar, some of its members were among the main cyberactivists leading the information war against the regime during the revolt.

Distorted narratives of the new media

Tariq Ramadan stated recently in his book *L'Islam et le réveil arabe* (*Islam and the Arab Awakening*) that US NGOs, companies, and the State Department trained the cyberactivists who supposedly engineered the civil disobedience movements in Tunisia and Egypt.[14] He made special mention of "evidence" of links with the Serbian youth movement Otpor (Resistance) under the guidance of US NGOs associated with the State Department. While he distanced himself from embracing any conspiracy theories, his videos summarizing this narrative are shared widely on the internet with comments referring specifically to conspiracy theories such as that the whole "Arab Spring" was plotted by the US government. Ironically, though, Ramadan's story, which seems highly anti-imperialist, was actually originally created and shaped in the US, as I demonstrate below.

Only four days after the fall of Ben Ali, the US-based *Foreign Policy Journal* (a website very firmly invested in all sorts of conspiracy theories) published an article penned by one of its main contributors, "Dr. K R Bolton." Dr. Bolton, usually described as a sympathizer with "neo-Nazi" movements from New Zealand, was the first to write an article suggesting that what happened in Tunisia was not spontaneous but was fabricated by a group of internet activists trained by US NGOs linked to the State Department who suggested that they follow the model of Otpor! This is basically the same story told later by Ramadan.[15] Needless to say, Bolton's piece was widely shared, even beyond conspiracy circles, with the basic story being picked up by mainstream US media. For instance, David Kirkpatrick and David Sanger of *The New York Times* wrote a report reproducing the same thesis: that what made the Tunisian and Egyptian revolutions possible was the connection between certain cyberactivists and Otpor!, as well as the influence of Gene Sharp's *Waging Non-Violent Struggle: 20th Century Practice and 21st Century Potential* (2005). They mention that the group of activists behind what happened in Tunisia was called "Progressive Youth of Tunisia."[16]

Some of the information included in these narratives may be true. In the Tunisian case, for instance, a few internet activists, including Lina Ben Mhenni, had indeed attended workshops organized by foundations linked to the State Department. Yet these affiliations were fiercely debated among Tunisian bloggers, causing conflict, disunity, and malaise, to say the least.[17] My own sources tell me that perhaps a handful of people attended a workshop organized by Otpor! but most Tunisian internet activists had never heard of the Serbian organization, or at least knew little about them, let alone were trained by them. I have never met anyone, however, who is aware of the so-called "Progressive Youth of Tunisia" as an organization involved in cyberactivism. These details aside, the cyberactivists who attended US-sponsored workshops were neither the initiators nor the organizers of the Tunisian revolt. At best, they were involved in sharing and at times filtering the information coming from the ground. As discussed in a recent radio show, several important internet activists on the ground, who remain mostly anonymous, were indeed the real sources for bloggers and journalists in urban and cosmopolitan locales. Among them, I should mention union activists from Sidi Bouzid and Kasserine, including Lamine Bouazizi, Slimane Rouissi and Belgacem Sayehi.[18] Finally, I should also point out here that the spontaneous strategy of Tunisian protesters hardly tried to lure the security forces away from the regime. This happened only with the army, and only after the army already showed signs of passive involvement in the repressive efforts of the regime. Mostly, there was a constant tendency toward confrontation led by the largely young protesters after several years of experiencing police repression. Clearly, then, my own participation in the revolts from the very beginning helps to further debunk these and other related myths. In fact, the story of this link between bloggers, local sources, and the old media merits considerable elaboration and clarification.

The "new media" and the revolt

Around December 17, 2010, a few people on Facebook started to share videos coming from Sidi Bouzid made by activists (mainly union and student activists such as old friends Slimane Rouissi and Lamine Bouazizi) about the growing protests across the province. A closed Facebook group created by activists from Sidi Bouzid and including several internet activists was used to share and spread information.[19] The two major Tunisian Facebook pages ("Ma Tunisie" and "Tunisia_تونس_Tunisie", which then had 500,000 and 300,000 members respectively) were closely connected to the Sidi Bouzid Committee and became a platform for sharing and conveying information to a wider public.[20] Facebook was a very effective platform for two reasons: first, it reached a relatively large audience of around 2 million Tunisian users (out of a population of 11 million), not including "secondhand" users who would learn about what transpired on Facebook through their children, neighbors, and friends. Second, national censors could not access Facebook's closed network. This has allowed anyone to receive information from censored pages and profiles through the "News Feed" tab and using the secure "https" links.

In fact, one of the major contributions of cyberactivism was the role played by Facebook pages with large numbers of members in propagating information leaked from the Wikileaks documents about the regime's "Mafia" family. What is really important about these revelations was not necessarily the raw information included in them, although the details about the lifestyle of Ben Ali's family members were shocking, but the fact that they had an official aspect. It was only a few weeks before December 17 and it was not especially difficult for the demonstrators in Sidi Bouzid to see the obvious link between the kleptocratic system in their province and that at the top of the state. The publication and translation into French and Arabic by Nawaat.com of the cables of the US embassy in Tunis from the Wikileaks documents was crucial but it was also highly influential, all the more so as a result of the involvement of widely read Facebook pages.[21]

Meanwhile, my friends on Facebook who are Al-Jazeera journalists broadcast some of the information and videos on Al-Jazeera primetime programs after checking the information with local sources. Though at first spontaneous, this soon turned into a more organized effort. My close relationship with an Al-Jazeera producer, Noureddine al-Idoudi, was one such strong and trusted partnership in this effort. Since the second week of the revolution, most Tunisians had been avidly following Al-Jazeera's primetime news programs (*Haṣād al-Yawm* and *Al-Ḥaṣād al-Maghāribī*, both of which focused almost entirely on Tunisia). This crucial link between Facebook and TV satellite channels, notably Al-Jazeera, proved to be devastating to the Tunisian official propaganda machine, leading to the downfall of the regime's media weeks before that of Ben Ali himself.

By early December 2010, the number of Tunisians on Twitter was not as high as those on Facebook, but it allowed wide Arab and international exposure. As early as December 17, I (@t_kahlaoui) called for a hashtag to relay the unfolding events and Taieb Moalla (@moalla), a journalist in Quebec, suggested #SidiBouzid. Tunisian and Arab activists and friends (including @TunObs, @ifikra, @yassayari, @Malek, @Asudrabal, @benmhennilina, @sofinos, @slim404, @weedady, and @Dima_Khatib to name a few) and groups (including @nawaat and @takriz) led the efforts to relay all available information, especially that coming from Facebook, into Twitter. By late December, #SidiBouzid appeared on Twitter's list of trending topics within Tunisia. These were the first acts that established the basic structures of using the social networks as an effective media branch of the unfolding Tunisian revolution.

In the first weeks of the revolution, inaccurate information was used by the official propaganda machine to discredit the credibility of social networks as a new media source. This happened mainly via TV stations, especially the national official TV station, TV 7. The media scene in Tunisia was always dominated by official media, enabled and watched over by the power of the dictatorship. Because of the wide reception of satellite TV stations in the 1990s, especially Al-Jazeera and the new, much freer information they carried with them, the regime seemed fragile and had to make some changes. It is in this context that a series of "private" and supposedly "independent" TV stations (Nessma TV and Hannibal TV) and radio stations (Mosaïque FM, Express FM, and Shems FM) were founded starting from 2003. Yet they were headed mostly by entrepreneurs very close to or even part of the ruling family.[22]

The propaganda of TV stations was mainly through news programs (on TV 7) that presented distorted versions of whatever was happening on the ground. In the days leading up to January 14, 2011, talk shows (on TV 7, Nessma TV, and Hannibal TV) followed the basic line of propaganda, and reiterated ad infinitum that the regime was well meaning and that foreign TV networks (namely Al-Jazeera) were plotting against the stability of Tunisia, all the while avoiding any mention of police brutality and the regime's criminality.

By the end of the third week of the Tunisian revolution, when Ben Ali's security forces committed a massacre in the province of Kasserine, I coordinated with eight friends (including trained journalists Ghassen Ben Khlifa and Ismail Dbara, among others[23]) to establish a Facebook page that would try to act as a semi-professional news platform. We called it "The News Agency of the Protests of the Tunisian Street" ("*Wikālat Anbāʾ Taḥarrukāt Al-Shariʿ al-Tūnsī*"). Using professional methods like a news room and contacts on the ground to check and re-check the flow of information, we worked around the clock to establish credibility. When the platform was eventually blocked by Facebook administrators (presumably the result of massive reporting by the old regime's supporters), we created a second page, which gathered more than 20,000 members in two days.[24]

The postrevolution media

Since January 14, 2011, Facebook and Twitter have increasingly shaped public opinion and facilitated the coordination of the continuing popular street demonstrations. Their pressure has resulted in street protests against the acting government and what was left of the old ruling party, which forced the old regime's leading figures to make continuous concessions. Even with the major changes in the official media scene, social networks are still leading the media along with the foreign TV satellite channels.

The changes in mainstream media are for the moment affecting newspapers with the emergence of new major newspapers on the scene, such as *Al-Maghrib*, founded by Omar Shabou, a veteran journalist since the 1980s, which is competing with leading papers from the time of the Ben Ali era such as *Al-Chourouk* and *Al-Sabah*. The audiovisual scene remains unchanged. None of the TV and radio projects that were given official authorization by the transitional government, following the suggestions of the Higher Authority for Information and Communication Reform (Instance Nationale pour la Réforme de l'Information et de la Communication, INRIC), are operative. Financial difficulties might be the reason in many of these cases. Exceptions include the case of Ettounsiya, a TV station based in Tunisia and broadcasting from abroad, led by Sami Fehri, a media figure of the old regime and the director of a media production company "Cactus prod," owned by Belhassan Trabelsi, a prominent member of the Ben Ali family.

The new media is evolving slowly into a more organized and institutional format. For instance, the former cyberdissident website Nawaat took the form of an association with funding streamed from abroad and journalists and activists hired to provide regular news to its website (nawaat.org). Our team that created the Facebook page "The News Agency of the Protests of the Tunisian Street" also became the association of *Al-Machhad al-Tunisi* (The Tunisian Scene) with a website (machhad.com) and volunteers led by trained journalists providing news in Arabic. Journalists from mainstream media also founded electronic news websites, notably the commentator of Mosaïque FM, Noureddine Ben Ticha, a figure close to the old regime, who founded Aljarida.com. Yet, it is fair to say that Facebook remains as influential as before, especially as an alternative to the TV stations, which continue to be perceived largely as part of the old regime.

Notes

1. The IMF published a report a few months before the start of the revolt, which failed to grasp the gravity of the economic situation. See International Monetary Fund, "Tunisia: 2010 Article IV Consultation – Staff Report; Public Information Notice

on the Executive Board Discussion; and Statement by the Executive Director for Tunisia." IMF Country Report No. 10/282, accessed March 7, 2012, www.imf.org/external/pubs/ft/scr/2010/cr10282.pdf. Former IMF president Dominique Strauss-Kahn was a strong defendant of the regime, describing it frequently as a "model" for the region, as was the case during a visit to Tunisia on November 18, 2008. See http://youtu.be/xEA9X6j7b_U.

2. As is the case in an article on the Daily Beast website, "Tunisia Protests: The Facebook Revolution," January 15, 2011, accessed March 4, 2011, www.thedailybeast.com/articles/2011/01/15/tunisa-protests-the-facebook-revolution.html. The "Twitter Revolution" was mentioned notably in an ABC news report dated January 16, 2011, accessed March 4, 2011, http://abcnews.go.com/WNT/video/twitter-revolution-tunisia-strongman-ruling-leader-12629386.
3. On the censorship of Ben Ali's regime as it evolved over the years, see, for example, Sami Ben Gharbia, "Silencing Online Speech in Tunisia," August 20, 2008, accessed March 4, 2011, http://advocacy.globalvoicesonline.org/2008/08/20/silencing-online-speech-in-tunisia.
4. Bruce Wilkinson, "Tunisia: Security Environment to 2010" (Masters thesis, Naval Postgraduate School, 1999).
5. Tunezine is particularly interesting since it was founded by the late Zouhair Yahyaoui, the first cyberactivist to have been arrested by the regime; he died as a result of torture shortly after his release. Yahyaoui is a rare example of an activist who used the internet as an effective tool against the regime in the years when Ben Ali was in total control of the cyber scene in Tunisia. For an account of Tunisian cyberactivism (whose history remains to be written), see Sami Ben Gharbia, "Anti-Censorship Movement in Tunisia: Creativity, Courage and Hope," *Global Voices Advocacy*, May 27, 2010, accessed March 25, 2011, http://advocacy.globalvoicesonline.org/2010/05/27/anti-censorship-movement-in-tunisia-creativity-courage-and-hope.
6. I started blogging in 2004 using the pseudonym "Taher Laswad" and writing anti-regime articles. It was not until 2007, however, that I started blogging on political issues regarding Tunisia using my real name in a blog entitled "Afkar Layliyya" ("Nocturnal Thoughts") in which I wrote in Arabic and in the Tunisian dialect, which was one of the distinguishing characteristics of the Tunisian blogosphere compared to the "old media." The center of this community was "tn-blogs.com," an aggregator started by Houssein Ben Amor.
7. This group included: Sami Ben Gharbia ("Nawaat"), "El Clandestino" (Issam), Aymen Jemni, "Gouverneur" (Wissem Tlili), Tarek Kahlaoui, Amira Yahyaoui, Lina Ben Mhenni, and "Khmais Bandi" (Hatem Saidi).
8. See Lina Ben Mhenni, "Tunisia: Censorship Again and Again!" February 8, 2010, accessed January 23, 2011, http://globalvoicesonline.org/2010/02/08/tunisia-censhorship-again-and-again. By early May 2010 more than 100 blogs were censored, including very mildly politicized and even culinary blogs. See Lina Ben Mhenni, "A Black Day for Bloggers," May 5, 2010, accessed January 23, 2011, http://globalvoicesonline.org/2010/05/05/tunisia-a-black-day-for-bloggers.
9. The two notes were written in Arabic. The first was dated April 3, 2010, and entitled "Suggestions towards moving effectively against cyber censorship" (see www.facebook.com/note.php?note_id=402664910801) while the second, dated April 23, 2010,

was entitled "For a popular initiative to resist cyber censorship" (see www.facebook.com/note.php?note_id=409208710801).

10. Among the administrators of this page, I should mention Riadh Hammi, Haythem Mekki, Aymen Mekki, Wael Souihli, and myself. See www.facebook.com/tisayeb sala7.
11. Among the administrators of this page and this group of activists are Amira Yahyaoui, Malek Khadhraoui ("Nawaat"), Nabil Farhat, "Aarabasta," Yassine Ayayri, Wael Souihli, Slim Amamou, Lina Ben Mhenni, Azyz Amami and myself. Given that the members of this group were scattered throughout the world (some of whom are independent journalists such as Sofiene Chourabi and Ismail Dbara), coordinating throughout the summer of 2010 via Skype and especially via Google groups. See www.facebook.com/nhar3la3ammar.
12. For a brief account of the demonstration of May 22, 2010, see Ben Gharbia, "Anti-Censorship Movement in Tunisia."
13. I led the efforts to organize the flashmob as I was in Tunisia that summer. Unlike prior actions, I tended to include activists from political parties and not only cyber-activists. The flashmob was heavily cracked down upon and activists were prevented from reaching their endpoint by the secret police which ended up using heavy force in the streets.
14. Tariq Ramadan, *L'islam et le réveil arabe* (Paris: Presses du Châtelet, 2011), 21–5.
15. See K. R. Bolton, "Another Soros/NED Jack Up?" *Foreign Policy Journal*, January 18, 2011, accessed January 26, 2012, www.foreignpolicyjournal.com/2011/01/18/tunisian-revolt-another-sorosned-jack-up.
16. David Kirkpatrick and David Sanger, "A Tunisian-Egyptian Link that Shook Arab History," *The New York Times*, February 13, 2011, accessed March 3, 2012, www.nytimes.com/2011/02/14/world/middleeast/14egypt-tunisia-protests.html?_r=1.
17. I was among the bloggers who did not see any benefit from attending these workshops. I took part in various debates in which I defended this position to other participants.
18. On the occasion of the first anniversary of the revolution, on December 18, 2011, I was invited onto an Express.FM radio show with Lamine Bouazizi and Azyz Amami where we discussed some aspects of this media battle. See www.radioexpressfm.com/podcast/show/les-vrais-blogueurs-de-la-revolution (accessed May 4, 2012).
19. The Facebook group initiated by a Sidibouzid group that was leading some of the protests on the ground was called "The Committee of Citizenship and Defense of the Victims of Marginalization in Sidi Bouzid." See www.facebook.com/groups/140635172657879.
20. See www.facebook.com/MaTunisie (I was briefly an administrator of this page, which was originally created by an internet geek turned activist, Imed Amri) and www.facebook.com/touwenssa.
21. One of the founders of "Nawaat," Sami Ben Gharbia, was able to reach a deal with Wikileaks.org to publish exclusively the Tunisian documents on a dedicated website, https://tunileaks.appspot.com/ (note that the link is no longer operational).
22. See Rikke Hostrup Haugbølle's chapter in this book as well as her article co-written with Franceso Cavatorta, "*Vive la grande famille des médias tunisiens*: Media Reform, Authoritarian Resilience and Societal Responses," *The Journal of North African Studies* 17.1 (2012): 97–112.

23. Others included Ramzi Masoudi, Anis Mansouri, Nabil Farhat, and Malek Sghiri.
24. See respectively, www.facebook.com/pages/وكالة-أنباء-تحرّكات-الشارع-التونسي/189381554411547 and www.facebook.com/anba2.tn.

CHAPTER 7

Rethinking the Role of the Media in the Tunisian Uprising

Rikke Hostrup Haugbølle

Many early newspaper articles and blogs as well as later academic writings labeled the events in Tunisia from December 17, 2010 to January 14, 2011 a "Facebook Revolution," pointing to the decisive role of Facebook, Twitter, blogs, and the internet in the uprising. Ten days after the fall of Ben Ali, Nick O'Neill wrote that coordination efforts existed prior to the uprising but that "the social network [that is, Facebook] played the most significant role of any web technology used during the revolution."[1] A few weeks later, Noureddine Miladi wrote that because of the censorship of Ben Ali's regime, "Tunisians flocked to the social media networks" and the regime was then "faced with a fierce and unprecedented cyber war."[2] Howard and Hussein argue that social networks and social capital "materialized in the streets"[3] thanks to cellphones and Twitter. They singled out bloggers and cyberactivists as the protagonists of the uprising, the ones who were "producing alternative online newscasts, creating virtual spaces for anonymous political discussions."[4] The tribute to bloggers led to awards being given by, among others, the Oslo Freedom Forum to the Tunisian blogger Lina Ben Mhenni.[5]

Against the hype over the role of social media, Alterman critically remarks that "it is tempting to be swept away by this narrative."[6] He argues that it was not the new social media but rather "the power of 20th-century media"[7]—television and more accurately satellite TV—that was a decisive factor in the uprising. Similarly, Marc Lynch stressed on his blog the day after Ben Ali fled Tunisia that "calling Tunisia a 'Twitter Revolution' would be simplistic"[8] and argued that the question is not whether the uprising was driven by the new social media or by the "old" satellite TV stations but rather that they collectively transformed "a complex and potent evolving media space."[9] So neither Alterman nor Lynch rejects the assumption that media played a role; they shift the focus from social media to television and to the interaction between satellite media and new social media.

Such a focus of new social media and satellite TV and their role in the Tunisian uprising follows on from the argument Lynch and other scholars[10] put forward in the 2000s in discussions of the role and impact of Al-Jazeera. Addressing the question of Al-Jazeera and its contribution to democratization, Lynch argued in 2006 that the new satellite media and what he called the "new Arab public" were transforming Arab political culture because these new media eliminated "the sense of distance among Arabs and Muslims, bringing them together in real time and in a common language alongside intense images and a shared political discourse."[11] Because of the creation of a new transnational Arab community and its access to "independent" news, knowledge, and uncensored criticism of the national authoritarian regimes, the new Arab satellite media were seen as playing an important role in undermining them. In line with this argument, Seib argued that

> in the past, governments could control much of the information flow and therefore keep tight rein on political change. That is no longer the case. Governments can jail some bloggers and knock some satellite stations off the air, but the flood of information, and the intellectual freedom it fosters, is relentless.[12]

Furthermore Al-Jazeera's use of critical journalism and the introduction of Arab debate programs led some scholars to point to the possibility of the development of a new Arab public sphere where media free of state censorship could contribute to the development of democracy.[13] The linkage was derived from the democratization paradigm which at that time attracted much attention among Western scholars.[14] In this light, the challenge coming from satellite channels to the authoritarian regimes' monopoly on information was seen as an important precondition for regime change.

While all these accounts of the contribution by the new social media and satellite media to the Arab Spring certainly have a degree of validity they also have a number of shortcomings. First, studies about Al-Jazeera and satellite media are for the most part media-centric with very little attention paid to how the audience actually uses the satellite media. In a critique of scholarly analysis of the new satellite channels, Kai Hafez argues that the quest for rapid information led to studies that represent "an essayistic culture," with weak analyses, lacking theoretical and methodological weight.[15] Second, the need for quick analyses and comments on how to understand the events in Tunisia and other Arab countries has resulted in studies that make you think as if media and the internet had not existed in Tunisia prior to the uprisings. Generally, these studies overlooked entirely the broadcasting media based in Tunisia and run by Tunisians, and therefore failed to approach the media as part of broader Tunisian political, social, and economic changes. A final shortcoming is that these studies take for granted the fact that the infrastructure and technology that would allow the flow of information through the internet or phones were in place. People cannot send text messages if there is no cellphone network; uploading from cellphones to the internet requires wireless internet. In addition, the use of Facebook and Twitter requires reading and writing skills, and using social media critically requires that citizens are used to engaging in discussions and expressing themselves freely. From this, it follows that the tribute paid only to social media and satellite television is inconsistent with the emphasis on the Arab uprisings as leaderless in terms of both personalities and organized groups because all generations and all social classes participated.[16] Given these shortcomings, then, how should we approach the role of the media in the Tunisian uprising? It seems necessary to raise questions that allow us to dig deeper into this issue and that can inform us more accurately about the role of the Tunisian media and about the broader conditions and developments prior to the uprising. Instead of asking, "Was it a Facebook Revolution?" the questions must be broadened to the following: What role did the internet and social media play? When? And how? Should the influence of satellite TV and especially Al-Jazeera be rejected? Did any other media play a role and if so what and how? Such questions are the point of departure for the following analysis of the role of the media in the Tunisian uprising. The chapter is divided into two major sections. The first section explores the historiography of various media reforms and initiatives that were carried out after Ben Ali came to power in 1987. I discuss the impact that the introduction of these media had on Tunisians. The mapping of the media ensemble reveals that while the first media reforms leading to, among other things, the introduction of the internet in Tunisia were part of a strategy of upgrading Tunisians' skills, later reforms were part of a strategy of upgrading the authoritarian regime. At any rate, all the media reforms were factors that contributed, however indirectly, to the fall of the regime. This becomes clear in the second section of the chapter which explores the question of the role of the various media in the 2010–11 uprising. I do this through a comparative study of the Gafsa uprising in 2008 and the uprising in 2010–11. Although the two uprisings have many similarities, they differ on one important point: the Gafsa uprising remained locally confined while the 2010–11 uprising came to national and transnational attention. One of the recent developments of the Tunisian media landscape is the introduction in 2010 of wireless internet and new providers of cellphone services. This seems to have played a decisive role in the first days of the uprisings in 2010, but was unavailable in Gafsa in 2008.

Media reforms and the creation of the 2010 media ensemble

Focusing on the immediate role of social media in the Tunisian uprising is certainly interesting and important given the fact that it is a new phenomenon, with Facebook being launched in 2004 and Twitter introduced in 2006. Changes in the Tunisian media landscape, however, cannot be reduced to the introduction of Facebook and Twitter. Rather, media reforms have been carried out continuously by the regimes of both Bourguiba and Ben Ali to their own peril.[17] Radio broadcasting was well established in Tunisia before independence in 1956, and by 1959 the state launched Radio Tunisienne, which reached all areas of the country. The first Tunisian TV channel was launched on May 31, 1966. Both were state-led and were used strategically in the building of the new nation state, becoming synonymous with the state and political broadcasting.[18] A little more than twenty years later, in 1983, Tunisians could watch the Italian channel Rai Uno. Many preferred this channel because of the poor content of the programs on national TV.[19] With regard to the written press, one of Tunisia's biggest newspapers, *La Presse*, was established in 1936 while its Arabic version, *Assahafa*, was launched in 1989. Tunisia's other big Arabic newspaper, *Assabah*, was launched in 1951, and its French version, *Le Temps*, was founded in 1975. The Tunisian magazine *Réalités* was launched in 1979 and was the only one to publish continuously until 2011. Needless to say, however, all the newspapers were tightly controlled by the successive regimes of Bourguiba and Ben Ali.

With the arrival to power of Ben Ali as president in 1987, the media sector underwent a number of important reforms. The Press Code was amended in 1988, 1993, and 2001 as part of a broader liberalization of the former state-led economy.[20] A consultative body, the Higher Council on Communication (Conseil Supérieur de la Communication), was established on January 30, 1989. The Council was under the prime ministry's administrative control. It had a consultative role as it advised Ben Ali on media matters such as legal texts, regulation of the media, communication, and information. It consisted of fifteen members whose main duties were to investigate and put forward proposals for the further development of communication policies. There are reasons to believe that the Council was reform-oriented and saw potential in the media for an upgrading of the skills and level of knowledge in Tunisian society. Three important reforms and changes carried through in the 1990s point toward this conclusion. The first is the launch of a number of local radio stations; the second the launch of the internet and the so-called Publinet; the third the legalization of satellite dishes.

In the 1980s, Tunisia was marked by social unrest and at that time the more neglected regions were leading the protests against Bourguiba's regime, which eventually led to the takeover of power by Ben Ali. One person who became a media adviser to Ben Ali explained that an idea he put forward to Ben Ali shortly after 1987 was to establish local radio stations in the regions in the south and the interior of the country.[21] For this media adviser, one reason for the discontent in these areas was the feeling of being excluded from the nation state which was articulated by the elite in Tunis, and the long distance between the ruling regime in Tunis and these regions. For him, "local radio stations could be a means of proximity; my idea was to set up *radios de proximité*. It would give the feeling that the centralized power had come to them [in the regions] to listen to them and their problems."[22] The ideas were turned into reality: local radios were established in remote regions far from Tunis. In 1991, Radio Kef was founded to cover the northwestern part of the country and Radio Gafsa reached out to the southwest; in 1993, Radio Tataouine covered the southeastern part of the country. According to the media adviser, the main function of the local radio stations was to inform and educate people, but each radio station was also encouraged to produce programs that reflected local specificities. His idea was "to let people feel included in the nation and that their local history was a part of the larger Tunisian history." In this way, these local radio stations became a first step after independence to articulate differences within the nation state, which somehow ran counter to the regime's emphasis on creating a homogeneous nation state. However, the regime was very aware that it could undermine the legitimization of Ben Ali if history was rewritten and especially if the role of Islam became a subject of local discussion.[23] As a result the local radio stations were under strict state control. The potential of these local radio stations to engage in horizontal communication with the audience through the inclusion of them and *their* problems and issues could not be realized until the launch of private broadcasting media in 2003. I shall return to this later.

A second major media reform initiated by Ben Ali and his advisors was the launch of the internet in Tunisia. In 1996 the Tunisian Internet Agency (Agence Tunisienne d'Internet, ATI) was created as a public agency in charge of promoting internet services. In the beginning the number of internet users was very modest. In the first months of 1997, there were only 200 internet subscribers but by November that year the number had already increased to 11,000.[24] By 2001, the number of internet subscribers had increased to 57,000. Although the number of users reached 550,000 in 2003,[25] only 47 percent of the population owned a computer in 2002.[26] Private internet connectivity remained costly and was only an option for wealthy Tunisians. The inability of the average Tunisian to purchase a computer led to the launch of Publinet in 1998, an "office" which is a type of internet café without the café. In a simple room or office a number of computers with internet access are available to the public for a low fee. The Publinet project sought to improve internet access particularly in rural regions, and to create new job opportunities for young Tunisians, as only young Tunisians with a university degree could obtain a license to run a Publinet office. In 1999, 100 Publinet offices were established all over the country. Ten years later, in 2009, the number had increased to 248.

The internet in Tunisia was run by the state and from its launch many web pages were not available because of censorship. Despite this, many young Tunisians spent hours, days, evenings, and nights in the Publinets, gradually improving their skills as internet users. The number of internet users rose equally gradually. In December 2009, there were 3.5 million internet users and by May 2011 the number had reached 4 million out of a total population of 11 million.[27] However, this also means that just over a third of the Tunisian population was using the internet in 2011 and only half (1,970,200[28]) of the total number of internet users had joined Facebook by January 2011. On the one hand, the overall conclusion is that not all Tunisians were using the internet or Facebook in the years prior to the regime change in 2011. On the other hand, there are reasons to believe that the launch of Publinet played a significant role for those who eventually did use the internet, cellphones, and social media in the uprising, thereby contributing significantly to it. It is often stressed that the youth sector played a significant role in the uprising, and they did so because they were used to and trained in using the internet through the Publinet project. Although very little is known about the specific profile of Publinet users, they were mainly young people aged between fifteen and thirty-five. A study conducted by Sami Ben Sassi in 2002 concludes that only a particular section of the Tunisian population uses the new information technology and internet, namely students and the young new (and relatively young) well-educated upper middle class.[29] Those who were aged between fifteen and thirty-five in 1998, when Publinet was launched, would be between twenty-five and forty-five in 2010, and arguably would be familiar with and frequent users of cellphones, social networks, and wireless internet in the years before the uprising broke out.

At the same time as the internet and Publinet were introduced, the state and the state-led media faced a challenge coming from the illegal introduction of satellite dishes. This phenomenon led to a third reform in the media sector, whereby the government decided to legalize satellite dishes in 1996 after having initially banned them. In the same year, the satellite channel Al-Jazeera was launched and could be watched in Tunisia. Ordinary Tunisians were eager to purchase satellite dishes and although in the first few years the price of a satellite dish on the black market was equal to a month's salary for an average worker,[30] by the early 2000s the price had fallen to a level where most households could purchase a dish. Two crucial points about the introduction and use of satellite TV in Tunisia should be made here. First, the use of satellite TV was not an either/or: people watched the news both on Al-Jazeera and on state television because the two channels broadcast very different news. Al-Jazeera covered news from and offered insights into other Arab countries while state TV dealt with national issues such as agricultural forecasts, local problems of drought, and so on. As I pointed out earlier, we know very little about how Tunisian audiences used the different media and TV channels, but it would be too strong to argue that they only watched Al-Jazeera and that they only did so to listen to discussions and debates critical of the authoritarian regime.

Second, an often ignored dimension of the use of Al-Jazeera and other Arab satellite channels is the spoken language used on satellite channels. Due to their pan-Arab nature, they use the standard Arab language which can be understood by all Arabs who have learned Arabic in school. However, despite the high proportion of children who attend school in Tunisia, many Tunisians do not have advanced language skills in standard or classical Arabic. One reason is that because of changing education policies, teaching has in some periods been mainly in French. Another reason is that especially in urban areas children do not complete the compulsory nine years of schooling, which means that many

Tunisians do not learn Arabic well and can only speak the Tunisian dialect. Despite the often highlighted high level of education among Tunisian women, in 2004 only 65.3 percent of the female population over the age of fifteen could read and write compared to 83.4 percent of the male population.[31] As a consequence, they have difficulty understanding the programs on satellite channels with regard to both language and content when it comes to complex discussions. This left them in a "passive" state where they were watching Al-Jazeera and getting news but were not engaging with the media or participating in the discussion taking place on screen. While further examination of audience behaviour is required to get a more precise understanding of how Al-Jazeera and other satellite channels were used and understood by the Tunisian audience, the channels constituted an overall threat to the regime.

From upgrading society to upgrading authoritarianism

From his takeover in 1987 and well into the 1990s, Ben Ali's main concern was to consolidate and legitimize his power. In order to do so he had to respond to social unrest and meet the population's demand for jobs and better socioeconomic conditions. This was the principal reason behind the launch of a structural adjustment program in 1995 and the signing in the same year of the Association Agreement between Tunisia and the EU.[32] The aim of both policies was to create a liberal market attractive to European investors, so that more jobs could be created and privatization and liberalization of the economy became the mainstays of Tunisian economic policy. One way of making Tunisia more attractive to foreign investors was to carry out a thorough upgrading of the skills and education levels of the population, particularly the young. The launch of the internet and the ambition to make it accessible to the population at large through the spread of the Publinet should be seen in this context of reforms and job creation, which in turn would legitimize Ben Ali.

In the 2000s, crucial reforms and developments of the media sector continued to be carried out, but at that time the economic interests of Ben Ali's family and the close elite around them became the driving force of many of the reform initiatives. Ownership of the former state-led companies was simply transferred to members of Ben Ali's and his wife's family and their friends. It became clear that the reform process in Tunisia was no longer about creating structural changes, but was rather about the enrichment of a narrow elite and securing power—in the words of Steve Heydemann, this was an "upgrading of the authoritarian regime."[33] Furthermore, from 2003, the United States increased the focus on free media in the Arab world as part of its so-called War on Terror.[34] Given the close and good relations between the Tunisian government and the United States,[35] the regime found itself under pressure from two sides with regard to the media sector. On the one hand, Al-Jazeera journalists were criticising the regime and pointing to aspects of it that the regime did not want the United States and the European Union to become aware of. On the other hand, the new focus of the United States on the media put pressure on the regime to open up the media landscape. The growing economic interests of the Ben Ali family and the elites coupled with the pressure to open up the media sector led to two crucial media reforms in the 2000s.

The first reform was the legalization of private broadcasting media based in Tunisia. In a public speech in November 2003, Ben Ali announced that the Tunisian media sector was now open to private radio and TV channels.[36] This act was a response to the double pressure coming from Al-Jazeera and from the United States, but a closer look at the ownership of the radio and TV stations that were launched between 2003 and 2010 reveals that they all had a very close relationship to Ben Ali and his family. The first private broadcasting station to be launched was Radio Mosaïque, a radio station based in Tunis but reaching the whole country. The director of Radio Mosaïque was a member of the High Communication Council, which had the power to give operating licenses to launch private media stations. Furthermore, Radio Mosaïque was part of Karthago Group, the holding group headed by Ben Ali's brother-in-law, Belhassan Trabelsi. In 2005, a second radio channel, Radio Jawhara, was launched. The license for Radio Jawhara was granted to Néji Mhiri, a close friend of Ben Ali. Radio Jawhara broadcasts from the Sousse area, which is the hometown of Ben Ali and of many of the former members of the ruling party, the Constitutional Democratic Rally (Rassemblement Constitutionnel Démocratique, RCD). The same year, 2005, the first private Tunisian TV channel, Hannibal TV, was launched. Its owner, Larbi Nasra, has close family ties to Leila Ben Ali. In 2007, Tunisia's first Islamic radio station, Radio Zitouna, began broadcasting. Radio Zitouna was owned by Ben Ali's son-in-law, Sakhr El Materi, who comes from an important business family. In 2009, a second private TV channel, Nessma TV, in part owned by the Tunisian Karoui brothers, began broadcasting. Finally, in 2010, the two radio stations Shems FM, launched by Ben Ali's daughter Cyrine, and Express FM, financed by Belhassan Trabelsi, were set up. At the same time, a number of private media initiatives presented by opposition members were rejected when they applied for licenses. This is the case, for instance, of Radio Kalima and a number of private journals and magazines. The ownership of the new private media was often highlighted, especially by journalists who opposed the regime, to delegitimize it. There is no doubt that these media initiatives were launched as an attempt to consolidate the power base of Ben Ali and the ruling family.[37] Still, the new private media transformed the relationship between the audience and the media in a number of ways that cannot be overlooked in any objective reassessment of the role of the media in the uprising.

First, contrary to all other broadcasting channels, these new private media broadcast their programs in the Tunisian dialect. The importance of the use of Tunisian dialect on the new private stations should not be underestimated. To the people in underprivileged areas, these private radio and TV stations opened up a new world for them, as they could now engage with the programs and not just watch and listen passively, as was often the case with the programs on the satellite channels. Now they could understand every word of the programs on Tunisian radio and TV channels. Second, these channels introduced new styles of dynamic journalism and discussion programs tackling issues that until then had been taboos for the Tunisian public but were part of the everyday life of Tunisians. Issues such as unemployment, sexuality, and AIDS are just a few examples of the topics Tunisians all of a sudden could hear about, especially on Radio Mosaïque and Hannibal TV. In this way, these two private channels fulfilled the role that local radio stations had a decade earlier. They included the audience by taking *their* problems as the point of departure. Third, they employed horizontal communication skills focused on the inclusion of and dialogue with the audience,[38] something that local radio could not do before. Through the introduction of phone-in programs, ordinary Tunisians could call in and—in their own everyday dialect—tell their stories, give their comments, or ask questions about an issue dealt with in the studio.

However, the ability to call into a radio or TV studio requires access to a telephone. Such access increased at the same time as one new private media organization after the other was launched through the expansion of cellphone providers from 2002. This expansion, albeit not directly part of the media sector, had an important impact on the media scene by the 2010–11 uprising. Cellphones were introduced in 1998 by Tunisie Télécom, which at that time was state-owned, and the entire endeavor could be seen as one more attempt from Ben Ali's regime to make Tunisia attractive to foreign investors, with the latest telephone technology now available.[39] As was the case with satellite dishes, cellphones were at first very expensive and the network coverage very limited. It was not until the arrival of private cellphone companies that the number of lines increased significantly and cellphones could be purchased by average Tunisians. In 2002, the first private cellphone provider, Tunisiana, was launched in Tunisia. It was founded by the Egyptian giant Orascom and the Kuwaiti company Wataniya, but Orascom later withdrew with 25 percent of the shares transferred to Sakhr El Materi, Ben Ali's son-in-law and owner of Radio Zitouna. In 2003, Tunisiana's cellphone network covered 60 percent of the country; by 2005, it covered 99 percent of the country. By mid-2006 it had more than 2.5 million subscribers out of a total of 3,265,000—eight times more subscribers than in 2001. In 2010, it had 5.7 million subscribers.[40] In March 2009, Tunisie Télécom launched the cellphone company Elissa. It was specifically aimed at young Tunisians under the age of twenty-five. Elissa offered SIM cards for only 4 dinars, a small sum for many young people. In 2010, Elissa had more than 500,000 subscribers. This resulted in a total of 6.2 million cellphone subscribers in 2010. Another well-known businessman, Marouane Mabrouk,[41] married to Ben Ali's daughter Cyrine, the owner of Shems FM, entered the cellphone provider market in May 2010 when the French company Orange launched a Tunisian branch, of which Mabrouk held 51 percent of the shares. Orange was the first company to obtain the license to launch 3G in Tunisia and with it the first wireless internet. In July 2010, Orange had 8 percent of the total number of cellphone subscribers, including 65,000 3G subscribers. When it was launched, the Orange network covered 50 percent of the Tunisian territory but was expected to double its coverage by the end of the year.[42] With the new providers in place in 2010, more than half of all Tunisians had a cellphone when the uprising broke out in December that year. The following comparison between the Gafsa uprising in 2008 and the 2010–11 uprising demonstrates that this made a difference for the spread of the uprising in 2010–11 from a local to a national level.

The media in the Gafsa uprising of 2008

In January 2008, a popular uprising broke out in the mining area of Gafsa in the southwestern corner of Tunisia. Like Sidi Bouzid, the Gafsa area is extremely underdeveloped compared to the coastal areas and the capital.[43] Many young people in the area study at the university in Gafsa or in Sousse and Tunis but very often return to their families in their home towns after they graduate. In the Gafsa area, there is only one economic activity: phosphate mining through the Compagnie des Phosphates de Gafsa (CPG). Thus, young graduates either return home to face unemployment or to a job in mining if they have the right connections.[44] The situation worsened in January 2008 when CPG announced that they were reducing the number of employees from the local area from 11,000 to 5,000. A group of young, well-educated people occupied the office of the local branch of the workers' union while others pitched tents on the train tracks that transported the phosphate from the mines. In a very short time, unemployed people of all ages, their relatives, trade unionists, and even some of the staff of CPG joined the protest.[45] They demanded socioeconomic justice, development, and work—the same demands protesters made in 2010–11.

The protests were met with harsh repression, as the police opened fire on demonstrators. Very little information came out of Gafsa in 2008. While a few articles appeared in the international press in 2008 and 2009 about the events in Gafsa, Tunisian newspapers and magazines could not cover them. The state-controlled media were given orders not to disseminate information about the events, and journalists and human rights defenders could hardly come to the area as the police simply blocked all the roads. However, the opposition magazines *Attariq Al Jadid* and *El Maouqif* managed to cover parts of the uprising.[46]

One Tunisian journalist, Fahem Boukadous, managed to report on the uprising through the London-based TV satellite channel Al-Hiwar. "Hundreds of youths who had received a camera as a gift from relatives who had emigrated became journalists. I just had to collect these pictures and circulate them," he explained.[47] Three points have to be made clear about Boukadous's explanation. The first is that "camera" here refers to a video camera. Second, "to circulate" means to make copies of DVDs which then were passed from one person to another, a task complicated by the police's siege of the area. Third, this way of covering the Gafsa uprising was mainly the work of one activist, Boukadous. In 2008, the protesters in Gafsa might have had cellphones with lines provided by Tunisiana and they could arguably have uploaded photos to the web pages by using stationary computers. However, the number of cellphone subscribers increased significantly only in 2010. Furthermore, the very strict state control over everything that happened in Gafsa as well as over all cybertraffic at both private and public computers in Publinets meant that it was not possible for the protesters to upload pictures and film clips taken on the spot. Finally, in July 2008, Boukadous was sentenced to six years' imprisonment for covering the Gafsa events. Thus, no further pictures, films, or live reports reached the rest of the Tunisian population.

The media ensemble in the 2010–11 uprising

This was not the case in the 2010–11 uprising. By then, more than half the Tunisian population had cellphones, especially young people who benefited from the Elissa 3G special offer, and wireless internet had been introduced. But, as I have demonstrated, other new media such as private TV and radio stations had been launched in the years prior to the uprising. Thus a new media and communication set-up was in place shortly before the uprising broke out. To better capture the broad variety of the media operative in 2010, I suggest the notion of "the media ensemble;" this notion better describes this body of different kinds of media including the printed press, radio, television, cellphones, and wireless internet which had developed over decades and enabled Tunisians to communicate and disseminate information both face to face and using a mix of media and communication technologies. This Tunisian media ensemble was not created a few weeks before the uprising. Rather, as I have demonstrated, it had evolved over several years. These various parts of the media ensemble played different roles at different moments of the uprising.

In the first phase of the uprising, covering the period from December 17 to 27,[48] the media ensemble consisted of cellphones, satellite TV, international news agencies, and the state media. On December 18, photos and short film clips of firefighters and police in the streets of Sidi Bouzid were circulated on the internet. The next day, December 19, the international news agency Reuters brought news about the event, saying, "Witnesses report rioting in Tunisian town" and "Footage posted on Facebook,"[49] which clearly indicates that, contrary to the events in Gafsa in 2008, the protesters in Sidi Bouzid remained in contact with the outside world and could report the events from the very beginning. In December 2010, there was not one Boukadous but many activists uploading pictures on the internet and thus disseminating information. Everyone with a cellphone and, even better, any 3G subscriber could become an activist or citizen journalist. Thus the development of the media ensemble from 2008 to 2010 plays an important role for the evolution of events in 2010. However, cellphones and the internet were also used in concert with other media, which bespeaks a collaborative relationship between different types of media. The Al-Jazeera program *Al-Ḥaṣād al-Maghāribī* covered the events in Sidi Bouzid and used amateur film clips showing protesters in the streets. Al-Jazeera followed up with an article on the internet[50] and next to the article were two short amateur films originally posted on YouTube showing the protesters in Sidi Bouzid. This use of a YouTube clip by the "old media" turned out to be one of the characteristics not only of the Tunisian uprising but even more so of those in Egypt and Syria.

A study carried out by the Tunisian blogger Eli'coopter[51] clearly demonstrates that in the initial days of the 2010–11 uprising, Twitter did not support political activism. It was only from January 12 to 15, that is, during the final days of the uprising that activity on Twitter increased significantly. While some activists certainly used the internet and the new social media,[52] a decisive point was that of using Facebook and blogs, both of which required reading and writing skills. As already pointed out, not all Tunisians actually possessed these skills. Cellphones, on the contrary, do not require the same skills as phone calls are based on oral expression. With the introduction of low-cost cellphone lines, a growing number of Tunisians were in 2010 able to call their friends and relatives all over the country and tell them about the events in Sidi Bouzid. Second, text messages are short and can be written in the Tunisian dialect. This enabled Tunisians with poor writing skills to report what was going on. Finally, forwarding photos and film clips and uploading them to Facebook does not require writing skills and neither does looking at such photos and clips.

State TV, for its part, employed the same strategy that had proven effective in Gafsa two years earlier. The security forces and the police moved into the towns of Sidi Bouzid and Kesserine in the first few days; journalists were prevented from reaching the towns and the national media remained silent about what was going on. When they finally gave in and mentioned the events it was presented as a short news item in the 8 p.m. newscast on TV7 (now renamed El-Wataniya TV). The main focus, however, was not that protesters had taken to the streets but that "certain parties" were spreading "groundless rumors" about what had happened in Sidi Bouzid.[53] This was a well-known strategy that used to work for the regime, but it did not work in 2010. While TV7 tried to ignore what was going on, people watched and circulated the film clips and photos mentioned above and could follow the events on Al-Jazeera. The importance of the silence of state media should not be underestimated. Sadok Hammami has argued that the monopoly of the official media was not only ineffective, but detrimental to the regime. He points out that instead of lulling Tunisians into passive watching, the silence pushed them into exasperation.[54] The film clips available on the internet and Al-Jazeera coverage coupled with the (lack of) reaction from the state media meant that it became clear to people outside the two towns involved that the state and the state media were holding back information, and this provoked anger against the regime and thus solidarity with the population in Sidi Bouzid in a broader national context. The impact of the rise in cellphone subscribers in 2010 stands out as the clearest and more important factor in this first phase, but the media ensemble also consisted of satellite TV, the use of photos and film clips from the protesters in Sidi Bouzid, and the silence of the state-led media.

This led to the second phase of the uprising, characterized by the spread of demonstrations to the national level.[55] Al-Jazeera English wrote on December 27: "Tunisia protests spread to capital;"[56] this is the crucial difference with the 2008 uprising in Gafsa, where only one journalist could access the town, since the police succeeded in blocking the roads leading into it, and information therefore did not get out. In the second phase, media other than the internet and cellphones were important for the continued protests. First of all, the state media played a role. On December 28, *La Presse* published the rather grotesque photo of President Ben Ali visiting Mohammed Bouazizi at the hospital in Tunis. Bouazizi's entire body and head were wrapped in bandages so it is difficult to assess whether he was alive or already dead. The president is surrounded by doctors and nurses with serious faces. The photo gives the impression that the president was concerned about Mohammed Bouazizi and thus projecting the same concern about what was happening in Tunisia at that time. This concern is in stark contrast with what he said in his first public speech on state TV the same evening:

> While these events were triggered by *one* social case, of which we understand the circumstances and psychological factors and whose consequences are regrettable, the *exaggerated* turn that these events have taken, as a result of their political manipulation *by some parties who do not wish good to the homeland and resort to some foreign television* channels which broadcast false and unchecked allegations and rely on dramatization, fabrication and defamation hostile to Tunisia, requires from us to clarify some issues and confirm the truths that must be taken into consideration.[57]

The next day the Tunisian news agency quoted the political advisory group of President Ben Ali as saying that it "condemned the acts of disturbance carried out by *extremist groups* who exploited an isolated case."[58] Once again the ignorance of the regime and the speech made Tunisians furious. On the one hand, they could see on Facebook, YouTube, and satellite TV how many fellow citizens were shot and attacked by the police, while on the other hand the president called it an isolated case, and an act of extremists, blaming the foreign media and thereby completely ignoring the social situation of thousands of Tunisians in the same condition as the people in Sidi Bouzid. More importantly, the regime neglected to account for the fact that it was Tunisians themselves who this time were disseminating information and not foreign satellite channels. Thus, the national TV broadcast of the presidential speech also played a reverse role and strengthened the uprising at the national level. It obviously became clear to the regime that it could not continue this rhetoric and strategy and according to the journalist Jamel Arfaoui, advisers told Ben Ali that he had to "give a little bit of air to the protesters" and let people know something about what happened in Sidi Bouzid and neighboring towns.[59]

Nessma TV was selected as the only Tunisian TV station that was allowed to go to Sidi Bouzid and make a program covering the events. This resulted in a special program broadcast on December 30 at 8 p.m.: a primetime slot. The opening sequence of the program was the journalists' car driving along deserted roads to arrive in Sidi Bouzid. Once in town, the microphone was immediately offered to different inhabitants: young women and men, older people, poor people and well-educated businesspeople. They all expressed their discontent with the social and economic conditions and were rather direct in blaming the regime for the poor situation in which the town found itself. After these interviews, a very open round table discussion followed in the studio. It was new to hear such open expressions of discontent, as was the case with both the interviewees in Sidi Bouzid and the studio discussion. However, the argument here is that the terrain had been prepared in so far as the introduction of the style of dynamic journalism that the new private media had espoused since 2003 was an important precondition for the program broadcast that evening on Nessma TV. Tunisians had, in 2011, gradually become used to the possibility of expressing themselves to journalists on the private channels as they could use their Tunisian dialect and had become used to listening to what other Tunisians were saying in various types of programs, and to hear discussions that broke taboos. The program on Nessma TV was one factor out of several but contributed to the continued drive of the uprising, especially for those Tunisians who did not use the internet or social media. However, at the same time, the importance of the internet and social media was declining as there had been a clear awareness since December 30 that the internet was under increased surveillance. That day, the first Facebook pages were hacked and closed down by the regime.[60] The following day, Facebook pages and blogs covering the events in Sidi Bouzid were no longer accessible. The protests now spread to all regions of the country with all generations and social groups taking to the streets. It appears that national

TV, by blatantly ignoring the events, played a role in the second phase of the uprising, but it is also clear that the concept of audience discussion programs or talk shows on Tunisian private media came into play while the contributing role of the new social media is not as clear-cut in this period due to the fact that the regime intensified its control and censorship of the internet.

As Eli'coopter[61] clearly demonstrates, it was only from January 12 to January 15, 2011, the third and last phase of the uprising, that activity on Twitter increased significantly. By then, however, the uprising had moved massively into the streets with the highest participation on January 14 when Ben Ali eventually left the country. On that day there were two demonstrations in Tunis: one in front of the head office of the workers' union gathering members and others who were affiliated to the workers' union; and a second organized by the so-called "Facebook people" in front of the Ministry of the Interior. The mobilization for this demonstration had mainly been through the use of Facebook.[62] This composite demonstration is a good representation of the 2010–11 uprising.

Facebook, new social media, and cellphones did indeed play a crucial role in spreading information about the demonstrations taking place. The introduction of 3G in the summer of 2010 meant that for the first time, cellphone owners were no longer restricted to uploading on web pages and blogs through stationary computers but could now upload information, pictures, and film clips directly on the spot where they were situated. This new technical possibility, which enabled ordinary citizens to become reporters and journalists, is responsible for the label "Facebook Revolution."

However, as has been demonstrated, 3G and social networks were only a part of the entire complex and multidimensional media ensemble which gradually developed until a few months before the events in Sidi Bouzid in 2010. Media reforms had gradually been carried through since 1987 and expanded the media landscape which was until then dominated by the state TV, radio, and the printed press. Local radio stations became a feature of rural regions and gave Tunisians living in the interior a first, albeit limited, taste of diversity and the possibility of participating in the articulation of problems and identity in Tunisia. The introduction of the internet also reached these remote areas through the launch of Publinets. Young people gradually obtained better skills in using it despite—or perhaps because of— the censorship of the regime which meant that they had to search for alternative ways of accessing certain web pages. In the same period, the 1990s, satellite TV was introduced in Tunisia and became very popular, although Tunisians would still tune in to watch the national news on the state-governed TV7.

Many Tunisians watched the satellite channels without fully understanding what was discussed in the various programs. This, however, profoundly changed with the launch of private Tunisian broadcasting media. They engaged the Tunisian audience and accustomed Tunisians to the phenomenon of open and public discussions tackling subjects that had previously been taboo and covering ordinary Tunisians' everyday problems. The final change to the media ensemble came with the launch of private cellphone providers and a drop in prices for subscription to the wireless internet in 2010. All of the components of this media ensemble were in use in the 2010–11 uprising. Cellphones, 3G, and the internet were used in the first days of the initial phase to disseminate information about what was going on. The skills the younger generation had acquired in the Publinets (and, in the case of the more affluent, at home in front of the computer) were activated and used for uploading pictures and film clips to create blogs and Facebook pages which made it possible for the outside world to follow the events. State media also played a role: first, by their silence alone and later by ignoring the fact that Tunisians all over the country sympathized and identified with the protesters in Sidi Bouzid. The coverage of the events on national TV also provided a glaring contrast to the program broadcast by one of the new private media, Nessma TV. The program applied all the characteristics of the new private broadcasting media: the use of the Tunisian dialect, giving voice to ordinary Tunisians in interviews and conducting discussions that pushed through the "red lines."

The media ensemble after the uprising

The many components of the Tunisian media ensemble continue to play a significant role in postrevolutionary Tunisia. Facebook has increased its role as the medium whereby politics is debated and freedom of expression is used by "the man in the street."[63] The field of printed and broadcast media, however, demonstrates how new clashes between various actors and debates over values have unfolded and evolved since January 2011.

In the weeks after January 14, 2011 a number of independent journalists and civil society actors negotiated with then Prime Minister Mohamed Ghannouchi the constitution of a council that could discuss and draft new propositions with regard to media laws and regulations. As a result INRIC was launched on March 2, 2011.[64] It had consultative status to the interim government.[65] Other councils were also established, such as the Independent High Electoral Commission (Instance Supérieure Indépendante pour les Elections, ISIE). INRIC was composed of, among others, journalists who had led the journalists' fight against the Ben Ali regime and human rights activists who had for many years opposed Ben Ali. ISIE, for its part, was led by Kamel Jendoubi, a well-known human rights activist and opposition figure. In the first months, INRIC was engaged in the important task of reforming the national news agency, TAP, and worked toward making the public media independent from the political authorities. ISIE had the task of preparing and seeing through the first elections after the uprising for the National Constituent Assembly (Assemblée Nationale

Constituante, ANC) in October 2011. During the summer of 2011—a few months before the elections—the first tension between INRIC and ISIE on one side and various actors within the media landscape on the other broke out into the open. One dispute revolved around Nessma TV. When the channel was launched in 2009 it had a clear strategy of featuring sport and entertainment but no news and political programs.[66] However, this strategy was set aside after the uprising and Nessma TV broadcast daily programs with political discussions. In Ramadan 2011, which was in August that year and thus two months before the elections, Nessma TV decided to screen a program showing how various politicians and politically active Tunisians were breaking the fast in their homes during Ramadan. This did not go unnoticed by ISIE who directed a letter to Nessma TV highlighting ISIE's decision that the Tunisian broadcasting media were prevented from inviting politicians into the studio and thus granting them time on the airwaves before the real election campaign took off. In a press meeting one of the owners of Nessma TV, Nabil Karoui, said:

> I have received a letter. It is a nightmare. It is from Kamel Jendoubi who is telling us to stop some of our spots because a politician appears in one of them. The Tunisian TV channels are prevented from inviting politicians while Al-Jazeera can invite all they want.[67]

He then continued to criticize Kamel Jendoubi. The personal dimension of the dispute—the relationship between Karoui and Jendoubi—stands out as one important aspect. Nessma TV is owned and directed by a handful of people, including Nabil Karoui and his brother, who had a very close relationship with Ben Ali and the regime. After the uprising many attempts were made to stop the power and functioning of Nessma TV, and the intervention of ISIE led by a prominent opposition figure can be seen as an attempt to "clean" the branch of old regime supporters and as a showdown between the old opposition and old regime supporters.

Another example of how the media sector has been an arena of personal fights rooted in past relations between various wings within the political landscape under Ben Ali also occurred in the months leading up to the elections. While Ennahda had been completely prevented from participating in any political or civil society activities since 1991, the left wing had enjoyed some degree of tolerance. The popular support Ennahda garnered, which became clear from the polls in the months before the elections, came as a shock to many secular Tunisians who had partly believed in the myth of Tunisia as a secular country where Islam only played an insignificant role. They therefore became very outspoken in their critique and scepticism of the future role and dominance of Islam in Tunisia. Radio Zitouna, which was owned by Ben Ali's son-in-law, Sakhr El Materi, became a space for debating the resurgence of political Islam. Many in the secular opposition perceived Radio Zitouna as the mouthpiece of the regime and an outlet of state-defined Islam.[68] After the uprising the daily management of Radio Zitouna was handed over to Cheikh Mohammed Machfar, a popular presenter at the radio station. However, in December 2011, INRIC decided to appoint a female professor, Iqbal Gharbi, as new manager of the radio station. The appointment led to a real drama. Iqbal Gharbi holds a degree in psychology from a French university, and in 1993 she was appointed director of the newly reopened Zitouna Faculty in Tunis. Her task was to ensure that Islamic studies were not politicized. She seemed to be a good choice for this position as she is also known as a secular and left-wing militant, belonging to a group of hardcore Tunisian secular feminists. Her appointment as director of Radio Zitouna was a very provocative act which spoke directly to the ongoing battle over values and the role of Islam in Tunisia. Cheikh Machfar and the employees at Radio Zitouna refused to hand over any documents to Gharbi and told her to stay away. The government stepped in and a new director was appointed.

Reforming the media sector after the uprising has turned out to be as complex as it was during the decades of Ben Ali's rule but for very different reasons. Disputes between various actors have broken out and have taken place within the media sector. While these disputes are also about reforms and new media laws they have a lot to do with clashes between old, pre-uprising actors. They are about secular voices against Islam as represented by the Ennahda-led government. They are about Islamic voices claiming their right to run media with a focus on Islam. They are about old human rights militants and old opposition journalists continuing their fight for freedom of expression. They are about finding out how to live side by side with old regime supporters. The reform of the media sector is part of an overall effort to face the challenges of securing freedom of expression for journalists and Tunisians irrespective of their faith and political convictions, of reconciling with the past, and of accepting one important aspect of democracy, the will to compromise.

Notes

The author is grateful to Nouri Gana and Francesco Cavatorta for useful comments and suggestions.

1. Nick O'Neill, "How Facebook Kept The Tunisian Revolution Alive," *All Facebook*, January 24, 2011, accessed January 4, 2012, http://allfacebook.com/how-facebook-kept-the-tunisian-revolution-alive_b30229.
2. Noureddinne Miladi, "Tunisia: A Media Led Revolution?" *Al-Jazeera*, January 17, 2011, accessed April 3, 2013, www.aljazeera.com/indepth/opinion/2011/01/2011116142317498666.html.
3. Philip N. Howard and Muzammil M. Hussain, "The Role of Digital Media," *Journal of Democracy* 22.3 (July 2011): 36.

4. Howard and Hussain, "The Role," 36.
5. See www.oslofreedomforum.com/speakers/lina_ben_mhenni.html.
6. Jon B. Alterman, "The Revolution Will Not Be Tweeted," *The Washington Quarterly* 34.4. (2011): 103.
7. Alterman, "The Revolution."
8. Marc Lynch, "Tunisia and the New Arab Media Space," *Foreign Policy*, January 13, 2011, accessed June 7, 2012, http://lynch.foreignpolicy.com/posts/2011/01/15/tunisia_and_the_new_arab_media_space.
9. Lynch, "Tunisia and the New Arab Media Space," 1.
10. See, for instance, Khalil Rinnawi, *Instant Nationalism: McArabism, Al-Jazeera, and Transnational Media in the Arab World* (Lanham, MD: University Press of America, 2006).
11. Marc Lynch, *Voices of the New Arab Public. Iraq. Al-Jazeera, and Middle East Politics Today* (New York: Columbia University Press, 2006), 41.
12. Phillip Seib, *The Al Jazeera Effect: How the New Global Media Are Reshaping World Politic* (Washington, DC: Potomac Books Inc., 2008).
13. Jon B. Alterman and Ibrahim Karawan, "New Media, New Politics? From Satellite Television to the Internet in the Arab World," The Washington Institute for Near East Policy, PolicyWatch #356: Special Forum Report, December 11, 1998.
14. See, for instance, Morten Valbjørn and André Bank, "Examining the 'Post' in Post-democratization – The Future of Middle Eastern Political Rule through Lenses of the Past," *Middle East Critique* 19.3 (2010): 303–19.
15. Kai Hafez, *Arab Media. Power and Weakness* (New York: Continuum, 2008), 9.
16. See Tarek Kahlaoui's firsthand account in this book.
17. Media in Tunisia is a relatively understudied area. For literature about the early years of Tunisian media, see Noureddine Sraïeb, *Le mouvement littéraire et intellectuel en Tunisie* (Tunis: Alif, 1998), 171–83. On state radio and TV in the period 1956–90, see Ridha Najar and Fethi Houidi, *Presse, Radio et Television en Tunisie* (Tunis: Maison Tunisienne de l'Édition, 1983), and Thouraya Snoussi, *La télévision tunisienne dans les années 1990: Problématique entre monopole politique et les exigences de l'internationalisation* (Tunis: Publi Press, 2007). For studies of the new private media in Tunisia, see Riadh Ferjani, "Du rôle de l'état dans le champ télévisuel en Tunisie: Les paradoxes de l'internationalisation," and Larbi Chouikha, "Les identités au miroir des temporalités télévisuelles: Le ramadan et le réveillon du jour de l'an à Tunis à travers le petit écran," in *Mondialisation et nouveaux médias dans l'espace arabe*, ed. Franck Mermier (Lyon: Maison de l'Orient et de la Méditerranée, 2003), 153–83.
18. Donald R. Browne, "International Broadcasting in Arabic. Tunisia," in *Broadcasting in the Arab world, a Survey of the Electronic Media in the Middle East*, ed. Douglas A. Boyd (Ames, IA: Iowa State University Press, 1999), 261–78.
19. Snoussi, *La télévision tunisienne*, 49.
20. See Emma Murphy, *Economic and Political Change in Tunisia: From Bourguiba to Ben Ali* (London: Macmillan, 1999).
21. Interview conducted by the author in Tunis, January and February 2010. The informant wishes to remain anonymous.
22. Interview conducted by the author in Tunis, January 2010.
23. Rikke Hostrup Haugbølle and Francesco Cavatorta, "Beyond Ghannouchi: Islamism and Social Change in Tunisia," *Middle East Report* 262 (2012): 20–5.

24. Arab Network for Human Rights Information, "Tunisia, the First, the Worst," accessed December 28, 2011, www.anhri.net/en/reports/net2004/tunis.shtml.
25. Arab Network for Human Rights Information, "Tunisia, the First, the Worst."
26. Sami Ben Sassi, "Les Publinets de Tunis," accessed May 1, 2013, http://www.gdri-netsuds.org/IMG/pdf/Samider.pdf.
27. See www.internetworldstats.com/stats19.htm, accessed December 28, 2011.
28. See www.socialbakers.com/facebook-statistics, accessed January 5, 2011.
29. Ben Sassi, "Les Publinets."
30. Lotfi Ben Sassi, "Le retour de la parabole," *La Presse Magazine* 501 (May 18, 1997).
31. *The CIA World Fact Book.* While the rate of school attendance is high compared to other Arab countries, government records revealed in 2007 that the highest rates of illiteracy in the 10–29 year old categories were 14.98 percent in Kairouan in the interior of Tunisia, followed by Kasserine in the northwest, where the initial 2010 uprising took place, at 13.93 percent. The capital city had the lowest rate, with 1.92 percent. National Institute of Statistics, Tunis, 2009.
32. Fathi Chamkhi, "La politique de privatisation." *Confluences Méditerranée* 35 (autumn 2000): 103–9.
33. For a critical approach to the reform process and privatizations in Tunisia see, for instance, Stephen King, *Liberalization Against Democracy* (Bloomington, IN: Indiana University Press, 2003); S. Erdle, "Tunisia. Economic Transformation and Political Restoration," in *Arab Elites: Negotiating the Politics of Change*, ed. V. Perthes (Boulder, CO: Lynne Rienner, 2004); Béatrice Hibou, "Domination and Control in Tunisia: Economic Levers for the Exercise of Authoritarian Power," *Review of African Political Economy* 33.108 (June 2006): 185–206; Bradford Dillman, "International Markets and Partial Reforms in North Africa: What Impact on Democratization," *Democratization* 9 (2002): 63–86; and Eva Bellin, *Stalled Democracy* (Ithaca, NY and London: Cornell University Press, 2002).
34. In December 2002, the US Secretary of State, Colin Powell, launched the Middle East Partnership Initiative (MEPI) to address the need for political reform in the region. One of the two regional MEPI offices is situated in Tunis at the American Embassy.
35. Vincent Durac and Francesco Cavatorta, "Strengthening Authoritarian Rule through Democracy Promotion? Examining the Paradox of the US and EU Security Strategies: The Case of Bin Ali's Tunisia," *British Journal of Middle Eastern Studies*, 36.1 (2009): 3–19.
36. Speech by president Zine El Abedine Ben Ali on the occasion of the sixteenth anniversary of his accession to power on November 7, 1987, accessed January 10, 2011, www.changement.tn/english (page is no longer accessible).
37. For a discussion of the use of the media in the upgrading of the authoritarian regime, see Rikke Hostrup Haugbølle, "'La Famille' og nye private medier i Tunesien," *Tidsskriftet Babylon* 2 (2011): 86–97.
38. Thomas Tufte and Florencia Enghel, *Youth Engaging with the World. Media, Communication and Social Change* (Gothenburg: The International Clearing House on Children, Youth and Media, Nordicom, 2009).
39. In 2006, the state-owned Tunisie Télécom went through a partial privatization as 35 percent of its capital was transferred to Emirates International Telecommunications (part of Emirates Financial Funds).

40. In 2001 there were 380,255 cellphone subscribers. See www.tunisia-today.com/archives/11 (accessed January 25, 2012). For 2010, see www.itp.net/582863-wataniya-princesse-holdings-to-acquire-tunisiana (accessed January 28, 2012).
41. The Mabrouk family and the Groupe Mabrouk was one of the most important business elites in Tunisia until 2011. See http://nawaat.org/portail/2011/08/12/les-mabrouk-dans-la-nouvelle-tunisie (accessed May 17, 2012).
42. "Orange Tunisie: 676.000 abonnés et sponsor du CSS et l'ESS," accessed January 27, 2012, www.tekiano.com/phone/operateurs/1-1-2447/orange-tunisie-676-000-abonnes-et-sponsor-du-css-et-l-ess.html.
43. Amnesty International, "Behind Tunisia's "Economic Miracle": Inequality and Criminalization of Protest," June 2009, accessed January 27, 2012, http://www.amnesty.org/en/library/info/MDE30/003/2009.
44. Amin Allal, "La 'reconversion' problématique du bassin minier de Gafsa en Tunisie. Réformes néolibérales, clientélismes et protestations en situation politique autoritaire," *Politique Africaine* 117 (March 2010): 107–26.
45. Allal, "La 'reconversion'."
46. See the archives at www.attariq.org.
47. Alma Allende, "Interview with Fahem Boukadous, Member of the Communist Workers Party of Tunisia," accessed August 1, 2011, http://links.org.au/node/2151.
48. See interview in Antoine Perraud, "Al Jazeera a donné le la. Les autres télés satellitaires ont suivi," *Mediapart*, January 18, 2011, accessed May 30, 2012, www.mediapart.fr/journal/culture-idees/180111/al-jazeera-donne-le-la-les-autres-teles-satellitaires-ont-suivi
49. http://af.reuters.com/article/topNews/idAFJOE6BI06U20101219.
50. www.aljazeera.com/news/africa/2010/12/201012206374582893l.html.
51. Eli'coopter, "Quelle Twitter révolution en Tunisie?" Nawaat, January 19, 2011, accessed January 24, 2012, http://nawaat.org/portail/2011/01/19/quelle-twitter-revolution-en-tunisie.
52. See Tarek Kahlaoui's firsthand account in this book.
53. See, for instance, www.espacemanager.com/macro/tunisie-des-precisions-concernant-l-incident-survenu-a-sidi-bouzid.html (accessed January 27, 2012).
54. Perraud, "Al Jazeera a donné le la."
55. See interview in Perraud, "Al Jazeera a donné le la."
56. www.aljazeera.com/video/middleeast/2010/12/2010122622502l489335.html
57. TAP, accessed December 29, 2010, www.tap.info.tn/en/index.php?option=com_content&task=view&id=13597&Itemid=46 (the link is no longer available).
58. TAP, accessed December 29, 2010, www.tap.info.tn/en/index.php?option=com_content&task=view&id=13596&Itemid=65 (the link is no longer available).
59. Interviews and conversations between the author and Jamel Arfaoui in January, February, May, and December 2011.
60. My own experience: I wanted to download all the information on Nawwat relating to Sidi Bouzid and the uprising, and the special pages on Facebook named "Sidi Bouzid" to keep them as documents for later analysis and reference. Later the same day, however, I could no longer find the pages on Facebook and I noted that my friends' Facebook pages had been hacked. Other friends were no longer willing to use Skype as they knew that it was under surveillance.
61. Eli'coopter, "Quelle Twitter révolution."

62. Interview with Selma Jabbes, owmer of the Librairie al Kitab bookstore in Tunis, February 24, 2011.
63. See Tarek Kahlaoui's firsthand account in this book.
64. In French: Instance Nationale pour la Réforme de l'Information et de la Communication.
65. See INRIC Report, April 2012, accessed March 4, 2013, www.inric.tn/fr/INRIC-Report-Eng-final.pdf.
66. Interview by author with Moez Sinaoui, communications director of Nessma TV, September 2009.
67. *Kapitalis*, "Tunisie. Nabil Karoui tire sur tout ce qui bouge," Kapitalis, August 13, 2011, accessed May 21, 2012, www.kapitalis.com/kanal/61-medias/5381-tunisie-nabil-karoui-tire-sur-tout-ce-qui-bouge.html.
68. This was, however, not the entire story of Radio Zitouna's broadcasting. See Rikke Hostrup Haugbølle, "Old and New Expressions of Islam in Tunisia: The Regimes and the Islamic *Radio Zitouna*" (in Danish), The Forum for Islam Research (FIFO), accessed May 1, 2013, http://islamforskning.dk/files/journal/2013/FIFO-2013-1-del2.pdf.

CHAPTER 8

Visions of Dissent, Voices of Discontent: Postcolonial Tunisian Film and Song

Nouri Gana

There is hardly a public debate in postrevolutionary Tunisia that does not ultimately devolve into a "blamestorming" exercise, in which the participants apportion blame to some figures of the *ancien régime*, discredit or champion others, and in the process establish their own revolutionary credentials. This obsessive return to the prerevolutionary situation in an all-out war of positions, which has become a constant feature of political and public debate, has cast its long shadow on the cultural scene. Not infrequently, concerts were cancelled, screenings picketed, and artists attacked, especially on Facebook and other social media. The Ministry of Culture itself had often succumbed to popular opinion: for instance, it had extended and then withdrawn an invitation to Lotfi Bouchnaq to perform in the opening ceremony of the 2011 Carthage Festival precisely because of his association in the (still green) collective memory of Tunisians with Ben Ali's regime. Bouchnaq's name appeared on a petition signed by many public figures—including lawyers, businesspeople, artists, journalists, athletes, doctors, and university professors—calling on Ben Ali to run for re-election in 2014. Quite suggestively, Bouchnaq was replaced by El Général, along with a host of other rappers, singers, and musical troupes associated with the Revolution of Freedom and Dignity.

The value of artists and public intellectuals in postrevolutionary Tunisia has come to be routinely reassessed depending on the degree of their past association with or the nature of their relationship (if one exists) to Ben Ali's regime, especially given that bloggers and cyberactivists had already made public several lists of all the artists and public figures who allegedly supported Ben Ali in his bid for re-election in 2014. Quite disturbingly, one of these lists included the names of iconic filmmakers Moufida Tlatli and Abdellatif Ben Ammar, and actors Hind Sabri and Hichem Rostom, as well as several famous singers such as Latifa al-Arfaoui, Nabiha Karaouli, Amina Fakhit, Sonia M'barek, and Saber Rebaï, in addition to the aforementioned Bouchnaq. These celebrities might not have chosen out of their own free will to be on the list of signatories, but instead were selected by Ben Ali's entourage and included on the list with or without their consent. They might not be entirely guilty of complicity but they are not exempt of it either; it was definitely less a matter of principle than of convenience.

While many artists, especially popular singers, who thrived under Ben Ali experienced a rude awakening, a fall from grace of sorts, after December 17,

2010, others who opposed Ben Ali and had been forced to disappear underground were catapulted to instantaneous, albeit long overdue, fame. Many of those whose reputation declined in the wake of January 14, 2011 have attempted to hitch their wagon to the train of revolution and have managed, at least partly, to redeem themselves. Those who enjoyed overnight fame, or belated acknowledgment of their revolutionary credentials, had in turn found themselves caught in the polarizing and polarized political atmosphere of postrevolutionary Tunisia. Not infrequently, their political views or stances vis-à-vis unfolding events have made them targets of Blamespeak or hate speech on Facebook and elsewhere in the public sphere writ large.

With the postrevolutionary overdose of politics and political debates in social media/public space, not to mention the exponential proliferation of political parties, the cultural sphere risks becoming further captive of and captivated by everyday political events and developments. The countrywide unity that brought thousands of Tunisians together in mass demonstrations against Ben Ali's regime has now largely given way to disunity and divisiveness along ideological lines and party politics. While Islamists, secularists, leftists, Arab nationalists, and salafis, among others, have variably contributed as sociopolitical actors to the toppling of Ben Ali, their combined histories of victimhood, resistance, and struggle has hardly resulted in a common agenda in postauthoritarian Tunisia. The same can be said about artists and intellectuals whose positions (the way they position themselves vis-à-vis public debates) and positioning (the way they were positioned by debaters and audiences in those debates) has come to override the commonalities of their pre-revolutionary struggles against Ben Ali's regime.

This chapter will not delve into the ideological rifts and political drifts of postrevolutionary Tunisia, for it is too soon to study a postrevolutionary cultural scene that is very much in the pull of an amorphous and fluid political reality. It seeks instead to disentangle the common genealogies of resistance and dissidence that have characterized the artistic ventures of a number of artists in postcolonial Tunisia and that seem, regrettably, to have been completely forgotten amidst the vociferous and politically driven debates that have come to characterize postrevolutionary Tunisia. In the process, I will shed light on the artists whose approval, if not support, of Ben Ali has amounted to nothing less than complicity in the injustices his regime has committed. I leave out of consideration many cultural forms of expression (namely, theater and literature, both of which I nonetheless discuss extensively in the Introduction) and focus in particular on the two most vital elements of Tunisian culture: music and film.

In the years that preceded the revolution, Tunisian music and film ran the gamut from conformity and consent to resistance and dissent. In the first part of this chapter, I outline the trajectory of Tunisian film from its amateurish beginnings in the 1960s and its rise to prominence in the 1980s with a generation of innovative and committed filmmakers whose vision has shaped the cinematic landscape of Tunisia today. I devote the second part to a discussion of popular music. I compare and contrast two genres of popular music and examine the crucial role that rap music has played in capturing and articulating Tunisian mass discontent with Ben Ali's authoritarian regime as well as in inspiring the popular uprising that has shaken the country and the entire region ever since December 17, 2010.

Postcolonial film: allegories of discontent, visions of dissent

By indirections find directions out

Shakespeare, *Hamlet* (2.2.66)

From its early beginnings to the present, Tunisian cinema has relied largely on the financial support of the postcolonial state (the Ministry of Culture, to be precise), which found in film and visual culture at large a viable means of promoting its national image and ideological discourse, which is why it founded the Tunisian broadcasting company ERTT (Établissement de la Radiodiffusion-Télévision Tunisienne) and the production company SATPEC (Société Anonyme Tunisienne de Production et d'Expansion Cinématographique), along with the Carthage Film Festival for Arab and African Cinema.[1] The early films emerged out of the amateur film movement and were understandably nationalist in content and purpose as they sought to document and represent the realities of the anticolonial struggle of Tunisia against French colonialism, particularly after World War II. Of note here are Omar Khlifi's films, especially his *al-Fajr* (1966, *L'aube/The Dawn*), arguably the first Tunisian feature film, and Abdellatif Ben Ammar's *Sejnene* (1973). *Al-Fajr* delved into the epic national struggle against French colonialism in documentary fashion and *Sejnene* focused on the particular role of the Tunisian general labor union (Union Générale Tunisienne du Travail, UGTT) in the events of 1952–4 leading up to independence. With Brahim Babai's *Wa Ghadan* (1972, *Et Demain/And Tomorrow*) and Naceur Ktari's *al-Sufarāʾ* (1975, *Les Ambassadeurs/The Ambassadors*), as well as Ridha Behi's film *Shams al-Dibāʿ* (1976, *Soleil des Hyenes/Hyenas' Sun*), counter-colonial revisionary critique of Tunisian history has opened up to realist social critique of the postcolonial state and its socioeconomic policies. *Wa Ghadan* addressed the social problems that result from rural exodus to towns and cities while *al-Sufarāʾ* addressed the challenges of racism and integration that Tunisian migrants face in the Goutte d'Or district in Paris, France. *Shams al-Dibāʿ* zeroed in on the neocolonial and sociocultural devastation caused by tourism well before the economic pitfalls and social malaise of the tourist industry were severely exposed by Nouri Bouzid's *Bezness* (1992). Both Behi and Bouzid, to use Kmar Kchir-Bendana's conclusion, "mounted a critique in which the ravages of the tourist industry were perceived as acts of rape."[2]

Gradually but steadily, the venture of Tunisian film has come to approach the plight of postcolonial nationhood in terms of individual struggles for social recognition, political redress, and, above all, justice and freedom of expression (especially at a time when Bourguiba had consolidated power in his own hands, proclaiming himself president for life in the mid-1970s, neutralizing the role of the Tunisian general labor union (Union Générale Tunisienne du Travail, UGTT), and crippling any existing or aspiring political opposition). There were manifest traces of this tendency already operative in Omar Khlifi's *Khlīfa Lagraʿ* (1968, *Khlifa le teigneux/Khlifa Ringworm*), Sadok Ben Aicha's *Mokhtar* (1968), Abderrazak Hammami's *Ummi Traki* (1972), and especially Salma Baccar's *Fatma 1975* (1976), but this neorealist approach has programmatically taken off with Nouri Bouzid's *Riḥ Essed* (1986, *L'homme de cendres/Man of Ashes*) and *Ṣafāʾiḥ min Dhahab* (1988, *Les Sabots en or/Golden Horseshoes*), and consolidated itself with Moufida Tlatli's *Ṣamt al-Quṣūr* (1994, *Les Silences du palais/Silences of the Palace*), Mohamed Zran's *Essaida* (1996), Naceur Ktari's *Ḥulu wa Murr* (2000, *Sois mon amie/Sweet and Bitter*), and Jilani Saidi's *'Urs al-Dhīb* (2006, *Tendresse du loup/Tender is the Wolf*) as well as Fadhil Jaibi's *Junūn* (Madness) of the same year. The latter films constitute the period of maturity of Tunisian cinema: whether in terms of their exemplary attention to real-life stories, to the complexity and density of character and character development, or in terms of their esthetic and stylistic sophistications, these films have defined the direction of Tunisian cinema toward art film, as opposed to commercial and melodramatic tendencies of other national cinemas, particularly the major corpus of Egyptian cinema.

It is not for nothing that the emergence of this trend of auteur filmmaking, in which much of the material for the films comes directly from the private stories of the filmmakers themselves, has gone almost hand in hand with the rise of private production companies, namely Tarek Ben Ammar's Carthago Films and Ahmed Baha Eddine Attia's Cinétéléfilms. The latter came into existence in order to produce Nouri Bouzid's groundbreaking *Man of Ashes* after it was turned down by Ben Ammar's review team.[3] Attia went on to produce singlehandedly the films that would constitute the golden age of Tunisian filmmaking in the 1980s and 1990s, including Bouzid's *Golden Horseshoes*, Boughedir's *Halfaouine* and Tlatli's *Silences*.[4] Most of the films that came after Bouzid's trailblazing *Man of Ashes* have focused on marginal and marginalized individuals from defeated leftists, prostitutes, gravediggers, failed singers, thieves, suicide bombers, lovers, and so on, as if defeat, powerlessness, and marginalization were the new chronotopes or overlooked spaces of empowerment in Tunisia's cinematic discourse.

While the emergence of female filmmakers (like Salma Baccar, Nejia Ben Mabrouk, Kalthoum Bornaz, Moufida Tlatli, Naida El Fani, and Raja Amari) has brought to the fore a variegated and peculiar focus on women characters, their lived experiences and past struggles, male filmmakers have all along approached women in their films as part and parcel of their agenda, namely the revalorization of the individual, gender equality, and freedom (from injustices). Take, for instance, Ali Abdelwaheb's *Um ʿAbbes* (1969), Rachid Ferchiou's *Yusra* (1971), Khilifi's *Ṣurākh* (1972, *Hurlements/Screams*), and Sadok Ben Aicha's *ʿĀridat al-Aziāʾ* (1978, *Mannequin*), or Boughedir's *Ṣaif Ḥalq Elwed* (1996, *Un été à La Goulette/A Summer in La Goulette*) and Khaled Ghorbal's *Fatma* (2001), not to mention Bouzid's *Bent Familia* (1997, *Tunisiennes/Girls from a Good Family*) and his *ʿArāʾis Ṭein* (2002, *Poupées d'argile/Clay Dolls*): they all visualized the particular stories of a heterogeneous number of female characters while breaking social and religious taboos relating to gender roles, adultery, sex before marriage, nudity, interfaith relations, virginity, child molestation, and child labor, among other hot button issues. While both Bourguiba and Ben Ali encouraged and even cultivated the rhetoric of women's rights hoping that it might appropriate attention away from their authoritarian conduct, male filmmakers have approached the treatment of female issues in their films as a rehearsal, or allegorical detour of sorts, to broach politics proper.

I find Moufida Tlatli's observation here of particular relevance to the indirect routes or figurative detours that male filmmakers take in their cinematic dissidences:

> I often wondered why it was that male directors should be so preoccupied with the question of women. Until I realized that, for them, woman was symbol of freedom of expression, and of all kinds of liberation. It was like a litmus test for Arab society: if one could discuss the liberation of women then one could discuss other freedoms.[5]

Each of the films I mentioned above and many more I have not mentioned constitute, at least retrospectively, a continuum of visual dissidence and critique that is of paramount importance to an understanding of the long-term and cumulative cultural forces that have propelled the popular protests following Bouazizi's suicide attempt on December 17, 2010.

In what follows I focus on a handful of films that I believe to be fairly representative of the diverse but cohesive critical venture of postcolonial Tunisian cinema. Nouri Bouzid's *Man of Ashes* and Férid Boughedir's *Halfaouine* along with Moufida Tlatli's *The Silences of the Palace* and Mahamed Zran's *Essaïda* as well as Moncef Dhouib's *The TV's Coming* chart a subtle genealogy of dissent from normative representations of Tunisia, Tunisianness in mainstream media, history, and state rhetoric. The crucial importance of these films lies in their ability to challenge the sociocultural status quo and form the basis for challenging the governmental and political state apparatus itself. The obsession with sex and the female body in Tunisian cinema bespeaks an allegorical obsession with the body politic. Breaking sociocultural taboos has become a style of political expression and subversion in its own right. And why not? Dissidence is contagious: once you practice it somewhere, the chances are you will be able to practice it elsewhere, even in the forbidden realm of grand politics, which had been practically unheard of in Ben Ali's Tunisia until December 17, 2010.

Moufida Tlatli's *The Silences of the Palace* (1994, *Ṣamt al-Quṣūr*)
Set in beylical Tunisia (the Hussein dynasty of Beys 1705–1957), which is technically part of the Ottoman Empire but in reality a French protectorate, *Silences* travels back and forth (through the cinematic economy of the flashback) between Tunisia on the eve of independence and postcolonial Tunisia, ten years later, in order to compare and contrast the fate of the nation and that of its male and female subjects, particularly Alia, the protagonist. The aim of *Silences* is not only to reclaim the lived experiences and expose the unspoken sufferings of women servants (who were practically slaves) under the beys but also to assess the extent to which the independence of Tunisia from French colonialism has intersected with their emancipation from patriarchal bondage. The fervent and enlightened nationalist Lotfi (Sami Bouajila) had already assured the young Alia (Hend Sabri) of this promissory future before she eloped with him the night her mother died trying to abort the child resulting from the recent rape by the evil Bey character, Si Bechir (Hichem Rostom): "You're as indecisive as our country. One word thrills you, the next scares you," Lotfi reproaches the young Alia, before reassuring her, "Things are going to change. A new future awaits us. You will be a great singer. Your voice will enchant everyone."

In the very same manner that many are now questioning whether anything significant has really changed after the January 14 popular revolution in Tunisia, the adult Alia (Ghalia Lacroix) went through that same process of questioning in the 1960s, only to find out that postcolonial Tunisia did not offer her a fate any different from that of her mother, Khedija (Amel Hedhili). After all, Lotfi proved more conditioned by the patriarchal constrains that sealed Alia's fate as an illegitimate child than by his idealistic vision of a free Tunisia, uninhibited by the past. After presenting the viewer with a series of extended flashbacks that recapture Alia's story in screen memory style (oscillating comparatively between past and present), the film ends ambivalently with Alia finally apprehending the extremity of her mother's suffering and addressing her in a moving inner monologue, expressive of Alia's entrapment and her defiance:

> I thought Lotfi would save me; I have not been saved. Like you, I've suffered, I've sweated. Like you, I've lived in sin. My life has been a series of abortions; I could never express myself; my songs were stillborn. And even the child inside me Lotfi wants me to abort. This child, however, I feel has taken root in me; I feel it bringing me back to life, brining me back to you. I hope it will be a girl; I'll call her Khedija.

Alia's decision to keep the baby can be seen as a sign of a better and fruitful future different from her abortive past, but it is simultaneously a *future past* in the sense that it is in the end nothing but a re-enactment of her mother's past insofar as her mother brought her up as an illegitimate child. Her choice not to obey Lotfi, however, is not something that her mother could have possibly chosen, let alone exercised. Here, it becomes clear that Alia's childhood rebelliousness against her mother's obeisance to the Beys served her well in her subsequent rebelliousness against Lotfi. Not only that: her courage to break the wall of silence on what was going on outside the palace and sing the forbidden national anthem in the middle of Sara's engagement party is at once a vindication of national and female self-determination.

This scene that constitutes the film's finale elevates Alia to a powerful yet vulnerable position: at the same time that she asserts her voice and the voice of a nation in the throes of a war for independence, her audience deserts her for fear of complicity and her mother passes away in a shadowy room in the palace following a failed attempt to perform an abortion on herself. Yet this seems to me to be an important lesson of the film that is of particular relevance to postrevolutionary Tunisia: the power and responsibility to speak up—when only few can—should necessarily override the fear of being left alone and exposed. This scene therefore acts as an economic foil to a previous very evocative scene in which Alia is portrayed—as if caught in a nightmare—screaming hysterically and running as fast as her legs could carry her toward the open gates of the palace after witnessing her mother being raped by Si Bechir, but the closer she gets to the gates, the faster the doors shut in front of her, locking her in—her scream visible but unhearable, muted but deafening, drowns in the crashing silence of the impervious night.

Even though the film is entitled *Silences of the Palace*, its ultimate goal is not only to show how agentive silence might be by virtue of being *endured* by the women servants thanks to their communal solidarity (where *ṣamt*, silence, equals *ṣumūd*, endurance), but also to point toward the inevitability of breaking or reneging the contract of silence that Khalti Hadda evokes when she says, "We are taught one rule in the palace: Silence." The image of the muted scream remains, however, a poetic epitaph to generations and generations of Tunisian women whose voices were forever lost in the chatter of nationalist discourse: their particular stories of pain and suffering were real but never saw the light. The image of the muted scream raises the question of whether anything that happened and that is now lost without a trace could be belatedly acknowledged even if it cannot be verified. If Alia's scream cannot be heard, the question is not only whether it can be acknowledged but also whether it actually happened.

The challenge for *Silences* is to reclaim and reinscribe that scream which is not a scream. The poetic significance of the image of the muted scream derives primarily from the fact that it is performative of the very question that haunts the ethical and esthetic endeavors of the entire film: how much pain has gone into the making of the Tunisian postcolonial nationalist discourse and how much of it has gone unacknowledged either because it did not count or because there were no available means of counting and quantifying it (by virtue of its interiority). The image of the muted scream becomes of paramount importance here because it is the performative materialization of the interior scream that persists invisibly in the flesh even while it escapes or is denied signification. The slow-paced motion of the camera, the impeccable *mise-en-scène*, the slow rhythm of the film, and the accomplished editing as well as the measured deployment of close-up scenes and long shots might all be seen as aesthetic investments typical of art film, but they are here simultaneously thematic pursuits insofar as they map and signify in minute detail the unquantifiable silences that seal the fate of the women inside the palace and simultaneously inside their very own bodies (which they can neither own nor disown). *Silences* delivers a lasting lesson that the Tunisians who hurried to the streets to break the wall of fear and the media wall of silence and protest against corruption, cronyism, and the travesty of human rights know very well: silence about (sexual or political) abuse does not help overcome it.

Finally, the fact that we do not see the French colonial forces in action in the streets—but only hear about them indirectly through the radio or the conversations in the kitchen or upstairs—is in my view an allegory of the invisible forces of neocolonialism at work in Tunisia. Neither Alia, nor Lotfi, nor postcolonial Tunisia is fully free. Neither Tunisian men, Tunisian women, nor Tunisia itself are fully free from the conditions of bondage that continue to constrain their global postcolonial present. By bringing into intimate collisions multiple and multidirectional correspondences between men and women and their national state of affairs, the film presents itself as a literal allegory of discontent inside Tunisia (as a postcolonial nation gone awry) and outside Tunisia (as a postcolonial nation still very much in the pull of the former colonizer). The film is nothing less than a call for action: to complete the decolonial project of freedom from injustice. It is an allegory of nationhood only in the sense that it literalizes the crisis of the postcolonial nation in the making.

Nouri Bouzid's 1986 *Man of Ashes* (*Riḥ Essed*)

Film represents for Tlatli what music in the film represents for Alia: a means of expression and empowerment. Alia's scream after she witnesses Si Bechir rape her mother comes muted not because it is less of a scream, but because in order for a scream to be a scream it needs to be heard and acknowledged. The muted scream puts the viewer on the qui vive for any signals or instances of injustice that might go unnoticed because of a lack of vigilance and empathy on our part and not necessarily because of a lack of means of expression on the part of the originator of the scream. The subaltern screams, but if they are not heard, did they really scream? The organizing principle of narrative in *Silences* is the following question: Does a scream that is not heard count? What counts as a scream and what counts as less than a scream? This very same set of questions has also been broached by Nouri Bouzid in his directorial début, *Man of Ashes*, as the protagonist of the film searches in vain for an empathic ear capable of listening to the story of his childhood rape by his master carpenter.

Man of Ashes chronicles the experiences of two childhood friends, Hachemi (Imad Maalal) and Farfat (Khaled Ksouri)—the former is about to tie the knot while the latter is kicked out of his father's house following the swirl of rumor, gossip, and street graffiti that call his manhood into question. When they were apprenticed youths, Hachemi and Farfat were molested by their carpentry mentor, Ameur (Mustafa Adouani); they both grew up indelibly marked and bound by this secret trauma. Now that that traumatic and tragic episode has come back to haunt them, they find themselves frantically scrambling for a final exit. There follows their obsessions with and anxieties over their virility, masculinity, and manhood within an allegedly heterosexual community they can neither desert nor reintegrate into.

Bouzid shrewdly broaches the question of homosexuality in Tunisia (and in the entire Arab Muslim world) through the crime of child molestation. The film not only exposes the naturalized hypocrisy and moral vagaries of a society in which homosexual panic overrides pederasty, but also distinguishes unequivocally between masculinity and manhood on the one hand, and between homosociality and homosexuality on the other. The bond between Hachemi and Farfat is homosocial and not homosexual. Bouzid is interested not only in raising the question of homosexuality to challenge sexual heteronormativity, but also in underscoring the extent to which homosexual panic has come to undermine homosocial bonds in Arab societies. In the brothel scene at the end of the film, for instance, homosocial desire quickly gives way to homosexual panic which, in turn, gives way to the reassertion of normative heterosexuality, best illustrated by the rivalry between Farfat and Azaiez (Mohamed Dhrif) to sleep with one of the two prostitutes.

While Tlatli's film stretches colonial and postcolonial times, Bouzid's film situates itself squarely in postcolonial Tunisia and in the post-1967 Arab world where the culture of defeat (and defeatism) became rampant. Bouzid's main interest is to examine how Hachemi's and Farfat's generation was penetrated by adult violence and its enduring psychic demarcations in the very same manner that Palestine was raped and dispossessed by Israel following the 1967 Six Day War. In other words, and as Jeffrey Ruoff rightly suggests, "While Bouzid's cinema is conscious of defeat, it is not defeatist."[6] More precisely, Bouzid is interested in the privatized experience of defeat that is at once structural (pertaining to being human) and historical (pertaining to being Arab at this particular historical juncture). Bouzid argues:

> What interests me in this business of defeat is the idea that the conflict is internal. Not only internal, the conflict is borne by every individual and it cannot

> be settled except by each individual. *The Man of Ashes* was a notable film in this respect, it was almost a key film, and that continued with *The Golden Horseshoes*. The first film speaks of the destruction and rape of a child; the second speaks of another form of destruction and rape of an adult.[7]

Specifically, *Golden Horseshoes* retells Bouzid's own experience of torture during his imprisonment for more than five years (1973–9) because of his political involvement in the leftist movement Perspectives. Bouzid's film—which was released shortly after Bourguiba's deposition from power in 1987—is a very bold indictment of Bourguiba's clampdown on leftists, his abuse of human rights by systematic recourse to repressing, torturing, and "disappearing" his political opponents. Like the carpenter-father in *Man of Ashes*, Bourguiba saw himself as the father of Tunisia and Tunisians, a father who would not hesitate to sacrifice (in an Abrahamesque fashion) some of them. Both Bouzid's films aspire to transform this Abrahamesque and sacrificial relationship to the father of the nation (and to all the powers that be) into an oedipal relationship and therefore rebellious confrontation. His revisionary approach to Tunisia's and the Arab world's postcolonial history through the lenses of defeat should not only be understood as an expression of discontent but also as an allegorical conjuration of a future free from injustice.

By staging broken and defeated individuals to Tunisian audiences, Bouzid not only makes it possible for viewers to identify with and distance themselves from those individuals on the screen, but also—and simultaneously—offers them an opportunity to immunize themselves against the psychology of defeat and the state apparatuses that perpetuate it. In the final analysis, the cinematic tendency to grapple with and visualize the experience of defeat indirectly becomes the basis for fostering strategies of empowerment.[8]

Férid Boughedir's 1990 *Halfaouine: Boy of the Terraces* (*'Asfūr al-Sṭaḥ*)

Toward the end of *Man of Ashes*, Farfat kills Ameur, exacting a long overdue vengeance on the man who "initiated" him sexually and professionally. Interestingly, however, while the plan to kill Ameur was premeditated, it only happened following Farfat's sexual encounter with one of the prostitutes in the brothel. After raising the question of homosexuality, the film seems to settle for normative heterosexual practice as the midwife to Farfat's manhood, revenge, and freedom from the trammels of the past. Farfat has at last become what he wanted to be at the beginning of the film, "a rooftop bird": at the same time that he is portrayed in the film's finale running away from the police, jumping in front of a moving train, and leaping across rooftops, the graffiti that called his manhood into question was being erased. While the film ends with Farfat's ultimate conformity to a conservative and patriarchal apparatus of manhood, its goal is to expose and critique it rather than to reenact and reinscribe it. The same can be said about Boughedir's *Halfaouine* where the rituals of becoming man in patriarchal society are unraveled in greater detail and far lighter register than *Man of Ashes*.

Halfaouine is the story of Noura (Selim Boughedir), a boy going through the trials of puberty and trying to reconcile the demands of his body to those of the social body and vice versa. Not infrequently, he gets confused about what he wants and what is wanted from him by those around him and thus he finds himself attempting to reconcile irreconcilables. For instance, his impatience to join the club of men matches only his eagerness to retain the privileges of childhood, namely accompanying his mother to the women's hammam to gaze at local beauties and satisfy his growing sexual curiosity. Boughedir assembles an inventory of the different steps involved in Noura's becoming a man, which include circumcision, banishment from the women's hammam, and, above all, sex. Little wonder, then, that Noura's first sexual experience with an orphan-girl servant leads immediately to his revolt against his father, Si Azzouz (Mustapha Adouani), which is a signal of his triumphant resolution of the oedipal struggle and mastery of the fear of castration—really, his ascension to manhood (qua masculinity/virility).

The importance of *Halfaouine* from a postrevolutionary perspective lies not only in Noura's ability to break through all the spatial and gendered boundaries that regiment the private and the public (which is never more to be desired than in the political life of a police state in which secrecy is of the essence of governance), but also in his exposure to political dissidence as an indispensable component of responsible manhood. Noura witnesses the arrest of Salih (Mohammed Driss), an unmarried cobbler, playwright, musician, and public opponent of Bourguiba's obsolete dictatorship, particularly in the 1980s when his health deteriorated and his neurotic obsession with power bordered on psychosis. It bears mentioning here that the scene in which Noura asks Salih, "When does one become a man?" is followed immediately by one in which Noura helps Salih stand on an upturned bucket to cross out the graffiti on the wall that reads, "Our Leader's idea is all that matters" and to write above it, "Our idea is all that matters and without a Leader," which is an apt and prophetic qualification of the Tunisian revolution.

Mahamed Zran's 1996 *Essaïda*

Zran's directorial debut, *Essaïda*, delves into the living conditions of a popular neighborhood (Essaïda, part of the bidonville around Tunis) to expose the socio-political reality of Tunisia in the mid-1990s at a time when it entered de facto into the global economy by signing an association agreement with the European Union. The neoliberal restructuring of the economy, however, aggravated rather than resolved the problem of unemployment and fostered a culture of corruption, crime and cronyism that affected all Tunisians except the very few at the top who were its beneficiaries. The film starts with a chance encounter in downtown Tunis between Amine (Hichem Rostom), a painter in search of a source of inspiration, and Nidal (Chadli Bouzayen), a wretched youngster begging for money. Nidal's gaze, which condenses Essaïda's (and Tunisia's) many stories of poverty, pain, and suffering, captivates the attention of Amine such that he offers Nidal money to draw portraits of him. Eventually, Amine moves on to live in Essaïda to experience firsthand life in a popular neighborhood where poverty, crime, and unemployment prevail. As if immersing himself completely in the world of Nidal and Essaïda would not be complete by relocating there, Amine breaks up with Sonia (Myriam Amarouchene), his fiancée who drives a fancy car and lives in Carthage, insulated from the everyday reality of the lives of the majority of Tunisians.

As an engaged filmmaker, Zran finds in Amine the artist the mouthpiece for the expression of his own cinematic preoccupations and in his portraits, especially the final portrait of the entire neighborhood, an apt metaphor for his own socialist realist portrayal of Essaïda in the film. By making Amine descend from his Carthage ivory tower, where he lived with his fiancée, Zran is not only advocating that art should return to social reality, but is also decrying how out of touch artists, not to mention the politicians in Palace Carthage, have become with what is going on at the margins of the capital and the coastal cities, in the interior, and in the southern parts of Tunisia, where the latest protests that led to Ben Ali's deposition began.

Zran's *Essaïda* takes us on a disturbing journey through the life of Nidal, a downtrodden youth, chronically beaten by his father and ostracized by his peers, as he begs, steals, and eventually kills to make money. There is nothing special about Nidal, Zran seems to suggest: he is every Tunisian youth insofar as he dreams of a better life. Nidal might be somewhat eccentric to aspire to be smuggled into the United States rather than into Italy or France (both of which he thinks are already full of Arabs), but we cannot fail to read in his gaze the bitterness and adversity of life in Essaïda, life in Ben Ali's Tunisia.

This bitterness is best captured at the end of the film. When chased by the police for murdering a cab driver, Nidal deserts his motorbike, climbs up a tall, high-voltage steel tower, and starts screaming loudly at the crowds pleading with him to come down: "I'm fed up with you, do you not hear me? I'm going to die here in front of you and you will all be relieved. I want to live. I'm fed up, fed up." In the end, Nidal shows compliance with his pleading father and starts descending from the tower, only to accidentally fall or deliberately jump to certain death. Zran's *Essaïda* paints a bleak vision of Ben Ali's Tunisia which, needless to say, has proven prophetic in the wake of Mohammad Bouazizi's self-immolation in Sidi Bouzid. Even while the film had prophesied and cautioned about Bouazizi's suicidal protest through Nidal's, it is tragically ironic that its full lesson had not been learned then. It's disturbingly ironic that that lesson has not yet been learned in postrevolutionary Tunisia, and that several young men have already committed suicidal acts to protest against the practices of the postrevolutionary interim governments who have so far not fully achieved any of the goals of the revolution: easing the challenge of unemployment by drawing foreign investments and creating jobs; offering reparations to the families of the martyrs and curing the injured; bringing the members of the old regime to justice; reforming the justice and media systems; and, above all, fighting corruption, which is still the burning issue. If suicide has become a fashionable form of protest for some observers, it is because they have not been attentive to or have failed to attend to the visionary tale of Zran's *Essaïda* and the cautionary implications of Nidal's fate.

Dhouib's 2006 *The TV's Coming* (*Ettelvza Jāyya*)

Moncef Dhouib's *The TV's Coming* was released in 2006, the same year that Tunisia was celebrating the fiftieth anniversary of its independence from France. While a celebratory mood runs throughout the film, the main thrust of director Dhouib is clearly to poke fun at the rosy rhetoric of state nationalism and the ways in which mainstream media (here, TV and radio) have become the vehicle (and as such the engineer) of a false and fabricated reality that boasts of democracy, stability, and prosperity. Not even El-Malga, a remote village in the interior of the country (where the film is set) is immune from the poison of simulated happiness, overall festiveness, and enthused consent to support and serve the powers that be in Palace Carthage.

The satirical unfolding of the plot of the film is set in motion following a phone call from a top official in the capital informing Fitouri (Ammar Bouthelja), the leader of the village's cultural committee, that a German TV crew will be coming for a visit the next month. We later learn that the German crew is coming to make a documentary about the deadly scorpions of North Africa in the hope that they might find a vaccine, but Fitouri thinks they will be making a documentary about the village. The entire script of the film hinges on this miscommunication which is not revealed to viewers until the very end of the film. The scramble of the cultural committee to primp itself for the imminent visit, however, becomes symptomatic of the ways in which the official rhetoric of postcolonial Tunisia dissimulates its moral bankruptcy and simulates colorful images of stability and prosperity for both local and foreign consumption. In no small measure, this is the poison for which Ben Ali's Tunisia did not bother looking for a cure but let it spread to the entire country until it was out of control and had taken Bouazizi's life as well as those of many other innocent people.

When, at the beginning of the film, a Tunisian official makes a visit to the village on National Tree Day, he is presented with various kinds of bribes which he declined, to the dismay of the villagers. The German crew, however, would be served differently: they are presented with a version of Tunisian history that is friendly to Euro-sensibilities and therefore sanitized from any forms of offensive authenticity. Hence, a Sufi group is, for instance, instructed to clean up its act and not follow its own singular path of dances and trances, and the owner of a local café full of jobless villagers is instructed to host fake book and newspaper readers to give a good and positive impression about El-Malga (and by implication Tunisia) to the Germans and Europeans.

The film is saturated with jokes and comic encounters but its ultimate goal is didactic and critical. It exposes how Tunisian officialdom was able to produce and disseminate a totally falsified image of Tunisia to Tunisians and non-Tunisians alike while unemployment, corruption, and national disillusionment were briskly thrusting the country to the brink of insurrection. The satiric comic register has commonly been used by playwrights and comedians in postcolonial Tunisia to evade state censorship and deliver sociopolitical critique. Dhouib's film is no exception. The risks attached to this register are common: neither the message nor the messenger may be taken seriously. This is perhaps the point at which the indirect medium of cinema, with its satirical detours and allegory of discontent, needs to be complemented by the more content-oriented style of rap music.

From compliance to defiance: from mizwid to rap

> A lot of the music that comes from here, from the region, is pop. It's all the same and it isn't art. They're making harmful actions to arts, actually. There's no engagement. And music without engagement isn't art.
>
> El Général[9]

When asked in early June 2011 by the private radio station Mosaïque FM whether he preferred rap music or *mizwid*,[10] Rachid Ghannouchi, the leader of Ennahda—the previously banned Islamic party and now one of the major players in Tunisia's postrevolutionary coalition government—did not hesitate to say "rap." When asked again by Samir Elwafi three months later about the kind of music he listens to, he singled out rap and applauded it for its contribution to the Tunisian revolution.[11] It is distinctly ironic that an Islamic party leader who has been routinely dismissed by his detractors as a "regressivist," "salafi," and "integrist" (or, in the Tunisian dialect, *khwānjī*, a derogative, if not incriminating, reference to the Muslim Brothers) should opt for the more "liberal" and "progressive" choice—rap music—over the more traditional and culturally authentic one—mizwid. Yet, there is method in Ghannouchi's choice of rap over mizwid. While mizwid contributed to the entrenchment and longevity of Ben Ali's regime, rap helped in the insurrectionary civic effort to dismantle it.

Mizwid came to Tunisia from Sudan and Libya in the late nineteenth century and then became the favorite means of entertainment for colonized Tunisians in farms and plantation fields, which is why the gestures of dance that accompany the music and singing initially tended to emulate and re-enact those very same gestures of menial labor. In other words, mizwid had been a very convenient, not to say pacifying, genre of music for French colonialism insofar as it channeled (that is, released and neutralized) whatever pent-up anger Tunisians must have had against the colonial system. Even when it staged socioeconomic miseries and mishaps, it simultaneously offered itself as a means of escape from them. In the wake of independence and the rural exodus to Tunis, mizwid had spread in the shanty towns surrounding the capital and become the main form of working-class entertainment. Despite the crucial psychosocial role it played in the daily lives of menial workers, it had quickly been categorized as a sign of cultural decadence, not only because of its lowbrow language but also because of its association with violence, sex, and the consumption of alcohol. No wonder, then, that under Bourguiba's rule mizwid was dismissed as a form of cultural degradation and was banned from national TV.

Yet, notwithstanding its reputed notoriety and overall marginalization, mizwid continued to flourish on the outskirts of mainstream culture, especially with the rise of Imail al-Hattab, Salah al-Farzit, and al-Hedi Habbouba as creative and diverse mizwid artists. By the time Ben Ali took power, mizwid had become the unacknowledged opium of everyday Tunisians, widely popular yet frantically quarantined from the public sphere. Unlike the Francophile and eccentric Bourguiba, Ben Ali, a military general and security agent by training, did not hold mizwid in popular disfavor. On the contrary, Ben Ali must have recognized the "virtues" of mizwid in depoliticizing Tunisians, and this is partly why after his ascendance to power it became the hegemonic form of popular music par excellence.[12] Note, for instance, that the first time that mizwid was broadcast on national TV was in 1988, just a few months after Ben Ali's assumption of power on November 7, 1987. While the broadcast was immediately met with public outcry against indecency and cultural decadence, mizwid was gradually and programmatically hammered home in the end, especially after the wide success of the 1991 *nuba* show, a hybrid spectacle that stealthily grafted mizwid performances onto spiritual and religious dances and songs.

By the end of the millennium, it had become all too obvious that the hegemony of the mizwid industry matched only the culture of corruption that Ben Ali's regime fostered. Not that mizwid stars such as Hedi Donia, Hedi Habbouba, Samir Loucif, Fawzi Ben Gamra, Lotfi Jermana, Noureddin el-Kahlaoui, Fatma Bousaha, and Zina el-Gasriniya somehow conspired to encourage corruption, but that they, like other popular icons, artists, and beneficiaries of the entertainment industry writ large, did very little, if anything, to raise awareness of the political and ideological origins of most of the derivative sociocultural issues they had been wont to address in their popular songs. Given mizwid's predilection for dance rhythms over lyrics, which mostly revolved around social, family, and emotional matters or more or less empty verbiage, it has hardly ventured into subjects even remotely political.

At the same time that Ben Ali encouraged mizwid, he forced all the musical groups and singers that were practicing what was called *al-ughniya al-multazima* ("committed song") to either turn to commercial music or go underground, if not give up their careers altogether. Many talented musicians and promising musical groups (such as Amel al-Hamrouni, Mohamed Bhar, al-Baḥth al-Mousīqī, ʿUshāq al-Waṭan, Awled al-Manājim) have subsequently given up singing or gone underground in the late 1980s and early 1990s while others who opted for commercial music prospered and became pop stars in Tunisia and across the Arab world (such as Lotif Boushnaq, Latifa al-Arfaoui, and Amina Fakhit).[13] The same set of choices was later offered to rappers and rap crews. Some of them took the more beneficial path while others stayed the course despite the complete crackdown on their activities (concerts, recordings, and dissemination). Until it came to popular attention in the early years of the new millennium with the rise of Balti as the first professional rapper, Tunisian rap remained more or less obscure (not to say absent) in the 1980s and 1990s, so much so that mizwid was perceived by many as Tunisia's indigenous version of or cultural equivalent to Algerian raï and/or American rap music.[14]

Despite its subsequent discomfiting complicity with Ben Ali's regime (as is variably the case with Wled Bled, Balti, Wajdi, Mascott, T-Men, DJ Costa, and others), Tunisian rap music had initially emerged as a democratizing force not only in the field of music and arts as a whole where a great number of marginalized youth found in it a viable career path and an accessible means to intervene in the highly commercial and competitive fiefdoms of mizwid and pop culture, but also in the public sphere where rappers adopted an activist agenda and spoken loudly in the name of the poor and underprivileged, conveying their political and socioeconomic malaise to the powers that be. Unlike mizwid, which foregrounded dance over lyrics (especially in the *R'boukh* version), the intensely content-based form of Tunisian rap music made it immediately amenable to transparent, straightforward, and dense yet unequivocal articulations of popular sentiments and sociopolitical grievances as well as of transformative, feasible, and perfectible futures.

After more than a decade, from the early experiments of Slim Larnaout, Wled Bled, T-Men, Filozof, and FTR, among others, in the 1990s to Balti's unprecedented commercial success in the early years of 2000, rap music had increased in popularity but its overall weight paled into insignificance in comparison with that of mizwid. Its novelty (unaccompanied by a daring political message) was nothing new for Tunisians, nor much of a threat to mizwid's popularity as the main engine of popular entertainment, not to say of mass diversion and distraction. Few courageous Tunisian rappers, however, were adamant about turning rap into an agent of political critique (and not just a means of social criticism, as was the case with Balti, Nizar T-Men and others). Lak3y, Delahoja, Psyco M and El Général, among very few others, took rap where everyone else feared to tread—to the realm of sociopolitical critique (which was, it bears mentioning here, of foundational importance to the rise and prominence of American rap from Grandmaster Flash to 2Pac and Public Enemy).

In 2005, the young rapper Lak3y (aka Mohamed Ben Salem) from the coastal city of Bizerte organized an antigovernment concert in which he tore down an RCD (Constitutional Democratic Rally, Ben Ali's party) banner hung by RCD representatives over the stage. This earned him a good beating after the concert by a handful of Ben Ali's policemen. Lak3y went underground afterwards, but he continued to be active in Tunisia's largely amateur and obscure rap scene until he came to prominence with his December 2010 prorevolutionary hit, "Touche Pas à Ma Tunisie" ("Don't Touch My Tunisia"). His earlier hit adopted an ironic title, "Tounes Bikhayr" ("Tunisia is well-off"), in order to debunk the official governmental rhetoric that Tunisia is a well-off society. Lak3y exposes socioeconomic inequality, cronyism, and the culture of corruption in a language and underground style similar to El Général's "Rais Lebled." The same can be said here about DJ Costa's "Royal Mafia" and Fami DKF's "Révolution," both of which convey searing criticisms of Ben Ali's system without naming names.

In the same year, another Tunisian rapper, Férid El Extranjero (aka Delahoja), an original member of Filozof, released a damning song titled "3bed Fi Terkina" ("People in a Prison Corner"), which exposed police brutality, the use of torture, and the overall ruthlessness of Ben Ali's criminal regime. The song begins as follows: "We live in a prison corner, our flesh is cut with a knife/Not only that, but the police insult and humiliate us/Poverty, woes and problems—it's a fish-eat-fish world." Delahoja released the song from Spain, where he has now lived for quite some time after short stays in Italy and France. He has experienced firsthand police brutality, imprisonment, and humiliation; he left Tunisia in the late 1990s following a fight with a policeman who insulted and cursed him and his family. He released the song upon his return to Spain after a short stay in Tunisia in 2005 (during which he was, not surprisingly, arrested at the airport). The song contained a few explicit words, but its language was on the whole nowhere near as explicit as the language of the notorious Karkadan or Mos Anif Mossa.[15] When the song reached Tunisia and became an underground hit, it drew the attention of Ben Ali's police, which exerted further pressure on rappers and left them with very limited choices. Delahoja was officially banned from re-entering the country. Many went back underground while others were more than ever convinced that they should stick to commercial rap and steer clear of political subjects. Chief among the latter group is Balti, whose career thrived, while others' careers were further jeopardized.[16]

The venture of Tunisian rap music had taken a completely sociopolitical turn by the year 2010, the same year that the United Nations General Assembly proclaimed, following Ben Ali's initiative, International Youth Year. Little did Ben Ali know at the time that those very youth he championed would initiate his eventual deposition from power after twenty-three years of authoritarian rule. At the same time that an orchestrated campaign calling on Ben Ali to run for the 2014 presidential elections was well underway (backed up by a petition that sixty-five Tunisian celebrities and public figures allegedly signed), rappers, along with a wide range of youth spokespersons, cyberactivists, dissident politicians, and journalists, initiated a counter-campaign calling for democratization.

Rap music has become more and more vocal and controversial in its critique of social and public issues that range from drugs, prostitution, and corruption to sound pollution (namely, the proposal that called for the reduction of the volume of *adhan*, or call for prayer, a proposal that launched a public uproar). B4 Clan decried the proposal in their song, "Contre-Attaque" ("Counter-Attack"), and several other rappers and rap crews did the same, all the while calling for a revalorization of Islam and Islamic values. Because Ben Ali's regime denigrated everyday Islamic practices (e.g., intimidation and harassment of veiled women and bearded men, mosque-goers, and so on), Tunisian rap took a more and more Islamic bent insofar as it denounced moral bankruptcy, the loosening of traditional values, and the rampancy of corruption. Apart from El Général's "Rais Lebled," two songs in particular gave rise to public controversy and brought rap to unprecedented musical prominence in 2010.

Balti's "Passe Partout" (a damning portrait with real pictures of Tunisian girls as prostitutes and one-night-standers) provoked public responses from parents and families as well as from rappers (such as DJ Costa, Emino, and Lotfi Abdelli who collaborated on "Chawahtou som3et lebled," or "You Stained the Reputation of the Country," a response song and corrective to Balti's invective) because one version of the video clip contained the pictures of real Tunisian girls caught on camera partying in various nightclubs. The shots of the anonymous girls featured were not particularly flattering, even though it was later found out that the pictures were actually taken from Facebook pages and edited by Balti's fans into the original clip of the song which did not contain any such pictures. At any rate, the song provoked so much brouhaha, rage, and fury that it officially gave rise to the phenomenon of "rap clashes," long associated with the West Coast/East Coast rivalries and diatribes between Tupac Shakur and Notorious B.I.G. and later between Nas and Jay-Z. Despite his cooption by Ben Ali's regime, Balti can be credited for writing songs that contain a measure of constructive ambiguity capable of igniting controversy and debate, which is not a negligible feat within dictatorships. Constructive ambiguity here means simply the attempt to raise questions indirectly about the regime's social and cultural policies, not to mention its moral values insofar as they are reflected in the video clip.

The other shock-song is "Manipulation" by Psyco M (aka Mohamed El Jandoubi). The song was released later in the year and mounted a sweeping attack on, among others, Arab nationalists and secularists alike, accusing them of involvement in a Euro-Zionist plot against Islam. The fifteen-minute song included an explicit attack on such public figures as Sawsen Maalej, an actress who used to appear regularly on Nessma TV, and Olfa Youssef, the author of the highly contentious book *Ḥayrat Muslima* (The Bewilderment of a Muslim Woman). Maalej and Youssef created a public uproar, the former for making an explicit reference to the male sexual organ of her colleague on a popular TV show and the latter for pointing out that the Qur'an is inconclusive about female inheritance, homosexuality, and masturbation, among other hot-button issues. Both ended up filing a defamation suit against Psyco M following the serious toll the song took on their reputation and the death threats they received because of its high-speed cyber-reach.

Filmmaker Nouri Bouzid had also filed a complaint against Ennahda and Psyco M whom he accuses of issuing a death threat against him in a public rally organized by Ennahda on April 17, 2011. The lyrics of the song in question, "La Guerre Psychologique" ("Psychological War") express Psyco M's passing wish to use a "Kalashnikov" on all those behind the global media campaign against Islam, including Nouri Bouzid whose films allegedly disparage Islam and equate it with terrorism. The song, however, dates back to 2009, when Ennahda was not officially in business. In his defense, Psyco M claimed that he used the word "Kalashnikov" metaphorically to refer to the powers and devastating effects of his rhymes. As for Bouzid, he pointed out time and again that he was not troubled by Psyco M as an artist whose right to artistic freedom ought to remain intact, but rather by the regressivist-salafi ideologies that inform his songs.

Many have associated Psyco M, who was banned from performing under Ben Ali, with extremism, fanaticism, and fundamentalist trends spearheaded by the unlicensed Hizb al-Tahrir (Liberation Party), whose central political project revolves around the reinstitution of the Islamic Caliphate. Others, however, support him for his bravery and informed invectives against the equally orthodox and fundamentalist tendencies of some Francophile secularists. Psyco M was elected the best rapper for 2010 on Facebook, where he enjoys a great reputation not only as a provocateur rapper but also as an anti-imperialist (albeit ideologically driven) artist.

Notwithstanding the regressivist-salafi tendencies of his songs, Psyco M has clearly emerged as one of the effortless masters of the flow, oftentimes associated with the Algerian rapper Lotfi Double Kanon who also enjoys a good reputation in Tunisia. The sheer length and scope, not to mention the amount of information and provocation contained in his lyrics, combine to make of Psyco M easily one of the most important, albeit controversial, rappers in the entire Arab world.

It might be a contradiction in terms for rappers to adopt a non-traditional musical genre such as rap music to preach a return to traditional Islamic values, but this is surely the logical outcome of Ben Ali's corrupt and corrupted secularist practices. Despite his notoriety and the controversial nature of his songs, the importance of Psyco M lies in the fact that he clearly upped the ante of critique and paved the way for the emergence of raw criticisms of Ben Ali's regime. Other rappers soon followed suit while few others consolidated further their already contestatory credentials, including Guito'N, RTM, Weld el 15, Wistar, Gadour, L'Imbattable, Mohamed Ali Ben Jemaa, Black Eye, Sincero, Kenzi, and, above all, El Général.

El Général took on the risky task of sending direct messages to Ben Ali twice. The first was titled "Sidi El-Rais" ("Mr. President") and was not substantially different from his second and now greatest claim to national and international fame, "Rais Lebled" ("Head of State"). Like Psyco M and several other rappers and rap crews, El Général called for the revalorization of Islam and Islamic values, but he went way further than most and addressed not only the sensitive question of state oppression and repression, but also, and above all, the question of corruption. In a leaked cable, the US ambassador to Tunis, Robert F. Godec, called corruption the "elephant in the room": every Tunisian knows about it but no one dares to address it. El Général dared the president to step down from his ivory tower in Palace Carthage and make a real field trip to the gray zones of Tunisia (and not the kind of "surprise" but elaborately planned and premeditated trips he had been known for since the early years of his presidency). He addressed Ben Ali in the persona of a schoolboy, as evidenced by the opening footage from one of Ben Ali's 1990s surprise trips to two underdeveloped areas in the interior of the country.

El Général's lyrics are raw and frank but his style is on the whole diplomatic, which is why the song worked quite well with audiences worldwide and was seductive and persuasive even to Ben Ali's supporters. The refrain of the song paints an apocalyptic picture of Tunisia and has become the rallying cry of protests from Avenue Bourguiba to Tahrir Square:

Rais lebled, sha'bik met
Barsha 'bed mizibla klet
Hek tshouf esh qā'id ṣāyir fil-bled
Ma'āsī partout we'bed mal-qātish wīn tbet
Hānī niḥkī bi'sm eshsha'b illī tzalmū willī 'indāsū bissubbāṭ

Mr. President, your people are dead
Many, today, on garbage fed
As you can obviously see what's going on nationwide,
Miseries everywhere and people find nowhere to sleep
I speak on behalf of those who were wronged and ground under feet

The audacity and courage of El Général's song is unmistakable, all the more so given that it was uploaded to Facebook at a time when Ben Ali was celebrating the twenty-third anniversary of his rise to power on November 7, 1987 (aka, the Blessed Change). The song was obviously censored and El Général arrested in a dramatic manner following presidential orders on January 6, 2011. By then the song had become the anthem of the uprising throughout the country, and El Général was released three days afterwards. Unlike many rap songs produced about the Arab revolutions after they unfolded, El Général's "Rais Lebled" was a leap in the dark, a sort of *cri-de-cœur* or scream, uttered way before the revolution started or took shape, at a time when very few would dare address Ben Ali publicly. No wonder he was celebrated by *Time* magazine as the seventy-fourth most influential person in the world, ahead of US president Barack Obama, FC Barcelona and Argentina soccer superstar Lionel Messi, and Israel's notorious prime minister Benjamin Netanyahu.

"Rais Lebled" has now become a classic in Tunisian and Arab rap music. It has been emulated by numerous wannabe MCs, and El Général's international recognition has resulted in an overdose of revolutionary and patriotic rap songs. Ben Ali and his wife, Leila Trabelsi, have excited much of the pent-up ire of postrevolutionary rappers but with the exception of those who were overtly or covertly the beneficiaries of Ben Ali's regime (like Balti and Mascott), most rappers hitched their wagon to the promissory train of the Revolution of Freedom and Dignity. In postrevolutionary Tunisia, all rappers (new and old) have become vociferous claimants to revolutionary credentials. While underground contestatory rap is now being commodified and coopted by the market economy, it remains unclear how it will remain on target as a politically engaged musical genre, shot through with insurrection and revolt. Counting more than a hundred new rappers, the postrevolutionary Tunisian rap scene is flourishing, for sure, but the political role of rap might well be in decline once its main thematic axis—the revolution—exhausts itself. Whether rap music will continue to exert pressure and garner the kind of attention it did in Tunisia during the revolution is yet to be seen but one thing is clear for now: post-Ben Ali regimes would be well advised to have open and perceptive ears because if they fail to listen, they will hardly survive the new brave voice of Tunisian youth, namely their favorite weapon of mass insurrection: rap music.

Notes

1. Arguably, the very creation of ERTT in 1961 and SATPEC in 1964 to facilitate the distribution of information and the production of local films came as a response to the refusal of a French laboratory to return the processed film of the massacre (of 1,300 Tunisians) the French army committed in Bizerte, northwestern Tunisia, in 1961. For more on the entanglements of cinema and state, see Florence Martin's short but

substantial account, "Cinema and State," in *Film in the Middle East and North Africa: Creative Dissidence,* ed. Josef Gugler (Austin, TX: University of Texas Press, 2011), 271–83.

2. See Kmar Kchir-Bendana, "*Ideologies of the Nation in Tunisian Cinema,*" *The Journal of North African Studies* 8.1 (2003): 38. The article offers an elegant panoramic view of Tunisian cinema around the question of nation and national identity (*tunisianité*). Whether or not, though, Tunisian cinema, as Kchir-Bendana concludes, is "obliged to organise and present itself as 'national cinema' in a market where it has to face other national cinemas" (42) remains a debatable contention that, if tenable, risks homogenizing both the production and the consumption of Tunisian cinema, which would not redound to anyone's benefit, except to that of the market industry.
3. See Hédi Khelil, *Le parcours et la trace: Témoignages et documents sur le cinéma tunisien* (Salammbô: MediaCon, 2002), 387.
4. See Roy Armes, *Post-colonial Images: Studies in North African Film* (Bloomington, IN: Indiana University Press, 2005), 48.
5. Laura Mulvey, "Moving Bodies: Interview with Moufida Tlatli," *Sight and Sound* 5.3 (1995): 18.
6. Jeffrey Ruoff, "The Gulf War, the Iraq War, and Nouri Bouzid's Cinema of Defeat: *It's Scheherazade We're Killing* (1993) and *Making of*," *South Central Review* 28.1 (2011): 31.
7. Nouri Bouzid, "On Inspiration," in *African Experiences of Cinema*, ed. Imruh Bakari and Mbye B. Cham (London: British Film Institute, 1996), 54.
8. For more on this, see Nouri Gana, "Bourguiba's Sons: Melancholy Manhood in Modern Tunisian Cinema," *The Journal of North African Studies* 15.1 (2010): 105–26.
9. See Lauren E. Bohn's interview with El Général, "Rapping the Revolution," *Foreign Policy*, July 22, 2011, accessed December 30, 2011, http://mideast.foreignpolicy.com/posts/2011/07/22/rapping_the_revolution.
10. *Mizwid* is Tunisia's most popular *sha'bi* or folk music whose name derives from the main instrument that accompanies the singing, i.e., the goatskin bagpipe. The interview with Ghannouchi occurred on June 6, 2011, on the radio program *Men Antom?* (*Who Are You?*).
11. The interview by Samir Elwafi took place on September 11, 2011, on his program *Fi Al- ṣarāḥa Rāḥa* (*In Frankness, there is Relief*), which airs weekly on the private TV channel Hannibal.
12. Under Ben Ali, 80 percent of the commercial recordings available on the Tunisian market and 70 percent of the cassettes sold by the company Phonie were of mizwid. See Kathryn Stapley, "Mizwid: An Urban Music With Rural Roots," *Journal of Ethnic and Migration Studies* 32.2 (2006): 254. Numbers are not necessarily very accurate but what is clear is that on several occasions in the last few years, many organizers of summer festivals have had recourse to mizwid stars (namely, Fatma Bousaha) to avoid bankruptcy.
13. It bears mentioning here that the names of Lotfi Bouchnaq, Latifa al-Arfaoui, Nabiha Karaouli, Amina Fakhit, Sonia M'barek, and Saber Reba'i appeared on a list of public figures calling on Ben Ali to run again for reelection in 2014. Bloggers and cyberactivists who made the list public called it the "list of shame" ("*Qā'imat al- 'ār*").
14. See Kathryn Stapley, "Mizwid: An Urban Music With Rural Roots," *Journal of Ethnic and Migration Studies* 32.2 (2006): 254.
15. One of Karkadan's early hits curses the day the police caught the rapper by surprise

at home, and the song is thus entitled "*Zokom ak nhar*" ("Fuck that Day"). Mos Anif Mossa's hit song "*Taḥchi Fih*" ("Liar") exposes the widespread culture of hypocrisy and lying that mediates all forms of sociality in Ben Ali's Tunisia.

16. Balti claims that he was summoned to the Ministry of the Interior for questioning after the release of Delahoja's devastating video. The experience further convinced Balti of the entailments or potential risks of treating political subjects in his music. Both Balti and Mascott participated in concerts during Ben Ali's electoral campaigns in 2004 and 2009. In his account, David Peisner relates how Balti became a "potential revenue source" for government officials and their business associates in ways that redounded to everyone's benefit (or share of the cake), see "Inside Tunisia's Hip-Hop Revolution," *Spin*, August 24, 2011, accessed April 25, 2012, www.spin.com/articles/inside-tunisias-hip-hop-revolution.www.spin.com/articles/inside-tunisias-hip-hop-revolution. After the revolution Balti made a song titled "Matloumounich," in which he tries to redeem himself, explaining why he steered clear of politics and recounting how he was routinely persecuted and arrested by Ben Ali's regime.

PART 3

Prospects: The Postrevolutionary Moment

unclear. I first examine the way in which the notion of civility was conceptualized by Ghannouchi before the revolution. I then show the challenges and pitfalls inherent to the transformation of this notion from a theoretical category of resistance to an operational category of governance.

Islam and democracy

Ghannouchi's theory of the compatibility of Islam and democracy has evolved around three related arguments: a postcolonial critique of the secularist ruling elite, a denunciation of the state hegemony over religion, and a call for the re-enactment of cultural authenticity.

Postcolonial critique

The French protectorate, Ghannouchi argues, has had a devastating effect on Tunisia's social structure and cultural identity. Ruining Tunisian authentic traditions, colonization left the country destroyed and disoriented. Moreover, French rule contributed to the formation of a westernized elite, who became increasingly fascinated by the Francophone-secular understanding of modernity and rejected its Arabic-Islamic roots as a form of backwardness. After independence, this westernized elite began oppressing the Tunisian people, in a way that mirrored French colonial rule. The authoritarian rule established by President Habib Bourguiba after 1956 was a consequence and reproduction of the colonial way of ruling. According to Ghannouchi, the opposition between oppressors and oppressed, rather than a conflict between religion and politics, is the relevant paradigm of analysis of Tunisian affairs in the postcolonial era.

> The conflict is not a religious one. Nor is it even a conflict between religion and the Western concept of secularism. It is a political conflict between the oppressor and the oppressed, between a people that has been struggling for its freedom and dignity, for power sharing as well as resource sharing, and an absolute corrupt ruler who has turned the state into a tool for repression. Like snakes, despotic rulers keep changing their skins. In the past Bourguiba practiced repression in the name of national unity, while Nassir did it in the name of liberating Palestine and uniting the Arabs. Today, it is practiced in the name of democracy, human rights, defending civil society, and making peace with Israel.[10]

In other words, secularism is rejected not as a form of arrangement of the relationship between religion and politics, but as the expression of an inauthentic mode of governance, imposed by the postcolonial elite.

State hegemony over religion

The corollary of this anti-domination approach is a denunciation of the monopolizing nature of the postcolonial nation state. In his struggle to modernize the country, President Bourguiba worked at diminishing the power of important institutions of civil society such as religious endowments, mosques, and charities. The personal status code of 1957 was primarily intended to dismantle tribes and social structures that could possibly threaten or unbalance the power of the state. Ghannouchi's rejection of secularism is essentially a consequence of his denunciation of state intrusion into people's minds, hearts, and customs. In order to assert state's hegemony over society, Bourguiba turned all religious institutions into a sort of "church," separate from, and controlled by, the state. "*Imams* in mosques are appointed by the state, which administers their affairs and may even dictate to them what to say and what not to say during the Friday sermons."[11]

The nationalization of religion by a secularist, westernized elite blocked the natural progress of Islamic thinking and threw Tunisian society into a state of ignorance and disarray. The key question, therefore, argues Ghannouchi, is not how to impose religion on politics, but how to liberate religion from the state. Democracy and the empowerment of civil society are the only remedy against the domination of what he calls a secular autocracy.

The search for authenticity

While strongly supporting the compatibility between Islam and democracy, Ghannouchi's thought remains structured around a series of binaries: tradition and modernity, society and state, Islam and secularism, despotism and democracy. The notion that there exists such a thing as an authentic cultural identity of Tunisia is central to the thought of Ennahda's leader. This authentic reality has allegedly been distorted by colonialism and nationalist-secular despotism. To the false modernity imposed by colonizers, Ghannouchi has long opposed a genuine, Islamic form of modernity. The argument for authenticity translates into a strong rejection of the liberal-secularist idea of a separation of spheres (private and public, religious and political). Ghannouchi's definition of the relationship between religion and politics is not an uncompromising one,[12] to the extent that he refuses the idea that beliefs and practice can be imposed on someone. He develops, however, a comprehensive view of politics, in which no separation between moral values and pragmatic affairs is needed. Ghannouchi speaks of development rather than of modernization. His understanding of development is based on a teleological, religiously inspired conception of history, whereby humanity's morality is meant to improve through scientific education and moral formation. In this process, the use of modern technologies and learning of modern scientific methods is perfectly commendable, but the notion of a separation between two distinct spheres of activities, religious and political, is dismissed as foreign and inauthentic. Human rights are defended within this teleological framework: they essentially designate the rights and duties of mankind to progress, i.e. to move away from its original condition of bestiality, barbarity, and ignorance. Ghannouchi's view resonates to a large extent with the notion, proposed by Iranian philosopher Abdelkarim Soroush,[13] of religious democracy. This concept defines a political situation where society is religious, but the state refrains from interfering with religious affairs, while allowing for the development of piety and virtue. The concept of religious democracy, just like Ghannouchi's notion of civil state, are contrary not to secularism as such, but rather to what is denounced as the moral relativism of liberalism.

Civility

In the past two decades, Ghannouchi has written extensively on the concept of civil society, which he sees at once as the victim of, and the solution to, the hegemony of the authoritarian state. Contrary to some Egyptian Islamic thinkers,[14] he insists on not giving up the term *madaniyya* to secularists. A cornerstone of a political order defined by innocuous state institutions, civil society represents both a form of political utopia and an ideal model of social contract. According to Ghannouchi, the Islamic movement plays a key role in revivifying this ideal model and in inverting the balance between the autocratic state and the weakened civil society:

> The Islamic Movement has succeeded in breathing a new life in civil society by tilting the balance in favour of the people's state rather than the state's people. This, and the potential threat it poses to the ruling autocracy, prompted the police state to intervene with all forms of repression and persecution, and with staging an election in which the president and his party won 99.99 percent of the votes.[15]

Civil society as described by Ghannouchi bears resemblance with the utopic Medina community, and defines a political order in which the will of the people had precedence over illegitimate state institutions. Pre-colonial Tunisian society was, according to him, close to such an ideal model: it was an autonomous, lively, self-regulating community that had succeeded in maintaining the integrity of its culture, language, and identity. The notion of civil society, while drawing upon this utopian model, also defines a rejection of the state of nature. The civil feeling of belonging to a same community (*umma*) replaces former tribal or ethnical allegiances. In this voluntary association, law, not passion, governs interpersonal relations. Good manners and civility, however, stem from the sharing of a common faith, not from the adhesion to secular principles. Likewise, the rule of law is meant to guarantee the improvement of the community's faith and virtue, rather than protect individuals from one another. According to Ghannouchi, faith feeds and protects civil sentiment. In contrast, the liberal, individualistic foundation of civility leads to the weakening and destruction of social relations. He uses the term *tawaḥush* (return to a state of barbarity) to describe the fake civility that characterizes liberal Western societies.[16]

Piety and civility are inextricably linked: the more pious people are, the more civil they become; and the more civil they are, the more pious they become. The state's function is reduced to a minimum: its main role is to enable citizens to become virtuous (civil and pious).[17] In this narrative, the secularist idea of a separation of worldly and otherworldly affairs is useless and counterproductive.[18] As explained by Gudrun Kramer, in such a political project

> the ruler is the agent and representative of the Muslim community, entrusted with executing god's law. He has no religious authority whatsoever, though some of his tasks such as the implementation of the Sharia or the propagation of the jihad, would by Western standards be classified as religious. Thus, while the state rests on a religious foundation, its leadership carries no religious sanction. It is to emphasize this distinction, [. . .] that many Muslim authors insist on saying that the ideal Islamic state is not a theocracy, which would be ruled by men of religion or a ruler of divine grace, but that it is a civil, or, to be more precise, a lay state.[19]

The state merely fulfills a technical function, but the essential objective of an Islamist policy, as defined by Ghannouchi, is to resist and block arbitrary rule.

To a certain extent, Islamists' notion of civility resonates with the concept of civil religion[20] as it is used to describe American understanding of religion and politics. The American paradigm of civil religion defines an order based on the principle of separation between church and state, but that recognizes a positive role of religion in the public space. Likewise, Ghannouchi vehemently rejects the state's interference with religious affairs. He does, however, advocate for the nurturing and development of a lively religious life within civil society: the society is all the more religious than the state is civil. Just as the notion of civil religion was originally crafted in a context defined by an understanding of America as an essentially Protestant country,[21] likewise the concept of civil state is closely linked, in the mind of Tunisian Islamists, with the idea of a nation that needs to reconnect with its Arab and Islamic heritage. From this point of view, civil religion and civil state are arguably two comparable expressions of nationalist projects. The two normative models found a political order where plurality is theoretically recognized as a social good, but only to the extent that it enriches and feeds the collective sentiment of belonging to a united nation, and of committing to a common good.

The Islamist concept of civil state, however, is distinct from the American notion of civil religion in one major aspect. Its relationship to the liberal principle of individuals' rights and freedoms remains unclear. Islamists reject the possibility of religious coercion, and they endorse the concept of pluralism, but they do so from an illiberal perspective. They conceive religious freedom and pluralism as necessary instruments for the moral development of the community. Individual's rights are not an end in themselves, and individualism is strongly criticized as an expression of the morally decadent West. This is also what separates Islamists' definition of the civil state from the way in which politicians and intellectuals from the secular left approach it. Indeed, while the concept is now endorsed both by Islamists and by seculars, as an appropriate third term between the Sharia state and the secular state (*ʿalmāniyya*), the two groups conceptualize it differently. While secular thinkers and Islamists both agree on depicting secularism as a notion imported from the West that has inadequately distorted Tunisian "authentic" identity, they hold divergent views of the primacy of individuals' rights. The conception propounded by secular intellectuals[22] is closer to the one articulated by the Sudanese-American scholar Abdullahi An-Naʿim. In *Islam and the Secular State*, An-Naʿim argues that constitutional democracy, and individual human rights guaranteed by a secular state are necessary conditions for the development of Islam in contemporary Muslim societies. Rejecting the model of the Sharia state, An-Naʿim contends that Muslims can only develop their faith and piety freely, without compulsion, in a secular state. Such a state "is more consistent with the inherent nature of Sharia and the history of Islamic societies than are false and counterproductive assertions of a so-called Islamic state or the alleged enforcement of Sharia as state law."[23] While the state should be prevented from interfering with religious affairs, religion, on the other hand, has a role in the public space. An-Naʿim refers to the term "civic reason" to designate both the inclusion of religion in the public space and its disconnection from the state:

> I believe religion has a public role, we cannot really exclude it from politics. I simply make a distinction between State and politics: religion and State are to be separate, but religion and politics can't and shouldn't be separated. Believers will act politically as believers, and we have to confront with the paradox to keep State and religion separated in a reality where religion and politics are interconnected. This is why I introduce the notion of *civic reason* to distinguish it from John Rawl's "public reason" which is too prescriptive and also too limited in the side of participation[24].

No matter how close this conception is to the way in which Islamists define the civil state, it remains based on entirely different premises. An-Naʿim's perspective, just like the analysis of Tunisian seculars, is based on the unconditional endorsement of liberal principles of individual rights and constitutional democracy. In contrast, Islamists' endorsement of democracy and civil state is illiberal, to the extent that it submits individual rights to the moral and religious edification of the community.

Dawla madaniyya as a principle of democratic governance

Tunisian Islamists' insistence on the establishment of a civil state thus draws upon a long series of analyses on the relationship between the state, civil society, and religion. This long-established political theory shows that accusations according to which Islamists' support for democracy is merely circumstantial are unfounded. But if the concept of civil state appears as a promising paradigm of government, it does pose a number of problems, to which Islamist have so far not provided an answer. An essential question is how the notion of civility, originally conceptualized as a category of resistance to state authoritarianism, can turn into a category of democratic governance. From the various statements, programs, and interviews of Islamist leaders, one can delineate four major characteristics of what a civil state is:

(1) A civil state is a state that is neither a military state, ruled by a military commission, nor a theocratic state, that seeks to implement Sharia as the only source of legislation.
(2) A civil state protects the freedom of expression, of belief, of worship. The state does not intrude into individuals' hearts and minds.
(3) The only legitimate source of legislation is the people's will. That will has to be respected without conditions, although the rights of minorities should also be protected.
(4) The civil state does not speak in the name of Islam, but accepts a fair political competition among parties that are based on a reference to Islam, and secular parties.

Consistently with an argument that Ghannouchi has emphasized since the 1980s, Islamist proponents of the notion of civil state strongly reject the Islamist v. secularist binary as an artefact that the Ben Ali regime used to divide and rule. The key distinction, Islamists argue, is between democracy and despotism. The revolutionaries' call for dignity has proven that the distinction between Islamism and secularism is utterly irrelevant. While it is true that this binary has been exploited by the regime of Ben Ali and its secularist supporters in order to justify the crushing of any form of political opposition, it is problematic to dismiss this binary as a sheer fantasy or linguistic construction. Admittedly, Tunisian society is far less polarized than alarmist reports or biased commentators may suggest. Nonetheless, it is not as united and homogeneous as Islamists' insistence on the unity of the people may suggest. Simply dismissing the secular-religious divide as a fake disciplinary strategy of the former regime will not help anyone to understand how to regulate the possible conflicts that may arise from the diversity and plurality of Tunisian society. In the political theory of Tunisian Islamism, society is strong and self-regulating, while the state is reduced to a mere enabler of this process. Presumably, society, not the state, solves conflict through education, social welfare, and religious associations. Islamists have been relatively elusive about the precise type of institution and laws that a civil state entails. In particular, they have evaded the question of how exactly the state would regulate social conflicts. In a somewhat tautological reasoning, they argue that a democratic society would inevitably know how to self-regulate its inner conflicts. The indeterminacy regarding the exact standards on the basis of which potential conflicts between majority and minorities could be solved may indeed be a matter of circumstances. Admittedly, it could also be argued that the very force of the concept of civil state comes from its indeterminacy. As a conceptual third term between secularism and theocracy, it contributes to avoid the polarization of the Tunisian public. It produces what political scientist Jean-Noël Ferrié[25] calls a negative type of consensus, that is, a consensus that is made possible by the very blurriness of the norm about which different people seem to agree. The main achievement of such a consensus is to offer a basis for further discussions and for the collective definition of a more positive consensus.

That being said, the pitfalls inherent to the concept of *dawla madaniyya* in the project of Tunisian Islamists are not merely a matter of circumstances. The promotion of this political concept raises two fundamental questions as to the type of democratic polity that Islamists envision. One, "civilism," that is, the unrestrained praise of people's authority, does entail the risk of a rise of populism. Second, rejecting the binary between Islamism and secularism does not suffice to define the standards on which law should be based in a democratic community as defined by Islamists.

Popular constitutionalism

A significant part of the Tunisian public worries that Islamists' insistence on defining the people's will as the only source of legitimacy actually conceals a hidden plan to establish a Sharia state. According to this reasoning, the Islamists' plan is to seduce the people into supporting a Sharia state. Islamists could then argue that, as a result of the people's will, this choice is unquestionable. Focused on the unlikely implementation of such a scenario, most critiques of Islamism neglect a more fundamental problem that lies at the heart of Islamists' unrestrained celebration of people's will. While conceding that some mechanisms should be elaborated to protect minority rights against the majority, Islamists remain eloquently vague as to what these mechanisms should be. Instead, they merely insist on how the people's will is the only legitimate source of legislation. This anti-elitist view of democratic politics strongly echoes the popular constitutionalist approach that has informed many important social movements in the US, such as the abolitionist, civil rights, or feminist movements. It does, however, entail a similar risk of a shift from "civilism" to populism, such as the one that has occurred recently with the growth of the Tea Party movement.[26] Tunisian Islamists, just like supporters of popular constitutionalism, argue that democracy is best protected when the people, rather than the elite, have control over the meanings and purpose of the constitution. This view, however, is based on the assumption that the people fundamentally want the same thing. But what happens when the individuals who compose the people hold conflicting views? Just as Tea Party activists argue that the constitution suffices to resolve all these differences, Islamists suggest that as long as the constitution is freely chosen by the people—preferably in accordance with some Islamic-inspired principles—the fundamental values that bind individuals together will be clear, and no discussion will arise. No matter how strongly one resents the manipulation of the secularist-religious divide by the Ben Ali regime, this romantic view of a united, self-righteous people does not provide a clear, realistic basis of democratic government.

Standard of conflict resolution

In Islamists' worldview, Tunisian people are fundamentally united in their quest for freedom, dignity, and social justice. The state simply serves as a mediator that helps by arbitrating among different groups. But the question of the standards on which conflict arbitration should be based remains unanswered. When asked about the specific standards of legislation, Islamists keep referring to the people's will. They do, however, have a normative understanding of the people. They define it, in a conservative way, as a community that is essentially based on family and aspires to the same goal, not as a series of individuals. They talk about human rights, using the nouns *shakhṣ* (person) and *ʾinsān* (human), as opposed to animals or individuals living in a state of nature. But they rarely use the notion of individual or *fard* and strongly reject the liberal principle of individualism. While defining the notion of pluralism *taʿaduddiyya* as natural and acceptable, they reject the possibility of division *taqsīm* as a consequence of the decadent state of liberal Western societies. Islamists contend that they do not want to implement a Sharia state, that the notion of *ḥudūd* is irrelevant and that they are a party with an Islamic referent,[27]not a religious party. Between a Sharia-based legislation and a secular one, there is, however, a wide spectrum of possible norms, and it is not clear what type of law and norms Islamists would support. If Sharia is the standard of definition of acceptable policy in an Islamic state, what is the standard of definition of an acceptable practice within a state "with an Islamic reference" (*à référentiel islamique*)? No matter how strongly Islamists reject the idea of separation and insist on the self-regulating capacity of society, individuals, policymakers, and judges need to know how the boundary between civil and uncivil practice is defined in the Islamic vision of a civil state.

Two controversies that broke out in Tunisia in the spring and summer of 2012 made the limitations of the reference to civil state more apparent. The first controversy regards the trial of Nabil Karoui, head of the Tunisian private television channel Nessma TV, who was charged by a group of 140 lawyers of "infringing sacred values and morals" and "disrupting public order" for allowing the movie *Persepolis*, by the French-Iranian director Marjane Satrapi, to be broadcast, on October 7, 2011. One scene in this movie particularly angered the plaintiffs as it shows God speaking to the main character. On the day of the trial, January 23, 2012, Ennahda issued a public statement firmly condemning the trial and insisting on the movement's attachment to the principle of freedom of expression. (Ennahda party), reads the statement, considers that the charges against the head of Nessma TV do not represent the best solution to address the question of how to find a balance "between the identity of the people and the attachment to the sacred on the one hand, and freedom of expression on the other."[28] The statement concludes by calling for a "national consensus among media, civil society and policymakers regarding questions of freedom of information and worship." Such a statement clearly illustrates the pitfalls of Ennahda's understanding of a civil state. The problem of Ennahda's endorsement of a civil state does not lie in its supposed ambiguity or lack of sincerity. Sincerity is not the issue here. What is at stake is, rather, the comprehensive vision of society on which such a conception rests. For Ennahda leaders, what is at stake in the *Persepolis* controversy is the collective definition of an equilibrium between the safeguarding of identity and sacred values, and fundamental principles such as freedom of expression. This equilibrium, according to Ennahda, can be found through education and debate, that ultimately will lead to a consensus. In other words, this statement suggests that society is capable of, and committed to, finding such an equilibrium on its own. Similarly, the response of Ennahda officials to the occupation of La Manouba University by extremist Salafi groups who advocate for the right of female students to wear niqab has been perceived as too slow and too timid. In an effort not to further radicalize Salafi groups and possibly to alienate the more radical fringe of their electoral basis, Ennahda leaders have been reluctant to take a firm stance in the Manouba controversy. This attitude is not merely related to an electoral strategy. More profoundly, it is based on Ennahda's faith in the capacity of a virtuous society to heal and reconcile through piety, charity, and education.

The pitfalls inherent to Islamists' conceptualization of the civil state have become even more apparent in the discussions that have taken place in the Constitutional Assembly about the place of religion. A heated debate broke out in February 2012 after the draft of a constitutional project attributed to Ennahda was leaked to the social networks. According to Article 10 of this draft, Sharia should be established as the main source of legislation. Article 20 of this same draft stipulated that freedom of expression should be limited out of respect for the sacred. On February 3 of that year, Habib Kehder, an Ennahda member of parliament and rapporteur in the commission in charge of the constitution, contended in a radio interview that Sharia would indeed be a major source of inspiration of the constitution.[29] For many secularist intellectuals and activists, the draft came as just another sign of how threatening and untrustworthy the Ennahda-led government was. A large part of the Tunisian public stood for the upholding of Article 1 of the 1959 constitution that states that "Tunisia is a free, independent and sovereign state: its religion is Islam, its language is Arabic, and its regime the Republic." For many, this article was arguably, in all its vagueness and ambiguity, the best way to deal with possible conflicts and disagreements concerning identity and religion. The Sharia debate also served as a catalyst for stimulating profound and ancient tensions within the Islamist party movement itself. Not only is Ennahda ideologically divided between a radical trend (led by Sadok Shourrou) and a pragmatic one (led by Rachid Ghannouchi and Meherzia Labidi); it is also divided on matters of strategy. While most Ennahdawi agree on a similar objective—a progressive Islamization of society— they still disagree on what is the best strategy to achieve this end. A significant number of Ennahda supporters worry that the party's participation in government will contribute to its becoming part of the mainstream, and ultimately its neutralization and ideological destruction. According to them, Ennahda should primarily be a social and cultural movement, not a political party.

Originally, the majority of Ennahda members were in favor of the inclusion of Sharia in the constitution. The rationale of the pro-Sharia side ranged from an aggressive desire to assert Tunisia's Islamic identity to a milder observation that Sharia was already the material source of a large part of Tunisian legislation. The Personal Status Code, aspects of contract law, rules regarding business transactions are indeed essentially informed by parts of Maliki law. A minority of members were worried about the consequences that the inclusion of Sharia might have on Tunisia's international image, and attempted to demonstrate that Article 1 was sufficient to assert Tunisia's Islamic identity. A few intellectuals tried to propose a middle ground, by suggesting that the objectives of Sharia (*Maqāṣid al-Sharia*), rather than Sharia, should be included, in the preamble of the constitution. Eventually, under the pressure of public opinion and the two secular parties of the Troika, Ennahda decided to abandon the reference to Sharia. On March 26, 2012, Ghannouchi publicly expressed, during a press conference, Ennahda's renouncement of the reference to Sharia. This term, he explained, is "a little blurred" and there is no need to add "ambiguous definitions" in the constitutional text that might "divide the people." The same day, Ennahda issued an official statement, declaring that the Bureau Exécutif had voted against the inclusion of Sharia. Immediately after March 26, Ennahda deputies gave up the fight for Sharia in the Assembly.

The Sharia affair has shown the complexity of Ennahda's attitude both in government and in the Assembly. To a large extent, it has shown Ennahda's interest in sustaining the compromise with the other parties of the Troika, and in defending the image of a moderate and civil party. Prominent Ennahda figures seize any opportunity to insist on the party's commitment to notions of civil state, rule of law, and freedom of religion. Ghannouchi published a significant number of articles, issued several statements, and participated in many public events in order to emphasize his belief in an open form of secularity.

Several public statements or new propositions of Ennahda deputies, however, regularly seem to contradict this attitude of moderation and praising of liberal-friendly norms and institutions. Sadok Shourou, an Ennahda member of parliament, proposed in April to cut the hands of all those who went on strike, in order to force strikers to resume work. A number of Ennahda deputies are strongly in favor of maintaining the death penalty. In November 2011, Souad Abderrahmanne condemned the sinful life of single mothers on a public radio show. It has often been suggested that the discrepancy between the attempts made by numerous Ennahda figures to assert their commitment to a civil state and human rights, and the statements of other Ennahda deputies and their allies from other parties is evidence of Ennahda's so-called doublespeak. Rather than the expression of a deliberate strategy of deception, this discrepancy can be seen as the reflection at once of a somewhat erratic process of governance learning, and of a tendency to "strategize as you go." The Sharia debate has shown Ennahda's capacity to adjust to circumstances and to adapt their strategy according to the response of the public. In other words, sporadic statements regarding single mothers, the caliphate, limitation of freedom of expression, *ḥudūd*, and so on are not the "true" face of an otherwise presentable and deceptive leadership. They are, rather, both the reflection of what some Ennahda supporters truly think and a way for the representatives of these people to test the water, to gauge the feelings of the public, to experiment with various responses, and then adjust their strategy accordingly.

The discussions that took place around the second draft of the constitution, produced in December 2012, reveal an even more complex and ambiguous shift in the Islamists' approach to the concept of civility. A central aspect of Ghannouchi's thinking is the close link between his rejection of secularism and his rejection of state intrusion into society's choices. In the specific context of Tunisian postcolonial history, he argues, the secular principle of separation between state and religion has been distorted into a principle that authorizes the state to strictly monitor religious affairs, thereby stifling the development of a genuine and authentic religious identity. The second draft of the constitution, however, suggests that some Islamists have departed from this approach and now advocate for a clear designation of Islam as the religion of the state, and not simply as the religion of Tunisia. They insisted on the inclusion of Article 148, which states that "no amendment to the Constitution may be prejudiced to Islam," and defines Islam as "the religion of the state." For secularists, the explicit definition of Islam as the religion of the state ruins the positive ambiguity of Article 1: "Tunisia is a free, independent and sovereign state. Its religion is Islam, its language is Arabic and its form of government is a republic." Due to its syntactic ambiguity, Article 1 could imply that Islam is either the religion of the state, or the religion of Tunisia. By unilaterally choosing from these two possible meanings, secularists argue, Islamists are trying to impose a vision of Tunisia whereby politics and religion are not separated, and that seems to contradict the whole conceptualization of civility. Admittedly, the problem raised by Article 148 is counterbalanced by other changes that secularists have welcomed as positive for human rights and freedoms. Previously proposed articles relating to the criminalization of the offense to the sacred were suppressed. An article that formerly described the relationship between men and women as based on "complementarity" rather than equality was also dropped. But a number of questions remain open, in addition to the inclusion of Article 148. In particular, secularists frequently criticize Article 15, which considers international treaties to be of inferior value than the constitution. They argue that this would enable an Islamist-led government to disengage from treaties concerning women's rights that were signed in the past. They also argue against the Article that states that only Muslim individuals can run for a presidential election. This provision is contradictory to Article 5, which states that "all citizens, males and females alike, shall have equal rights and obligations and shall be equal before the law, without discrimination of any kind."

Conclusion

In a recent article on the relationship between the state, religion, and secularism, Islamist thinker Ajmi Lourimi[30] insists on how imperative it is for Tunisia to "enter a new period, that goes beyond the fracture between the secular islamists and the modernists." He draws a clear distinction between a positive and inclusive form of democracy that is defined by its capacity to include diversity and an exclusive form of democracy that is based on the rejection of differences. The first, he argues, corresponds to the model of the "Medina democracy," whereas the second is based on the model of the "Athens democracy." The role of the state is to permit the people to develop dignity and liberty, and to progress, not to impose secularism from above. In order to do so, the state has to find a balance between the preservation of the "Oriental pages of the history of the country" and the promise of the "pages of a better future." One can only agree with the necessity of countering the polarization of the public sphere and of avoiding the trap of a perpetuation of the secularist-Islamist divide. As I have shown in this chapter, Islamists' endorsement of the notion of civility and civil state is based on several decades of debate and reflection on the relationship between religion and democracy. From this point of view, it is unfair to discredit Islamists' discourse and policy as evidence of a so-called hidden agenda or a form of doublespeak. The question remains, however, of the concrete and legal tools through which this ideal of a civil state may be implemented. While Islamists' conception rests on a comprehensive and optimistic view of society, seen as an organic body that can reach piety and virtue through education and development, this view seems contradicted by the controversies that have repeatedly broken out in Tunisia since the revolution. As long as the concepts of civility and civil state are not judicially and constitutionally specified, reference to this concept will be insufficient for the resolution of conflicts and the protection of individual liberties. This process of legal and constitutional characterization is indeed the responsibility not only of Islamist politicians and intellectuals, but of all Tunisian citizens together.

Notes

1. Philip Gorski, "Barack Obama and Civil Religion," in *Rethinking Obama (Political Power and Social Theory, Volume 22)*, ed. Julian Go (Bingley: Emerald Group Publishing Limited, 2011), 179–214.
2. Talal Asad, *Genealogies of Religion: Discipline and Reasons of Power in Christianity and Islam* (Baltimore, MD: The Johns Hopkins University Press, 2003).
3. Paul Kahn, *Political Theology: Four New Chapters on the Concept of Sovereignty* (New York: Columbia University Press, 2011).
4. Charles Taylor, *A Secular Age* (Cambridge, MA: The Belknap Press, Harvard University Press, 2007).
5. Michel Camau and Vincent Geisser, *Le syndrome autoritaire. Politique en Tunisie de Bourguiba à Ben Ali* (Paris: Presses de Sciences-Po, 2003).
6. Azzam Tamimi, *Rachid Ghannouchi: A Democrat within Islamism* (New York: Oxford University Press, 2001); Linda G. Jones, "Portrait of Rashid al-Ghannoushi," *Middle East Report* 153 (1988): 19–22, accessed March 4, 2012, www.merip.org/mer/mer153/portrait-rachid-al-ghannouchi?ip_login_no_cache=91a60e239d148864e6810 12bd1751d4e.
7. In this chapter, I use "secular" as a generic term to designate politicians and intellectuals who believe in the need to distinguish political authority from religious authority. I use "secularists" to designate those who advocate for a radical form of secularism, modeled on the French or Turkish experience, and who believe the state should monitor religious activities for fear of radicalization. The terms "secularists" and "Islamists" should be understood as relational and contingent categories, and not as the description of fixed ideologies. All supporters of secularism are not secularists. Most importantly, some Islamists are ironically more secular than secularists, to the extent that they advocate for a strict separation of religion and the state, whereas secularists want the state to monitor religious affairs strictly.
8. See the debate that took place between Rachid Ghannouchi and Neila Silini at the Hamra Theater in Tunis on April 16, 2011, www.youtube.com/watch?v=KPWFGEdR3V0. The scandal that broke out when film director Nadia el Fani released her provocative documentary about secularism, *Ni Allah, ni maître*, triggered numerous discussions in which the "doublespeak" argument played a major role. See, for example, Ons Bouali, "Non musulmans, pas moins Tunisiens, l'affaire Nadia El Fani", May 23, 2011, accessed August 14, 2011, http://nawaat.org/portail/2011/05/23/non-musulmans-pas-moins-tunisiens-laffaire-nadia-al-fani.
9. François Burgat and William Dowell, *Islamist Movements in North Africa* (Austin, TX: University of Texas, 1993).
10. Ghannouchi, "The Conflict Between the West and Islam, The Tunisian Case: Reality

and Prospects" (paper presented at the Royal Institute of International Affairs, Chatham House, London, May 9, 1995).

11. Quoted in Tamimi, *Rachid Ghannouchi*, 12. "Secularism in the Arab Maghreb ... What Secularism?" (paper presented at the Collapse of Secularism seminar, Centre for the Study of Democracy, University of Westminster, London, June 10, 1994).
12. I refer here to the distinction between *intransigeantisme* (an uncompromising and fundamentalist attitude toward the sacred text) and *intégralisme* (a conception of world affairs that refutes the idea of a separation between religion and politics), developed by Jean-Marie Donegani in Jean-Marie Donegani, *La liberté de choisir: pluralisme religieux et pluralisme politique dans le catholicisme français contemporain* (Paris, Presses de Sciences-Po, 1993).
13. Mahmoud Sadri and Ahmad Sadri, eds., *Reason, Freedom and Democracy in Islam, Essential writings of Abdolkarim Soroush* (Oxford: Oxford University Press, 2000).
14. This disagreement came up at a conference organized in Cairo: "The Civil State v. The Islamic state," in which many Egyptian Islamists argued that the term *ahli* is a more accurate way to translate "civil" into Arabic. See Fahmi Huwaidi, *Al-Islam Wad-Dimuqratiyah* [*Islam and Democracy*] (Cairo: Al-Ahram Translation and Publishing Centre, 1993), 192.
15. Rachid Ghannouchi, "Al-Harakah al-Islamiyah Wal-Mujtama' al-Madani" ["The Islamic Movement and Civil Society"] (paper presented at Pretoria University, South Africa, August 1994).
16. See interview with Azzam Tamimi in Tamimi, *Rachid Ghannouchi.*
17. Olivier Roy, *The Failure of Political Islam* (Cambridge, MA: Harvard University Press, 1994).
18. Ghannouchi, "Al-Harakah al-Islamiyah Wal-Mujtama' al-Madani."
19. Gudrun Kramer, "Islamist Notions of Democracy," *Middle East Report* 183 (1993): 2–8.
20. Robert Bellah, "Civil Religion in America," *Daedalus* 96.1 (winter 1967): 1–21; Richard D. Hecht, "Active Versus Passive Pluralism, a Changing Style of Civil Religion?," *The Annals of the American Academy of Political Science* 612 (2007): 133–51.
21. Hecht, "Active Versus Passive Pluralism."
22. I here refer to seculars who are open to dialogue and collaboration with the Islamists, and who argue for the necessity of going beyond past polarizations and binaries. This is the position held by members of the two secular parties of the center, Ettakatol and Congress for the Republic. Secularists, in contrast, continue to advocate for a model that follows the French view of *laïcité*.
23. Abdullahi An-Na'im, *Islam and the Secular State, Negotiating the Future of Shari'a* (Cambridge, MA: Harvard University Press, 2008), 268.
24. *Abdullahi An-Na'im, "Secular State and Civil Reason," October 13, 2011, accessed May 4, 2012,* www.resetdoc.org/story/00000021779.
25. Jean-Noël Ferrié, *Le régime de la civilité en Egypte* (Paris, Éditions du CNRS, 2004).
26. Ilya Somin, "The Tea Party Movement and Popular Constitutionalism," *Northwestern University Law Review Colloquy* 105 (December 2011): 300–16.
27. Ennahda's program was at www.365p.info/livre/index.html (link no longer active). "Islam is a moderate referential (*marja'iyya wasatiyya*) ... that interacts with all human experience (*khibra bachariyya*)." The press conference given by Rachid Ghannouchi

when Ennahda's program was presented in September 2011 and available at www.365p.info but the link has now been removed.

28. Accessed May 4, 2012, www.monmag.com/communiques/ennahdha-soutient-nessma-tv-et-defend-la-liberte-d%E2%80%99expression.html (access now forbidden).
29. See www.mosaiquefm.net/index/a/ActuDetail/Element/18129-Habib-Khedher-rap porteur-g%C3%A9n%C3%A9ral-de-la-constitution-parce-que-je-le-vaux-bien.html (accessed May 4, 2012).
30. Ajmi Lourimi, "Secularism is not the Role of the State," April 1, 2011, accessed March 4, 2012, www.nahdha.info/arabe/News-file-article-sid-4570.html.

CHAPTER 10

Women's Rights before and after the Revolution

Monica Marks

While Tunisians of all ages, class backgrounds, and religious persuasions united in opposition against Ben Ali's sclerotic regime, their unity quickly collapsed when he fled on January 14, 2011. Simmering tensions between Ennahda and its secular rivals spilled into public debate, and dozens of new NGOs and political parties—some with just a handful of members—sprung up around the country. Amidst this clamorous atmosphere, Tunisian and outside observers struggled to predict how emerging political dynamics might affect women's status.

Women's rights stood out as one of the most fiercely contested issues in the campaigning that preceded Tunisia's October 23, 2011 elections, a somewhat surprising development given that economic malaise, corruption, and police brutality—not suppression of women—provided the impetus for Bouazizi's suicide and the revolution itself. For competing political parties, however, women's rights represented a useful wedge issue—one that could deflect attention from hastily constructed economic programs and isolate electoral opponents as either "too secular" or "too Islamist" to please the population at large.[1]

Despite the prominence of outspoken *Nahdawiyāt* (Ennahda women), flashpoint conflicts between Islamist and secular trends—over such issues as single mothers' status and women's supposed "complementarity" to men—have raised concern over the future of women's rights. Seen through the distorting filter of Tunisian and international media, which focus heavily on such flashpoints, Islamism might seem to threaten Tunisian women's rights more seriously than less discussed structural issues, such as the state's historical monopolization of feminism or challenges arising from corroded legal and institutional frameworks.

Press-oriented alarmist renderings have powerfully shaped the postrevolution discussion surrounding women's rights, overshadowing both historical context and critical institutional challenges facing Tunisian women. During the 2011 campaign, domestic media—largely untrained in the investigative arts of deep institutional or economics reporting—naturally tended to cover ideological conflicts more than substantive, platform-related differences.[2] Western (meaning mostly French and English) media outlets similarly eschewed dryer coverage of socioeconomic and institutional issues for comparatively marketable stories about whether Ennahda's rise augured a setback for women. Though Western media generally applauded Tunisia as a regional leader on women's rights before the revolution, coverage soured during mid-2011 as local campaign coverage grew more ideological in tone, Ennahda gained traction in the polls, and Tunisian feminist groups—stricken for a time by their proximity to the old regime—recovered their voice.[3] The deteriorating situation for women in Egypt also biased coverage on Tunisia. As Egyptian women began facing serious abuses in Tahrir Square during autumn 2011, Western journalists and analysts started giving short shrift to the specificities of Tunisian women's situation, instead lumping them into an Egypt-centric narrative that characterized the Arab Spring as increasingly "bad for women."[4]

Tunisia's election results did not assuage such concerns. Instead, Ennahda's 41 percent plurality, paired with Islamist victories throughout the region, stoked fears of bearded patriarchy for many local secularists and international observers.[5] Ironically, forty-two out of the forty-nine women elected to the 217-member Constituent Assembly represented Ennahda, in part because it was the only major party to fully respect the gender parity rules for electoral lists, and because it mobilized many female activists to win over undecided voters and get people to the polls.[6] While female activists in Ennahda claimed the party's victory opened doors for Tunisian women, critics warned it would wage an Iran-style war on women's rights—mandating hijab and enforcing a separate spheres ethos aimed at returning Tunisia's *femmes féministes* to their kitchens.[7]

Pitched competition between *Nahdawīs* (Ennahda supporters) and *laïcistes* (supporters of a more aggressive French-inspired secularism, or laicism) has re-politicized historical narratives, blurring boundaries between fact and interpretation regarding Tunisia's record on women's rights.[8] Some have painted Ennahda's rise as a dramatic fall from grace—the tragic descent of a once secular, pro-women's rights country into a backward regime run by Islamist misogynists. While the nostalgic appeal of this narrative remains powerful for many of Ennahda's critics—particularly older feminists who remember the 1960s and 70s as unveiled decades—it oversimplifies a more complex historical reality in which Tunisia's postindependence presidents manipulated women's rights in conjunction with religious discourse to maintain one-party rule.

This chapter seeks to contextualize the discussion regarding Tunisian women's rights, injecting historical and institutional dimensions into what is often narrowly portrayed as a conflict between two supposedly dichotomous ideologies (Islamism vs. feminism). Special attention is devoted to the means by which Bourguiba and Ben Ali manipulated the intertwined discourses of religious authority and women's rights long before the 2011 elections, as well as challenges posed by the weak state institutions they left behind.

The first section explores three of the most salient themes that have characterized the modern Tunisian state's relationship to women's rights: pursuit of power, monopolization of women's rights, and the performance-oriented nature of Tunisian state progressivism. Understanding these historical patterns will help contextualize contemporary, often politicized narratives and preview trends that may continue affecting the Tunisian state's handling of women's rights in the future. The second section focuses attention on challenges affecting women in postrevolutionary Tunisia, briefly highlighting six issues of importance to women's rights in the transitional context: constitutional drafting, reform of the Personal Status Code (PSC), judicial reform, the rights of single mothers, transitional justice, and security reform. I argue that in the context of Tunisians' efforts to forge a truly democratic polity, threats to women's rights are more likely to stem from deeply embedded social norms and weak institutions than from deliberate machinations of Islamist ideology.

Religion and women's rights: a question of ends and means

The divisiveness of the "woman question" during Tunisia's 2011 election surprised many observers, but was not without precedent. Instrumentalizing women's rights in service of political ends has been a hallmark of modern Tunisian power politics. As in many societies, women's status and religious symbolism have represented intertwined repositories of traditional identity and legitimacy—compelling sources of cultural influence that politicians routinely draw upon in bids to shore up power. This section examines three crucial trends that have triangulated the relationship of state power, religious symbolism, and women's rights in Tunisia: (1) state pursuit of political objectives; (2) state monopolization of women's rights; and (3) the performance-oriented nature of seemingly progressive state policies.

State pursuit of political objectives

The Tunisian state's support for women's rights and religious freedoms has tended to fluctuate as a function of shifting political objectives and threats.[9] Presidents Habib Bourguiba (1957–87) and Zine El Abidine Ben Ali (1987–2011) instrumentalized religious rhetoric and the women's rights cause to consolidate power—a process that began even before Tunisia had won its independence.

From the 1920s until independence, Tunisia's nationalist leadership sought to maintain a unified front against the French, who had sought to marginalize veiling and other traditional practices.[10] Modernists such as Habib Bourguiba made common cause with more religious nationalists like Salah Ben Youssef and took a conservative approach to the women's issue, emphasizing the importance of customs like veiling which, in Bourguiba's words, constituted "the last defense of a national identity in danger."[11] Bourguiba encouraged women to wear the *sefseri*, a traditional white shawl drawn over the hair and entire body, as a means of consolidating cultural solidarity against the colonial occupier. The nationalist leadership likewise responded with swift condemnation when one woman, Habiba Menchari, attended a meeting unveiled, and exerted constant pressure on the women's rights advocate Tahar Haddad to cease his activism.[12]

Nationalist leaders also made creative application of Islamic symbols and institutions. They routinely held meetings in mosques and *zawāyā* (Sufi lodges) and urged Tunisians to pray for national martyrs five times a day.[13] During this period, Habib Bourguiba adopted the religiously infused title *al-mujāhid al-akbar* (the supreme combatant) as he led Tunisians in a sanctified jihad, or struggle, against French colonial forces.[14]

When Tunisia became independent in 1956, however, Bourguiba gradually shifted strategy. In his capacity as president, he scorned the *sefseri* as a symbol of backwardness—an "odious rag"—and encouraged women to remove it in service of national advancement.[15] Political objectives had changed. Aided by the French, who preferred to back the Paris-educated modernizer when they realized Tunisian independence was inevitable, Bourguiba and his faction ultimately wrested control of the Neo-Destour Party and Tunisia's fledgling state from Ben Youssef.[16] As William Zartman and Larbi Sadiki have noted, the dominant *ʿaṣabiyya* (social kinship group) that supported Bourguiba was the *Baldī-ṣaḥeli* (coastal bourgeois class), which was comparatively francophone and French-educated. Ben Youssef's faction, by contrast, was more representative of interior regions and the religious establishment.[17]

Upon taking power, Bourguiba reneged on his strategy of cooperation and pushed through a number of policies that contravened Youssefist demands. Although biographical evidence suggests Bourguiba was committed to the altruistic value of certain liberalizing reforms, such as expanding girls' education, political expediency also factored into his decisions.[18] The 1956 PSC did more than prohibit polygamy and grant women the right to divorce—it also served a politically useful function, hastening the marginalization of religious and kin-based forms of authority from which Bourguiba's Youssefist opponents drew strength.[19]

The relatively unchallenged nature of Bourguiba's leadership during the 1950s and 60s allowed him to pursue modernizing reforms that sidelined the religious establishment and undercut potentially restive power centers.[20] By the late 1960s, however, many Tunisians had grown skeptical of Bourguiba's policies. A weak economy and failed land collectivization program had left numerous Tunisians unemployed, and by the early 1970s Bourguiba increasingly sought a means of counterbalancing the growing threat of leftist and labor union unrest.[21]

Hoping to neutralize leftists' criticisms, Bourguiba began giving limited space to emerging Islamic currents in the 1970s. Instead of imprisoning Rachid Ghannouchi or the young sheikhs who attended his *ḥalqa* (discussion circle) sessions, Bourguiba allowed them to operate whilst simultaneously stressing his own religious credentials. In 1973, the government even facilitated distribution of Egyptian Muslim Brotherhood writings, likely hoping Islamism would siphon Marxist support.[22] Headlines such as "The Islamic Origins of Bourguiba's Thought" and photo-ops of him making the pilgrimage to Mecca ran routinely in *al-'Amal*, the government newspaper.[23] During the 1970s, the government reactivated religious symbols and retrenched on women's rights when deemed politically expedient.[24] In Mounira Charrad's words, Bourguiba "oscillated between mild reforms and outright retrenchment" throughout the 1970s, admonishing women to remember "their family responsibilities as wives, mothers, and homemakers."[25]

Rather than rectifying economic inequalities or genuinely liberalizing Tunisia's political system, Bourguiba employed Islamic rhetoric to quell criticism. Predictably, the country's general labor union (Union Générale Tunisienne du Travail, UGTT), remained dissatisfied. In 1981, likely to neutralize the union's demands, Bourguiba tried a more liberal approach, granting amnesty to condemned UGTT leaders, affirming the union's right to autonomy, and announcing a move toward multiparty elections. Ghannouchi and his fellow Islamists, who had recently reorganized under the name *al-Ittijāh al-Islāmī*, the Islamic Tendency Movement (Mouvement de la Tendance Islamique, MTI), declared themselves a political party ready to compete in elections.[26]

The MTI's explicit opposition to despotism, economic exploitation, and dependency on Western sources of income and value structures positioned the movement in opposition to Bourguiba's regime. Sensing a threat, Bourguiba abandoned his promise of multiparty reform in summer, 1981. He banned *ḥalqa* sessions, arrested sixty-one MTI members, and condemned a number of the movement's leaders to prison sentences ranging from two to ten years.[27] In 1981, Bourguiba passed Decree 108 banning Tunisian women from wearing sectarian dresss (hijab) in government buildings and forbade high school students from wearing hijab and long beards. He went even farther in 1985, extending the hijab ban to institutes of higher education.[28]

Bourguiba's successor similarly reneged on promises to hold free and fair multiparty elections. Eager to demonstrate legitimacy during his early days in power, Ben Ali rhetorically prioritized human rights and democracy as key objectives of *changement* and vowed to hold multiparty elections in 1989. The MTI changed its name to Ennahda to comply with the government's ban on parties having religious names, but failed to win recognition as a licensed party. However, Ennahda managed to field a number of independent candidates who won an estimated 15 to 17 percent of the overall vote. Before the election could be completed, though, Ben Ali reversed course and used the candidates' names to identify, imprison, and torture thousands of Ennahda members and suspected party supporters. Between the latter half of 1990 and 2011, Ennahda members fled the country, were jailed, or hunkered underground. While Islamists bore the brunt of Ben Ali's persecution, any individuals who dared to vocally oppose the regime—including leftists, outspoken trade unionists, and citizen activists—were also targeted.

Many of the most influential Tunisian feminist organizations, including the Tunisian Association of Democratic Women (Association Tunisienne des Femmes Démocrates, ATFD) and the Center for Arab Women Training and Research (CAWTAR) rose to prominence during the early 1990s, largely to safeguard women's gains against the perceived threats of Islamist fundamentalism and extremism. While not granted the freedom to seriously contest the regime or its record on human rights, women's rights groups enjoyed more latitude than most other civil society organizations under Ben Ali. The ATFD, for instance, focused mainly on efforts to mitigate domestic violence, while CAWTAR fostered research on issues related to gender equality and women's socioeconomic development in Tunisia. It is important to note that only secularly oriented women's organizations were allowed to form and operate under Ben Ali. The reasons for this had more to do with Ben Ali's political objectives than personal commitment to egalitarian gender relations.

While Bourguiba could lay a legitimate claim to the mantle of sincere modernizer, Ben Ali's manipulation of women's rights proved transparently self-serving. For Ben Ali, women's rights represented little more than a smokescreen—an illusion of modernity that distracted many secular-leaning Tunisians and some foreign observers alike from scrutinizing the country's numerous human rights abuses. Propping himself up as a defender of women's rights gave Ben Ali a bully pulpit for suppressing the Islamist resistance, which he portrayed as regressive, violent, and staunchly opposed to Tunisia's "modern" way of life.

Promoting this dichotomy was a relatively easy task in Tunisia, which lacked an independent watchdog group permitted to challenge erroneous statements made by the regime. Manufacturing a Manichean conflict between Islamist terrorists and women's liberation helped Ben Ali convince many international observers and a broad swath of the *Baldī-ṣaḥeli* class, including many women's rights activists, that he was the sole guarantor of their rights and privileges. In her interviews with feminist activists in the early 1990s, Souad Chater repeatedly encountered women who framed their rights and Islamism in a purely oppositional context:

> We know that the gains made by women are defended by the highest authorities of the country and, at present, there is no reason to fear that things will change. However, the PSC would certainly be in danger if power fell into the hands of the Islamic fundamentalists.[29]

Some feminist activists, including members of leading feminist groups like the ATFD, bought into the assumption that Ben Ali's dictatorship would defend their liberties more than a democratic form of government, concluding that the rise of Islamism was necessarily opposed to the protection of women's rights.

Others whom Chater interviewed expressed appreciation for Ben Ali's regime, characterizing it as a necessary—if flawed—bulwark against the impending rise of Islamist extremists. "If power falls into the hands of the Islamic fundamentalists," one woman remarked, "the PSC will fall too and then nobody will be able to do anything about it."[30]

Ben Ali did relatively little to substantively advance women's rights in Tunisia, though a bundle of reforms passed in 1993 did represent some progress towards equality of the sexes. These laws granted women greater child custody rights in the event of a divorce and removed a clause from the PSC which stipulated that women must obey their husbands. Wage discrimination in agricultural work was legally abolished, mothers gained the right to pass nationality onto their children with the father's approval, and the government set up a fund to assist needy divorced women and their children.

Still, Ben Ali left the most problematic portion of the PSC—regarding women's inheritance—untouched. Deeply entrenched social norms concerning the primacy of males in family matters made reforming the inheritance code politically unpalatable. Unmarried women and their children remained unrecognized under the law. Labor laws for women did not improve, nor did women gain access to meaningful, democratic representation in local and national decision-making bodies.

Most importantly, Ben Ali's regime came to be characterized by extreme oppression, kleptocracy, and police abuse that systematically targeted Islamists and their relatives. Women suspected of having any familial or political affiliation with banned political parties—most notably Ennahda and the Tunisian Communist Workers Party (POCT)—were routinely harassed, held under incommunicado detention, imprisoned, tortured, and sometimes sexually abused.[31] Others who dared to defend Islamist women or oppose the regime's human rights abuses—including civil society organizers, academics, and lawyers like Radhia Nasraoui, were "forced gradually to retreat from public life."[32]

Despite these abuses, Ben Ali's insistence that Tunisians faced an either/or choice—his own stable, secular dictatorship vs. an unpredictable democratic government ruled by illiberal Islamist rabble—convinced many Western observers and some local onlookers that his regime represented the lesser of two evils.

State monopolization of women's rights

Well before his death in 2000, Habib Bourguiba began laying plans for his final resting place—a strikingly opulent mausoleum in Monastir, his coastal hometown. Visitors approaching the mausoleum today must pass through a heavy door embossed with three gold epithets—*al-mujāhid al-akbar* (the supreme combatant), *bānī Tūnis al-jadīda* (the architect of new Tunisia), and *muḥarrir al-mara'a* (the liberator of women). These titles aptly summarize the legacy Bourguiba sought to leave behind and betray one of the chief tendencies that have characterized the Tunisian state's relationship to women's rights over the past sixty years: the drive to monopolize control of women's rights—a trend often termed "state feminism."[33]

Bourguiba's efforts to enact and popularize the 1956 PSC make an interesting case study in regime feminism.[34] Indeed, executive monopolization of the women's rights cause was one of the most important trends that emerged during Tunisia's state formation in the 1950s and 1960s. As numerous scholars have noted, feminism was not a salient civil society movement in Tunisia until the 1990s. Noura Bousali, a prominent writer and feminist, said recently that the PSC came "on a silver platter" handed top-down to women from a paternalistic, benevolently autocratic government.[35] Independent interest group lobbying, feminist organizing, and critical human rights activism were seen as impediments to single-party rule and were largely smothered throughout the Bourguiba years. The government coopted the women's rights movement, for example, by founding the National Union of Tunisian Women (Union Nationale des Femmes de Tunisie, UNFT) in 1961. Especially vocal women who championed rights-based causes were encouraged to join the UNFT, which "functioned as the women's auxiliary of the PSD [Parti Socialiste Destourien: Bourguiba's party]" and ultimately played little role in grooming women for political participation.[36]

Elements of the PSC that women's rights activists might have opposed, such as the stipulation that daughters continue to inherit half as much as male heirs, and Article 23, which stated that wives should "obey" their husbands, went largely unnoticed. In crafting the PSC, Bourguiba had sought to include something for everyone. He left more ingrained elements of Sharia-based law, such as unequal inheritance codes, untouched—a move that enabled him to justify more reformist portions of the code among conservative Tunisians using religious argumentation. Though the goal—forging a fresh consensus that mixed traditions with reforms—was laudatory, the PSC's results were mixed. The code granted Tunisian women more legal protections than their Middle East and North Africa (MENA) region counterparts, but also placated citizens and helped neutralize the development of critical, independent power centers.

The PSC extended government control over public institutions and personal status matters into rural areas, disrupting traditional life and increasing dependency on the Bourguibist state. Bourguiba glossed over opposition to the law in rural regions, among urban migrants, and in religious sectors, downplaying the *'ulama'*'s sharp divisions of opinion concerning the law. While fourteen leading religious scholars had swiftly issued fatwas condemning the PSC, others accepted positions as judges defending it.[37] Support from some *'ulama'* enabled Bourguiba to portray the PSC as harmonizing consistently with Islamic legal precepts. However, Bourguiba himself ultimately demanded the code's passage and portrayed it as a tacit—if not transparent or democratic—agreement between Tunisian Islamic traditionalism and forces of modernist nationalism. Today, the code is widely remembered as a product of Atatürk-style benign despotism—the work of one man, rather than the grassroots reflection of shifting societal consensus for women's rights.

Ben Ali's efforts to monopolize women's rights discourse took a more sinister turn. After falsifying the 1989 election results and waging a broad attack on Ennahda and suspected Islamist sympathizers, Ben Ali endeavored to ingratiate himself with the country's secular opposition as an indispensable figure committed to protecting their "modern" lifestyles. Semi-independent women's rights organizations that formed shortly after the 1989 election crackdown—including the ATFD, founded in 1989, and CAWTAR, founded in 1990—were tolerated provided they had no dealings with Islamists, muted their criticisms of Ben Ali, and accepted the regime's heavy involvement in coopting women's rights conferences and other civil society activities.

Members of the ATFD and other secular-laicist feminist groups complain today that they were not allowed to operate freely under the Ben Ali regime. Ben Ali often coopted various elements of their agenda to promote his own power rather than extend free speech and personal freedoms to Tunisian women in general. Ben Ali's wife, the much-loathed Leila Trabelsi, became the face of Tunisian feminism, and her picture appeared on virtually all conference materials and news releases concerning Tunisian women. As Sadiki notes, the Tunisian state under Ben Ali "possessed the democratic process," squelching any space for NGOs or non-party actors.[38] Although the regime's heavy involvement angered and alienated feminist activists, shared opposition to the perceived threat of Islamist misogyny united them in partial alliance with Ben Ali and a strained partnership developed between the two sides.[39]

The performance-oriented nature of Tunisian state progressivism

The performance-oriented praxis of Bourguiba's and, to a much greater extent, Ben Ali's seemingly progressive gender policies constitutes a significant pattern of state behavior in its own right. Tracing the evolution of religion and women's rights as connected discourses in recent Tunisian history forces a critical rethinking of what some scholars have dubbed Tunisia's "master narrative of modernity."[40] Both Bourguiba and Ben Ali attempted to popularize an image of Tunisian modernity as progressively linear, secular, and inherently supportive of women's rights. Bourguiba himself contributed powerfully to the production and performance of this narrative, as demonstrated by his mausoleum epitaphs. The Bourguibist narrative is an inspiring tale that pits a courageous secular modernizer, Bourguiba himself, against a recalcitrant and often backward Tunisia which he somehow manages to wrest from its cow paths onto the thoroughfare of liberal reforms. Ben Ali attempted to maintain this legitimizing narrative, portraying himself to Tunisians and the world as reliable bulwark devoted to thwarting the "Islamic fundamentalists" and preserving the rights of women, provided they refrained from expressing political criticisms or Islamist tendencies.

At the center of this performance-oriented progressivism has been the assumption that Tunisia represents a modernizing outlier state—a secular oasis in an otherwise patriarchal desert. Contrary to this perception, however, both Bourguiba and Ben Ali actively sought to politicize Islam, forging Islamic repertoires of personal legitimacy whilst simultaneously prohibiting oppositional actors from drawing on sacralized discourse and symbols, including the hijab.[41] Secularism in Tunisia had little to do with regime separation from religious matters. Like Bourguiba, who adopted religiously resonant titles such as *al-mujāhid al-akbar*, Ben Ali sought to build his reputation as a *munqudh* (savior), opening his speeches with the basmala (invocation of the name of God) and portraying himself as "*protecteur de la religion et des femmes*."[42] Ben Ali created a Ministry of Religious Affairs and oversaw extensive bureaucratization of religious practice.[43]

Tunisia's status as a secular outlier was associated with symbols and performance more than any clear separation between mosque and state. International actors considered Tunisia as a secular state primarily because its women frequently went unveiled and because they enjoyed more equality, despite the fact that the nation's leaders appropriated religious rhetoric and tightly controlled religious expression in schools, mosques, state offices, and the media.

Similarly, Tunisia's international reputation as a women-friendly backwater surrounded by patriarchal states was the result of considerable image manipulation and regime performance. Tunisia's adoption of the Convention to Eliminate All Forms of Discrimination Against Women (CEDAW) in 1985 epitomized the country's deeply contradictory approach to women's rights. While Tunisia allowed the adoption of CEDAW to proceed, it stipulated a number of reservations based on religious and traditional heritage.[44] More critical, though, was the stark disconnect between Tunisia's international accolades and its internal suppression of politically dissident women, most of whom were Islamists. While the UN, United States, and various European countries praised Tunisia's acceptance of CEDAW, Bourguiba—motivated by fears of rising Islamist political opposition—overtly circumscribed women's rights to religious self-expression, coordinating harsh crackdowns on forms of religious dress like the hijab, tolerating police harassment of Islamist women, and dismissing as pro-Islamist female (and male) political opponents who criticized his rule. A number of Bourguiba's reforms—most notably the expansion of universal education and the PSC—had a net positive impact for Tunisian women. Nevertheless, these reforms were enforced in a top-down manner alongside highly restrictive decrees that thwarted women's right to politically organize, express themselves religiously, or criticize the regime.

If advancements for women's rights followed a one-step-forward, one-step-back trajectory under Bourguiba, they slowed to one-step-forward, three-steps-back under Ben Ali. Ben Ali intuitively understood how to bend the Western-inflected liberal rights lexicon to suit his autocratic ends. He trumpeted his support for women's rights activities, contrasting his regime's stable secularity with Islamists, whom he portrayed as reactionary terrorists stubbornly opposed to women's advances. The regime trumpeted women's rights as a legitimizing badge of equality and democracy in the international community. Ben Ali's wife Leila stood at the helm of numerous women's organizations, including the Arab League of Women, the Tunisian Mothers' Association, and the World Association of Women Entrepreneurs.[45] Referring to the Tunisian Mothers' Association, Emna Jeblaoui of the Tunis-based Arab Institute for Human Rights recalled the following:

> It stunk. The organization was propaganda, just window dressing for the country. They gave clichéd speeches outside Tunisia and only held one or two events inside—just enough to say "we're here" then they sent their people outside—especially to France and, to a lesser extent, to the US—to encourage them to lay off human rights abuses at home.[46]

Under Ben Ali's presidency, outspoken activists of all stripes—most notably Islamists, but also a number of feminists and human rights campaigners such as Radhia Nasraoui and Sihem Ben Sedrine—were targeted by the regime, and prisoners of conscience numbered in the yet-undocumented thousands.[47] Ben Ali's constant efforts to trumpet a much-massaged version of Tunisia's record on women's rights to the outside world did not sit well with many Tunisians, who now tend to associate feminism with a project of dictatorial self-marketing that deflected international attention from the very grave human rights abuses happening within Tunisia.

The Tunisian revolution: opportunities and challenges

For the first time in living memory, most Tunisians are enjoying freedom to openly criticize their government. This openness poses both opportunities and challenges for the future of women's rights. Tunisians are finally able to contest the legacy of regime feminism and craft a more representative framework for guiding the state's relationship with women's rights. However, many secular-laicist women have worried that democracy might unleash long-percolating conservative trends in Tunisian society, the most dangerous of which they generally consider to be Islamist currents and significantly less popular, but nonetheless increasingly visible, Salafi trends.[48] While Tunisia has taken important steps regarding human and women's rights since the revolution, significant obstacles—mostly related to the weakness of state institutions—remain.

One significant step forward came in the form of a progressive parity law passed in May, 2011—just months before Tunisians elected the National Constituent Assembly (*al-Majlis al-Waṭanī al-Ta'sīsī*), a 217-member body charged with dual tasks of governing and writing a constitution reflective of the people's will. The parity law stipulated that women must comprise 50 percent of the candidates on each party's electoral lists, and that men and women's names must alternate down the lists in a so-called "zipper system." Most parties—many of which only formed after the revolution—opposed the law, realizing they would have difficulty finding enough female candidates to fill their lists. Ennahda, however, supported the law, confident that its support base was broad enough to field significant numbers of women candidates in most districts. Ennahda ultimately ran more female candidates in more electoral districts than any of its competitors and was the only major party to fully follow the rule both in spirit and in letter.

Women's advent to corridors of power was an unexpected consequence of Ennahda's victory. Women currently comprise 24 percent of the Constituent Assembly (49 out of 217) representatives, outpacing their counterparts in the French, British, and American legislatures. Whether or not the parity principle (*mabda' al-tanāṣuf*) will apply in Tunisia's next elections remains to be seen. Regardless of future gender quotas, women in the Constituent Assembly have played a crucial role in drafting constitutional articles, arguing for and against key pieces of legislation, and representing their parties' platforms and policies in the media.

Despite their front-and-center role in the Constituent Assembly, women still face a number of obstacles. These are largely a product of existing structural weaknesses that continue to plague key institutions of Tunisian society and governance, such as the yet-unreformed judicial and security sectors. The following section highlights six particularly critical issues affecting the future of women's rights in postrevolutionary Tunisia—constitutional drafting and debate, reform of the PSC, judicial reform, the rights of unmarried women, transitional justice, and security reform. I emphasize ways in which underdeveloped institutions—rather than ideological differences seized upon by the media and politically polarized actors—may present the most problematic challenges for Tunisian women's rights in the near future.

Constitutional drafting and debate

By August 14, 2012, each of the Constituent Assembly's six subcommittees had submitted their drafts to the Coordination Committee, which began to revise these drafts into a single edited, cohesive constitution in September. Three portions of August's draft constitution elicited varying degrees of criticism: Article

3, which called for the "criminalization of all attacks on that which is sacred"; Article 45, which sought to determine whether the president should be elected by popular vote or parliamentary vote; and Article 28, which defined the status of women. The proposed Article 28, as it was formulated in early August, stated verbatim that:

> The state guarantees the protection of women and supports their achievements, considering them as men's veritable partners in building the nation, and the roles of men and women complement one another within the family. The state guarantees equal opportunity between men and women in carrying out different responsibilities. The state guarantees the elimination of all forms of violence against women.[49]

Before the draft was even released, rumors that Article 28 referred to women as "men's complements" and "associates" (i.e. dependents) leaked from Ettakatol MP Salma Mabrouk's Facebook page into Tunisian and international news media.[50] Western wire services, Reuters, and other media outlets reproduced the mistranslations as direct quotes, and a report from the UN Working Group on Tunisian Women cited similar incorrect translations.[51] Even academics and prominent policy analysts based sharp criticisms off the mistranslations.[52] Article 28 provoked a firestorm of controversy, generating more coverage in foreign French and English language news sources than practically any single Tunisian event in 2012.

Though Western media sources failed to refer to the exact text of Article 28—in part because the draft constitution was released only in Arabic—there was no question that its language did depart from the standard liberal, individualistic template of Western human rights norms. The conjugated Arabic verb *yetekāmelu* (in the imperfect tense) translated above as "complement one another" has a deeper sense of enriching or integrating two parts to form a unified whole.[53] Such relational terminology reflects Ennahda's more Islamist-tinged philosophy that individuals are interconnected within an *'umma*, or community of believers, comprised of different but equal/complementary components, and that men and women are similarly connected in their contributions and responsibilities within the marriage bond. Both male and female Ennahda members tend to believe that while the sexes were created equal under God in terms of their *taqwā* (piety), *ḥuqūq* (rights), and *wājibāt* (obligations) they nonetheless remain distinctive in terms of certain biological roles and culturally determined familial obligations.

Female Ennahda representatives, including Ferida Labidi and Monia Brahim—MPs who sit on the Rights and Liberties subcommittee that drafted Article 28—felt that the article was mistranslated and taken deliberately out of context by the party's detractors. Labidi appeared repeatedly on radio and television, claiming that Ennahda's opponents ignored the fact that equality of all citizens had already been established in Article 22 of the draft. Brahim explained that the flurry of impassioned attacks against Article 28 "took us by surprise":

> We should have thought to release an English or French translation along with the Arabic draft. We didn't expect that the mistranslations of the text would be that bad—I don't think most Western journalists even read it . . . What we tried to say between Article 22 and Article 28 was that men and women are equal and complementary.[54]

Regardless of Ennahda's attempts to downplay and defuse the fallout over Article 28, the underlying concept of "equal complementarity" was nonetheless ambiguous. Although Article 28 did not explicitly contravene any portion of the 1956 PSC, its convoluted wording left wide scope for interpretation on the part of future legislators and local judges. The insertion of unclear, relational language into Article 28 generated mistrust amongst Tunisian feminists, some of whom feared the article might represent the much-feared first step in an insidious program of *Nahdawī* Islamization.

The National Constituent Assembly (Assemblée Nationale Constituante, ANC) eventually opted to delete the complementarity clause from the constitution in late September 2012, replacing Article 28 with a much clearer article (Article 37 and Article 45 in the June 1, 2013 version) stating that "all male and female citizens are equal in rights and duties."[55] This decision demonstrated the generally inclusive nature of Tunisia's constitution-building process, which has tended to respond to civil society input. Throughout the month of August and much of September, local women's rights groups, international organizations, and regular Tunisian citizens advocated forcefully in favor of using the term *musāwāt* (equality) rather than complementarity-centric language. On National Women's Day (August 13), an estimated 7,000 Tunisians thronged through a major boulevard in downtown Tunis protesting Article 28.[56] Public figures—from Sihem Badi, Tunisia's Minister of Women's Affairs, to Souad Abderrahim, an Ennahda MP—called for the Article's revision. On September 12, the ANC launched a consultative mechanism on its official website to welcome feedback from citizens. Soon thereafter, the ANC held two days of debate and discussion with Tunisian civil society organizations. Though some influential civil society organizations—including the Tunisian League of Human Rights (Ligue Tunisienne de Droits de l'Homme, LTDH) and the ATFD—boycotted the event, more than 300 organizations participated.[57]

The ANC sought input from civil society and swiftly reversed the complementarity clause, demonstrating that the "Troika" coalition at its helm, including Ennahda, were open to compromise. Rather than clinging to ideological positions regarding women's role in the family unit, Ennahda took a more flexible, pragmatic approach, accommodating public opinion to a considerable degree. Besides refusing to enshrine Sharia law in Article 1 of the constitution—a unique step for any allegedly Islamist party—Ennahda compromised on another piece of draft legislation and deleted the criminalization clause from Article 4 following criticism from local CSOs and international organizations.[58]

Though the controversy over Article 28 was resolved, important legal obstacles still remain for Tunisian women concerning inheritance and child custody rights. These laws were bundled into Tunisia's 1956 PSC, an unwieldy blend of French civil law and Sharia-based jurisprudence. Ennahda leaders sometimes claim that the PSC's Sharia-based inheritance law functions as a kind of legitimizing lynchpin that justifies the code as a religiously authoritative, culturally valid legal source in the eyes of many Tunisians.

A series of focus groups exploring public opinion on women's political participation conducted by the National Democratic Institute (NDI) found that support for the existing inheritance law is indeed widespread throughout the country. "When discussing heritage [*sic*]," the report noted, "most participants, across gender and different age groups, favored a literal interpretation of the *Sharia*." The report quoted a twenty-one-year-old female student from Gafsa as saying, "No equality in inheritance. This is a religious issue; we can have equality in other matters but not in questions that are related to religion."[59] Any mention of altering the inheritance law—or the comparatively progressive PSC in which it is enshrined—would be a risky move for almost any politician. During the 2011 campaign season, only one party leader—Moncef Marzouki of the Congress for the Republic (Congrès pour la République, CPR)—dared to publicly call for changing the law.[60]

The revised constitutional draft goes farther than the 1956 PSC, explicitly elevating equality between men and women to the constitutional level. There is a slim chance this could catalyze certain reforms of Tunisia's PSC that secular women's rights activists have championed, including a revised inheritance code. As the Troika's willingness to compromise on key portions of Articles 4 and 28 have demonstrated, Ennahda, primarily concerned with maintaining popularity beyond its core base of supporters, will back off from ideological issues to quell public outcry. However, as the NDI's report indicates, public opinion in favor of the inheritance law is strong, meaning politicians will be unlikely to change the law until a shift in popular demand renders such a change politically expedient.

The Personal Status Code

One important point of consensus that bodes well for women's future is the widespread support that exists for Tunisia's 1956 PSC. As noted above, a handful of prominent sheikhs at Zitouna mosque pushed against the code in the late 1950s and early 1960s on the grounds that some of its statutes, particularly those concerning divorce and polygamy, contradicted the tenets of Sharia. Ennahda's forerunner, the MTI, criticized the PSC during the 1980s.

Over the past three decades, however, Ennahda's position has evolved significantly, and the vast majority of Tunisians—save for the country's ultraconservative Salafi minority—seem to embrace the code as a proud piece of national legislation that advances women's rights and authentically represents what many indigenize as "Tunisian Islam"—an Islam characterized by tolerance, moderation, and progressive openness to the outside world. Today, members of Ennahda throughout the country, both at leadership and grassroots levels, say the PSC is grounded in Sharia-based jurisprudence. Farida Labidi, the above-mentioned human rights lawyer who sits on Ennahda's guiding shura council, claims to have written her dissertation on the topic of the PSC's basis in Sharia law.[61]

When questioned about the matter of *taʿadud e-zawjāt* (polygamy)—an illegal and largely frowned-upon practice in Tunisia—Ennahda members categorically deny harboring any desire to legislate the practice, claiming the Prophet Mohamed instituted this as both a progressive reform and a last-resort practice at a time when there were no limitations on the number of wives a man could take. Ennahda leaders have made repeated statements exonerating the PSC, and tend to feel that those who accuse the party of supporting pro-polygamy legislation are misinformed or grasping at straws. Most Tunisians' shared belief that the PSC represents a fundamental baseline for women's rights ensures a relatively moderate framework and considerable common ground for future discussions concerning women's legal status in Tunisia.[62]

Judicial reform

While constitutional pitfalls seem to have been largely avoided, Tunisian women may find the absence of an independent judiciary to be a significant obstacle to their well-being in the long term. Though the Ennahda-led government has spearheaded detailed roadmaps regarding judicial reform, these plans have yet to be implemented. So far, reform of Tunisia's corrupted judiciary has been limited mainly to wanton purges of former regime elements rather than deeper, critically important structural reforms. The main mechanism by which Ben Ali controlled the judiciary—the Conseil supérieur de la magistrature (Supreme Council of Magistrates)—remains under the near-total control of the executive power, contrasting bleakly with the strict separation of powers found in more mature, stable democracies.[63]

As Nathan Brown and Adel Omar Sharif have pointed out, judicial independence is critical for protecting human rights, facilitating political stability and fairness, and developing sound economies.[64] Widespread abuses of women's rights—including Islamist women's rights and the rights of critical political activists like Sihem Ben Sedrine—occurred under the Ben Ali regime in large part because the country lacked a legal system that had the independence and authority to protect constitutionally endowed rights. From courthouse lawyers to judges, Tunisia's legal system remains under the control of the executive branch. Recent dismissals of seventy-five judges on corruption charges re-emphasized the extent to which the rights of all Tunisians—both men and women—may be vulnerable to the whims of governing executive powers.[65] Tunisia's weak judiciary represents a little-discussed, but highly important institutional threat to securing human and women's rights in the future.

Rights of single mothers

Unmarried women and their children remain in a state of non-recognition under Tunisian law. Mothers whose babies are born out of wedlock face extreme difficulties registering their children for government services and are not eligible for state-provided forms of special assistance. While some families end up assisting the young men and women whose children are born out of wedlock, deeply entrenched cultural biases against unmarried couples who have children have rendered political discussions of the problem taboo.

Fortunately, the conversation surrounding this issue began to open up following a heated debate in November 2011 between Ennahda representative Souad Abderrahim (a Tunis-based pharmacist and the sole female Ennahda MP who does not wear a hijab) and supporters of single mothers' rights. Shortly after winning her seat to the ANC, Abderrahim retorted that single mothers "do not have a right to exist" when a radio presenter suggested that they should be protected under Tunisian law. "I am ashamed of Arab and Muslim countries that try to make excuses for people who have sinned," Abderrahim said, adding that "there is no room for full and absolute freedom."[66]

While the backlash to Abderrahim's statements came primarily from Tunisia's more secular communities and pundits, it was nonetheless extremely vocal. Women's rights groups such as the ATFD fought back, and Abderrahim eventually retracted her comments, claiming that her views were distorted by an overly antagonistic radio presenter. "My real point . . . was that the state should not subsidize behavior that destroys families," she said.[67] The conflagration over Abderrahim's comments raised awareness of single mothers' plight in Tunisia, as well as outspoken societal currents that were unafraid to challenge existing taboos and fiercely contest unfair treatment in the law.

Abderrahim's comments also reflected a much deeper turmoil within Ennahda—and Tunisian society at large—concerning the tension between perceived political freedoms and moral freedoms. While leading *Nahdawī* women tend to voice support for political freedoms such as voting, protesting, and criticizing, their stand on matters of personal moral freedom—particularly regarding sexuality and religion—are consistent with conservative views, be they Christian, Jewish, or Muslim. Emphasis on narrow interpretations of sexual mores is the hallmark of religiously based conservative political positions worldwide. Still, Ennahda activists scorn ultraconservative interpretations of Sharia taken by many local Salafis and hardliner Wahhabis in the Saudi Arabian government and disparage policies such as mandating that women wear hijab.

Postrevolutionary reordering of administrative structures both nationally and municipally has opened a decentralized space for local actors to oppose state-mandated policies. Reports that certain doctors and public hospital workers have denied abortions to some women (particularly those who are unmarried) came out toward the end of 2012.[68] Abortion, which has been state-provided for all adult women in Tunisia since 1973—is acceptable during the first three months of pregnancy for married women under most interpretations of Sharia, but is considered religiously unacceptable for unmarried women, who have traditionally been chastised for having sexual relations outside the marriage bond.

Overcoming ideological conflicts: transitional justice and the search for common ground

Postrevolutionary Tunisia is riven with deep polarities pitting secularists and leftists against their more conservative *Nahdawī* counterparts, not to mention the Salafis who are routinely and uncritically lumped in the same basket as the *Nahdawīs*. Over the past year, fresh tensions have emerged between ultra-conservative Salafis—the most vocal of whom are young and increasingly opposed to what they see as Ennahda's overly pragmatic, US-accommodating approach—and other sectors of Tunisian society, including both secularists and more gradualist Islamists of the Ennahda leadership variety. Terrified of the Wahabbi-influenced Salafi trend, many secularists and laicists have conflated Ennahda and Salafi streams as part of the same "*menace islamiste*" (Islamist threat) and have grown even more radically opposed to dialoguing with Ennahda than they were at the outset of Tunisia's revolution.

This intense polarization is most visible regarding issues of women's rights. Tunisia's leading feminist organizations are decidedly secular and tend to view female *Nahdawī* activists as non-agentive actors content to exist in a duped stupor of Islamist patriarchy. On the other hand, Ennahda's activist women, along with significant numbers of center-right religious and rural women who frequently support Ennahda, harbor deep-seated resentments against secular feminists that stem largely from the Ben Ali years, when these groups were embraced by Ben Ali and voiced support for the regime's crackdown on women wearing hijab. Many Tunisians, *Nahdawī* women included, bring up the matter of a 2004 open letter that the ATFD allegedly sent to Ben Ali in which the group was rumored to have implored Ben Ali to continue the crackdown on women who chose to wear hijab. Many *Nahdawī* women entertain their own stereotypes of secular feminists, caricaturing them as an elite, French-speaking minority whose concerns are self-serving, superficial, and far removed from the lived realities of most Tunisian women.

Focus group studies conducted by the National Democratic Institute in February 2012 reveal that a majority of Tunisians—both men and women, and across Tunisia's various regions—tend to view high-profile secular feminist groups (the most famous of which is the ATFD) as elitist and out of touch with the needs of most Tunisians. When questioned about the "women's issues" that matter to them, many women in rural areas speak first about economic issues, i.e. access to jobs. Today the ATFD and other groups organize caravans of feminist activists who travel to the Tunisian interior. However, prior to the revolution these groups had little contact with women beyond the urban coastal centers. Instead, the women's rights associations have spent a great deal of time at internationally funded conferences for women's rights held in the capital city of Tunis and its environs. Combined with their relatively favored status under Ben Ali and the extent to which feminism became struck with the "curse of the first lady" as Leila Trabelsi made herself the face of Tunisian feminism, this sense of economic disconnect has rendered the ATFD and other secular feminist groups unpopular with large swathes of the Tunisian population.

While *muḥajjabāt* (veiled women) have become active in NGOs and political parties since the revolution, they are not represented in the leadership structures of Tunisia's most visible and best-funded women's rights groups. Instead, they have tended to coalesce their activism around newly formed groups, many of which are advocating to bridge gaps in regional economic disparity, assist homeless women, and collect dossiers of the (mostly Islamist) women who were victims of human rights violations under Ben Ali. Women in these organizations resent the perceived Western favoritism shown to urban, secular women's rights groups—such as constant invitations to international conferences both in Tunisia and abroad, favorable reports in foreign press, and better networks with grant-giving institutions.

Because groups perceived to be Islamist (ranging from charity foundations organized by hijab-wearing women to Qur'anic reading groups) were prohibited under the old regime, civil society activism organized by more visibly religious and rural women is a recent phenomenon in Tunisia. These groups are new, unsure how to navigate international conferences and funding channels, and have almost no experience in organizing and disseminating their messages and goals. Ibtihel Abdellatif, president and founder of Tunisian Women, an NGO that is compiling the dossiers of women who were victims of police abuse (including brutal arrests, imprisonment, and sexual violations), said:

> This is an uphill struggle. *Les Femmes Démocrates* [ATFD] were not there to help us when we were arrested and abused in prisons, when our husbands were in jail and the police came to our houses and abused us. But they are the first to be invited now to anything about transitional justice and defending women's rights. We are working hard every day, but it is like we are invisible.[69]

Transitional justice—uncovering and addressing the widespread human rights violations that occurred at the hands of regime officials—will be a lengthy and daunting process. The ATFD and other women's rights groups that operated, albeit with limitations, under the Ben Ali regime, appear nervous that truth commissions might uncover their lack of support among women who suffered serious human rights violations. Used to a privileged status under the old regime and traditional recipients of Western support, these associations are now faced with a radically altered paradigm of state-society relations: the same religiously conservative, Islamist individuals who were persecuted under Ben Ali have now taken key leadership posts, and women's rights groups must function in the absence of an authoritarian figure committed to bulwarking a secular feminist agenda.

For the transitional justice process to be successful, the schism between secular and more religiously conservative women must be addressed. Misunderstandings, prejudices, and justified outrage stem from a long period of repression and corrupted favoritism institutionalized under the old regime. Suspicions that laicist women were somehow a cat's paw for the French government, or that Islamist women were duped into wearing hijab or joining Ennahda by their terrorist/fundamentalist male family members, grew under the highly repressive environment of Ben Ali's Tunisia. Competition between the various political ideologies exists in abundance and represents a generally positive trend toward more democratic contestation. Even still, a truth-seeking period of historical honesty and mutual respect would greatly benefit Tunisian women's associations, perhaps enabling them to collaborate on shared issues of concern in the future, of which there are many (including opposition to domestic violence, efforts aimed at raising women's economic position, educational initiatives, and more). Such grassroots, "shawārma style" cooperation—chipping away at shared socioeconomic problems in small but effective ways—would be especially useful in today's political climate, as the Troika and secular opposition have been embattled in largely unproductive debates and have failed to achieve meaningful reform on the economic inequalities and security abuses that afflict most Tunisians.

Security sector reform: continued police brutality and lack of accountability

Another issue that may prove a serious obstacle to Tunisian democracy in general, and to women's rights in particular, is the country's weak and corruption-warped security sector. Although Tunisia did not experience a ferocious, out of control army à la Egypt or Algeria, the country's dictators instead ensured their control through the Ministry of the Interior's loyal network of national police and unnamed informants known as *al-būlīs al-siyāsi* (the political police). Bourguiba transformed internal security into a kind of personal

Praetorian guard, a tradition that Ben Ali continued. No code of police ethics is known to have existed under the Ben Ali regime, and rules governing proper professional practices amongst internal security forces (police, *garde nationale*, *protection civile*, and so on) and intelligence services were not codified or widely understood, even within the Ministry of the Interior itself. As one scholar has noted, Tunisia's internal security forces operated in a "legal void."[70]

Under Ben Ali, police abuse of innocent civilians went almost wholly unchecked. The threat of "*terrorisme*" became a frequent excuse for targeting political opponents, most commonly Islamist sympathizers, many of whom were tortured, raped, and blacklisted from employment.[71] A video tape of police officers forcing Ouidad Laarayedh to undress and stand in the nude was sent to her husband, prominent Ennahda member Ali Laarayedh, while he was being held in solitary confinement.[72] Ali Laarayedh, who was imprisoned for a total of fifteen years, recalls that the experience caused him to have a nervous breakdown.[73] Such abuses were not isolated incidents—men in Ennahda have testified that they themselves were sodomized with glass bottles, and have related stories of policemen raping members' wives on tape, then forcing imprisoned husbands to watch such videos.[74]

Despite the fact that many key positions of leadership are now held by elected Ennahda officials who suffered immensely under the old regime (including Ali Laarayedh, who—in an ironic and deeply significant twist of fate, became minister of the interior following the 2011 elections), surprisingly little action has been taken to reform Tunisia's security sector. The internal decrees that regulate the police force have not been made public. Similarly, laws that existed under Ben Ali's regime, such as the State of Emergency Law and the Law on Public Meetings, which give the executive authority extensive powers to prohibit and suppress public gatherings, have not been repealed. Reports of police impunity and torture remain widespread, and practically no action has been taken to develop an ethical code or educational system for reforming Tunisia's highly abusive police culture.

Such institutional weaknesses portend dangerous implications for women's rights. Shortly following the revolution, one woman complained that she had spotted her rapist—a local police officer—walking freely in her neighborhood. "He didn't show himself for a couple of months after the revolution," she said. "But now he's back on the street . . . I see no justice."[75]

Reports of police abusing their power to harass and rape women continue to appear in Tunisian media. One case that gained widespread coverage involved an anonymous young woman who was spotted engaging in "indecent behavior" with her boyfriend in a parked car then raped by two police officers.[76] The woman was subsequently tried for indecent conduct in public then acquitted in December 2012. Her assailants have been tried. While many reports framed the issue ideologically (with headlines hinting "Islamist government tries woman for being raped"), this incident provided a more direct indictment of the Tunisian security sector, which remains a chaotic, unregulated, and often dangerous force in the daily lives of many Tunisians and for women in particular.[77] It also shone light on Tunisian public opinion regarding the justifiability of sexual crimes. Many Tunisians seemed to feel that because the police discovered the woman engaged in sexual activity with her boyfriend, her rape was somehow less shocking or condemnable. "Women should protect themselves," one middle-aged Tunisian police officer told me. "She made it easy."

According to a 2012 NDI report, harassment of women, by police and civilians alike, seems to have increased since the revolution. Whereas police used to harass women wearing hijabs, sometimes tearing off their head coverings and spitting on them, there have been increasing reports of police stopping women whom they deem to be wearing inappropriate clothing or consorting too intimately with young men or foreigners. While some critics of the government insinuate that the police are only doing Ennahda's bidding, the reality is likely less conspirational. Without clear regulations and a clear chain of command, gun-shy police have often avoided law enforcement, contributing to an atmosphere of unregulated chaos in which instances of sexual harassment have grown more commonplace.

Conclusion

The Revolution of Freedom and Dignity represented a watershed moment for Tunisia and the MENA region as a whole. Although the revolution has redirected the state's relationship to women's and human rights, it has not entirely erased established patterns of political self-interest and heavily centralized monopolization. Features of regime feminism that long characterized the state's approach to women's rights—including political opportunism, stereotyped renderings of an over-simplified "Islamists vs. women's rights" conflict, and tensions between paternalistic leadership and the critical forces of civil society, may resurface in the future.

Since the revolution, much local coverage and virtually all foreign French and English language coverage of Tunisian women's issues has focused on the threat of Islamism. This chapter has argued that, although the revolution unleashed widely divergent ideological visions of women's role in society, the main challenges to women's rights in the early phase of Tunisia's transition have stemmed from ingrained social attitudes and institutional weaknesses—not Islamist ideology. Prejudice toward single mothers, widespread tolerance of domestic violence, and the lack of trust between feminists, Islamists, and many women in between did not originate overnight with the revolution. These tensions and attitudes have brewed for decades, and will take years to resolve. Similarly, creating a strong and independent judiciary, reforming Tunisia's police culture, and sorting through the sensitive issues of transitional justice will take much more time.

Ultimately, isolated discussions that carve "women's rights" away from more substantive issues of institutional reform and human dignity fail to resonate with many Tunisian women, who have criticized feminist groups and international NGOs for prioritizing headline-grabbing ideological issues over the nuts-and-bolts issues that impact their daily lives. Cumbersome matters like judicial independence, transitional justice, civilian oversight of internal security, and economic health might not seem directly related to women's rights, narrowly conceived. But these issues represent some of the gravest challenges to Tunisian women's current and future well-being. Future research on women's rights in the Tunisian context must resist the urge to focus exclusively on politicized conflicts pitting Islamists against secularists and instead shine light on deeply entrenched social attitudes and institutional norms which represent less obvious, but no less fundamental obstacles to women's progress.

Notes

1. Certain center-left and secular parties, the most vocally critical of which was Al-Tajdād (Movement of Renewal), jockeyed to paint Ennahda as a misogynist movement, but Ennahda fought back, renting a massive conference hall in downtown Tunis for its widely advertised National Women's Day celebration on August 13, 2011. The atmosphere at this event was both assertive and defensive, featuring an array of eminent Ennahda women who took to the podium to debunk detractors' claims that Ennahda was male dominated.
2. Secularly oriented news outlets like *Al-Maghreb* and Nessma TV jockeyed to boost readership and viewership, respectively, by focusing on ideologically polarizing elements of the campaign, including a possible Ennahda-led backtracking on women's rights.
3. For instance Brian Whitaker, "Tunisia is Leading the Way on Women's Rights in the Middle East," *The Guardian*, September 10, 2011.
4. Isobel Coleman, "Is the Arab Spring Bad for Women?" *Foreign Policy*, December 20, 2011, accessed June 12, 2012, www.foreignpolicy.com/articles/2011/12/20/arab_spring_women.
5. Although Ennahda won 41 percent of the vote, only 51 percent of all eligible voters in Tunisia turned out on election day.
6. Author interview with Bill Lawrence, North Africa Director at International Crisis Group, December 19, 2012. In May 2011, Tunisia's interim government adopted a progressive measure that required all parties to run exactly 50 percent female candidates, and to alternate men and women's names down party lists in a so-called "zipper" system.
7. Jonathan Mitchell, "Tunisia's Islamist Victory Good for Women, Says Female Figurehead," *The Telegraph*, November 1, 2011.
8. Like Turkey, Tunisia has experienced state-led imposition of laicism (in French, *laïcité*) which seeks to guarantee citizens state protection from religion, as opposed to

Anglo-Saxon models of secularism which seek to protect religion from the state. After the revolution, some Tunisian parties—including Ennahda and more center-left, soft secular parties like CPR and Ettakatol began backtracking from the laicist model. For further reading on the contrasts between laicism and Anglo-Saxon secularism with many parallels to the Tunisian context, see Semiha Topal, "Everybody Wants Secularism—But Which One? Contesting Definitions of Secularism in Contemporary Turkey," *International Journal of Politics, Culture, and Society* 25.1–3 (2011): 1–14.

9. Mounira Charrad has argued that contests over state power have powerfully shaped Tunisia's gender policies. This section owes much to her work. See, for instance, Mounira Charrad, "Policy Shifts: State, Islam, and Gender in Tunisia, 1930s–1990s," *Social Politics* 4.2 (1997): 284–319.
10. See, for instance, the collaboration between the so-called Old Turbans and the Young Tunisians in Benjamin Rivlin, "The Tunisian Nationalist Movement: Four Decades of Evolution," *Middle East Journal* 6.2 (1952): 168.
11. Charrad, "Policy Shifts," 292.
12. Sami Zlitni and Zeineb Touati, "Social Networks and Women's Mobilization in Tunisia," *Journal of International Women's Studies* 13.5 (2012): 47.
13. Marion Boulby, "The Islamic Challenge: Tunisia Since Independence," *Third World Quarterly* 10.2 (1988): 592.
14. Boulby, "The Islamic Challenge," 592.
15. Bourguiba speech delivered in Sfax, December 5, 1957. Quoted in Boulby, "The Islamic Challenge," 593.
16. Bourguiba and Ben Youssef vied for supremacy within the Neo-Destour Party. Bourguiba ultimately prevailed, had Ben Youssef assassinated, and, in 1964, changed the name of the Neo-Destour Party to the Socialist Destourian Party. For more details, see Kenneth Perkins's chapter in this book.
17. Larbi Sadiki, "The Search for Citizenship in Ben Ali's Tunisia: Democracy versus Unity," *Political Studies* 50 (2002): 499–500. See also William Zartman, "Introduction: Rewriting the Future of the Maghreb," in *Economic Crisis and Political Change in North Africa*, ed. Azzedine Layachi (London: Praeger, 1998), 1–5.
18. Derek Hopwood, *Habib Bourguiba of Tunisia: the Tragedy of Longevity* (Oxford: Palgrave Macmillan, 1992).
19. Charrad argues that the PSC extended government control into rural areas and broke clan-based, religiously mediated marital relations into discrete conjugal units controlled by centralized state bureaucracy. See Charrad, "Policy Shifts," 297.
20. Boulby, "The Islamic Challenge," 592–3. For more information on Bourguiba's sidelining of the religious establishment, see Kenneth Perkins's chapter in this volume.
21. Clement Henry Moore, "Tunisia and Bourguibisme: Twenty Years of Crisis," *Third World Quarterly* 10.1 (1988): 179.
22. Sophie Bessis and Souhayr Belhassen, *Femmes du Maghreb: L'Enjeu* (Tunis: Cérès Productions, 1992), 148–9.
23. Boulby, "The Islamic Challenge," 601.
24. See also Franck Fregosi, "Bourguiba et la régulation institutionelle de l'islam: les contours audacieux d'un gallicanisme politique à la tunisienne," in *Habib Bourguiba: la trace et l'héritage*, ed. Michel Camau and Vincent Geisser (Paris: Karthala, 2004), 80.
25. Charrad, "Policy Shifts," 299.
26. Although *ittijāh* translates as "direction," the group is now known in English as the

Islamic Tendency Movement, derived from its French name, which uses the word *tendance* (tendency).

27. Boulby, "The Islamic Challenge," 609.
28. Decree 108, which prohibited the wearing of hijab in educational establishments, has been enforced to varying degrees since its passage in 1985. Enforcement peaked in the early 1990s and again after 2006—times when Ben Ali was especially worried about the growth of Islamist currents (following Ennahda's success in the early stages of the 1989 election and armed clashes near the town of Soliman in late 2006 and early 2007).
29. Souad Chater, *Les Emancipées du Harem: Regard sur la femme tunisienne* (Tunis: Édition la Presse, 1992), via Charrad, "Policy Shifts," 303. I am indebted to Mounira Charrad for extracting and translating this quote.
30. Chater, *Les Emancipées du Harem.*
31. Amnesty International, *Amnesty International Report, 1994: Tunisia* (London: Amnesty International, 1994). For detailed accounts of Ennahda women held under arrest and/or imprisoned, see Doris H. Gray, "Tunisia after the Uprising: Islamist and Secular Quests for Women's Rights," *Mediterranean Politics* 17.3 (2012): 285–302.
32. Olfa Lamloum and Luiza Toscane, "The Two Faces of the Tunisian Regime: Women's Rights, but Only for Some," *Le Monde Diplomatique: English Edition*, February 12, 1998. See also Kamel Labidi, "Tunisia is Backtracking on Women's Rights," *The Guardian*, August 25, 2010.
33. Considerable work on "state feminism" exists. See, for example, Mervat Hatem, "Economic and Political Liberation in Egypt and the Demise of State Feminism," *International Journal of Middle East Studies* 24.2 (1992): 231–51 and Emma C. Murphy, "Women in Tunisia: Between State Feminism and Economic Reform," in *Women and Globalization in the Arab Middle East*, ed. D. E. Abdella and P. Posusney (Boulder, CO: Lynne Rienner, 2003), 169–93.
34. Mounira Charrad, *States and Women's Rights: The Making of Postcolonial Tunisia, Algeria, and Morocco* (Berkeley, CA: University of California Press, 2001); Laurie Brand, *Women, the State, and Political Liberalization* (New York: Columbia University Press, 2008); and Ilhem Marzouki, *Le mouvement des femmes en Tunisie au XXème siècle* (Tunis: Cérès Productions, 1993).
35. Noura Bousali, "Les acquis de la femme sont-ils menacés?" *Le Temps*, August 12, 2012.
36. Susan Waltz, "Another View of Feminine Networks: Tunisian Women and the Development of Political Efficacy," *International Journal of Middle East Studies* 22 (1990): 26. See also Emma C. Murphy, "Women in Tunisia: A Survey of Achievements and Challenges," *Journal of North African Studies* 1.2 (1996): 141.
37. Boulby, "The Islamic Challenge," 593.
38. Larbi Sadiki, "The Search for Citizenship in Bin Ali's Tunisia: Democracy versus Unity," *Political Studies* 50 (2002): 505.
39. As evidence of this partnership, many Tunisians cite open letters that the ATFD allegedly sent to Ben Ali in 2003 and 2007. In these letters, the ATFD tells Ben Ali that his crackdown on Isamists has not succeeded since hijab wearing is on the rise. The ATFD invites Ben Ali to use its human rights framework—which sees the hijab as a manifestation of oppression—saying that its approach would banish hijab once and for all. The ATFD makes no secret of being a secular organization strongly opposed

to Islamists' philosophical platforms and clothing styles. Along with other high-profile women's organizations in Tunisia, including the Tunisian Women's Association for Research and Development (Association des Femmes Tunisiennes pour la Recherche et le Développement, AFTURD) and the Women's Commission of the Tunisian League of Human Rights, the AFTD issued a manifesto in March 2011 in response to three major "threats to Tunisia's modernist way of life," two of which were the "appearance of niqab" and "authorization for women to have ID photos wearing a scarf" following the January 2011 revolution. See Khadija Arfaoui, "Women and Education in Tunisia: From Independence to the Jasmine Revolution." Paper delivered at "Women's Studies North and South," International conference in Bellagio, Italy: 13-17 September, 2011, accessed June 4, 2012, www.catunescomujer.org/catunesco_mujer/documents/bellagio_compendium_9-dec-final.pdf.

40. Simon Hawkins, "Who Wears Hijab with the President: Constructing a Modern Islam in Tunisia," *Journal of Religious Affairs in Africa* 41 (2011): 42.
41. See also Pierre-Jean Luizard, *Laïcités autoritaires en terre d'islam* (Paris: Fayard, 2008), 252–60.
42. Such invocations and titles were common in Ben Ali's public appearances and speeches. For further information see Asma Larif Béatrix, "Changement dans la symbolique du pouvoir en Tunisie," *Annuaire de l'Afrique du Nord* 28 (1989), 141–51. See also Fred Halliday, "Tunisia's Uncertain Future," *Middle East Report* (1990): 25–7.
43. Recommended talking points for Friday sermons, or *khutāb*, were prepared by the ministry of religious affairs and distributed to imams throughout the country. Police were frequently placed in mosques to ensure that the talking points were covered and that imams' *khutāb* did not stray into politically critical territory.
44. Human Rights Watch, "Tunisia: Government Lifts Restrictions on Women's Rights Treaty," *Human Rights Watch*, September 7, 2011, accessed April 2, 2012, www.hrw.org/news/2011/09/06/tunisia-government-lifts-restrictions-women-s-rights-treaty.
45. For further explanation of Leila Trabelsi's connections to women's rights organizations see Gray, "Tunisia after the Uprising," 288–9.
46. Author's interview with Emna Jeblaoui, August 29, 2011.
47. Documenting the exact number of political prisoners under Ben Ali has been difficult, since many were arrested without official documentation and held in incommunicado detention either in police stations or jail cells for varying lengths of time. Amnesty International and other rights watchdogs had limited access to Tunisian prisons, and have had difficulty establishing exact figures. Author interview in Tunis with Lotfi Azzouz, Amnesty International President, August 26, 2011.
48. See the chapter by Fabio Merone and Francesco Cavatorta in this volume.
49. This translation is my own. For another translation see Larbi Sadiki, "Tunisia: Women's Rights and the New Constitution," *Al-Jazeera*, September 21, 2012, accessed February 13, 2013, www.aljazeera.com/indepth/opinion/2012/09/2012918102423227362.html.
50. Salma Mabrouk sat on the Rights and Liberties Committee that drafted Article 28 of the constitution. The full draft of Article 28 was released on August 8 and can be accessed at www.alchourouk.com/Ar/article.php?code=565818.
51. Tarek Amara, "Thousands Rally in Tunisia for Women's Rights," *Reuters*, August 13, 2012, accessed March 30, 2013, http://uk.reuters.com/article/2012/08/14/us-tunisia-women-rights-idUSBRE87C16020120814. Also see UN Working Group

on Tunisian Women, "News Release, Tunisia: UN Expert Group Calls on New Government to Protect and Strengthen Achievements on Equality and Women's Human Rights," Geneva, August 21, 2012.

52. See, for example, Isobel Coleman, "Women, Free Speech, and the Tunisian Constitution," *CNN World*, August 16, 2012, accessed January 13, 2013, http://globalpublicsquare.blogs.cnn.com/2012/08/16/women-free-speech-and-the-tunisian-constitution.
53. One could argue that "complete one another" or "fulfill one another" are more accurate translations.
54. Author interview with Monia Brahim, September 4, 2012.
55. See Article 5 of the revised constitutional draft released in Arabic on December 14, 2012, accessed December 28, 2012, www.anc.tn/site/main/AR/docs/divers/divers.jsp?id=5.
56. Monica Marks, "Complementary Status for Tunisian Women," *Foreign Policy*, August 20, 2012, accessed March 1, 2013, http://mideast.foreignpolicy.com/posts/2012/08/20/complementary_status_for_tunisian_women.
57. Carter Center, "The Carter Center Recognizes Tunisia's National Constituent Assembly Progress; Calls for Increased Public Participation, Outreach, and Transparency," September 12, 2012, accessed January 1, 2013, www.cartercenter.org/resources/pdfs/news/pr/tunisia-092612-full-statement-en.pdf.
58. While Article 1 of Tunisia's constitution contains no explicit mention of Sharia, it does state that Tunisia's religion is Islam—a declaration that could be used to defend existing Sharia-based laws. Interestingly, although Tunisia's interim government removed the country's specific reservations to CEDAW in September 2011, it retained one general reservation stating that the country will not adopt legislation that violates Chapter 1 of the constitution.
59. Gabriella Borovsky and Asma Ben Yahia, "Women's Political Participation in Tunisia after the Revolution: Findings from Focus Groups in Tunisia Conducted February 16–28, 2012," National Democratic Institute, May 2012, accessed May 12, 2012, www.ndi.org/files/womens-political-participation-Tunisia-FG-2012-ENG.pdf.
60. Marzouki answered candidly when questioned about his views on inheritance during various political roundtables and campaign events before the 2011 elections. He also expressed his views on inheritance during an interview with the author at CPR's Tunis headquarters on August 26, 2011.
61. Author interview with Farida Labidi, July 8, 2011.
62. Salafis represent a noteworthy exception to this point of view. Unlike other Tunisians, who tend to applaud the PSC, Salafis—including both other so-called "scientific" Salafis and younger jihadi Salafis—criticize the PSC for violating key tenets of Sharia and do not see it as legitimate.
63. Derek Lutterbeck, "After the Fall: Security Sector Reform in post-Ben Ali Tunisia," *Arab Reform Initiative* (September 2012): 11.
64. Nathan J. Brown and Adel Omar Sharif, "Judicial Independence in the Arab World," United Nations Development Programme, accessed March 23, 2013, www.deontologie-judiciaire.umontreal.ca/fr/textes%20int/documents/ONU_jud-independence_MONDE_ARABE.pdf.
65. Human Rights Watch, "Tunisia: Mass Firings a Blow to Judicial Independence,"

Human Rights Watch, October 29, 2012, accessed January 25, 2013, www.hrw.org/news/2012/10/29/tunisia-mass-firings-blow-judicial-independence.

66. Souad Abderrahim's interview on Radio Monte Carlo can be heard at www.youtube.com/watch?v=nxOAMHKIRAA (accessed December 30, 2012).
67. Author's interview with Souad Abderrahim, January 9, 2012.
68. Farah Samti, "Tunisian Democratic Women Address Post-Revolution Access to Abortion Services," *Tunisia Live*, November 10, 2012, accessed January 27, 2013, www.tunisia-live.net/2012/11/10/tunisian-democratic-women-address-post-revolution-access-to-abortion-services.
69. Author interview with Ibtihel Abdellatif, September 14, 2012.
70. Lutterbeck, "After the Fall," 10.
71. See Béatrice Hibou, "Domination and Control in Tunisia: Economic Levers for the Exercise of Authoritarian Power," *Review of African Political Economy* 108 (2006): 185–206. See also Amnesty International, "In the Name of Security. Routine Abuses in Tunisia," June 2008; OHCHR, "Universal Periodic Review of Tunisia," June 4, 2008; Conseil National pour les Libertés en Tunisie, *Rapport sur l'état des libertés en Tunisie*, March 15, 2000.
72. Olfa Lamloum and Luiza Toscane, "The Two Faces of the Tunisian Regime: Women's Rights, but Only for Some," *Le Monde diplomatique*, July 12, 1998.
73. Wafa Sdiri, "Portrait de Ali Larayedh, futur ministre de l'intérieur dans le gouvernement de Jebali," *Tunisie Numérique*, December 20, 2011.
74. See Amnesty International, *Amnesty International Report, 2004: Tunisia* (London: Amnesty International, 2004) and *Amnesty International Report, 2008*: Tunisia (London: Amnesty International, 2008). This section draws primarily on material related to the author in interviews with Ennahda members during July–August 2011 and January 2012.
75. Quote taken from interview with the author, August 22, 2011.
76. Ségolène Allemandou, "Violée par des policiers tunisiens, ma fiancée est accusée d'attentat à la pudeur," France24.com, September 27, 2012, accessed May 1, 2013, www.france24.com/fr/20120926-tunisie-societe-justice-islamisme-femme-violee-accusee-atteinte-pudeur-justice-condition-feminine.
77. See "Tunisie: lutter contre l'impunité, restaurer la sécurité," International Crisis Group, May 9, 2012, accessed December 20, 2012, at www.crisisgroup.org/en/regions/middle-east-north-africa/north-africa/tunisia/123-tunisia-combatting-impunity-restoring-security.aspx?alt_lang=fr.

CHAPTER 11

The Rise of Salafism and the Future of Democratization

Fabio Merone and Francesco Cavatorta

At the end of October 2012, the poor marginalized neighborhood of Douar Hicher in the suburbs of Tunis witnessed a few days of uncontrolled violence between the police and Salafi youths. The origins of the riots are contested, but the outcome is not. Two men belonging to the salafi movement, including the imam of the local mosque, died during the clashes, with a number of policemen also injured. Just like the attacks on the US embassy on September 11, 2012, or the rallies to demand a clear reference to Sharia law in the new constitutional text, the events of Douar Hicher highlighted the continued presence of Salafism on the public scene since the fall of the regime. Furthermore, this episode highlighted how Salafism has become a significant social force in many of the poorer neighborhoods of the country and it further reinforced the presumed association between Salafism and violence in so far as the police had to intervene to put an end to the riots.[1] For most Tunisians, the rise of Salafism in such a short period of time is extremely surprising because there was no indication that the phenomenon even existed in the country. At the same time, Tunisians are also fearful of Salafism because it is perceived to be a major destabilizing factor in the construction of a new political system due to its rejection of both democracy and liberalism.

Following the riots in Douar Hicher, the private Tunisian TV channel Ettounsiya broadcast a debate on its programme *Al-Tāsiʿa masāʾ* on November 1, 2012 to discuss the significance of such incidents. The anchor of the programme, Moez Ben Gharbia, invited the then minister of the interior and an Ennahda leader Ali Laarayedh; the minister for human rights and Ennahda member Samir Dilou; and representatives of the political opposition. The new imam of the mosque at the center of the events in Douar Hicher also participated in the discussion, but not from the studio. During the debate, the imam, displaying his *kafn* (burial cloth), claimed that he was ready to fight to the death for the sake of Allah and invited all salafis to do the same. Following this televised debate, the national press and a significant number of commentators claimed that the imam's intervention was a call for violence that had no place in contemporary Tunisia. A second televised debate on the same issue took place a week later and Moaz Ben Gharbia invited Bilel Chaouachi as representative of jihadi Salafism together with Béchir Ben Hassen, a salafi scholar involved in educational activities, Abdelfattah Mourou, Ennahda co-founder well-known for his moderate positions, and the late Chokri Belaïd, member of the left-wing Popular Front.

The student of religion and young imam Chaouachi (aged twenty-six) more than held his own during the debate with more consummate politicians and sheikhs, displaying not only his religiosity but also his revolutionary language and credentials. He insisted that *takfir* (declaration of unbelief directed at other Muslims) is part of Islam and anyone who contradicts God's law must be declared *kāfir* (unbeliever). It follows that Sharia must be the only source of legislation and that whoever promulgates laws that go against God's laws is not only *kāfir*, but also *ṭāghūt* (idolater), which is worse than *kāfir*. When asked what the punishment should be for those who legislate against God's law, Chaouachi replied, "In the name of Sheikhs Ben Laden and al-Zawahiri this [Tunisia] is the land of *daʿwa* (preaching) and not jihad. Jihad should be conducted when specific conditions materialize and such conditions today in Tunisia do not exist." The anchor pushed Chaouachi on this point and asked what would happen if the Tunisian Communist Party, for example, were to win the elections; would the salafi movement conduct a jihad then? Chaouachi replied that "when the real terrorists who live in this country take up arms against the people only then we will make jihad to defend the people," implying that the salafis are defenders of the revolution against the return of dictatorship. When accused of inciting violence, Chaouchi simply stated that he was "not inciting anyone to use violence, but simply laying out his political position." The anchor again pushed the young man on his reference to Ben Laden. Chaouchi argued that "Ben Laden made the *umma* walk tall and proud and he did not fear speaking the truth." At this point Mourou intervened in the debate and provocatively asked Chaouachi whether Ben Laden was to be considered an *ʿālim* (scholar), to which the young salafi replied, "Yes, he is. Whoever is not afraid to speak the truth is *ʿālim*. He is an *ʿālim* in practice [through his concrete actions rather than academic scholarship], in his deeds and not in words or in his scientific production." Following on from this, Ben Hassen, almost exasperated, stated that "the problem of these young men [the jihadi salafis] is that they do not recognize the [primacy] of the *ʿulamaʾ*. In order to get their respect you must have gone to prison and wore a military fatigue. If not, you are enslaved to petro-dollars and to the USA."

The two televised debates crystallize the way Salafism in Tunisia is regarded. Its opponents highlight its foreign nature, its links to Al-Qaedism as an ideology, and its lack of respect for traditional Islamic scholarship. Its proponents display different understandings and practices of Salafism, pointing to divergences from within, and highlight its revolutionary nature. This chapter provides first an account of the emergence of Salafism in Tunisia, arguing that it is the product of domestic social, political, and economic circumstances and not of external interference (although there are transnational links at play). The chapter goes on to analyze the complexity of Salafism in Tunisia, which on the one hand reflects the traditional divisions that scholars have pointed out in the past and on the other points to specificities and peculiarities that need to be accounted for. Finally, the chapter highlights the evolution, support basis, and strategic choices that Tunisian Salafism, in its different components, has undertaken during the ongoing process of democratization to voice its dissent.

The emergence of Salafism

Since the fall of the Ben Ali regime, Tunisian public opinion has had to adapt progressively to the terminology and categories through which Islam is used in public political debates. Contrary to many other parts of the Arab world, in Tunisia this was never really possible before the uprising because what had prevailed since independence was a radical closure of the political system towards political and, at times, social expressions of Islam. Both Bourguiba and Ben Ali subscribed to a Western, and notably French, model of modernization whereby public and political displays of religiosity were perceived solely in terms of threat and a return to a backwardness that Tunisians had to mobilize against.[2] State repression was accompanied for a time by what can be termed "societal exclusion" of religious *intégrisme* whereby significant sectors of Tunisian society had bought into the modernization process the ruling elites offered and perceived religious *intégrisme* as a threat, forcing it in part to moderate its stances progressively over time in order to remain politically relevant.[3] The combination of repression and a rather widespread social refusal of *intégrisme* meant that the image of a secular country that had definitively relegated religious practices to the private sphere became dominant. Regime propaganda, sectors of Tunisian society, and the international community all perceived Islamist actors as undermining Tunisian specificity and its apparently successful economic model.[4] Thus, this image and self-perception of a secular Tunisia was part and parcel of the propaganda effort of the Ben Ali regime to appease the Western international community,[5] but was also shared in many liberal middle-class circles who had benefited from the economic reforms of the regime and the repression of those who wanted to offer a different path to social and political development. Following the revolution, the emergence of both Ennahda as the principal political party and the rise of Salafism put to rest the mythology of *laïcité*[6] therefore reaffirming the necessity for Tunisian society to reconcile its effective social and political pluralism not only with the categories of Western modernization, but also with its Muslim-Arab identity.

The opening up of the political system and the electoral victory of Ennahda have allowed the proponents of a much stronger adherence to the Muslim-Arab identity in the construction of the postauthoritarian state to engage with the proponents of West-inspired modernity from a position of relative strength. However, rather than pushing for the creation of an Islamic state based on the application of Sharia as the sole source for legislation, what has emerged is a compromise between the secular sector of society and Ennahda around the notion of civil state and the subsequent marginalization of Sharia law. This political and institutional compromise finds its concrete expression in a draft constitutional text that places at its center the mechanisms of democracy as the only legitimate tools through which one is to govern society. Ennahda had already accepted the principle of democracy in the 1980s and despite the skepticism surrounding the party in the aftermath of the October 2011 elections, it has stuck to its position. Those who have reappeared on the political scene after the fall of the regime, both within the secular and Islamist camp, are those whom the dictatorship had silenced and who had worked together in exile to come up with a shared vision of a post-Ben Ali Tunisia. Paradoxically, a youth-led revolution has given rise to a political system where the cross-ideological debates and discussions about the identity and developmental path of Tunisia reprise those that took place in the 1980s, often with the same, and now much older, leaders at the helm. Within the Islamist camp, we have the re-emergence of Ennahda and its leader Ghannouchi confirming the choice of democracy made in the past. We also have the re-emergence of those Islamists who were against Ghannouchi and his group when they sought an ideological and intellectual reconciliation between Islam and democracy. Activists such as Mohammed Khouja and Rafik Aouni, who had broken with Ennahda in the early 1980s to begin a more radical engagement in jihadism, are today at the helm of the Front of Reform, one of a number of salafi parties that emerged in postrevolutionary Tunisia. Other salafi parties are Asala, led by Ali Mouladi Jihadi, and Arrahma, led by Said Jaziri. These parties took part in the October 2011 elections with independent lists because they had yet to be legalized, but obtained no seats. It is worth emphasizing again that these parties and their leaders represent the re-emergence of an old debate within Tunisian Islamism between *Nahdawīs* favorable to the civil state and salafis favorable to the instauration of Sharia law, having rejected the reformist path of Ennahda. The party Hizb at-Tahrir, a radical Islamist party and not necessarily a salafi one, active illegally in Tunisia since the 1980s, is also part of these debates about the nature of the state and the identity and institutions it should have. By virtue of its transnational character and political plan aiming at the re-instauration of the caliphate under the guidance of an enlightened leader, it enjoys a degree of credibility among young salafis. Having been legalized by the authorities, it might attract part of the protest vote and radical support at elections. This type of debating is, incidentally, the same for the secular and left-wing camp where, once again, old leaders reprised their role and continue the same discussions they have had among themselves and with Islamists since as far back as the 1980s. Thus, while President Moncef Marzouki argues in favor of compromise with the Islamists of Ennahda and accepts the importance of an Arab-Muslim identity, other leftists and liberals are very suspicious of Ennahda and prone French-style secularism.

The revolutionary process in Tunisia has, however, also allowed the entry onto the political and social scene of a social group previously very marginal, the *muhammashūn* (marginalized), who were the protagonists of the street effort to challenge and eventually defeat the regime. This does not mean that it was the only social block that actively participated in the revolution, which certainly had a cross-class and cross-ideological dimension. However, it should be underscored that the effective and violent presence on the streets against the security services makes the *muhammashūn* genuine revolutionary subjects. In any case, the middle class, either liberal and linked to the center left or more conservative and linked to Ennahda, took the lead of the postrevolutionary process rather quickly, managing the transition without engaging in any serious attempt to include the swathes of young disenfranchised people who demanded a radical departure from the socioeconomic policies of the past. Thus, a new generation has entered the scene through the politics of contestation and dissent. This new generation finds its ideological roots in the jihadi radicalism of those salafi activists who participated in the international jihad in some of the great pan-Muslim causes such as Bosnia, Chechnya, Afghanistan, and Iraq. The formative experiences in exile of a number of Tunisians who left the country because of the authoritarian nature of the Ben Ali regime were in the jihadi circles in Afghanistan and Iraq as well as in European cities where ideological training and organizational skills were learned. There are three key figures who symbolize and influence how postrevolutionary Salafism in Tunisia is beginning to think of its role: Tarek Maaroufi, Sami Essid, and Abou Iyadh (Seifallah Ben Hassine). Of these figures, Abou Iyadh emerges as the charismatic leader of the salafi group Ansar al-Sharia because of his participation in international jihadi causes and the time he spent in prison in Tunisia. In many ways his charisma, credibility, and following derive precisely from what Bechir Ben Hassen, a non-jihadi Salafi scholar with good relations with the current authorities, had so exasperatedly pointed out in the TV debate mentioned earlier: war and prison. Jihadism in Tunisia already existed and had begun to mobilize in the latter years of the Ben Ali regime and it is this that Abou Iyadh built on when leaving prison in the aftermath of the revolution. While there are very clear links with international causes, and some members did indeed participate in the jihad in Afghanistan and Iraq, it should be emphasized that the connection with Tunisia was never lost. In a sense Tunisian salafis were forced to go away because of the nature of the Tunisian regime and they are therefore the by-product of its repressive policies. In addition, in Tunisia itself, the little contestation that existed against the Ben Ali regime was not confined to the socioeconomic demands that emerged in Gafsa, for instance,[7] or to the public order disturbances that youths caused at football matches,[8] but instead included episodes and social behaviors that can be linked to jihadi Salafism. On the security front, the Jerba terrorist attack against the synagogue and the fire-fights in 2006 and 2007 between jihadists and security forces suggest that a challenge for the Ben Ali regime existed from within. The regime dealt with this threat through increased repression, with many young Tunisians incarcerated for their political-religious beliefs. On the social front, it became noticeable that society was also Islamizing from below and it would again be misleading to see increased personal religiosity as a product of the postrevolutionary period. The regime dealt with this in a different way and rather than resorting to sheer repression it attempted to play up its own religious legitimacy through the promotion of a Tunisia-specific Islam to counter *wahhabi* influences. It is no coincidence that the regime allowed for the launch of a religious radio station and an Islamic bank in the late 2000s. This combination of repression and concessions suggests, therefore, that a dynamic and active Islamization in certain sectors of society was in place before the end of the regime.

Thus, even before the revolution we had the development of two parallel phenomena. On the one hand, there is the spread and adoption of religious practices and behavior that can be described as puritanical but are strictly apolitical because there is still the need to appease the regime for fear of repression. This is the case, for instance, of Qur'anic schools.[9] On the other hand, there exists the political radicalization of a segment of the disenfranchised youth which finds its raison d'être in the mythology of international jihadism and in opposition to a regime that is not only authoritarian, but also increasingly incapable of delivering material goods.[10] It is this latter jihadi camp that emerges more forcefully after the revolution because it adopts policy positions and concrete behaviors that challenge the liberal-democratic consensus.

A number of points emerge from this. First is the confirmation that Salafism, with its ideological rejection of democracy, emphasis on the primacy of Sharia law, and support for international jihadism, has strong domestic roots dating back to the 1980s debate within Ennahda on its controversial reformist choice. While the majority of the party followed the pro-democracy line of Ghannouchi, a minority rejected it and embraced political violence against the regime or became involved in jihadi groups fighting abroad. Many salafis of that generation have come back to Tunisia from exile or have resurfaced from jail to form political movements demanding the application of Sharia, although they accept democratic procedures and play the game of elections. These salafis are not particularly influential, but they are testimony to the fact that Salafism has a history in the country. Second is the generation gap. The youth that had been the protagonists of the revolution are virtually absent from the new institutions being constructed and have to find other channels of political and social participation. This is true of both the Islamist and the secular camps. When it comes to the religious camp, the early enthusiasm of the youth for the Ennahda project has waned significantly because socioeconomic changes have not occurred quickly enough. Part of the youth, particularly in disenfranchised areas of the country, have therefore turned to Salafism as an ideology and guide to private and public behavior that allows them to take control of their own destiny and express their political demands. In this way Salafism has become a vehicle through which part of the Tunisian youth remains a protagonist of a revolution that they see being hijacked by a generation of old politicians. Third is the class aspect of the revolution. The protagonist of the process of democratization is, broadly speaking, the middle class in its different ideological references ranging from the Francophone/Francophile bourgeoisie to the religiously conservative one. The new political system is built on a compromise between these two sectors of the same class. This leads to the question of what type of political and social representation exists for a large mass of the disenfranchised, particularly young men, which is the pool from where Salafism draws its strength.

The complexity of Tunisian Salafism

In order to make sense of the complexity of Tunisian Salafism and highlight its specificity, it is necessary to examine it in the context of broader studies on Salafism. The definition of Salafism is still quite controversial in academic circles because of its internal fragmentation, which makes it difficult to neatly outline its main ideological tenets. In any case its contemporary use refers to an ideology that tends toward the purification of Islam, involving a return to a purist original version as practiced by the "pious ancestors."[11] Following on from this, a number of scholars have attempted to categorize the different strands of Salafism that have emerged over the last few decades as an alternative to the ideological moderation and open political engagement of the Muslim Brotherhoods across the region. For instance, Wiktorowicz identifies three forms of Salafism: purist (scientific), political, and jihadist.[12] Purist salafis are focused on maintaining the purity of Islam, in compliance with the religious requirements of the sacred texts. Purist or scientific salafis emphasize the need for preaching (*daʿwa*) and education (*tarbiyya*) in order to change individual lives. In this context, overt institutional political activism is shunned and purist salafis favor quietism. In short, the strategy purist Salafism follows results in a kind of isolationism or retreat from political institutions. In this perspective, political movements and jihadists are criticized because their actions are counterproductive and actually lead to the repression of Islamist activism. Political salafis are instead moved to political activism precisely because they argue that purist salafis are unable to break out of their small circle and that political action is required in order to see the objective of Salafism, notably the application of Sharia law, realized. Finally, jihadist Salafism is a form of violent opposition to "unjust rule" aimed at establishing an Islamic state ruled through Sharia law. Unlike political Salafism, where training takes place in Islamic universities and is based on the classic texts of Salafism, "jihadists have received their political training on the battlefields."[13] A number of other scholars such as Amghar[14] and Bonnefoy[15] classify Salafism in similar categories. In many ways the complexity of Tunisian Salafism reflects such categorization, but it also displays new characteristics and traits that derive from the uniqueness of the Tunisian situation. Thus there are, as mentioned, a number of salafi political parties that openly subscribe to the idea that salafi objectives should be pursued through institutional participation, representing what has been termed political Salafism. In addition, there are different groups and associations that can be defined as quietist, promoting purist or scientific Salafism that through preaching and education attempts to Islamize society from below. This is the case, for instance, in the work that sheikhs such as Bechir Ben Hassen are doing through institutions such as the Imam Malek private university of Sharia Science. Such sheikhs, however, are often accused in more radical salafi circles of being too close to the ruling authorities. Finally, and most significantly, is jihadi Salafism, which is best represented by Ansar al-Sharia and other looser groupings usually based around neighborhood mosques. It is this jihadi Salafism that seems to function as a potential spoiler of democratization because it does not recognize the validity of the model on offer. This "spoiler" label is due to two interconnected factors.

First is the place that democracy has within the ideological construction of Salafism. On this point, it is important to note that jihadi salafis ideologically reject the liberal-democratic model. However, the issue is slightly more complicated in the sense that jihadi salafis do not necessarily reject democratic mechanisms; they simply see them as being of use in a context where Sharia law is the absolute framework for decision making. As Hassan Brik, *daʿwa* officer of Ansar al-Sharia, stated:

> We do not believe in democracy, but this does not mean that we are against elections or consultations as a mechanism to elect representatives of the community. The point is that until we live in a society where seculars and people who do not want the application of Sharia law also live, we cannot conceive of the fact that in the name of the principle of majority rule God's law can be contradicted. In the framework of a community where Sharia law is applied we have nothing against the method of choosing one's own representative.[16]

In some sense, therefore, jihadi Salafism does not want to be outside of modernity. Members of the jihadi group Ansar al-Sharia place conditions, albeit very significant ones, on democratic mechanisms, but do not reject them per se because this would simply embolden those who argue that they are anti-modern. The difference with the other two salafi trends emerges quite forcefully on this issue, particularly with the political salafis who have accepted to play the game of democracy and elections before having Sharia law in place.

In terms of differences with the scientific ones, this is fairly obvious in the sense that scientific salafis profoundly disagree with any activism that might endanger preaching and education: confrontation with the state would represent precisely such a danger. At the same time this is also the factor that distinguishes Tunisia from other contexts because jihadi Salafism has to reconcile its ideological rejection of liberal democracy with the fact that it is precisely the nascent liberal and democratic institutional framework that allows it to organize, occupy the public space, carry out its political and social activities, and, generally speaking, be present on the public scene without suffering from systematic repression. This is a novelty for jihadi Salafism and therefore the traditional automatic choice of political violence against the state has to be pondered in much more depth. In this respect, Tunisian jihadi Salafism begins to adopt positions close to the scientific strand.

Second is the often-made link between jihadism and what has been termed al-Qaedism. Jihadism represents the necessity of a part of the Arab world to respond to the injustices that the international order has created over time, first and foremost the Palestinian issue. In addition, the domestic repression that prevented the free expression of society made Arab regimes appear silly puppets in the hands of Western powers, which, through their empty rhetoric about democracy and their concrete policies of political and military support, undermined the effective self-determination of the Arab world. In this context, the jihadi reaction in its qaedist form is initially, if not supported, at least looked at with a degree of admiration in so far as there is a man and a method that make the West take notice of such injustices. Jihadi Salafism in Tunisia is not immune to the attraction of such a discourse and the adoption of the "Afghan" look on the part of activists together with the violence of the slogans and, at times, the actual use of violence are traits that are present on the Tunisian scene. However, the initial thrust of qaedism cannot be sustained for long and loses its appeal, whereas a more complex understanding and practice of jihadism does not. This is because the latter can take different forms and at a time when authoritarian domestic regimes begin to fall new dynamics develop within jihadi Salafism. It is here once again that Tunisia constitutes a novel laboratory where these dynamics can be expressed and worked out. As Abdullah a-Tunisi, a prominent jihadi salafi sheikh, argued quite cogently, "Ben Laden should not be considered a learned man of religion and Zawahiri has limited influence because his theoretical contribution is minimal in terms of his writings."[17] This indicates that there is a much wider world of jihadism out there that cannot be exhaustively subsumed within Al-Qaeda and its practices.

The previous discussion of these two factors permits a clearer understanding of Tunisian Salafism, which operates today in a context that is profoundly novel due to the "freedom" of the country in the aftermath of the revolution, reducing therefore the distance between its different trends. Thus, while there is certainly an anti-systemic dimension to Tunisian Salafism, particularly in its jihadi version, this is tempered by the realization that the system allows Salafism as a whole to propagate its message and, potentially, to grow. The impact of this novelty has profound consequences for the way in which Salafism as a whole organizes and pursues its objectives.

The evolution of Tunisian Salafism

In his study of Salafism, Roel Meijer convincingly argues that "in a contentious age, Salafism transforms the humiliated, the downtrodden, disgruntled young people, the ostracized migrant, or the politically repressed into a chosen sect (*al-firqa al-nājia*) that immediately gains privileged access to the Truth."[18] This certainly applies in the Tunisian case where a significant sector of the youth aged between twenty and thirty, following on from their revolutionary experience, have occupied the social and religious scene in numerous working-class and poorer neighborhoods after the disappearance of the authoritarian structures that used to channel consensus or repress dissent. There is therefore a sort of lumpenproletariat on the scene, which has very little class conscience and which can be mobilized through the immediately understood language and symbolism of religion in its salafi version, particularly the jihadi trend.[19] This constitutes the base of a new kind of political-theological socialization that has been defined elsewhere as "sheikhism."[20] Today young people under the age of thirty are on pulpits at different mosques and appointed imams with wide popular consensus, generating a quasi-direct revolutionary democracy whereby the personnel of old committees that managed the affairs of the mosque are replaced with a new generation. This is a rather broad social phenomenon in some neighborhoods and has allowed a sort of civic participation on the part of a youth that has always been marginalized and that the system under construction has failed to include. This is one of the very few places where the youth has occupied the public space in a truly revolutionary manner and therefore this worries both the authorities and the wider public because they operate with rules, references, and symbolism owing to jihadi Salafism. It follows that demands for repression on the part of sectors of domestic society and Western powers have been made on the ruling Troika. The government partly acceded to them, jailing a number of young salafis and initiating a repressive campaign aiming at isolating the violent elements, and this has a significant influence on the salafi *mouvance* and its evolution because it triggered an intense debate on "what to do" next. The decision taken in the spring of 2013 to deny permission to Ansar al-Sharia to hold its annual rally in Kairouan has furthered these internal discussions.

Two different camps within jihadi Salafism emerged. On the one hand is Abou Iyadh, who insisted on the necessity of structuration and formal organization just as he had done with Ansar al-Sharia. On the other is Sheikh Khatib Idrissi who is more reluctant about formal organizations and put forth the idea of a looser Council of Sheikhs with the necessary religious training and scholarly authority to have a degree of coordination that would prevent the excesses that might be committed in the name of jihadi Salafism through the provision of precise rules of behavior. The repressive actions of the Ennahda-led government determined the apparent victory of Idrissi's camp in the sense that it is indeed a selected number of Sheikhs drawn from the Council Idrissi had set up who were asked to visit the presidential palace in the autumn of 2012 and in some ways negotiate on behalf of the whole movement, implicitly marginalizing Abu Iyadh and Ansar al-Sharia. The problem is that this move does not really have much of an effect on the ground where the vast majority of the young sheikhs view the older sheikhs with a degree of suspicion and are still attracted by the social and political plan Ansar al-Sharia put forth and are therefore keen to replicate its organizational forms. The point of contention among jihadi salafis is how to provide a framework for the young radicals who are joining the movement and are attracted by the purity of the message, its religious undertones, and the example it sets for social behavior. This framework is rendered necessary because many of these young people still "live" in revolutionary times and operate accordingly, while to the more political savvy older and religiously educated leadership the new political environment offers ways to develop the movement that had not existed in the past. This development, however, should be undertaken without attracting the ire of the authorities, making the Idrissi camp closer to the position of the purist salafis. For their part, Ansar al-Sharia and the other looser groupings are not concerned with the reactions that they might provoke from the state and wider society because they still think and behave in a revolutionary fashion, with the objective of radically altering the system in which they operate. In addition to these internal debates over the evolution of Salafism and the forms it should take there is the influence of international jihadi scholars and activists who have become interested in Tunisia because it can offer new avenues and ways to mobilize young people attracted to jihadi Salafism. Important sheikhs such as the Moroccan Haddushi and the Egyptian Hanni al-Sibai therefore intervened in the domestic debate about what the movement should do. The former attempted to convince the young "hotheads" to calm down and encouraged a type of behavior that should not attract repression, implicitly recognizing that the way in which Idrissi wants to take the whole movement is the correct one. The latter theorizes how important it is to create an organization that would structure the varied and different demands that young people legitimately have. Al-Sibai is very much in favor of following the Ansar al-Sharia path of structuration and argues that it is necessary to have a formal organization that can operate as support for the activities of the movement. He clearly states:

> you, young men who are interested in charity and social work need a degree of coordination, you need someone who takes care of this or takes care of that, don't you? You do not like the name Ansar al-Sharia? It does not matter, find another one. You do not like the word *jamāʿa* because it gives rise to problematic doctrinal matters? Do not use it; pick some other name . . . whether it is association, school, whatever you want. The objective here is purely organizational and administrative.[21]

This internal debate on the evolution of jihadi Salafism is not only crucial for the balance of power within the movement, but is also of significance for the process of democratization as a whole because the degree, intensity, and level of structuration can indicate the willingness, or lack thereof, to become institutionalized actors. While some may argue that the progressive and externally sanctioned formal structuration along the lines of Ansar al-Sharia might constitute a problem in so far as it might give strength to an illiberal and anti-democratic movement, it can also be argued that such structuration would permit the identification of clear interlocutors and representatives of the instances of a social group that needs to be somehow included in the new Tunisia if the construction of a renewed political system is to be successful. There is no escaping this. The "other Tunisia" that the revolution brought to the fore is in need of answers and for the moment Salafism is the framework through which such answers are provided, but ultimately it is the responsibility of the new political system to offer traditionally marginalized and downtrodden groups a stake in society.

In addition, a higher level of structuration would further expose the differences that exist within the jihadi salafi movement and within Salafism more broadly. On the one hand, the difficulty of the Council of Sheikhs to be seen as the legitimate representative of young people in the poorer neighborhoods who have espoused jihadi Salafism is due to the re-emergence of the generation gap whereby these sheikhs replicate, consciously or not, the same fault lines that exist in wider society, appropriating the radicalism of the youth to lead it towards patience and compromise. Thus jihadi Salafism is not a unified force. On the other hand, a clear structuration along jihadi salafi lines would continue to reduce the gap that exists between jihadis and scientific salafis because both would be focused on *daʿwa*, which is therefore much less threatening than jihad itself. When the revolutionary spirit is tempered and when violence is out of the question because Tunisia is a land of *daʿwa*, there is no longer much in practice that differentiates jihadis from purist salafis who are more interested in cultural, spiritual, and welfare provision activities. The non-jihadi salafi camp is usually identified with a cultural and associative trend heavily influenced by *wahhabism*. Purist or scientific Salafism follows some sort of hyper-puritanical approach which aims at transforming the Muslim believer into a devout religious radical in terms of its moral integrity and behavior, while rendering him quietist on political matters. This is, for instance, the objective of salafis such as Wissam

Othmani who came to prominence when he was nominated spokesperson of the movement supporting the wearing of the niqab at university.[22] His concern was not with jihad or altering the whole political system, but with the right to live his very conservative interpretation of Islam in all aspects of his life without interference from the state. Banning the niqab in schools certainly represents for him such an intrusion and should be challenged without, however, resorting to violence. The central point in this context is the concept of *walī al-ʾamr* (the legitimate ruler). For scientific salafis, obedience is due to the ruler no matter what his policy choices are as long as he is legitimately Muslim according to legal scholarship. Jihadi salafists do not subscribe to this principle and almost by definition defy the political order in place both nationally and internationally. When, as in postrevolutionary Tunisia, the case of the illegitimacy of the ruler is much more difficult to make for jihadi salafis because the current rulers are not yet applying repressive means against Islam and do not offend religion, a convergence between scientific and jihadi salafis can occur around the concept of *daʿwa*.

As mentioned above, a non-confrontational structuration of jihadi Salafism in Tunisia has the potential to diffuse its political radicalism, forcing it to shift towards the positions of scientific Salafism, which is already reasonably active in the country and partly sanctioned by the authorities. In this sense a shared focus on *daʿwa* would legitimate a political system that allows it to take place without impediments. An effective convergence has yet to occur in Tunisia and might not materialize because at the ideological level there are still many jihadi salafis who still subscribe in principle to the idea that the current rulers are not entirely legitimate because they do not apply Sharia law. In addition, a significantly repressive turn of the authorities against Salafism might alter the perception of the legitimacy of rulers. In practice, however, this is an argument that is increasingly difficult to make insofar as Tunisian society as a whole seems to have espoused the idea that an elected government might be incompetent, but not illegitimate. Thus, the division between jihadists and scientific salafis is still present, but there are elements of proximity that might lead the jihadi trend to move away from their most radical domestic positions towards convergence. The state authorities, Ennahda, and the political establishment hope that this convergence will eventually be the end-point of the journey of jihadists because despite the tensions and incidents involving them since the transition, no open calls to violence against the state and society have been made within the movement. Ghannouchi himself, displaying some sympathy for their positions, is favorable to their integration into the political system through political parties, and underlines that even Abou Iyadh never called for the violent overthrow of the regime. In this respect, the work of scientific salafis like Béchir Ben Hassen should be emphasized. He shares the same educational background as Khatib Idrissi and other members of the Council of Sheikhs and he is of primary importance for the state and Ennahda because he is the proponent of what can be termed "Salafism lite." Ben Hassen is prominent because he attempts to promote a campaign to de-radicalize the jihadi youth following the example of what was done in the Arabian peninsula.[23] At the moment, this type of activism is perceived with great skepticism in jihadi circles, but it indicates that there are still profound divisions within the salafi galaxy on how to operate in and approach a political system that allows for far greater freedoms than anywhere else in the Arab world.

Finally, and probably most importantly, structuration is of significance in so far as increased institutionalization would lead the salafi movement as a whole to have a much clearer idea of the sociopolitical plan it hopes to achieve outside the easy sloganeering and references to the trite "Islam is the solution." As it stands in postrevolutionary Tunisia, jihadi Salafism is more than able to represent and be the vehicle of widespread social frustration in numerous poorer neighborhoods, but it is still unable to offer an alternative social plan that has content and meaning beyond simplistic and unrealistic solutions. For instance, the absence of salafis from engagement in social movements that have very practical and political objectives is glaring and significant. The Siliana crisis is but one example of this. In early December 2012 in Siliana a number of protests against the poor socioeconomic conditions of the town and the inability of the political parties to do anything about it despite the promises of the postrevolutionary period shook the country because they were paradigmatic of the sense of frustration that permeates Tunisia. The whole town marched in protest at having been abandoned by the state and the Tunisian general labor union (Union Générale Tunisienne du Travail, UGTT) organized the marchers, becoming the interlocutor which the government had to deal with to solve the crisis. Eventually concessions were made by the authorities and the UGTT was widely perceived as the winner in this struggle. When these types of protest with very complex economic, developmental and practical undertones occur, salafis seem to be at a loss on how to react and channel them. It is as if once campaigns linked to the defense of religion are over, the movement has nothing to say about what else happens in the country. As a young jihadi salafi leader[24] almost naively stated:

> We do not deal with these issues because they are squabbles between political parties. We do not want to be drawn in and we do not want to be used. What happens in Siliana is between Ennahda and the trade union movement.[25]

In many ways the negotiations over socioeconomic issues in Siliana were indeed between Ennahda and the trade union, but that is precisely the problem in so far as it turns out that the salafi movement has nothing to say about socioeconomic conditions in the country and, even worse, does not really want to be drawn into that debate. If you have very little or nothing to say about the greatest priority of the majority of Tunisian citizens, the room for growing the movement might be very limited. What emerges clearly from the crisis in Siliana and from other countless examples of social mobilization on economic issues is that the UGTT is still very much the only actor capable of interpreting and framing these explosions of rage, turning them into coherent political demands that can be discussed and negotiated with those who have political power.[26] While the outcome of the Siliana crisis might not be replicated nationally, the UGTT still has a significant degree of both legitimacy and mobilizational strength that can be harnessed to support or confront the government. For its part, the absence of jihadi salafis from these kinds of debates and actions is potentially positive in the sense that sectors of Tunisian society will not find what they are looking for in jihadi Salafism, confining its appeal to a young underclass. This inability to represent social dynamics with conflictual economic issues at their core points to the complexity and also the vitality of Tunisian civil society, which finds avenues of expression in a host of different political and social actors, negating by implication the primacy of jihadi salafis.

Conclusion

Tunisian Salafism, including the jihadi component, is part of a much larger process of restructuration of the political and social system typical of a country in transition. In many ways, Tunisian Salafism is the latest stage of *ṣaḥwa islamiyya* (Islamic awakening), a phenomenon that has characterized the Arab world over the last few decades. In Tunisia, it has found a fertile terrain among the youth of poorer neighborhoods where the lumpenproletariat bypassed by economic growth lives and where we see a further cycle of social contestation that is deeply unsatisfied with the outcome of the revolution. Traditional political parties are unable or unwilling to give a representative voice to this social group for a number of reasons. First, the management of the transition to democracy has fallen quite quickly with an older generation of politicians and leaders. This is immediately offputting for many young people. Second, the consensus around the political structures, values, and identity that will govern the new Tunisia, albeit difficult to achieve and still potentially in the balance, is very much a compromise between a conservative religious middle class that identifies with Ghannouchi and a more liberal and secular one that identifies with the neo-Destourian parties of the center-left. This is not a negative outcome per se because it opens the door to the very real possibility that a new pluralistic political system will indeed be consolidated, but it is based on the continued exclusion of the disenfranchised, which, ultimately, could be a destabilizing factor. Third, the current economic, foreign, and social policies that the ruling coalition implemented have yet to prove successful, generating wider frustration which can at some stage be mobilized. At the moment, Salafism is unable to speak for the whole of—or even for the majority of—society because it does not have a credible alternative plan for it, but this might change in the future. What is certain, however, is that the salafi youth involved in social, political, and even violent activities across the country can only find in religious categories the language of self-affirmation and mobilization. This is due to the relative popularity of Salafism in specific areas of the country even before the revolution. This built on the subscription to both the formative international causes of jihadism such as Iraq and Afghanistan and to the contentious domestic politics approach against the authoritarianism of Ben Ali, which led many young people to prison and marginalization, instilling at the same time a spirit of radicalism liberated after the revolution. The admittedly incoherent and facile demands of the salafi movement are couched in religious language and are therefore difficult to dismiss in the context of a society where a much wider debate on how to adapt specific historical and cultural categories derived from religion to the requirements of modernity is taking place. The rise of Salafism is a more extreme aspect of this very significant debate. This in part explains why there is a rather complex relationship between Ennahda and the salafis. Ennahda is actively promoting the institutionalization of the salafis in order to bring them around to the idea that a high degree of personal religiosity and behavior is compatible with the construction of a democratic Tunisia. This means that the party has seen with a degree of satisfaction the creation of salafi political parties that will compete with others for votes in the upcoming elections. It has also supported the idea of scientific salafis attempting to moderate the views and beliefs of the jihadi component. It also discusses the phenomenon of Salafism through historical relativism, meaning that it attempts to interpret it as having the same starting positions. In the past, Ennahda only moved toward moderation over time and after numerous and intense internal ideological debates. Ghannouchi's belief is that eventually the social consensus and toleration of plural identities of which many Tunisian intellectuals speak will have a moderating influence on the salafis; time is what is needed.[27] Finally, Ennahda has taken it reasonably easy with the repressive option, although there are indications that the new executive formed in the aftermath of the assassination of Belaïd in the spring of 2013 might take a firmer approach. All this suggests that when the Ennahda leadership uses religious language in its discussions with and about the jihadi salafis it is not necessarily contradicting the modern democratic language with which it speaks to secular and liberal society. The party is often accused of doublespeak and of having a hidden agenda of Iranian-style Islamization, but it is more likely that this doublespeak is the product of having to engage a constituency, the salafis, who can only be really talked to through the use of traditional Islamic concepts.

There is no doubt that it is necessary for the whole of Tunisian society if it is to be successful in the transformation of the political system to integrate in some manner the social and, importantly, economic demands that, however incoherent, the jihadi salafis make after having been excluded and marginalized for a long time. Behind the at times shocking and harsh language infused with a terminology that is often reminiscent of violence lies a demand for social integration and the challenge for the political establishment is to take it seriously and engage, not agree, with it. On its part, Tunisian Salafism is conscious of operating in a novel situation where its ideological certainties about the evils of democracy and liberalism are challenged daily by the fact that it is benefiting precisely from the environment it so despises. To the more intellectual and politicized elements within the movement this is becoming increasingly clear and there are therefore both domestic and international pressures from within wider jihadi Salafism to better organize and create structures that can engage with a state that tolerates rather than represses their views. This progressive structuration can also have the unintended consequence of increasing the mobilization of that part of society that rejects Salafism and supports an entirely different set of values because it can take advantage of the fact that Salafism seems unable to provide an alternative plan of society when it comes to dealing with economic and developmental issues. While Tunisian Salafism is often perceived as a threat to democratization, and it certainly is at times, it can also present an opportunity to strengthen the transition. The political establishment and the international community have to be aware of both possibilities.

Notes

The authors are grateful to the Gerda Henkel Foundation for funding this research in the context of the program "From over-estimation to under-estimation: the trajectory of political Islam in five MENA countries."

1. For a "contested" official account of the events at Douar Hicher see Mischa Benoit-Lavelle, "Shooting of Salafists in Tunisia May Spur More Attacks," *Al Monitor*, November 1, 2012, accessed January 23, 2013, www.al-monitor.com/pulse/originals/2012/al-monitor/salafist-shooting-tunisia.html.
2. Christopher Alexander, *Tunisia. Stability and Reform in the Modern Maghreb* (London: Routledge, 2010).
3. Alaya Allani, "The Islamists in Tunisia between Confrontation and Participation: 1980–2008," *Journal of North African Studies* 14 (2009): 257–72.
4. Antoine Sfeir, *Tunisie. Terre de Paradoxes* (Paris: L'Archipel, 2006).
5. Vincent Durac and Francesco Cavatorta, "Strengthening Authoritarian Rule through Democracy Promotion? Examining the Paradox of the US and EU Security Strategies. The Case of Tunisia," *British Journal of Middle Eastern Studies* 36 (2009): 3–19.
6. Francesco Cavatorta and Rikke Hostrup Haugbølle, "The End of Authoritarian Rule and the Mythology of Tunisia under Ben Ali," *Mediterranean Politics* 17 (2012): 179–95.
7. Amin Allal, "Ici ça ne bouge pas ça n'avance pas. Les mobilisations protestataires dans la région minière de Gafsa en 2008," in *L'État face aux débordements du social*

au Maghreb, ed. Myriam Catusse, Blandine Destremau, and Eric Verdier (Paris: IREMAM/Khartala, 2010), 173–86.

8. Laryssa Chomiak and John Entelis, "Contesting Order in Tunisia: Crafting Political Identity," in *Civil Society Activism under Authoritarian Rule*, ed. Francesco Cavatorta (London: Routledge, 2012), 73–93.
9. Rikke Hostrup Haugbølle and Francesco Cavatorta, "Beyond Ghannouchi. Islamism and Social Change in Tunisia," *Middle East Report* 262 (2012): 20–5.
10. Béatrice Hibou, *La force de l'obéissance* (Paris: La Découverte, 2006).
11. Bernard Haykel, "On the Nature and Thought of Salafist Action," in *Global Salafism*, ed. Roel Meijer (London: Hurst & Co., 2009), 33–57.
12. Quintan Wiktorowicz, "Anatomy of the Salafi Movement," *Studies in Conflict and Terrorism* 29 (2006): 207–39.
13. Wiktorowicz, "Anatomy of the Salafi Movement," 225.
14. Samir Amghar, *Le salafisme d'aujourd'hui. Mouvements sectaires en Occident* (Paris: Michalon, 2011).
15. Laurent Bonnefoy, *Salafism in Yemen. Transnationalism and Religious Identity* (London: Hurst & Co., 2011).
16. Interview with authors, Yasminette, Tunis, September 22, 2012.
17. Interview with authors, Sidi Bouzid, October 2012.
18. Roel Meijer, "Introduction," in *Global Salafism*, ed. Roel Meijer (London: Hurst & Co., 2009), 13.
19. We are thankful to Yahia Zoubir for alerting us to this point.
20. Fabio Merone and Francesco Cavatorta, "Salafist *Mouvance* and Sheikh-ism in the Tunisian Transition," Center for International Studies, Working Paper No. 7 (2012), accessed January 1, 2013, http://doras.dcu.ie/17570/1/1207.pdf.
21. Skype conference on November 28, 2012 with a group of youth in Mahdia. The conference has been repeated with different groups. Accessed December 20, 2012, www.youtube.com/watch_popup?v=FMMNhqMngPE&feature=youtu.be.
22. Interview with authors, Tunis, October 31, 2012.
23. Omar Ashour, *The Deradicalization of Jihadists: Transforming Armed Islamist Movements* (London: Routledge, 2009).
24. The interviewee was wanted by the authorities at the time of writing and wished to remain anonymous.
25. Interview with authors, Tunis, December 15, 2012.
26. Héla Yousfi, "Ce syndicat qui incarne l'opposition tunisienne," *Le Monde Diplomatique*, 704 (2012):17.
27. Interview with authors, Tunis, October 30, 2012.

CHAPTER 12

The Fragile Tunisian Democracy—What Prospects for the Future?

Lise Storm

This chapter explores the prospects for democracy in Tunisia following the Arab Spring. The core argument put forward is that while Tunisia has, indeed, undergone significant transformation and a transition to democracy, democracy is still to be consolidated and, furthermore, the quality of democracy currently in place leaves a lot to be desired. While many have emphasized factors such as Islamism and the state of the country's economy as the key to understanding the fragility of the recently established democracy, the analysis in this chapter demonstrates that the core factors stalling the democratization process in Tunisia are the character of the country's party system, the nature of the political parties, and the level of maturity and/or democratic commitment of some of the chief politicians.

Beginning with the character of the party system and the political parties, the analysis shows how, despite the fragmented nature of the party system, the vast majority of the parties that successfully contested the first post-Arab Spring elections were, in fact, headed by familiar faces. These parties were not externally created, that is, originating from the citizenry and with a clear and coherent party program, but internally created parties—offshoots or transformations of already existing parties, and led by well-known members of the political elite.[1] The only new entity of any significance was Al-Aridha (the Popular Petition for Freedom, Justice and Development, PP), a populist party without much substance, headed by the television mogul Mohamed Hechmi Hamdi.

Taking into account the reality that political parties are viewed as a cornerstone of democracy—an element without which democracy cannot survive—it is hardly surprising that the young Tunisian democracy appears to be fragile indeed. In addition to being internally created, most of the political parties are without a clear and coherent party program and have feeble links to society at best. This latter problem is further exacerbated by the fact that the electorate struggles to differentiate between the parties, not only because of a lack of local party offices, but also due to the very fragmented nature of the party system in the wake of the fall of Ben Ali's regime. In short, at present, the Tunisian party system is predominantly populated by entities that can only be classified as political parties at a stretch—most are simply office-seeking, while neglecting policy-seeking and their representative functions.

A good illustration of how personalistic politics has damaged the Tunisian democratization process is the power struggle within the first Hamadi Jebali cabinet. As the months passed, it became very clear that this was not simply a case of secularists vs. Islamists, or those supporting parliamentarism vs. those in favor of presidentialism. This battle had nothing to do with ideology, and everything to do with the distribution of power (now and in the future) and political maturity. In other words, there is every indication that the primary concern of those involved in this battle was, on the one hand, who governs and who will govern and, on the other, who had most popular legitimacy. The key parties and politicians on both sides of the fence seemed rather indifferent to the question of what was best for the country's democratization process in the longer run, because it was certainly clear that the right way forward was not to give in to popular pressure at a time when strong leadership and a clear counterweight within the government was most needed, and nor was it, in true authoritarian style, to seek to restructure the cabinet and replace (difficult) elected representatives with compliant technocrats.

What is democracy?

Before one can address such questions as the quality of the new Tunisian democracy and the prospects for its future, it is, of course, necessary to define what is meant by democracy. This is particularly true given that democracy is a so-called "essentially contested concept", that is, one that is defined in numerous ways. The definition of democracy applied in this chapter is neither minimalist—emphasizing solely the holding of free, fair and competitive elections—nor maximalist, that is, stipulating (in addition to the electoral element) the need for basic civil liberties, effective power to govern of the elected government, and various additional economic, social, and political factors associated with industrial democracy.[2]

If the minimalist and maximalist definitions of democracy are viewed as the two endpoints on a continuum, the definition of democracy used in this chapter can be located somewhere in the middle as it stresses three of the elements of democracy present in the group of maximalist definitions, namely free, fair, and competitive elections; the respect for and protection of basic civil liberties; and the elected government having effective power to govern. By using a relatively broad definition, one ensures that democracy is not simply equated with the holding of elections, something that is terribly important in a Middle Eastern and North African setting, where non-democratic rulers—like many of their counterparts elsewhere—have often turned this so-called "instrument of democracy" into one of authoritarianism, thereby effectively rendering elections as a yardstick of democracy meaningless.[3] Equally, by adopting a definition that is less extensive than those belonging to the maximalist group, one avoids the pitfall of making democracy a virtually exclusively Western phenomenon.

Finally, a word on institutions is fitting. The emphasis in the selected definition of democracy on the elected government having effective power to govern as well as basic civil liberties being respected and protected underlines the necessity of strong institutions, institutions capable of assisting not only in the consolidation of democracy, but in the consolidation of a democracy with substance—a genuine democracy with good prospects of longevity, and not merely a façade.[4] Of course it is important to bear in mind that the building of strong and stable institutions in new democracies takes time, but even in new democracies there are usually clear indications of the way in which key institutions (such as the judiciary, the legislature, and the political parties) are heading, partly via their response to the new political environment in the wake of the transition to democracy, but also based on their previous track record over the past few decades, even if under authoritarian rule.

The crucial role of political parties

As just mentioned, there are a number of institutions that are key to ensuring that what is established following a transition to democracy is not simply a shallow, short-lived experiment that turns into a façade for what is essentially a non-democratic regime. Without strong and stable institutions, the quality of democracy is poor, and the likelihood of democratic breakdown great. Hence, in a case like Tunisia, the prospects for democracy in the long-term perspective are invariably tied to the state of the country's core political institutions. Of the various institutions that help foster genuine democracy, the political parties are perhaps the most crucial.[5] Amongst the academic community there is almost unanimous agreement that without political parties, democracy does not work, and therefore cannot survive in the longer run.[6]

There are several reasons why parties are crucial for the survival of democracy, but the two most important are undeniably their representative and procedural functions. Parties are, on the one hand, the articulators and aggregators of interests, the formulators of public policy, as well as the main vehicles of citizen integration and mobilization. On the other hand, parties recruit political leaders, they organize parliament and the government, and they nominate candidates to public office.[7] It is by fulfilling these functions—both types—that the political parties provide their fundamental contribution to making democracy the "only game in town," that is, creating a situation in which no significant political groups seriously attempt to overthrow the democratic regime, and where all actors in the polity have become habituated to the resolution of conflict via constitutionalized democratic norms. Democracy has, in other words, become consolidated—routinized behaviorally, attitudinally, and constitutionally.[8]

The 2011 legislative elections: the problem with political parties

The Tunisian legislative elections of 2011 took place in an atmosphere of tremendous hope and excitement. After years of going to the polls in elections that were nominally competitive, but whose results were already known prior to balloting, the country's electorate was heading to the polls to cast its vote in what everyone hoped would be the country's first genuinely competitive, free and fair legislative elections.[9]

On voting day, October 23, 2011, the electorate was faced with a choice between more than 100 different parties, the vast majority of which had sprung up following the fall of the Ben Ali regime on January 14, i.e. only a few months prior to the elections.[10] Despite the mushrooming of new parties in the wake of the Revolution of Freedom and Dignity, the numerous independent candidates, the presence of a large number of international observers, the keen interest from the media (whether domestic or international), and, of course, the end of an era with the exit of Ben Ali and the dissolution of the regime party the Democratic Constitutional Rally (Rassemblement Constitutionnel Démocratique, RCD) on March 9, the electorate was somewhat lukewarm in its support for the process.[11] Regardless of the many reports of difficulties with voter registration, there is no denying that it was a very disturbing reality indeed that a staggering 46.8 percent of the eligible voters did not register. Hence, the low voter turnout of 52 percent—if measured on the basis of eligible voters—was hardly a great surprise, but simply a very damning sign.[12]

Of the many parties that contested the first post-Arab Spring elections in Tunisia, only a relatively small proportion gained representation in the new legislature. To be more exact, nineteen parties succeeded in winning seats, the vast majority of these simply gaining minimal representation—only three parties won a seat share in excess of 10 percent, while fourteen parties each commanded less than 3 percent of the seats up for contestation (see Table 12.1).[13] The main winners of the elections was Rachid Ghannouchi's Islamist Ennahda (Renaissance Party) with 41.0 percent of the seats and a vote share of 37.0 percent, while the party's nearest rival—the Congress for the Republic (Congrès pour la République, CPR) headed by the human rights activist Moncef Marzouki—won a less impressive seat share of 13.4 percent, and an even smaller vote share of 8.7 percent. Not far behind came the above-mentioned new entity, the PP, which succeeded in winning 12.0 percent of the seats up for contestation, despite only receiving 6.7 percent of the valid votes cast. Finally, in fourth and fifth place respectively, came the Democratic Forum for Labor and Liberties (Forum Démocratique pour le Travail et les Libertés, FDTL) and the Progressive Democratic Party (Parti Démocrate Progressiste, PDP), the former being allocated 9.2 percent of the seats and the latter 7.4 percent, which corresponded to sixteen seats.

Table 12.1 Results of the 2011 legislative elections

Party	Votes (No.)	Seats (No.)
Ennahda	1,498,905	89
CPR	352,825	29
PP	280,382	26
FDTL	285,530	20
PDP	160,692	16
PDM	113,094	5
LI	129,215	5
AT	76,643	4
PCOT	60,620	3
MP	31,793	2
MDS	22,842	2
UPL	51,594	1
MPD	32,306	1
PLM	13,053	1
PNSD	15,572	1
Parti Néodestourien	15,459	1
PLP	9,329	1
MPUP	7,619	1
PNCU	5,581	1
Independents	81,464	8
TOTAL	3,244,518*	217

*A total of 4,053,905 valid votes were cast, but nearly 20 percent of these were wasted.

Source: L'Instance Supérieure Indépendante pour les Élections (www.isie.tn).

The state of the political parties

The problem with the 2011 legislative elections was not, in other words, the contest itself. The elections were highly competitive, international observers as well as the national monitoring body, the Instance Supérieure Indépendante pour les Élections (Higher Independent Authority for the Elections, ISIE), agreed that they were largely free and fair, and suffrage was, of course, universal as it had been during the entire postindependence period. Rather, the problem with the first post-Arab Spring elections lay with the political parties.

In line with the trend elsewhere in the Maghreb, the Tunisian parties that presented candidates in the 2011 elections—and succeeded in having one or more of these elected—were all so-called personalistic parties, that is, political parties which were hardly anything more than personal vehicles for the party leader to amass further power, wealth, and prestige. The main goal of these parties was, in other words, to further the career of the party leader and, to some extent, his inner circle. The representative and procedural functions of parties were not of primary importance, which explains why were few—if any—of the parties contesting the elections could be said to have a clear and coherent policy agenda, Ennahda undoubtedly coming across the best, given the party's Islamist credentials, which made it easy to identify vis-à-vis its closest competitors, most of which were secular.[14]

Taking the above into consideration, it is hardly astonishing that a significant proportion of the electorate did not identify strongly with a party and, furthermore, that voters found it difficult to differentiate between the various parties, not only because of their sheer number and (in most cases) relative youth. Many were also so depoliticized that they did not know the date of elections or, indeed, what type of elections were to take place.[15] Given the absence of strong policy profiles, it appears that those Tunisian voters that did turn out on election day chose to vote for familiar faces, which explains why the chief legal opposition parties during Ben Ali's reign, most notably the PDP and the FDTL, did rather well, as did the two main clandestine opposition entities, Ennahda and the CPR, whose leaders were welcomed onto Tunisian soil as veritable heroes after Ben Ali's departure. Furthermore, it was hardly a surprise that the PP did as well as it did with party leader Hamdi being a well-known figure due to his ownership of the TV station el-Mustakilla.

Of the nineteen parties that gained election to parliament, only one—the PP—can be described as an entirely new entity. In other words, despite the overthrow of the Ben Ali regime, the opening up of the political system, and the licensing of some 100 new parties, only one of the successful parties was a so-called externally created party, that is, not the result of a fission or fusion of already existing entities. That said, the party landscape had, of course, been enriched with no fewer than eighteen new entries going by Sartori's definition, as all of the parties represented in the legislature following the 2011 elections, save for the Mouvement des Démocrates Socialistes (Democratic and Social Movement, MDS), had not presented candidates in the previous legislative elections of 2009, or had been unsuccessful in these.[16] These other eighteen parties, however, either (1) had existed as clandestine parties during Ben Ali's reign; (2) had been coopted/neutralized by the previous regime; or (3) were somehow linked to a party in either group (1) or (2) and, therefore, internally created parties.

The dynamics of the political system following the 2011 elections

The very fragmented nature of the Tunisian party system, particularly in terms of the number of parties contesting the legislative elections of 2011, but also to a certain extent if measured by the effective number of parties, which came to 4.6 (equivalent to limited pluralism), has assisted in paving the way for a highly unstable political system and therefore also a very fragile new democracy.[17]

In the postindependence period, Tunisia has experienced different forms of party systems, depending on the nature of the authoritarian regime in place. For many years, the country was governed by one party, and although nominal competition was allowed during the elections held during 1956–9 and again from 1981 until 1989, there was never any illusion that power would be shared—the effective number of parties was one, just as under the single-party system, which was in place at the time of the legislative elections held in the period from 1964 until 1979. It was not until the tentative political opening—or, rather, the façade opening—of 1994 that so-called opposition parties were allowed a modicum of political power in the form of seats in parliament and, eventually, low-ranking cabinet portfolios.[18]

Even with Ben Ali's façade opening of the early 1990s, the Tunisian electorate was never actually presented with any genuine choice on election day. There was no element of uncertainty surrounding the outcome of the various legislative elections; it was always a given that the regime party, the RCD, was going to win the elections, and while it was not clear by how large a margin, it was certain that it was going to be considerable indeed.[19] As a consequence of the almost total domination by the regime party in the postindependence period, the Tunisian politicians—and the electorate—have virtually no experience with democratic power sharing and, therefore, perhaps very little patience.

In the past, the president and the regime party governed. There was a monopoly on power, and decisions were consequently made swiftly and efficiently. In comparison to such a power structure, the new-look political system born out of the Revolution of Freedom and Dignity and the legislative elections of 2011, with its different centers of power, was always going to struggle to perform in terms of efficiency and was, therefore, always going to face the wrath of the citizenry at some point. With popular protests being en vogue in the Middle East and North Africa with the onset of the Arab Spring, in all likelihood the face of the regime, that is, the first government formed on the basis of the results of democratic elections, was going to face displays of popular dissatisfaction sooner rather than later. And that was, indeed, what happened. The question is, was this necessarily a bad sign for Tunisia and the long-term prospects for democracy?

The newfound voice of the citizenry

Arguably, the clear displays of dissatisfaction with the country's new leadership—including calls for the prime minister and the government to step down—were signs that the political system was yet to stabilize.[20] There was evidently a lot of anger and resentment amongst part of the population vis-à-vis the newly elected government, and particularly its Ennahda component, which some argued was seeking to abandon secularism and turn Tunisia into an Islamic state. To some observers, these accusations were wholly unfounded, while with others, they struck a chord. That said, regardless of one's position on the issue of the agenda of Ennahda and, hence, the party's character (as in democratic or anti-systemic), there is no denying that the act of protest was in itself a positive sign. The Tunisian citizenry, while apparently happy with Ben Ali's exit, did not settle for merely a replacement, that is, for just a new regime. The success of the Revolution of Freedom and Dignity had taught people that not only civil unrest but also peaceful popular protests can indeed make a difference.

Hence, when dissatisfied with the new regime, Tunisians took to the streets once again. Admittedly not in the same spirit as that of the Revolution of Freedom and Dignity, and far from at the same scale and level of intensity, but they did take to the streets. They carried out protests. They used their newfound rights, most notably the freedoms of speech and assembly.[21] And they did their best to keep the new political leadership in check. In short, after decades of playing powerless actors in the show that was Ben Ali's façade democracy, with the Revolution of Freedom and Dignity the Tunisian citizenry had become a meaningful actor, if not respected, then at least feared by the political elite due to its sheer size and newfound voice. This fear—the uncertainty instilled—amongst the key components of the new regime regarding the potential for a long term in office is arguably one of the chief signs that, although fragile, the new Tunisian democracy is heading in the right direction.

Post-Ben Ali power-sharing: good or bad?

A further indication that things are going well in Tunisia is, rather absurdly, the serious difficulties that have faced the governing Troika since its coming to power in December 2011. Difficulties on the inside. Not from the outside. But difficulties that have unquestionably led to political instability and a certain degree of uncertainty. What is referred to here is essentially the very difficult working relationship within the governing Troika, consisting of Ennahda, the CPR, and the FDTL, leaving aside—for a brief moment—the events that led to the fall of the Jebali cabinet in February 2013.

The fact is that the governing Troika was always going to find it challenging to work as a coherent entity, not only because of the lack of a democratic history in Tunisia, and due to the clandestine nature of Ennahda and the CPR for so many years—a reality that deprived them of even an authoritarian bargaining experience—but mainly for the reason that the parties of the Troika have such different outlooks. Only with serious difficulties were an Islamist party, a center-left party, and a markedly left-wing/socialist party going to develop a shared platform because, as Tunisians are becoming increasingly aware, coalition government is not simply a numbers game.[22] Just because Ennahda dominates the legislature and the cabinet, commanding 41 percent of the seats in the former and initially sitting on fourteen out of thirty cabinet portfolios, the party cannot simply push through its own agenda.[23] It needs a majority in parliament and, more importantly, it must make sure that it does not alienate its coalition partners to the extent that they choose to end the partnership.

This latter point, that is, the uncertainty of the survival of the governing coalition, is crucial. This is where the new Tunisian democracy has demonstrated its potential for consolidation. While some would argue that the governing Troika's inability to agree on the wording of certain clauses of the new constitution, most notably the character of the country's political system in the future (that is, presidentialism, semi-presidentialism, or parliamentarism), and the fall-outs over issues such as the status of the Sharia and women's rights, are signs of political immaturity and also bode badly for the future of the democratic process in Tunisia given the uncertainty that a lack of a new constitution imposes, the argument put forward here is completely the opposite, namely that this is actually quite a positive sign.[24] It would be worrying if the governing Troika, given the diverse backgrounds of its components, simply agreed on everything to do with such an important document as the new constitution, even if under tremendous domestic and international pressure to reach a speedy solution.[25] Unlike Ben Ali, neither President Marzouki and his party, nor the Ennahda and its prime minister, have carte blanche to govern as they see fit. They must consult, coordinate, bargain. The fracas over the design of the new constitution is an example of the democratic method being applied in Tunisia. It may not be pretty, but the parties are playing by the rules of the democratic game.[26]

The assassination of Chokri Belaïd and the Jebali affair

Taking the above into consideration, one could get the impression that Tunisia after the transition to democracy is in a rather rosy state. That is not wholly true. The critics of the new regime are not entirely without justification in their worried arguments. Most notably, their fear of authoritarian regression seems only to have been confirmed.

The fear of authoritarian regression and the onset of an "Islamist Winter"

Not long after the first government formed on the basis of post-Arab Spring elections took office, protesters—including some parliamentarians—took to the street, voicing their fear that the country would be abandoning the principle of secularism and Tunisia turned into an Islamic state given Ennahda's dominance in the legislature and within the cabinet. The protesters were arguing that there was a very real risk that the democratic advances made during the Revolution of Freedom and Dignity would be not only stalled, but turned back, hence Tunisia was about to witness authoritarian regression.[27] The fear of Ennahda was so great that in addition to participating in public demonstrations, some parliamentarians and political actors outside of parliament decided to join forces, leading parties to merge—the two main examples being Ahmed Brahim's Al-Massar (Social Democratic Path) and Al-Jumhuri (Republican Party, PR), which is dominated by former PDP members and led by Ahmed Najib Chebbi.[28]

The protesters, as well as other critics of the new regime, based their fear of authoritarian regression almost entirely on the Islamist character of Ennahda, arguing that the party had simply utilized the democratic process to ascend to power, after which the party would slowly but surely begin to Islamisize the country. The fear of authoritarian regression was not, in other words, linked to the country's authoritarian legacy, which arguably lasted the entire postindependence period until the Revolution of Freedom and Dignity and the holding of the country's first free and fair, competitive elections.

This reality seems somewhat unfair, and also rather inexplicable, given that the authoritarian regime in place for so long in Tunisia was secular, not Islamist. In fact, one of the mechanisms of regime survival deployed by Ben Ali (and Bourguiba before him) was the portrayal of the Islamist alternative as a great danger, something which to a certain extent legitimized the regime's repression and persecution of Islamists and suspected Islamists.[29] In short, the argument that an Islamist(-dominated) government is going to result in (the return to) authoritarian rule, albeit with a religious flavor, is not new. It has been put forward in other countries too, for instance in Turkey after the victories of the Adalet ve Kalkınma Partisi (Justice and Development Party, AKP) in the legislative and presidential elections in 2002 and 2007, and the Parti de la Justice et du Développement (Party of Justice and Development, PJD) in neighboring Morocco in 2011.[30]

It is important to underline that the fear that Islamist electoral victories would lead to authoritarian regression was not simply a domestic concern, but shared by many Western policymakers and academics, some arguing that the Middle East and North Africa was moving from an Arab Spring into a so-called "Islamist Winter," a term used to describe either a "freezing" of the democratization process or outright authoritarian regression. That said, there did appear to be somewhat of a transatlantic divide on the issue, with the American contributors to the debate being particularly fearful, undoubtedly due to their largely right-wing background.[31]

To give one example, Bruce Thornton—a fellow at the Hoover Institution—asserted that recent developments in Tunisia, Egypt, and Libya called into question the optimistic predictions regarding the long-term outcome of the Arab Spring.[32] With reference to Tunisia, Thornton speculated that the promises of moderation made by Ennahda were perhaps "tactical deceptions, given the party's more hard-line base and Muslim Brothers roots."[33] Continuing in a similar vein, but talking about the rise to power of Islamists in general, Thornton stated that "it is more likely that Islamist participation in democratic institutions is a temporary tactic in the long-term strategy of creating an Islamic government similar to that in Iran,"[34] going on to quote Turkish prime minister Recep Tayyip Erdoğan for once saying that "Democracy is like a train. We shall get out when we arrive at the station we want."[35]

Somewhat more restrained in his analysis, David Schenker at the Washington Institute for Near East Policy found that the most likely outcome of the Arab Spring was "populist and Islamist politics," adding that of course these "too can be voted out of power. That is, provided that these states continue to hold elections and viable alternatives are not snuffed out."[36]

In contrast to the Americans, the European academics—most notably the French—were much more skeptical, questioning whether we were really beginning to witness "*un hiver islamiste*" or "*un automne islamiste*," and arguing that it was important not to forget that the Islamist parties that had recently arrived in power in the Middle East and North Africa were not a monolithic group, but rather diverse.[37] According to Bertrand Badie, a professor at the Sciences Po in Paris, speaking of an Islamist Winter presently would appear incorrect—the term tends to be used by those in the West who fear the region. Of course, Badie argues, Islamism has experienced a surge in popularity as a consequence of the Arab Spring, but it is a heterogeneous phenomenon, and its future is uncertain. Much depends on the Islamist parties who have recently witnessed an electoral boost, most notably in Egypt, Morocco, and Tunisia, but it is still too soon to interpret the impact of their victories.[38]

Jebali makes a move: murder, dissent, and disagreements

While, so far, there are no indications that an Islamist Winter is taking hold in countries such as Morocco, Turkey, and Tunisia, regardless of how one defines the concept, there have indeed been signs that the fears of authoritarian regression are not unfounded in the Tunisian case. What is being referred to here in particular is the attempt by Prime Minister Jebali to reshuffle the cabinet in the wake of the assassination of the opposition figure Chokri Belaïd on February 6, 2013. However, Jebali's move was personally motivated and not supported by the upper echelons of Ennahda. The attempt at concentrating powers in Jebali's hands did not, in other words, have an Islamist flavor—the objective was not to strengthen the party or further some Islamist cause, it was to advance Jebali under the guise of "what is best for Tunisia" at a time of looming instability with protesters taking to the street once again, accusing Ennahda of killing off its opponents Ben Ali style.[39]

Who assassinated Belaïd is still not entirely clear, although suspects have been arrested and they apparently have Islamist sympathies.[40] But, in fact, no matter the tragedy of Belaïd's terrible death, who did the evil deed is not the most crucial aspect if seen from the point of view of the country's democratization process. The reality is that Belaïd was relatively unimportant. Yes, he was a longstanding political activist, voicing his opposition to Ben Ali's regime and later the new government due to Ennahda dominance, and Belaïd was also the leader of a political party, the Mouvement des Patriotes Démocrates (Movement of Patriotic Democrats, MPD), which was legalized in 2011 after years of clandestine activity. However, commanding only one parliamentary seat out of 217, the MPD was not, by any means, a relevant party, and Belaïd was hardly an opposition leader, although he was certainly a familiar face. Yet, despite this reality, his assassination was turned into a major political event as everyone, whether Jebali, the parties of the governing coalition, the opposition, or those amongst the general population who were simply anti-Ennahda (or anti-Islamist) tried to hijack the situation and use it to their own advantage politically.

Jebali, as mentioned above, attempted to concentrate power in his own hands. And he moved very swiftly indeed. In fact, it appears that Jebali used the assassination of Belaïd to get himself out of a political stalemate, not only with dignity, but also strengthened, something that had appeared unlikely only a week earlier when the CPR threatened to withdraw its cabinet ministers and resign from the governing coalition should Jebali fail to reach an agreement on key political and economic issues as well as deliver the promised cabinet reshuffle originally scheduled for January 14, 2013.[41] By dismissing the cabinet on February 6, the day of Belaïd's killing, arguing that the political situation had changed dramatically with this event, and that Tunisia was accordingly not only in need of a new cabinet as promised, but one devoid of party ties so that the new ministers would not be blinkered by partisan interests but would only have what was best for the country at heart, Jebali sought to eliminate his critics within the regime in a manner that he undoubtedly hoped would come across as legitimate to the electorate, most notably the angry protesters. As a further means of appeasing the citizenry, Jebali made clear that the cabinet of technocrats would only be a temporary measure—a so-called "caretaker" government—that would step down following legislative elections that he envisioned would take place sometime in the autumn of 2013.[42]

The response

Rather unsurprisingly, Jebali's move was met with fierce opposition from the CPR, which looked set to lose all its influence within the cabinet.

Barely twenty-four hours after the prime minister's announcement, the CPR's Abdelwaheb Maatar made it very clear that the party was seriously unimpressed with Jebali, arguing that he was seeking to legitimize what was essentially nothing but an attempt at a dirty coup, and that the CPR refused to accept a cabinet composed of technocrats. Such an entity was not, declared Maatar, in the spirit of the Revolution of Freedom and Dignity and, moreover, it would not have a clear program and therefore would not be able to do very much, an assessment that was echoed by another central party figure only a few days later.[43] On February 10, the CPR left the governing Troika, albeit only to reverse its decision and return the following day, giving talks an extra chance.[44]

More importantly, however, the prime minister did not have his own party on board. The decision to dismiss the cabinet, and the idea of appointing a cabinet of technocrats were Jebali's own—he had not consulted the party leadership, but was hoping that Ennahda (along with the CPR and the FDTL) would support the move.[45] As it turned out, the party did not. It did not take long for key figures within Ennahda to publicly condemn Jebali's actions, stating that not only had they not been consulted, the party was also not in agreement with the prime minister.[46] Faced with opposition from several fronts, Jebali responded by declaring that if his plans for a cabinet of technocrats failed, he would resign from his post as prime minister.[47] What was undoubtedly a last-ditch attempt to force his vision through instead ended as political suicide. The CPR and Ennahda both refused to cave in, thereby ridding themselves of a difficult prime minister, and Ennahda effectively also of a disloyal and self-centered key party figure, who had spun out of control and was proving to be quite a liability. Hence, on February 19, Jebali stepped down.[48]

With Jebali's resignation, many people got what they wanted, others hoped they did. Fanning the anti-Islamist fire, Belaïd's widow publicly blamed Ennahda for her husband's death, and declared that "this government must resign today, not tomorrow or the day after tomorrow" and that "they must go, all of them, including the prime minister. The game is over."[49] Belaïd's wife got what she asked for, as did many of the demonstrators, but they were soon to be disappointed. As expected, rather than bowing to popular pressure, President Marzouki tasked Ennahda with nominating another prime minister as the party was the largest in the legislature.[50] On February 22, Marzouki proclaimed that the minister of the interior, Ali Laarayedh, had been identified as Jebali's successor.[51] Viewed as a hardliner by many, this was undoubtedly not what the anti-Ennahda and anti-Islamists on the street and in the legislature had hoped for.[52]

While it is still too soon to judge Laarayedh on the basis of his actions as prime minister, at first glance his appointment does not appear to be at all revolutionary. The cabinet formed by Laarayedh shortly after accepting the job includes a handful of ministers from the CPR, the FDTL, and Ennahda, as well as a number of technocrats. In fact, the whole Jebali affair concluded with what can best be described as a careful cabinet reshuffle, with a number of portfolios changing hands, but the balance of power within the Troika remaining much the same, although the weight of technocrats within the cabinet has arguably increased, to some extent at the expense of Ennahda, which agreed to hand over key portfolios to appease the critics, most notably the Ministry of the Interior, the Ministry of Justice, the Ministry of Defense, and the Ministry of Foreign Affairs.[53] In short, despite the various attempts to capitalize on the assassination of Belaïd, the political change that occurred as a result was largely insignificant—the Troika survived, and Ennahda remained the dominant actor within the alliance, albeit somewhat weakened.[54]

That said, there will arguably be some repercussions as popular legitimacy was dented in the process. A prime minister seeking to concentrate power in his own hands, a deep rift within the country's largest party becoming readily apparent to the general public,[55] the near political deadlock within the governing Troika, the CPR's threat to leave the coalition, the prime minister tying his continuation in the job to having his own ideas pushed through—all of those incidents came across very badly to the electorate as they bore witness of political immaturity, personalistic politics, and petty power struggles that did not have the interest of the Tunisian democratization process at heart, but instead that of individual politicians and, to some extent, that of individual political parties. This reality is undeniably linked to the fact that the components of the country's party system are mostly relatively young in terms of the date of their legalization and participation in the democratic process and, more importantly, virtually all can best be characterized as personal vehicles.

The future of Tunisia's fragile democracy

This chapter has sought to highlight that despite the sudden transition to democracy in Tunisia, the country's democratization process seems to be heading slowly in the right direction, that is, towards the consolidation of democracy. Legislative elections were held, they resulted in the formation of a coalition government representing quite diverse segments of society, and despite significant difficulties in working together within the governing Troika—partly brought on by the personalistic nature of the political parties as well as their inexperience with the democratic process—democracy does not appear to be at significant risk of breakdown. The components are working together, regardless of how strained the relationship, and there is clearly also a system of checks and balances in place as the Jebali affair illustrated.

That said, the new Tunisian democracy is arguably fragile. As the Jebali affair illustrates, democracy is yet to become the only game in town—there is simply no denying that the former prime minister did attempt to concentrate power in his own hands, although in the end he failed miserably. One of the main reasons why Jebali was unsuccessful—apart from him neglecting to consult his own party—was the existence of a coalition government. The refusal by the CPR, the second-largest party in the legislature, to accept his proposal of a cabinet of technocrats made it impossible for Jebali to simply push it through. While the coalition partners were by no means equal, even a much smaller partner can cause the government to fall, which is exactly what the CPR threatened to do. Consequently, when discussing how best to ensure the consolidation of democracy in Tunisia, it is important to bear in mind that while the design of the country's new constitution is of primary importance, one should not overlook other key legislative measures that can help institutionalize democracy—and a democracy of quality. At present, Tunisia is arguably an electoral democracy. The first elections held following the revolution were free and fair, and competitive. However, while the government has effective power to govern, not all of its key components were popularly elected—presidential elections are still to be held. With regard to the respect for and protection of basic civil liberties, the situation at present is much better than during the reign of Ben Ali, but it still leaves a lot to be desired. In other words, while Tunisia is now a democracy, the quality of democracy could be much improved, partially via legislative measures (in addition to a revised constitution) as alluded to above.

Most notably, the first post-Arab Spring elections and the Jebali affair have highlighted the importance of establishing a party system that is a much slimmed-down version of the current one. The level of fragmentation is extremely high, making it virtually impossible for the electorate to navigate the party system at election time, resulting in the loss of political legitimacy. Reducing the size of the party system, for instance by designing an election code with a sizeable national electoral threshold and constituencies of a moderate size, possibly with a district magnitude in the range of 3 to 5, would be one way of combatting the current depoliticization of the electorate, partly due to a less crowded party landscape, but also because the parties left on the scene would be forced to appeal to the electorate to a greater extent than they have had to do so far—via measures such as party conferences, the establishment of local party offices, and the development of clear and coherent party programs—as a consequence of the changed nature of competition.[56] This latter point, that is, the parties establishing stronger roots in society, would also help address the issue of the quality of democracy, which, as just mentioned, is currently a very genuine concern.

In light of the above, it should be noted that it is important not to reduce the party system to such a degree that coalition government will no longer be the norm. As the Jebali affair has proved, checks and balances are very important, and the more the better. This is also why the insistence by some politicians, mostly from Ennahda, on the adoption of a parliamentary rather than a semi-presidential or presidential system, seems like the best option for the design of the country's political system in the future. Although parliamentarism arguably carries a significant risk of deadlock, which can indeed be threatening to the survival of democracy (again as illustrated by the Jebali affair), the risk seems worth taking if the alternative is a system, that is, a form of presidentialism, where there is a very real likelihood that the president and the prime minister could originate from the same party, thereby concentrating power and, consequently, diminishing checks and balances.

Finally, it is of utmost importance that the Tunisian electorate will be given the opportunity to head to the polls again in the not too distant future, probably to cast a vote in favor of or against the new constitution, which will then set the scene for further elections, parliamentary for sure, presidential perhaps, depending on the chosen design of the country's political system.

Notes

1. For a discussion of the concepts of internally and externally created parties, please consult Maurice Duverger, *Political Parties: Their Organization and Activity in the Modern State* (London: Methuen, 1954).
2. For more on the veritable jungle of definitions of democracy, please refer to David Collier and Steven Levitsky, "Democracy with Adjectives: Conceptual Innovation in Comparative Research," *World Politics* 49 (1997): 430–51. See also Lise Storm, "An Elemental Definition of Democracy and its Advantages for Comparing Political Regime Types," *Democratization* 15.2 (2008): 215–29.
3. Andreas Schedler, *Electoral Authoritarianism: The Dynamics of Unfree Competition* (Boulder, CO: Lynne Rienner, 2006), 3.
4. For reflections on how to assess the quality of democracy, see Larry Diamond and Leonardo Morlino, *Assessing the Quality of Democracy* (Baltimore, MD: The Johns Hopkins University Press, 2005).
5. The definition of political parties applied here is that by Sartori, which stipulates that ". . . any political group identified by an official label that presents at elections, and is capable of placing through elections (free or non-free), candidates for public office" constitutes a political party. This definition is unquestionably of the minimalist kind, and has been chosen because of its emphasis on success and due to the fact that Sartori views non-democratic elections as qualifying, two aspects that are rather important in a Middle Eastern and North African setting where there is an abundance of so-called parties that only exist on paper, and where the elections are often not democratic. Giovanni Sartori, *Parties and Party Systems: A Framework for Analysis* (Cambridge: Cambridge University Press, 1976), 63.
6. See, among others, Seymour Lipset, "The Indispensability of Political Parties," *Journal of Democracy* 11.1 (2000): 48–55; Peter Mair, "Democracy Beyond Parties," Center for the Study of Democracy Working Paper Series 05/06 (Berkeley, CA: University of California Irvine, 2005); Sartori, *Parties and Party Systems*; E. Schattschneider, *Party Government* (New York: Rinehart, 1942); Joseph Schumpeter, *Capitalism, Socialism and Democracy* (New York: Harper and Row, 1942). Even Tocqueville was in agreement.
7. Peter Mair, "Populist Democracy *vs* Party Democracy," in *Democracies and the Populist*

Challenges, ed. Yves Mény and Yves Surel (Basingstoke: Palgrave Macmillan, 2002), 81–98.

8. Juan Linz and Alfred Stepan, *Problems of Democratic Transition and Consolidation: Southern Europe, South America, and Post-Communist Europe* (Baltimore, MD: The Johns Hopkins University Press, 1996), 5–6.
9. For more on the Tunisian elections (legislative and presidential) in the post-independence period, see Lise Storm, *Party Politics and Prospects for Democracy in North Africa* (Boulder, CO: Lynne Rienner, 2013).
10. Union Européenne, *Mission d'observation électorale: rapport final. Élections législatives Algérie 2012* (Brussels: Union Européenne, 2012); Union Européenne, *Mission d'observation électorale en Tunisie 2011. Élection de l'Assemblée Nationale Constituante* (Tunis: Union Européenne, 2011).
11. The elections were contested by 1,519 lists of which 54.6 percent were fielded by political parties, 43.3 percent by individual candidates, and the remaining 2.4 percent by so-called coalitions. See The Carter Center, *National Constituent Assembly Elections in Tunisia: October 23, 2011. Final Report* (Atlanta, GA: The Carter Center, 2012), 32.
12. The Carter Center, *National Constituent Assembly Elections in Tunisia*, 29, 54. Please note that 97.8 percent of the registered voters participated in the elections. Of the votes cast, no fewer than 255,740 (or 5.9 percent) were invalid.
13. The results were published online by L'Instance Supérieure Indépendante pour les Élections (www.isie.tn).
14. Roy and Filiu both agree with this assessment. See Christophe Boltanski, "La galaxie islamiste," *Le Nouvel Observateur*, December 8, 2011, accessed March 27, 2013, www.gremmo.mom.fr/sites/gremmo.mom.fr/files/docs/Activites/Medias/NouvelObsdec2011.pdf
15. International Foundation for Electoral Systems, *Tunisia Voter Registration and Voter Confidence Assessment Survey: May 2011* (Washington, DC: International Foundation for Electoral Systems, 2012).
16. For the results of the 2009 elections, see the Inter-Parliamentary Union online at www.ipu.org.
17. The effective number of parties is an indication of the number of parties with genuine power in the legislature. The measure takes into account a party's seat share as well as the seat share of the other parties in the legislature. See Markku Laakso and Rein Taagepera, "'Effective' Number of Parties: A Measure with Application to West Europe," *Comparative Political Studies* 12.1 (1979): 3–27.
18. Célina Braun, "À quoi servent les partis tunisiens? Sens et contre-sens d'une 'libéralisation' politique," *Revue des Mondes Musulmans et de la Méditerranée* 111–12 (2006): 15–61; Michel Camau and Vincent Geisser, *Le syndrome autoritaire: Politique en Tunisie de Bourguiba à Ben Ali* (Paris: Presses de Sciences Po, 2003).
19. On the topic of the importance of uncertainty and alternation, please refer to Adam Przeworski, *Democracy and Development: Political Institutions and Well-Being in the World, 1950–1990* (New York: Cambridge University Press, 2000); Adam Przeworski, "Some Problems in the Study of the Transition to Democracy," in *Transitions from Authoritarian Rule: Comparative Perspectives*, ed. Guillermo O'Donnell et al. (Baltimore, MD: The Johns Hopkins University Press, 1986), 47–63.
20. Eileen Byrne, "Tunisians Protest over Charges against Woman Allegedly Raped by Police," *The Guardian*, October 3, 2012, accessed March 27, 2013, www.guardian.

co.uk/world/2012/oct/03/tunisians-protest-charges-woman-police; "Protests in Tunisian Town Show Anger at Islamist Government," *Reuters*, December 2, 2012, accessed March 27, 2013, www.reuters.com/article/2012/12/02/us-tunisia-protests-idUSBRE8B108620121202; Tarek Amara, "Tunisians Take to Streets Two Years after Ben Ali's Fall," *Reuters*, January 14, 2013, accessed March 27, 2013, www.reuters.com/article/2013/01/14/us-tunisia-protests-idUSBRE90D0JY20130114.

21. This is not to say that the human rights situation in Tunisia had become completely idyllic in the wake of the Revolution of Freedom of Dignity. For a critical report, see "World Report 2012: Tunisia," Human Rights Watch, January 2012, accessed March 27, 2013, www.hrw.org/world-report-2012/world-report-2012-tunisia.
22. For a discussion of the uneasy nature of the alliance, see Andrea G. Brody-Barre, "The Impact of Political Parties and Coalition Building on Tunisia's Democratic Future," *Journal of North African Studies* 18.2 (2013): 217–18.
23. The Jebali cabinet saw fourteen seats awarded to Ennahda, five to the FDTL, and four to the CPR. Technocrats held an additional seven portfolios.
24. Duncan Pickard, "The Current Status of Constitution Making in Tunisia," *Carnegie Endowment Commentary*, April 19, 2012, accessed March 27, 2013, http://carnegieendowment.org/2012/04/19/current-status-of-constitution-making-in-tunisia.
25. For an European perspective, see "Parliament will Stand by Tunisia in its Transition to Democracy, say MEPs," *European Parliament News*, October 2, 2012, accessed March 27, 2013, www.europarl.europa.eu/news/en/pressroom/content/20121002IPR52722/html/Parliament-will-stand-by-Tunisia-in-its-transition-to-democracy-say-MEPs.
26. Roy concurs. See Boltanski, "La galaxie islamiste."
27. One of the parliamentarians voicing a fear that Tunisia would experience authoritarian regression under Islamist leadership was the leader of the (now defunct) PDP, Ahmed Najib Chebbi.
28. Brody-Barre, "The Impact of Political Parties," 218–21. Al-Massar encompasses members of the former Pole Démocratique Moderniste (Modernist Democratic Pole, PDM), primarily the Ettajdid (Movement for Renewal), and the Parti du Travail Tunisien (Tunisian Workers Party, PTT), while the PR is a merger between the PDP, Afek Tounes (Tunisian Aspirations, AT) and a number of smaller entities and independents.
29. For more on this topic, please refer to the chapter by Perkins in this volume.
30. "Morocco: Benkirane Denies Intention to Islamicise Society," *The Maghreb Daily*, February 22, 2013, accessed March 27, 2013, http://en.lemag.ma/Morocco-Benkirane-denies-intention-to-Islamisize-Society_a3377.html. See also the discussion of the compatibility of Islam and democracy in Brody-Barre, "The Impact of Political Parties," 214.
31. It is important to underline that while this was the view of many, it was certainly not shared by everyone. For an example of a more measured assessment, please refer to Tamara Cofman Wittes, "Learning to Live With the Islamist Winter," *Foreign Policy*, July 19, 2012, accessed March 27, 2013, www.foreignpolicy.com/articles/2012/07/19/learning_to_live_with_the_islamist_winter?page=0,0.
32. Bruce Thornton, "The Arab Winter Approaches," *Defining Ideas*, November 2011, accessed March 27, 2013, www.hoover.org/publications/defining-ideas/article/100526.

33. Thornton, "The Arab Winter Approaches."
34. Thornton, "The Arab Winter Approaches."
35. Thornton, "The Arab Winter Approaches."
36. David Schenker, "Arab Spring or Islamist Winter?" *World Affairs Journal*, January/February (2012), accessed March 27, 2013, www.worldaffairsjournal.org/article/arab-spring-or-islamist-winter-0
37. Olivier Roy, "Révolution post-islamiste," *Le Monde*, February 12, 2011, accessed March 27, 2013, www.lemonde.fr/idees/article/2011/02/12/revolution-post-islamiste_1478858_3232.html; Boltanski, "La galaxie islamiste."
38. "Bertrand Badie, 'Le printemps arabe a révélé l'existence d'un islamisme hétérogène et composite'", *Le Monde*, January 19, 2012, accessed March 27, 2013, www.lemonde.fr/international/article/2012/01/19/bertrand-badie-le-printemps-arabe-a-revele-l-existence-d-un-islamisme-heterogene-et-composite_1632134_3210.html. Please note that this view is shared by Brody-Barre, "The impact of political parties," 215.
39. Monica Marks and Kareem Fahim, "Tunisia Moves to Contain Fallout After Opposition Figure is Assassinated,' *New York Times*, February 6, 2013, accessed March 30, 2013, www.nytimes.com/2013/02/07/world/africa/chokri-belaid-tunisian-opposition-figure-is-killed.html?_r=0; Tarek Amara, "Démission du gouvernement tunisien après la mort d'un opposant," *Reuters*, February 6, 2013, accessed March 30, 2013, http://fr.reuters.com/article/topNews/idFRPAE91501B20130206?sp=true
40. Heba Saleh, "Tunisia Arrests Four over Belaid's Murder," *Financial Times*, February 26, 2013, accessed March 30, 2013, www.ft.com/cms/s/0/270106ae-8023-11e2-96ba-00144feabdc0.html#axzz2OpcJegRj
41. "Le parti du chef de l'État quitte le gouvernement tunisien," *Le Point*, February 10, 2013, accessed March 30, 2013, www.lepoint.fr/monde/le-parti-du-chef-de-l-etat-quitte-le-gouvernement-tunisien-10-02-2013-1625947_24.php; "Tunisian President's Party in Government 'U-turn'," *France 24*, February 11, 2013; accessed March 30, 2013, http://www.france24.com/en/20130211-tunisia-president-jebali-party-cpr-stay-in-government-u-turn; "Tunisia: Ali Larayedh Named New Prime Minister," *BBC News*, February 22, 2013, accessed March 30, 2013, www.bbc.co.uk/news/world-africa-21550375
42. Dan Rivers and Laura Smith-Spark, "Jebali Vows to Press on with Plans for Caretaker Government in Tunisia," *CNN*, February 9, 2013, accessed March 30, 2013, http://edition.cnn.com/2013/02/08/world/africa/tunisia-unrest; "Jebali to Form 'Mini Technocrat Government'," *TAP*, February 7, 2013, accessed March 30, 2013, www.tap.info.tn/en/index.php/politics2/5446-jebali-to-form-mini-technocrat-government. It is worth noting that calling for legislative elections appeared to be in the interest of Ennahda as opinion polls indicated that the party would emerge the winner again, albeit with a slightly smaller seat share. In contrast, the CPR looked set to lose nearly half of its mandates. See "Élections législatives: 38.5% des Tunisiens ne savent pas pour qui voter," *Direct Info*, March 21, 2013, accessed March 30, 2013, http://directinfo.webmanagercenter.com/2013/03/21/elections-legislatives-38-5-des-tunisiens-ne-savent-pas-pour-qui-voter/
43. "Abdelwahab Maater: 'le CPR refuse le gouvernement de technocrates et la décision de Hamadi Jebali est un coup "mauve" porté à la légitimité'," *Shams News*, February 7, 2013, accessed March 30, 2013, www.shemsfm.net/fr/actualite/abdelwahab-maater-le-cpr-refuse-le-gouvernement-de-technocrates-et-la-decision-de-hamadi-jebali-est-un

-coup-mauve-porte-a-la-legitimite?id=36153; "Le CPR refuse de participer à un gouvernement de technocrate," *Tunisie 14*, February 9, 2013, accessed March 30, 2013, http://tunisie14.tn/article/detail/le-cpr-refuse-de-participer-a-un-gouvernement-de-technocrate

44 "Le parti du chef de l'État quitte le gouvernement tunisien," *Le Point*, February 10, 2013, accessed March 30, 2013, www.lepoint.fr/monde/le-parti-du-chef-de-l-etat-quitte-le-gouvernement-tunisien-10-02-2013-1625947_24.php; "Tunisia's Moncef Marzouki's CPR 'Stays in Government'," *BBC News*, February 11, 2013, accessed March 30, 2013.

45. "Tunisia PM Jebali Pledges New Government 'By Next Week'," *BBC News*, February 9, 2013, accessed March 30, 2013, www.bbc.co.uk/news/world-africa-21394031; "Tunisia Political Crisis Deepens After Assassination," *BBC News*, February 7, 2013, accessed March 30, 2013, www.bbc.co.uk/news/world-africa-21366235; Rivers and Smith-Spark, "Jebali Vows to Press on with Plans for Caretaker Government in Tunisia."

46. "Tunisia PM Jebali Pledges New Government 'By Next Week'," *BBC News*, February 9, 2013, accessed March 30, 2013, www.bbc.co.uk/news/world-africa-21394031; "Tunisia Political Crisis Deepens After Assassination," *BBC News*, February 7, 2013, accessed March 30, 2013, www.bbc.co.uk/news/world-africa-21366235; Rivers and Smith-Spark, "Jebali Vows to Press on with Plans for Caretaker Government in Tunisia."

47. "Tunisia PM to Resign if New Cabinet Rejected," *Al-Jazeera*, February 10, 2013, accessed March 30, 2013, www.aljazeera.com/news/africa/2013/02/2013291157142522.html; Tarek Amara, "Tunisia PM Quits After Failing to Form New Government," *Reuters*, February 19, 2013, accessed March 30, 2013, www.reuters.com/article/2013/02/19/us-tunisia-pm-idUSBRE91I10J20130219

48. Amara, "Tunisia PM Quits After Failing to Form New Government."

49. Rivers and Smith-Spark, "Jebali Vows to Press on with Plans for Caretaker Government in Tunisia." See also "Tunisia Leader Says Unity Government Imminent," *Al-Jazeera*, February 12, 2013, accessed March 30, 2013, http://m.aljazeera.com/story/201321116616961398; "Tunisia's Moncef Marzouki's CPR 'Stays in Government'," *BBC News*, February 11, 2013, accessed March 30, 2013.

50. Tarek Amara, "Tunisian President asks Islamist to Form Government," *Reuters*, February 22, 2013, accessed March 30, 2013, http://uk.reuters.com/article/2013/02/22/uk-tunisia-politics-idUKBRE91L0F420130222

51. "Tunisia: Ali Larayedh Named New Prime Minister," *BBC News*, February 22, 2013, accessed March 30, 2013, www.bbc.co.uk/news/world-africa-21550375

52. Bouazza Ben Bouazza, "Tunisia Islamist Party Chooses New Prime Minister," *Huffington Post*, February 22, 2013, accessed March 30, 2013, www.huffingtonpost.com/huff-wires/20130222/ml-tunisia/?utm_hp_ref=homepage&ir=homepage;
Tarek Amara, "Tunisia's New Premier Promises Inclusive Government," *Reuters*, February 22, 2013, accessed March 30, 2013, www.reuters.com/article/2013/02/22/us-tunisia-politics-idUSBRE91L0F720130222

53. "Tunisie: Larayedh annonce la composition du nouveau cabinet," *Jeune Afrique*, March 8, 2013, accessed March 30, 2013, www.jeuneafrique.com/actu/20130308T154515Z20130308T154510Z/; Kareem Fahim, "Tunisia Includes Independents in New Cabinet," *The New York Times*, March 8, 2013, accessed March 30, 2013, www.

nytimes.com/2013/03/09/world/africa/to-ease-crisis-tunisia-includes-independents-in-new-cabinet.html?ref=tunisia&_r=1&; "Larayedh Unveils Tunisia Cabinet," *Magharebia*, March 8, 2013, accessed March 30, 2013, http://magharebia.com/en_GB/articles/awi/newsbriefs/general/2013/03/08/newsbrief-02.

54. This is unquestionably a controversial view given that only 51 percent of the members of the first Laarayedh cabinet are from the Troika. The other 49 percent are technocrats and independents. However, rather than looking at the workings of the cabinet (and government) as a mere numbers game, the position taken here is that what matters is the balance of power in terms of blackmail and coalition potential (i.e. where smaller partners threaten to leave the coalition or where there are clear alternatives to the governing coalition, such as for instance Ennahda joining forces with other parties).
55. Please note that dissent within Ennahda was far from a novel phenomenon. For more on the issue, see Brody-Barre, "The Impact of Political Parties," 216.
56. The new mergers, principally al-Massar and the PR, and potentially also the looser alliances, including Minbar al-Istiqlal (or Forum of Independence, comprising members of the right, liberal Destourians, and Islamists) and the effort by the former prime minister Béji Caïd Essebsi to unite the centrist, secular opposition, assist a little in reducing fragmentation. However, given the small size of these entities (in terms of parliamentary seats), their contribution is rather small. Furthermore, the formation of most of these new parties and alliances do not address the issue of the quality of democracy in Tunisia as they are all internally created and have feeble programs; indeed, the main defining feature of most being their position vis-à-vis Ennahda, which they are in opposition to. Regardless of what the various party leaders say, virtually all of the new creations are against Ennahda, not simply an alternative to the party. See Brody-Barre, "The Impact of Political Parties," 219–21.

Postscript: Preserving the Exemplar

Nouri Gana

Two and a half years ago, Tunisia was hailed across the world as the exemplar of a popular, leaderless and peaceful revolution. The power and promise of what happened in Tunisia was and remains overwhelming to this day: an entire people marching united, civilly and non-violently, calling proudly and loudly with one voice, "Ben Ali, out" before they delivered the final knockout—"Game over." Hope became infectious across the streets of Tunisia; long-overdue democratic and revolutionary change became, in turn, contagious, and what happened in Tunisia was bound to travel, as indeed it variably did, across the entire Arab World.

The real achievement of Tunisia is that it demonstrated that the hope for change was and continues to be alive and well despite the longevity of authoritarianism. The worst crime of European and US-backed Arab dictatorships is the politics of fear they use to engineer the consent of their people—the slow and steady dispossession of their will to freedom, to dignity and to self-determination. When this fear insinuates itself into the mind, not only does all memory of freedom disappear, but so too does the willingness to pay the price for it. The crucial importance of what happened in Tunisia on January 14, 2011, then, is that Arabs have shown such hunger for freedom from injustice that they no longer recognize themselves without it.

By the time the Egyptian and then the Libyan revolutions started in January and February, respectively, Tunisia had become the unofficial exporter of revolutionary change, even though the death toll incurred in the Egyptian and especially the Libyan revolutions undermined the quasi-peacefulness of what Tunisia achieved in January 2011. All the more so now, given the staggering human cost exacted by Syria's bitter revolution-cum-civil war. While the quasi-exemplary fashion in which Ben Ali was ousted was not replicated anywhere in the Arab world, not even in Egypt where the deposition of Mubarak cost so many lives, the bloody turn of the uprisings-cum-civil wars in Libya and especially in Syria have never ceased to cast a shadow of gloom on the transitional process in Tunisia.

After holding the first truly democratic elections in October 2011—a feat that seemed to consolidate its model leadership of the Arab uprisings—Tunisia found itself, though, gradually dragged into the ideological and geopolitical struggles of power and influence that have befallen the region. Tunisia's new leaders (i.e. the Troika: the tripartite coalition of Ennahda, CPR and Ettakatol) tried genuinely to steer the country clear from these burning regional struggles and simultaneously stand for the same principles that defined the Tunisian revolution, but failed in the end to remain neutral, much less to fully quarantine the young Tunisian democracy from those nightmarish scenarios taking shape in Libya, Syria and then Egypt. The governmental attitudes toward Syria, Libya, Qatar, and Algeria, among others, have all fueled tensions among the Troika and the opposition parties. What further complicated things for Tunisia is that other Arab countries, where revolutions have yet to take place, had an undeclared interest in tarnishing the Tunisian revolution for fear it might spill over to them.

With the unfolding events in Libya, Syria, and especially Egypt returning to haunt the Tunisian postrevolutionary scene, it might be fair to suggest that Tunisia is only reaping part of the disorder it sowed in the old order of Arab dictatorships. The problem remains, however, the tenacity and intransigence of that very same old order, those very same regional and international players—the neocolonial clans of European and US-backed Arab dictatorships—against which the Arab masses have risen up. After the fall of Ben Ali and the official dissolution of the RCD, Tunisians have given up too quickly the fight against old regime figures who continued, under the first two interim governments of Mohamed Ghannouchi and Béji Caïd Essebsi respectively, to reassemble politically and elude justice and accountability by destroying all archival evidence of their criminal activities. Instead, secularists and Islamists alike aligned themselves into parties/coalitions in power and others in the opposition and were too absorbed fighting each other to pay attention to the return of the *azlām* (the remnants of the old regime figures) to political life. In some cases, they even appealed to some of these figures in order to strengthen their parties/coalitions or to score political points against each other. At times, they used the *azlām* to tarnish each other's reputation, but while they were busy bickering and exploring how to do things with the *azlām*, the *azlām* were preying on their disunity and divisiveness so as to reclaim power and influence.

Dictators may die hard (Gaddafi and now Assad are just two cases in point), but dictatorships die even harder. The recent military coup in Egypt and the deposition of the democratically elected president—Mohamed Morsi—speaks volumes about the ways in which the old order is reasserting itself across the region. The Egyptian Tamarod (rebellion) movement, whose legitimate agitations against the failures of the Muslim Brotherhood resulted in the sudden deposition of Morsi by the military, had overnight been copied in Tunisia, and there followed a number of calls for the Tunisian military to depose the governing Troika and especially the Ennahda party, long associated with the Brotherhood's line of thinking. Were this to happen, Tunisia would practically change positions from being the vector of a revolutionary wave to becoming the victim of a counterrevolutionary tide. It would be seen to have sowed a revolution in Egypt and elsewhere in the Arab world only to reap a coup.

Not unlike Egypt, where the Muslim Brotherhood are partly responsible for the massive protests that resulted in their ousting by the military, the old regime forces in Tunisia have thrived on the mistakes, failures and general incompetence of the Troika (and Ennahda party in particular). Apart from its inability to fulfill much of the economic and social promises of the revolution and of its electoral campaign, the governing Troika's gravest mistake is its inability to introduce institutional reforms, to effect transitional justice, to bring old regime figures to justice, to open up the archives, and to fight corruption. Accountability is a word that has gone largely missing from the agenda of the Troika, which is why old regime figures have now started to flex their muscles. After having been the problem, old regime figures have now successfully refashioned themselves as part of the solution, if not the solution altogether; all the more so in the wake of the recent assassination of two opposition political figures: Chokri Belaïd on February 6, 2013 and Mohamed Brahmi on July 25, 2013.

Before these two recent assassinations, which have so far come to pose the biggest threat to the very existence of the Troika and the National Constituent Assembly (ANC), the beneficiaries of the October 2011 elections encountered a host of security challenges and social demands which they did not always address in the right way. This has in turn emboldened not only the opposition parties, which could be understandable, but also the old regime and RCD figures, which is outrageous, if lamentable and regrettable on the part of the Troika. Gradually, the Troika governing body found itself being compared to the former Ben Ali party, the RCD; what is worse, the beneficiaries of the old regime, along with some opposition leaders and disenchanted Tunisians, have begun to believe that the Troika and the RCD are disposed to acting not only similarly but identically. Wittingly or unwittingly, such comparisons serve more to dilute and disperse the crimes of the old regime than discredit the Troika.

Ever since they assumed power, shortly after the October 2011 elections, the Troika and Ennahda party in particular have been accused of continuing the same practices of the old regime of Ben Ali, especially given their recourse to excessive violence on multiple occasions to repress anti-government demonstrations. For instance, in late October 2012 riot police from the Brigades de l'Ordre Public ("les BOP") used tear gas and birdshot against Siliana protesters, which resulted in hundreds injured, several of whom lost or risked losing sight in one or both eyes from the birdshot. The use of rubber and lead birdshot pellets (small rubber or lead spheres fired in bursts from guns that can cause serious injury to soft tissue) is unprecedented in Tunisia and was largely seen as far worse than the repressive measures Ben Ali commonly adopted against demonstrators.

The then Minister of Interior (Ali Laaraydh, from Ennahda) had pointed out, though, that the riot police used birdshot as the only alternative to using lethal ammunition against protesters who were allegedly throwing rocks and Molotov cocktails in an attempt to storm the *wilāya* or the government building in the Siliana governorate. In contradistinction to the merciless use of birdshot pellets against the Siliana protesters, the Troika government and Ennahda party in particular have been accused of being lenient, if not complicit, with the so-called Leagues for the Protection of the Revolution (*Lijān ḥimāyit al-thwara*) whose members allegedly attacked the building of the UGTT in December 2012 at a time when UGTT members were gathered to mark the sixtieth anniversary of the assassination of UGTT founder Farhat Hached in 1946.

Moreover, the Ennahda-led Troika government was also accused of failing to protect art exhibitions, theaters and, more recently, Sufi shrines against the attacks of allegedly religious extremists. With the rise of Salafism to prominence, especially after the storming of the American embassy in September 2012, and its continual duel with laicism (or secularism *à la française*), there have been—and currently still are—security threats and fears that Tunisia runs the risk of sliding into a theocracy, if not reverting back into a secular autocracy; however, these fears are likely to remain unrealized, given the lively spirit of the public arena and the irrevocable rights of speech and protest that Tunisians have earned. What is remarkable here, perhaps not without some irony of course, is that at the very same time that the ruling Troika is being accused of continuing the same policies and practices of the deposed Benalite regime, the return of notorious old regime figures to the political scene has gained spectacular momentum: Borhane Bsaies (Ben Ali's spokesperson) and Slim Chiboub (Ben Ali's son-in-law) reappeared in the public sphere through TV interviews on Hannibal and Ettounsiya respectively. Leila Ben Ali wrote a memoir, cleaning her records and claiming innocence. In no time, a member of the ANC (Mohamed Karim Krifa) shouted at his detractors in the opposite aisle: "The RCD is your Master (*Sīdkum*)." The declaration came as a shock to many Tunisians but it only put a stamp of shamelessness on the return of the RCD to political life; all the more so with the formation of Nidaa Tounes (the Call of Tunisia Party Movement) as a hub for RCDists, led by the controversial veteran politician Béji Caïd Essebsi, who once confessed to Ahmed Mansour on al-Jazeera that, under Bourguiba, he consistently rigged elections. Now, if Nidaa Tounes keeps growing and pulling other opposition parties into its orbit, as it is indeed doing under the umbrella of the Union for Tunisia, it is not unthinkable for it to win the upcoming elections.

Such a scenario looks almost inevitable if we go by the recent polls which accord Nidaa Tounes pride of place in any future elections, presidential or parliamentary. All the more so given the continuing weakening of the Troika with the ongoing terrorist attacks and landmines in Mount Chaambi, which have resulted in several deaths and injuries—including the slaughter of eight soldiers on July 29, 2013. After the attacks on the American embassy in September

2012, Ennahda became more aggressive in fighting Salafi jihadists but has not always been successful in preventing terrorist attacks and assassinations. The murders of Chokri Belaïd and Mohamed Brahmi, political figures from the Popular Front coalition, dealt yet more blows to Ennahda and the Troika. After the assassination of Brahmi on Republic Day, massive demonstrations and an ongoing sit-in in front of the ANC in Bardo called for the dissolution of the government and the ANC altogether, and the formation of a government of technocrats and independents whose members would not take part in the upcoming elections. While the assassins of Belaïd and Brahmi are suspected to be religious extremists (Salafists associated with the Ansar al-Sharia movement, led by Abou Iyadh), it is unclear how Ennahda is said to be the beneficiary of these acts of murder. One of the most popularized slogans in the recent demonstrations went so far as to point the finger toward Rachid Ghannouchi himself: *Ya Ghannouchi ya saffāḥ, ya qattāl larwāḥ* (Ghannouchi assassin, killer of innocents).

What further muddies the waters is that these assassinations weakened the Troika and emboldened the opposition parties and the old regime figures. In fact, the Brahmi assassination came at a time when the ANC was preparing to discuss and ratify the fourth and last draft of the constitution (signed on June 1, 2013); more important by far, the assassination came at a time when the Law for the Protection of the Revolution from the old regime was about to be discussed and approved in the ANC, which would constitute a deadly blow to all the former regime figures, including Essebsi. This final phase of the transitional process has now been almost systematically hijacked by the murder of Brahmi, and a totally different agenda has ever since dominated the political scene—the Troika calling for the preservation of the ANC and a government constituted of politicians and the opposition parties, and the Salvation Front (including ex-ANC members) calling for the dissolution of the ANC and the formation of a non-political government composed of technocrats and independents who will not run for office in the upcoming elections.

The problem with a so-called government of technocrats and independents is that it is very hard, if not impossible, to come up with national figures who are genuinely independent and neutral in a profoundly polarized political milieu. Political bickering and petty disputes among the Troika, the opposition parties, the Salafis, and the UGTT have been a constant feature of the post-election scene. The atmosphere of mistrust and fear prevails: the opposition parties fear that Ennahda is turning into a monster (*taghawul*) taking over all institutions and, if left unattended, will definitely rig the upcoming elections to establish a new dictatorship, a theocracy. Ennahda, on the other hand, fears that it is being cornered and, if it fails to protect itself, will meet the same fate that it met before under Ben Ali—or the one met by the Muslim Brotherhood in Egypt. Ennahda did not hesitate, therefore, to dismiss the sit-in protests in Bardo as an example of coup-mongering *à l'égyptienne*.

With the ANC meetings being unilaterally suspended by ANC president Mustapha Ben Jafar for now (August 2013), Tunisia might be seen as drifting into uncharted waters, even though the Ghannouchi interview on Nessma TV (August 25, 2013) suggests that Ennahda and Nidaa Tounes are gearing up toward a way out of the political stalemate. The coming months will be decisive in determining whether or not Tunisia will have once again set itself apart as a model in settling its political disputes through dialogue, compromise, and national consensus. This is never more to be desired than at a time when the road to democratization, pluralism, and coexistence—not to mention freedom, justice, and dignity—must lead past a polarized political leadership and a divided public in a world braced for economic and financial crisis. While thousands of protesters flocked into Avenue Bourguiba on January 14, 2011 in a show of unity and singularity of purpose that prompted the unceremonious exit of Ben Ali, such action is near impossible in a country where political quarrels and positioning have almost completely turned all attention from the common goals that constituted the driving force of the revolution.

In the midst of these ongoing crises, the activities of the media have hardly been exemplary. Instead of discussing national debt, economic hurdles in rural areas, unemployment, the dozens of TV and radio political programs that have mushroomed lately focus on sensational topics such as Salafism versus Tunisianness, or secularism versus Islamism. The role of the media in the Tunisian revolution, and especially in the postrevolutionary transition to democracy, has left much to be desired. The very same state media, TV channels, radio stations, and newspapers that backed up Ben Ali's authoritarian reign refashioned themselves overnight into anti-state media. For instance, TV channels such as Nessma, Hannibal, Ettounisiya, and El-Wataniya (formerly known as TV7) have been biased in their criticism of Ennahda and the governing Troika and have often misrepresented or selectively focused on topics that foment sociopolitical tension. Following the agendas of their owners and producers, most of whom have continuing ties to the old regime, they have broadcast programs, political talk shows and ongoing coverage of protests (for example, recently, the sit-in in Bardo) that have gradually worn down the Troika and aggravated its apparent failure—much to the disenchantment of everyday Tunisians. Likewise, foreign (especially French) media have programmatically focused on Islamism and Salafism and applied the highest standards of scrutiny to the Troika rule in Tunisia, all the while producing the most reductionist and stereotypical reports, exaggerating the civilizational clash between secularism and Islamism and overlooking the particularities of the Tunisian experience and the many instances of constructive dialogues, collaborative efforts, and coalition building (which the Troika itself exemplifies).

In their concerted effort with the opposition parties to aggravate the different setbacks in the transitional process, the media have generally played into the hands of the counterrevolutionary forces—the forces who have been trying to regain control over the transitional government through different means, whether by violence or by promoting political parties that defend their right to re-enter the political field and resist government attempts to banish them by law from politics for a certain number of years. Ennahda and other political parties have been compelled to create alternative media, which has further blurred the political scene and deepened the secular-versus-Islamist divides that are already tearing the Tunisian public apart.

Given the military coup in Egypt, which is counterrevolutionary by all measures, Tunisia is fast transforming from the springboard of the Arab Spring to its last (lasting) frontier. True! Much is at stake and what began in Tunisia might as well end in Tunisia. Let me say, though, that what happened in Egypt may well have rid millions of Egyptians of an inefficient government and of a party that does not know (and has not learned) how to govern, but I would argue that the incompetence of an Islamist government might be the price that emerging Arab democracies have to pay (at least for a while) in order to persuade Islamists (including Salafists) of the validity of democracy. In Tunisia, where there has been a genuine effort to convince Salafists to found political parties and accept the rules of the democratic process, and where many have done so while others continue to refuse to follow suit, what happened in Egypt does nothing but recast the long shadow of mistrust that Salafists have always harbored concerning elections and democracy. It will take now further effort to persuade young Salafis about the tenability of democracy—really, it will take nothing less than preserving the indispensable institution, the ANC, that resulted from the October 2011 elections.

Despite the entrenchments of the counterrevolutionary forces to this day, and the manifold challenges encountered and still lying ahead, the Tunisian revolution does seem to be heading slowly in the right direction: the National Constituent Assembly—which resumed work after a month-long suspension—has almost completed writing the new constitution and electing the independent members of the Electoral Committee which will plan and oversee the next elections. The task now is to overcome the political stalemate resulting from the Brahmi assassination, to reach a workable national consensus, and to speed up the transition process, so that the transitional justice law might be passed and all hitherto stalled processes of reform in the media, justice, and security sectors—among others—can be finalized.

It is very hard to speculate on the future, however, partly because the policies of the current interim coalition government have proven unproductive and partly because the alternatives (or lack of them) of the opposition parties have proven counterproductive. Not unlike its predecessors, the coalition government has been quite reluctant to bring to justice the major players in the old regime along with the riot policemen and snipers who killed more than 300 protestors; what is worse, it has even allowed former Ben Ali men to reassemble, form political parties, and prepare for the upcoming elections.

What is reassuring, though, is that the Tunisian people, civil society organizations and the cyberspace community remain very vigilant. After all, it is not solely elections that will assess the health of democracy, or its durability, but the everyday practice of democracy by the people themselves in a climate of intense political differences, if not disunity. The whole process of unlearning the corrupted and corrupting habits of mind has just begun. It is too early to assess its progress, let alone judge the outcome. Pedagogy will play an important role in democratizing mentalities shaped by decades of brutal governance; indeed, the sedimentations of the culture of corruption that Ben Ali's regime fostered will take some time to eradicate and overcome. However, despite the many exogenous and internal variables that have threatened to derail the transitional process, Tunisia is still the exemplar of revolutionary change in the region. All one can hope, for now, is that Tunisians preserve the exemplar and prove worthy of the challenge they had set up (to) themselves. It might take time and great sacrifice, more sacrifice, for Tunisians to start reaping the fruits of the Revolution of Freedom and Dignity, but let me wager on my sense of resolve here and say that this has indeed become inevitable. Democratization is no longer an option now—it is a historical certainty—and the Tunisian revolution has more of a chance to succeed than the counterrevolution has of changing the course of history.

Bibliography

Abdul-Hamid, Yara. "The Euro-Mediterranean Agreements: Partnership or Penury?" Oxfam International, 2003.

Abrougui, Afef. "Tunisia: Hillary Clinton's Unwelcome Visit." Globalvoicesonline.org, March 19, 2011. Accessed May 4, 2011. http://globalvoicesonline.org/2011/03/19/tunisia-hillary-clintons-unwelcome-visit.

Aburish, Saïd K. *A Brutal Friendship: The West and the Arab Elite.* New York: St. Martin's Press, 1997.

Africa Focus Bulletin. "Tunisia: Democracy Deferred." *Africa Focus,* February 22, 2004. Accessed March 1, 2013. http://www.africafocus.org/docs04/tun0402.php.

Alami, Aida. "Tunisia Sinks Back into Turmoil." *The New York Times,* February 13, 2013.

Agence Tunisienne de Communication Extérieure. "La Femme dans le Projet Nahdhaoui." 1991.

Agence Tunisienne de Communication Extérieure. "Femme et Famille: Extraits de Discours du Président Zine El Abidine Ben Ali." 1991

Albers, Ronald, and Maarga Peeters. *Food and Energy Prices; Government Subsidies and Fiscal Balances in South Mediterranean Countries,* European Economy Papers 431. Brussels: European Commission, 2011.

Alexander, Christopher. "Opportunities, Organizations, and Ideas: Islamists and Workers in Tunisia and Algeria." *International Journal of Middle East Studies* 32.4 (2000): 465–90.

Alexander, Christopher. *Tunisia: Stability and Reform in the Modern Maghreb.* Abingdon: Routledge, 2010.

Allal, Amin, "La 'reconversion' problématique du bassin minier de Gafsa en Tunisie. Réformes néolibérales, clientélismes et protestations en situation politique autoritaire." *Politique Africaine* 117 (March 2010): 107–26.

Allal, Amin. "Ici ça ne bouge pas ça n'avance pas. Les mobilisations protestataires dans la région minière de Gafsa en 2008." In *L'État face aux débordements du social au Maghreb,* edited by Myriam Catusse, Blandine Destremau, and Eric Verdier, 173–86. Paris: IREMAM/Khartala, 2010.

Allal, Amin. "Réformes néolibérales, clientélismes et protestations en situation autoritaire. Les mouvements contestataires dans le bassin minier de Gafsa en Tunisie (2008)." *Politique africaine* 117 (2010): 107–25.

Allani, Allaya. "The Islamists in Tunisia between Confrontation and Participation: 1980–2008." *The Journal of North African Studies* 14 (2009): 257–72.

Allemandou, Ségolène. "Violée par des policiers tunisiens, ma fiancée est accusée d'attentat à la pudeur." September 27, 2012. Accessed May 1, 2013. http://www.france24.com/fr/20120926-tunisie-societe-justice-islamisme-femme-violee-accusee-atteinte-pudeur-justice-condition-feminine.

Allende, Alma. "Interview with Fahem Boukadous, Member of the Communist Workers Party of Tunisia." Accessed August 1, 2011. http://links.org.au/node/2151.

Al-Shabbi, Abul-Qasim. *Aghani al-Hayat* [Songs of Life]. Tunis: al-Dar al-tunisiya li-l-Nashar, 1966.

Alterman, Jon B. "The Revolution Will Not Be Tweeted." *The Washington Quarterly* 34.4 (2011): 103–16.

Alterman, Jon B. and Ibrahim Karawan. "New Media, New Politics? From Satellite Television to the Internet in the Arab World." The Washington Institute for Near East Policy, PolicyWatch #356: Special Forum Report, December 11, 1998.

Al-Turki, Nadia. "Tunisian Islamist Leader: Zionist Parties Fabricated Anti-Arab Monarchies Comment." *Al-Sharq al-Awsat*, December 17, 2011.

Al-Yousfi, Al-Amin. *Al-Haraka Annaqabiyya bi Tounis.* Tunis: Dar Mohammed Ali lil-nashr, 2011.

Amara, Tarek. "Thousands Rally in Tunisia for Women's Rights." *Reuters*, August 13, 2012. Accessed March 30, 2013. http://uk.reuters.com/article/2012/08/14/us-tunisia-women-rights-idUSBRE87C16020120814.

Amara, Tarek. "Tunisia Jails Salafist Leader in US Embassy Attack for One Year." *Reuters*, October 24, 2012. Accessed January 12, 2013. www.reuters.com/article/2012/10/24/us-tunisia-us-embassy-idUSBRE89N1QV20121024.

Amara, Tarek. "Tunisians Take to Streets Two Years after Ben Ali's Fall." *Reuters*, January 14, 2013. Accessed March 27, 2013. www.reuters.com/article/2013/01/14/us-tunisia-protests-idUSBRE90D0JY20130114.

Amara, Tarek. "Démission du gouvernement tunisien après la mort d'un opposant." *Reuters*, February 6, 2013. Accessed March 30, 2013. http://fr.reuters.com/article/topNews/idFRPAE91501B20130206?sp=true.

Amara, Tarek. "Tunisia PM Quits After Failing to Form New Government," *Reuters*, February 19, 2013. Accessed March 30, 2013. www.reuters.com/article/2013/02/19/us-tunisia-pm-idUSBRE91I10J20130219.

Amara, Tarek. "Tunisia's New Premier Promises Inclusive Government," *Reuters*, February 22, 2013. Accessed March 30, 2013. www.reuters.com/article/2013/02/22/us-tunisia-politics-idUSBRE91L0F720130222.

Amara, Tarek. "Tunisian President asks Islamist to Form Government," *Reuters*, February 22, 2013. Accessed March 30, 2013. http://uk.reuters.com/article/2013/02/22/uk-tunisia-politics-idUKBRE91L0F420130222.

Amghar, Samir. *Le salafisme d'aujourd'hui. Mouvements sectaires en Occident.* Paris: Michalon, 2011.

Amnesty International. "Behind Tunisia's 'Economic Miracle': Inequality and Criminalization of Protest," June 2009. Accessed May 28, 2013. http://www.amnesty.org/en/library/info/MDE30/003/2009.

Amnesty International. "In the Name of Security: Routine Abuses in Tunisia." Report, June 23, 2008. Accessed May 4, 2011. https://amnesty.org/en/news-and-updates/report/routine-abuses-name-security-tunisia-20080623

Amnesty International. *Tunisia: Rhetoric Versus Reality: The Failure of a Human Rights Bureaucracy.* New York: Amnesty International USA, 1994.

Amnesty International. *Tunisia: The Cycle of Injustice.* London: International Secretariat, 2003.

Amnesty International. *Amnesty International Report, 1994: Tunisia.* London: Amnesty International, 1994.

Amnesty International. *Amnesty International Report, 2004: Tunisia.* London: Amnesty International, 2004.

Amnesty International. *Amnesty International Report, 2008: Tunisia.* London: Amnesty International, 2008.

Amnesty International. *In the Name of Security. Routine Abuses in Tunisia.* London: Amnesty International, 2008.

Amroussia, Ammar. "Tunesië: een eerste balans van de opstand in het mijnbekken van Gafsa in 2008." *Marxistische Studies* 93 (2011): 61–75.

Anderson, Lisa. *The State and Social Transformation in Tunisia and Libya, 1830–1980.* Princeton, NJ: Princeton University Press, 1986.

Anderson, Lisa. "Friends and Foes: American Policy in North Africa." In *Africa in the 1990s and Beyond: US Policy Opportunities and Choices,* edited by Robert I. Rotberg, 168–88. Algonac, MI: Reference Publications, 1988.

Anderson, Lisa. "Democracy Frustrated: The Mzali Years in Tunisia." In *The Middle East and North Africa: Essays in Honor of J.C. Hurewitz,* edited by Reeva Simon, 185–203. New York: Columbia University Press, 1990.

Anderson, Lisa. "Demystifying the Arab Spring: Parsing the Differences between Tunisia, Egypt, and Libya." *Foreign Affairs* 90.3 (May/June 2011): 2–7.

Anderson, Perry. "On the Concatenation in the Arab World." *The New Left Review* 68 (2011): 5–16.

An-Naʿim Abdullahi. *Islam and the Secular State, Negotiating the Future of Shariʿa.* Cambridge, MA: Harvard University Press, 2008.

An-Naʿim, Abdullahi. "Secular State and Civil Reason." October 13, 2011. Accessed May 4, 2012. www.resetdoc.org/story/00000021779.

Arab Network for Human Rights Information. "Tunisia, the First, the Worst." Accessed December 28, 2011. www.anhri.net/en/reports/net2004/tunis.shtml.

Arfaoui, Khadija. "Women and Education in Tunisia: From Independence to the Jasmine Revolution." Paper delivered at "Women's Studies North and South." International conference in Bellagio, Italy: September 13–17, 2011. Accessed June 4, 2012. www.catunescomujer.org/catunesco_mujer/documents/bellagio_compendium_9-dec-final.pdf.

Arieff, Alexis. "Political Transition in Tunisia." Report RS21666. Washington, DC: Congressional Research Service, February 2, 2011.

Armes, Roy. *Post-colonial Images: Studies in North African Film.* Bloomington, IN: Indiana University Press, 2005.

Asad, Talal. *Genealogies of Religion: Discipline and Reasons of Power in Christianity and Islam.* Baltimore, MD: The Johns Hopkins University Press, 2003.

Ashour, Omar. *The Deradicalization of Jihadists: Transforming Armed Islamist Movements.* London: Routledge, 2009.

Associated Press. "Tunisia Supplied with US Arms." *Associated Press,* August 15, 1958.

Associated Press. "Tunisia Boss Vows Loyalty to the West." *Associated Press,* October 17, 1958.

Associated Press. "Tunisian President Says he Wants to Share Experience in Handling Islamic Extremism with Bush." *Associated Press,* February 13, 2004.

Associated Press. "Violence Plagues Tunisia's Politics 2 Years Later." *Associated Press,* January 14, 2013. Accessed March 2, 2013. www.viewheadlines.com/news/695380/Violence-plagues-Tunisia-s-politics-2-years-later.html.

Ayeb, Habib. "Social and Political Geography of the Tunisian Revolution: The Alfa Grass Revolution." *Review of African Political Economy* 38.129 (2011): 467–79.

Baker, James A. III. "Interview with James A. Baker III." *Middle East Quarterly* 1.3 (September 1994).

Balta, Paul. "Mitterrand et les Arabes." *Politique internationale* 13 (1981): 31–46.

Bannerman, Patrick. "The Mouvement de la Tendance Islamique in Tunisia." In *Islamic Fundamentalism*, edited by R. M. Burrell, 67–74. London: Royal Asiatic Society, 1989.

Baroud, Ramzy. "Islamists on Probation." *Al-Ahram Weekly* (Egypt), November 3–9, 2011.

Bayat, Asef. *Life as Politics: How Ordinary People Change the Middle East.* Stanford, CA: Stanford University Press, 2010.

Bchir, Mohamed Hedi, Mohamed Abdelbasset Chemingui, and Hakim Ben Hammouda. "Ten Years after Implementing the Barcelona Process: What Can Be Learned from the Tunisian Experience." *The Journal of North African Studies* 14.2 (2009): 123–44.

Beau, Nicolas, and Arnaud Muller. *Tunis et Paris: les liaisons dangereuses.* Paris: Jean-Claude Gawsewitch, 2011.

Beau, Nicolas, and Catherine Graciet. *La régente de Carthage: Main basse sur la Tunisie.* Paris: La Découverte, 2009.

Beau, Nicolas, and Jean-Pierre Tuquoi. *Notre ami Ben Ali: l'envers du "miracle Tunisien".* Paris: La Découverte, 1999.

Belhassen, Souhayr. "Le legs Bourguibiens de la répression." In *Habib Bourguiba: la trace et l'héritage*, edited by Michel Camau and Vincent Geisser, 391–404. Paris: Éditions Karthala, 2004.

Belhassine, Najy, Andrew Stone, Philip Keefer, Youssef Saadani Hassani, and Sameh Neguib Wahba. *From Privilege to Competition: Unlocking Private-Led Growth in the Middle East and North Africa.* MENA Development Report. Washington, DC: World Bank, 2009.

Belkhodja, Tahar. *Les trois décennies Bourguiba: témoignage.* Paris: Publisud, 1998.

Bellah, Robert. "Civil Religion in America." *Daedalus* 96.1 (winter 1967): 1–21.

Ben Bouazza, Bouazza. "Tunisia Islamist Party Chooses New Prime Pinister." *Huffington Post*, February 22, 2013. Accessed March 30, 2013. www.huffingtonpost.com/huff-wires/20130222/ml-tunisia/?utm_hp_ref=homepage&ir=homepage.

Ben Dhiaf, Issa. "Chronique tunisienne 1982." *Annuaire de l'Afrique du Nord 1982* 21 (1984): 655–97.

Ben Gharbia, Sami. "Anti-Censorship Movement in Tunisia: Creativity, Courage and Hope." *Global Voices Advocacy*. May 27, 2010. Accessed March 25, 2011. http://advocacy.globalvoicesonline.org/2010/05/27/anti-censorship-movement-in-tunisia-creativity-courage-and-hope.

Ben Gharbia, Sami. "Silencing Online Speech in Tunisia." Accessed March 4, 2011. http://advocacy.globalvoicesonline.org/2008/08/20/silencing-online-speech-in-tunisia.

Ben Hamida, Abdesselem. *Le syndicalisme tunisien de la deuxième guerre mondiale à l'autonomie interne.* Tunis: Publications de l'Université de Tunis, 1989.

Ben Mhenni, Lina. "A Black Day for Bloggers." Accessed January 23, 2013. http://globalvoicesonline.org/2010/05/05/tunisia-a-black-day-for-bloggers.

Ben Mhenni, Lina. "Tunisia: Censorship Again and Again!" Accessed January 23, 2011. http://globalvoicesonline.org/2010/02/08/tunisia-censhorship-again-and-again.

Ben Rejeb, Lotfi. "Tunisian–American Relations from 1942 to 1990: A 'Special Friendship'." *American-Arab Affairs* 33 (Summer 1990): 115–25.

Ben Romdhane, Mahmoud. "Social Policy and Development in Tunisia Since Independence: A Political Perspective." In *Social Policy in the Middle East: Political, Economic and Gender Dynamics*, edited by Massoud Karshenas and Valentine M. Moghadam, 31–77. London: Palgrave Macmillan, 2006.

Ben Romdhane, Mahmoud. *Tunisie: État, économie et société. Ressources politiques, légitimation, et régulations sociales*. Paris: Edisud, 2011.

Ben Sassi, Lotfi. "Le retour de la parabole." *La Presse Magazine* 501 (May 18, 1997): 3–5.

Ben Sassi, Sami. "Les Publinets de Tunis." Accessed May 1, 2013. http://www.gdri-netsuds.org/IMG/pdf/Samider.pdf.

Benoit-Lavelle, Mischa. "Shooting of Salafists in Tunisia May Spur More Attacks." *Al Monitor*, November 1, 2012. Accessed January 23, 2013. www.al-monitor.com/pulse/originals/2012/al-monitor/salafist-shooting-tunisia.html.

Bensedrine, Sihem and Omar Mestiri. *L'Europe et ses despotes: quand le soutien au 'modèle tunisien' dans le monde arabe fait le jeu du terrorisme islamiste*. Paris: La Découverte, 2004.

Bertelsmann Stiftung. "BTI 2010 Tunisia Country Report." Accessed September 27, 2011. www.bertelsmann-transformation-index.de/145.0.html?L=1.

Bessis, Juliette. "Le mouvement ouvrier tunisien: de ses origines à l'indépendance." *Le Mouvement Social* 89 (1974): 85–108.

Bessis, Sophie and Souhayr Belhassen. *Femmes du Maghreb: L'Enjeu*. Tunis: Cérès Productions, 1992, 148–9.

Bicchi, Federica. "'Our Size Fits All': Normative Power Europe and the Mediterranean." *Journal of European Public Policy* 13.2 (2006): 286–303.

Bohn, Lauren E. "Rapping the Revolution." *Foreign Policy*, July 22, 2011. Accessed December 30, 2011. http://mideast.foreignpolicy.com/posts/2011/07/22/rapping_the_revolution.

Boltanski, Christophe. "La galaxie islamiste." *Le Nouvel Observateur*, December 8, 2011. Accessed March 27, 2013. www.gremmo.mom.fr/sites/gremmo.mom.fr/files/docs/Activites/Medias/NouvelObsdec2011.pdf.

Bolton, K. R. "Another Soros/NED Jack Up?" *Foreign Policy Journal*, January 18, 2011. Accessed January 26, 2012. www.foreignpolicyjournal.com/2011/01/18/tunisian-revolt-another-sorosned-jack-up.

Bonnefoy, Laurent. *Salafism in Yemen. Transnationalism and Religious Identity*. London: Hurst & Co., 2011.

Borovsky, Gabriella, and Asma Ben Yahia. "Women's Political Participation in Tunisia after the Revolution: Findings from Focus Groups in Tunisia Conducted February 16–28, 2012." National Democratic Institute, May 2012. Accessed May 12, 2012. www.ndi.org/files/womens-political-participation-Tunisia-FG-2012-ENG.pdf

Boulby, Marion. "The Islamic Challenge: Tunisia Since Independence." *Third World Quarterly* 10.2 (1988): 590–614.

Bourguiba, Habib. "Le problème franco-tunisien est un problème de souveraineté." *Les Temps Modernes* 77 (1952): 1567–71.

Bourguiba, Habib. "Nationalism: Antidote to Communism." *Foreign Affairs* 35.4 (1957): 646–53.

Bourguiba, Habib. "The Tunisian Way." *Foreign Affairs* 44.3 (1966): 480–8.

Bourguiba, Habib. "We Choose the West." *Orbis* 2.3 (1958): 315–19.

Bousali, Noura. "Les acquis de la femme sont-ils menacés?" *Le Temps*, August 12, 2012.

Bouzid, Nouri. "On Inspiration." In *African Experiences of Cinema*, edited by Imruh Bakari and Mbye B. Cham, 48–59. London: British Film Institute, 1996.

Bradley, John R. *After the Arab Uprising: How Islamists Hijacked the Middle East Revolts*. New York: Palgrave Macmillan, 2012.

Bradley, Matt and Adam Entous. "US Reaches Out to Islamist Parties—Public, Private Warming Seen Toward Egypt and Tunisia Groups." *Wall Street Journal*, July 1, 2001.

Brand, Laurie. *Women, the State and Political Liberalization: Middle Eastern and North African Experiences*. New York: Columbia University Press, 1998.

Bras, Jean-Philippe. "Chronique Tunisie (chronologie et documents en annexe)." In *Annuaire de l'Afrique du nord*, edited by André Raymond and Hubert Michel, 957–1009. Paris: Éditions du CNRS, 1986.

Braun, Célina. "À quoi servent les partis tunisiens? Sens et contre-sens d'une 'libéralisation' politique." *Revue des Mondes Musulmans et de la Méditerranée* 111–12 (2006): 15–61.

Brody-Barre, Andrea G. "The Impact of Political Parties and Coalition Building on Tunisia's Democratic Future." *The Journal of North African Studies* 18.2 (2013): 211–30.

Brown, Nathan J., and Adel Omar Sharif. "Judicial Independence in the Arab World." United Nations Development Programme, 1–25. Accessed March 23, 2013. www.deontologie-judiciaire.umontreal.ca/fr/textes%20int/documents/ONU_jud-independence_MONDE_ARABE.pdf.

Browne, Donald R. "International Broadcasting in Arabic. Tunisia." In *Broadcasting in the Arab World, a Survey of the Electronic Media in the Middle East*, edited by Douglas A. Boyd, 261–78. Ames, IA: Iowa State University Press, 1999.

Burgat, François, and William Dowell. *Islamist Movements in North Africa*. Austin, TX: University of Texas, 1993.

Burghardt, Tom. "Secret Diplomatic Cables Reveal Microsoft's 'Win-Win' Deal with Tunisian Police State." *Dissident Voice*, September 12, 2011.

Burns, William J. "American Strategy in a New Middle East: Statement before the Senate Committee on Foreign Relations." US Department of State, March 17, 2011. Accessed May 2, 2012. http://www.state.gov/p/us/rm/2011/158516.htm.

Burns, William J. "W. J. Burns: 'The USA Multiplied Fifteen Times Assistance to Tunisia, Since the Revolution'." *Agence Tunis Afrique Presse* (Tunisia), June 28, 2011. Accessed September 25, 2013. www.thefreelibrary.com/W.J.+Burns%3A+%22The+USA+multiplied+fifteen+times+assistance+to+Tunisia,...-a0259999126.

Burns, William J. "State's Burns on US Middle East Policy." iipdigital.usembassy.gov, December 8, 2012. US Department of State, December 8, 2012. Accessed March 4, 2013. http://london.usembassy.gov/midest247.html.

Byrne, Eileen. "Tunisians Protest over Charges against Woman Allegedly Raped by Police." *The Guardian*, October 3, 2012. Accessed March 27, 2013. www.guardian.co.uk/world/2012y/oct/03/tunisians-protest-charges-woman-police.

Camau, Michel, and Vincent Geisser. *Le syndrome autoritaire. Politique en Tunisie de Bourguiba à Ben Ali*. Paris: Les Presses de Sciences Politiques, 2003.

Camau, Michel, and Vincent Geisser. *Habib Bourguiba: la trace et l'héritage*. Paris: Éditions Karthala, 2004.

Cardwell, Paul James. "Euromed, European Neighbourhood Policy and the Union for the Mediterranean: Overlapping Policy Frames in the EU's Governance of the Mediterranean." *Journal of Common Market Studies* 49.2 (2011): 219–41.

Carnegie Middle East Center. "A Conversation with Mustapha Nabli, Governor of Tunisia's Central Bank. The Economic Dimensions of Unrest in the Arab World", 2011. Accessed July 20, 2011. http://carnegie-mec.org/events/?fa=3165.

Carpenter, J. Scott. "Help Tunisia First." *Foreign Policy*, February 24, 2011. Accessed May 11, 2011. www.foreignpolicy.com/articles/2011/02/24/help_tunisia_first.

Carter Center. "The Carter Center Recognizes Tunisia's National Constituent Assembly Progress; Calls for Increased Public Participation, Outreach, and Transparency." September 12, 2012. Accessed January 1, 2013. www.cartercenter.org/resources/pdfs/news/pr/tunisia-092612-full-statement-en.pdf

Carter Center. *National Constituent Assembly Elections in Tunisia: October 23, 2011. Final Report.* Atlanta, GA: The Carter Center, 2012.

Cassarino, Jean-Pierre. "The EU-Tunisian Association Agreement and Tunisia's Structural Reform Program." *Middle East Journal* 53.1 (1999): 59–74.

Cavatorta, Francesco and Rikke Hostrup Haugbølle. "The End of Authoritarian Rule and the Mythology of Tunisia under Ben Ali." *Mediterranean Politics* 17 (2012): 179–95.

Chamkhi, Fathi. "La politique de privatisation." *Confluences Méditerranée* 35 (autumn 2000): 103–9.

Charrad, Mounira. "Policy Shifts: State, Islam, and Gender in Tunisia, 1930s–1990s." *Social Politics* 4.2 (1997): 284–319.

Charrad, Mounira. *States and Women's Rights: the Making of Postcolonial Tunisia, Algeria, and Morocco.* Berkeley, CA: University of California Press, 2001.

Chater, Souad. *Les Emancipées du Harem: Regard sur la femme tunisienne.* Tunis: Édition la Presse, 1992.

Chew, Kristina. "Ben Ali's Tunisia Tested Censorship Software For Western Companies." Care2.com, October 5, 2011. Accessed May 4, 2012. www.care2.com/causes/tunisia-tested-censorship-software-for-western-companies.html.

Chomiak, Laryssa. "The Making of a Revolution in Tunisia." *Middle East Law and Governance* 3.1/2 (2011): 68–83.

Chomiak, Laryssa, and John P. Entelis. "The Making of North Africa's Intifadas." *Middle East Report* 259 (2011): 8–15.

Chomiak, Laryssa, and John Entelis. "Contesting Order in Tunisia: Crafting Political Identity." In *Civil Society Activism under Authoritarian Rule*, edited by Francesco Cavatorta, 73–93. London: Routledge, 2012.

Chomsky, Noam. "The Manufacture of Consent." In *The Chomsky Reader*, edited by James Peck, 121–36. New York: Pantheon Books, 1987.

Chouikha, Larbi. "Les identités au miroir des temporalités télévisuelles: Le ramadan et le réveillon du jour de l'an à Tunis à travers le petit écran." In *Mondialisation et nouveaux médias dans l'espace arabe*, edited by Franck Mermier, 167–83. Paris: Maisonneuve & Larose, 2003.

Chouikha, Larbi, and Vincent Geisser. "Retour sur la révolte du bassin minier. Les cinq leçons politiques d'un conflit social inédit." *L'Année du Maghreb* (2010): 415–26.

CIA. "CIA Factbook, 2011." Accessed July 10, 2011. www.cia.gov/library/publications/the-world-factobook/geos/ts.html.

Clinton, Hillary. "Secretary Clinton's Town Hall Meeting in Tunis, Tunisia." US Department of State, March 17, 2011. Accessed May 4, 2012. http://iipdigital.usembassy.gov/st/english/texttrans/2011/03/20110318093629su2.725947e-02.html#axzz2UvmntqlM.

Coleman, Isobel. "Is the Arab Spring Bad for Women?" *Foreign Policy*, December 20, 2011. Accessed June 12, 2012. www.foreignpolicy.com/articles/2011/12/20/arab_spring_women.

Coleman, Isobel. "Women, Free Speech, and the Tunisian Constitution." *CNN World*, August 16, 2012. Accessed January 13, 2013. http://globalpublicsquare.blogs.cnn.com/2012/08/16/women-free-speech-and-the-tunisian-constitution.

Coller, Ian. *Arab France: Islam and the Making of Modern Europe, 1798–1831*. Berkeley, CA: University of California Press, 2010.

Collier, David, and Steven Levitsky. "Democracy with Adjectives: Conceptual Innovation in Comparative Research." *World Politics* 49 (1997): 430–51.

Conseil National pour les Libertés en Tunisie, *Rapport sur l'état des libertés en Tunisie*, March 15, 2000.

Curtis, Mark. *The Ambiguities of Power: British Foreign Policy since 1945*. London: Zed Books, 1995.

Curtis, Mark. *Unpeople: Britain's Secret Human Rights Abuses*. London: Vintage, 2004.

Daley, Suzanne. "Tensions on a Campus Mirror Turbulence in a New Tunisia." *The New York Times*, June 11, 2012.

De Certeau, Michel. *The Practice of Everyday Life*. Translated by Steven Rendall. Berkeley, CA: University of California Press, 1984.

Diamond, Larry, and Leonardo Morlino. *Assessing the Quality of Democracy*. Baltimore, MD: The Johns Hopkins University Press, 2005.

Disney, Nigel. "The Working Class Revolt in Tunisia." *MERIP Reports* 67 (1978): 12–14.

Donegani, Jean-Marie. *La liberté de choisir: pluralisme religieux et pluralisme politique dans le catholicisme français contemporain*. Paris: Presses de Sciences-Po, 1993.

Dreyfuss, Robert. *Devil's Game: How the United States Helped Unleash Fundamentalist Islam*. New York: Metropolitan Books, 2005.

Dunn, Michael C. "The Al-Nahda Movement in Tunisia: From Renaissance to Revolution." In *Islam and Secularism in North Africa*, edited by John Ruedy, 149–65. New York: St. Martin's Press, 1994.

Durac, Vincent, and Francesco Cavatorta. "Strengthening Authoritarian Rule through Democracy Promotion? Examining the Paradox of the US and EU Security Strategies. The Case of Tunisia." *British Journal of Middle Eastern Studies* 36 (2009): 3–19.

Duverger, Maurice. *Political Parties: Their Organization and Activity in the Modern State*. London: Methuen, 1954.

Dwyer, Kevin. *Arab Voices: The Human Rights Debate in the Middle East*. Berkeley, CA: University of California Press, 1991.

Eli'coopter. "Quelle Twitter révolution en Tunisie?" Nawaat, January 19, 2011. Accessed January 24, 2012. http://nawaat.org/portail/2011/01/19/quelle-twitter-revolution-en-tunisie.

Enloe, Cynthia. *Bananas, Beaches and Bases: Making Feminist Sense of International Politics*. Berkeley, CA: University of California Press, 2000.

Entelis, John P. "The Democratic Imperative vs. the Authoritarian Impulse: The Maghrib State Between Transition and Terrorism." *Middle East Journal* 59.4 (2005): 537–58.

Erdle, Steffen. *Ben Ali's "New Tunisia" (1987–2009): A Case Study of Authoritarian Modernization in the Arab World*. Berlin: Klaus Schwarz, 2010.

Executive Magazine. "Tunisia's Sell-off Slowdown." *Executive* 93 (April 2007). Accessed September 15, 2011. www.executive-magazine.com/special-report/Tunisias-selloff-slowdown/1247.

Faath, Sigrid. *Anti-Americanism in the Islamic World*. London: Hurst & Co., 2006.

Facts on File Weekly World News Digest. "Tunisia." *Facts on File Weekly World News Digest* (1985): 724.

Fahim, Kareem. "Tunisia Includes Independents in New Cabinet." *The New York Times,* March 8, 2013. Accessed March 30, 2013. www.nytimes.com/2013/03/09/world/africa/to-ease-crisis-tunisia-includes-independents-in-new-cabinet.html?ref=tunisia&_r=1&.

Falk, Richard. "Welcoming the Tunisian Revolution: Hopes and Fears." *Foreign Policy Journal,* January 24, 2011. Accessed March 12, 2013. www.foreignpolicyjournal.com/2011/01/24/welcoming-the-tunisian-revolution-hopes-and-fears.

Fanon, Frantz. *The Wretched of the Earth.* Preface by Jean-Paul Sartre, translated by Constance Farrington. New York: Grove Press, 1968.

Feldman, Greg. "Europe's Border Control with a Humanitarian Face." *Middle East Report* 261 (2011): 14–17.

Feldman, Gregory. *The Migration Apparatus: Security, Labor, and Policymaking in the European Union.* Stanford, CA: Stanford University Press, 2012.

Ferjani, Riadh. "Du rôle de l'état dans le champ télévisuel en Tunisie: Les paradoxes de l'internationalisation". In *Mondialisation et nouveaux médias dans l'espace arabe,* edited by Franck Mermier, 153–65. Paris: Maisonneuve & Larose, 2003.

Ferrié, Jean-Noël. *Le régime de la civilité en Egypte.* Paris: Éditions du CNRS, 2004.

Fisk, Robert. "The Brutal Truth about Tunisia." *The Independent,* January 17, 2011. Accessed January 20, 2011. www.independent.co.uk/voices/commentators/fisk/the-brutal-truth-about-tunisia-2186287.html.

Food and Agriculture Organization. "FAO Food Price Index." Accessed September 27, 2013. www.fao.org/worldfoodsituation/wfs-home/foodpricesindex/en.

Fregosi, Franck. "Bourguiba et la régulation institutionelle de l'islam: les contours audacieux d'un gallicanisme politique à la tunisienne." In *Habib Bourguiba: la trace et l'héritage,* edited by Michel Camau and Vincent Geisser, 79–100. Paris: Karthala, 2004.

Gana, Nouri. "Bourguiba's Sons: Melancholy Manhood in Modern Tunisian Cinema." *The Journal of North African Studies* 15.1 (2010), 105–26.

Gana, Nouri. "Let's Not Forget about Tunisia." *Jadaliyya,* January 30, 2011. Accessed January 30, 2011. www.jadaliyya.com/pages/index/500/lets-not-forget-about-tunisia.

Gana, Nouri. "Rap Rage Revolt." *Jadaliyya,* August 5, 2011. Accessed June 13, 2012. www.jadaliyya.com/pages/index/2320/rap-rage-revolt.

Geisser, Vincent. "Tunisie: des élections pour quoi faire? Enjeux et 'sens' du fait électoral de Bourguiba à Ben Ali." *Maghreb/Machreq* 168 (2000): 14–28.

Geisser, Vincent, and Amin Allal. "Tunisie: 'Révolution de jasmin' ou Intifada?" *Mouvements* 66 (2011). Accessed February 28, 2012. www.mouvements.info/Tunisie-Revolution-de-jasmin-ou.html.

Geisser, Vincent, and Aziz Zemouri. *Marianne et Allah: les politiques françaises face à la 'question musulmane.'* Paris: La Découverte, 2007.

Geisser, Vincent, and Eric Gobe. "Le président Ben Ali entre les jeux de coteries et l'échéance présidentielle de 2004." *Annuaire de l'Afrique du Nord 2003* 41 (2005): 291–320.

Gelvin, James. *The Arab Uprisings: What Everyone Needs to Know.* New York: Oxford University Press, 2012.

Geyer, Georgie Anne. "Interview: Zine El Abidine Ben Ali." *Middle East Policy* 6.2 (1998): 183–7.

Geyer, Georgie Anne. *Tunisia: A Journey Through a Country that Works*. London: Stacey International, 2003.

Ghannouchi, Rachid. "Al-Harakah al-Islamiyah Wal-Mujtama' al-Madani" [The Islamic Movement and Civil Society]. Paper presented at Pretoria University, South Africa, August 1994.

Ghannouchi, Rachid. "The Conflict Between the West and Islam, The Tunisian Case: Reality and Prospects." Paper presented at the Royal Institute of International Affairs, Chatham House, London, May 9, 1995.

Ghannouchi, Rachid. "Rachid Ghannouchi's Interview with *Al-Arab*." May 2, 2011. Accessed May 4, 2012. www.alarab.com.qa/details.php?docId=185944&issueNo=1181&secId=28.

Ghannouchi, Rachid. "Tunisia's Challenge: A Conversation with Rachid al-Ghannouchi." Washington, DC: Council on Foreign Relations, November 30, 2011. Accessed May 4, 2012. http://www.cfr.org/tunisia/tunisias-challenge-conversation-rachid-al-ghannouchi/p26660.

Gobe, Eric. "Politiques sociales et registres de légitimation d'un état néo-patrimonial: le cas tunisien." In *Solidarités et compétences: idéologies et pratiques*, edited by Monique Selim and Bernard Hours, 39–54. Paris: L'Harmattan, 2003.

Gobe, Eric. "Les syndicalismes arabes au prisme de l'autoritarisme et du corporatisme." In *Autoritarismes démocratiques et démocraties autoritaires au XIXe siècle. Convergences Nord/Sud*, edited by Olivier Dabène, Vincent Geisser, and Gilles Massardier, 267–84. Paris: La Découverte, 2008.

Gobe, Eric. "The Gafsa Mining Basin between Riots and a Social Movement: Meaning and Significance of a Protest Movement in Ben Ali's Tunisia," 2010. Accessed July 16, 2011. http://halshs.archives-ouvertes.fr/halshs-00557826.

Gobe, Eric, and Michael B. Ayari. "Les avocats dans la Tunisie de Ben Ali: une profession politisée." *L'Année du Maghreb Édition 2007*: 105–32.

Gordon, Michael R. "North Africa is a New Test." *The New York Times*, January 20, 2013. Accessed May 2, 2013. http://www.hrw.org/news/2004/02/13/tunisia-bush-should-call-end-repression.

Gorski, Philip. "Barack Obama and Civil Religion." In *Rethinking Obama (Political Power and Social Theory, Volume 22)*, edited by Julian Go, 179–214. Bingley: Emerald Group Publishing Limited, 2011.

Gourgouris, Stathis. "Withdrawing Consent." *The Immanent Frame*. Accessed February 2, 2013. http://blogs.ssrc.org/tif/2011/02/15/withdrawing-consent

Government of Tunisia. "Privatisation in Tunisia: The Value of a Strategic Investment." Accessed September 15, 2011. www.privatisation.gov.tn/www/en/doc.asp?mcat=1&mrub=50

Gray, Doris H. "Tunisia after the Uprising: Islamist and Secular Quests for Women's Rights." *Mediterranean Politics* 17.3 (2012): 285–302.

Grislain Karray, Cyril. *La prochaine guerre en Tunisie: La victoire en 5 batailles*. Tunis: Cérès Éditions, 2011.

Haddad, Tahar. *Les Travailleurs tunisiens et l'émergence du mouvement syndical*. Tunis: Maison Arabe du Livre, 1985 [1927].

Hafez, Kai. *Arab Media. Power and Weakness*. New York: Continuum, 2008.

Halliday, Fred. "Tunisia's Uncertain Future." *Middle East Report* 163 (1990): 25–7.

Hamdi, Mohamed Elhachmi. *The Politicization of Islam: A Case Study of Tunisia*. Boulder, CO: Westview Press, 1998.

Hamza, Hassine Raouf. *Communisme et nationalisme en Tunisie: de la libération jusqu'au l'indépendance (1943–1956)*. Tunis: Université de Tunis, 1994.

Hamzaoui, Salah. "Champ politique et syndicalisme en Tunisie." *Annuaire de l'Afrique du Nord 1999* 38 (2000): 369–80.

Hargreaves, Alec G. *Immigration, "Race" and Ethnicity in Contemporary France*. London: Routledge, 1995.

Hatem, Mervat. "Economic and Political Liberation in Egypt and the Demise of State Feminism." *International Journal of Middle East Studies* 24.2 (1992): 231–51.

Haugbølle, Rikke Hostrup, and Francesco Cavatorta. "Beyond Ghannouchi: Islamism and Social Change in Tunisia." *Middle East Report* 262 (2012): 20–5.

Haugbølle, Rikke Hostrup, and Franceso Cavatorta. "*Vive la grande famille des médias tunisiens*: Media Reform, Authoritarian Resilience and Societal Responses." *The Journal of North African Studies* 17.1 (2012): 97–112.

Hawkins, Simon. "Who Wears Hijab with the President: Constructing a Modern Islam in Tunisia." *Journal of Religious Affairs in Africa* 41 (2011): 35–58.

Haykel, Bernard. "On the Nature and Thought of Salafist Action." In *Global Salafism*, edited by Roel Mejer, 33–57. London: Hurst & Co., 2009.

Hazbun, Waleed. *Beaches, Ruins, Resorts: The Politics of Tourism in the Arab World*. Minneapolis, MN: University of Minnesota Press, 2008.

Hecht, Richard D. "Active Versus Passive Pluralism, a Changing Style of Civil Religion?" *The Annals of the American Academy of Political Science* 612 (2007): 133–51.

Henry, Clement. "Tunisia's 'Sweet Little' Regime." In *Worst of the Worst: Dealing with Repressive and Rogue Nations*, edited by Robert I. Rotberg, 300–23. Washington, DC: Brookings Institution Press, 2007.

Henry, Jean-Robert. "Chronique international." In *Annuaire de l'Afrique du nord*, edited by André Raymond and Hubert Michel, 737–55. Paris: Éditions du CNRS, 1986.

Hermassi, Abdelbeki. "The Rise and Fall of the Islamist Movement in Tunisia." In *The Islamist Dilemma: The Political Role of Islamist Movements in the Contemporary Arab World*, edited by Laura Guazzone, 105–27. London: Ithaca Press, 1995.

Hermassi, Elbaki. *État et société au Maghreb. Étude comparative*. Paris: Anthropos, 1975.

Heydemann, Steve. "Upgrading Authoritarianism in the Arab World." The Brookings Institutions, Analysis Paper 13 (2007): 1–37.

Hibou, Béatrice. "Les marges de manœuvre d'un 'bon élève' économique: la Tunisie de Ben Ali." *Les Études du CERI* 60 (1999): 1–33.

Hibou, Béatrice. "Tunisie: le coût d'un 'miracle'." *Critique internationale* 4 (1999): 48–56.

Hibou, Béatrice. "Domination and Control in Tunisia: Economic Levers for the Exercise of Authoritarian Power." *Review of African Political Economy* 33.108 (2006): 185–206.

Hibou, Béatrice. "Le partenariat en réanimation bureaucratique." *Critique internationale* 18 (2003): 117–28.

Hibou, Béatrice. *La force de l'obéissance. Economie politique de la répression en Tunisie*. Paris: La Découverte, 2006.

Hibou, Béatrice. *The Force of Obedience: The Political Economy of Repression in Tunisia*. Translated by Andrew Brown. Cambridge: Polity, 2011.

Holden, Patrick. "Development through Integration? EU Aid Reform and the Evolution of Mediterranean Aid Policy." *Journal of International Development* 20 (2008): 230–44.

Hopwood, Derek. *Habib Bourguiba of Tunisia: The Tragedy of Longevity*. Oxford: Palgrave Macmillan, 1992.

Howard, Philip N. and Muzammil M. Hussain. "The Role of Digital Media." *Journal of Democracy* 22.3 (July 2011): 35–48.

Human Rights Watch. "Tunisia: Bush Should Call for End to Repression: Tunisian President's US Visit Will Test Bush's Commitment to Mideast Democracy." February 14, 2004. Accessed April 2, 2012. www.hrw.org/news/2004/02/13/tunisia-bush-should-call-end-repression.

Human Rights Watch. "Tunisia: Government Lifts Restrictions on Women's Rights Treaty." *Human Rights Watch.* September 7, 2011. Accessed April 2, 2012. www.hrw.org/news/2011/09/06/tunisia-government-lifts-restrictions-women-s-rights-treaty.

Human Rights Watch. "Tunisia: Mass Firings a Blow to Judicial Independence." *Human Rights Watch.* October 29, 2012. Accessed January 25, 2013. www.hrw.org/news/2012/10/29/tunisia-mass-firings-blow-judicial-independence.

Huntington, Samuel. *The Third Wave: Democratization in the Late Twentieth Century*. Norman, OK: University of Oklahoma Press, 1991.

INRIC. INRIC Report, April 2012. Accessed March 4, 2013. www.inric.tn/fr/INRIC-Report-Eng-final.pdf.

International Crisis Group. "Tunisie: lutter contre l'impunité, restaurer la sécurité." May 9, 2012. Accessed December 20, 2012. www.crisisgroup.org/en/regions/middle-east-north-africa/north-africa/tunisia/123-tunisia-combatting-impunity-restoring-securi ty.aspx?alt_lang=fr.

International Crisis Group. "Soulèvements populaires en Afrique du nord et au Moyen-Orient (IV): la voie tunisienne." Rapport Moyen-Orient/Afrique du Nord 106, April 28, 2011. Accessed July 3, 2011. www.crisisgroup.org/en/regions/middle-east-north-africa/north-africa/tunisia/106-popular-protests-in-north-africa-and-the-middle-east-iv-tunisias-way.aspx.

International Foundation for Electoral Systems. *Tunisia Voter Registration and Voter Confidence Assessment Survey: May 2011*. Washington, DC: International Foundation for Electoral Systems, 2012.

International Monetary Fund. "Tunisia: Report on the Observance of Standards and Codes-Data Module; Response by the Authorities and Detailed Assessments Using the Data Quality Assessment Framework." IMF Country Report No. 06/300. August 2006. Accessed March 1, 2012. www.imf.org/external/pubs/ft/scr/2006/cr06300.pdf.

International Monetary Fund. "Tunisia: Selected Issues." IMF Country Report No. 10/109. May 2010. Accessed July 28, 2011. www.imf.org/external/pubs/ft/scr/2010/cr10109.pdf.

International Monetary Fund. "Mideast Unrest Shows Need to Consider Bigger Picture." IMF Survey Online. April 8, 2011. Accessed October 4, 2011. www.imf.org/external/pubs/ft/survey/so/2011/car040811b.htm.

International Monetary Fund. "Tunisia: 2010 Article IV Consultation – Staff Report; Public Information Notice on the Executive Board Discussion; and Statement by the Executive Director for Tunisia." IMF Country Report No. 10/282. Accessed July 28, 2011. www.imf.org/external/pubs/ft/scr/2010/cr10282.pdf.

International Monetary Fund. "Tunisia: 2007 Article IV Consulting Mission Preliminary Conclusions." IMF Country Report No. 02/122. Accessed July 28, 2011. www.imf.org/external/np/ms/2007/062907.htm.

International Monetary Fund. "Enabling Economic Transformation in the Middle East and North Africa." Speech given by David Lipton at the London School of Economics, November 13, 2012. Accessed March 25, 2013. www.imf.org/external/np/speeches/2012/111312.htm.

Jacinto, Leela. "'Secret' Video Stirs Islamist Fears in Tunisia." *France 24*, October 12, 2012. Accessed December 1, 2012. www.france24.com/en/20121011-tunisia-secret-video-stirs-salafist-islamist-radicalism-fears-ghannouchi-ennahda.

Joffé, George. "The European Union, Democracy and Counter-Terrorism in the Maghreb." *Journal of Common Market Studies* 46.1 (2008): 147–71.

Jones, Linda G. "Portrait of Rashid al-Ghannoushi." *Middle East Report* 153 (1988): 19–22. Accessed March 4, 2012. www.merip.org/mer/mer153/portrait-rachid-al-ghannouchi?ip_login_no_cache=91a60e239d148864e681012bd1751d4e.

Kahn, Paul. *Political Theology: Four New Chapters on the Concept of Sovereignty*. New York: Columbia University Press, 2011.

Kapitalis. "Tunisie. Nabil Karoui tire sur tout ce qui bouge." *Kapitalis*, August 13, 2011. Accessed May 21, 2012. www.kapitalis.com/kanal/61-medias/5381-tunisie-nabil-karoui-tire-sur-tout-ce-qui-bouge.html.

Kaufman, Stephen. "After Election, 'Real Politics' for Tunisian Coalition-Building." *IIP Digital*, October 28, 2011. Accessed July 23, 2012. http://iipdigital.usembassy.gov/st/english/article/2011/10/20111028154144nehpets0.7106134.html#axzz2UsQaEpdZ.

Kaufman, Stephen. "Panetta Sees Closer US Security Partnership with Tunisia." *IIP Digital*, July 31, 2012. Accessed July 23, 2012. http://iipdigital.usembassy.gov/st/english/article/2012/07/20120731142561.html#axzz2UsQaEpdZ

Kchir-Bendana, Kmar. "Ideologies of the Nation in Tunisian Cinema." *The Journal of North African Studies* 8.1 (2003): 35–42.

Khelil, Hédi. *Le parcours et la trace: Témoignages et documents sur le cinéma tunisien*. Salammbô: MediaCon, 2002.

Khiari, Sadri. "Reclassements et recompositions au sein de la bureaucratie syndicale depuis l'indépendance. La place de l'UGTT dans le système politique tunisien." Centres d'Études et de Recherches Internationales, Le Kiosque, 2000. www.ceri-sciencespo.com/archive/dec00/khiari.pdf.

Kilani, Mohamed. *La Révolution des braves*. Tunis: Impression Simpact, 2011.

King, Stephen J. *Liberalization against Democracy: The Local Politics of Economic Reform in Tunisia*. Bloomington, IN: Indiana University Press, 2003.

King, Stephen Juan. *The New Authoritarianism in the Middle East and North Africa*. Bloomington, IN: Indiana University Press, 2009.

Kirkpatrick, David, and David Sanger, "A Tunisian-Egyptian Link that Shook Arab History." *The New York Times*, February 13, 2011. Accessed March 3, 2012. www.nytimes.com/2011/02/14/world/middleeast/14egypt-tunisia-protests.html?_r=1.

Kramer, Gudrun. "Islamist Notions of Democracy." *Middle East Report* 183 (1993): 2–8.

Krichen, Aziz. *Le syndrome Bourguiba*. Tunis: Cérès Productions, 1993.

Kurlantzick, Joshua. "One Step Forward, Two Steps Back." *Foreign Policy*, March 4, 2013. Accessed May 12, 2013. www.foreignpolicy.com/articles/2013/03/04/one_step_forward_two_steps_back.

Laakso, Markku, and Rein Taagepera. "'Effective' Number of Parties: A Measure with Application to West Europe." *Comparative Political Studies* 12.1 (1979): 3–27.

Labidi, Kamel. "Tunisia is Backtracking on Women's Rights." *The Guardian*, August 25,

2010. Accessed March 27, 2011. www.guardian.co.uk/commentisfree/libertycentral/2010/aug/25/tunisia-backtracking-womens-rights.

Labidi, Naouar, and Erminio Sacco. "Food Security in Tunisia: Rapid Assessment Report." Rome: World Food Programme, 2011. Accessed July 17, 2011. http://home.wfp.org/stellent/groups/public/documents/ena/wfp235120.pdf.

Lachheb, Ahmed. "Investigation Committee Against Corruption Will Embarrass Tunisian Lawyers." August 14, 2011. *Tunisia Live*. Accessed October 4, 2011. www.tunisia-live.net/2011/08/14/investigation-committee-against-corruption-will-embarrass-tunisian-lawyers.

Lamloum, Olfa. "L'enjeu de l'islamisme au cœur du processus de Barcelone." *Critique internationale* 18 (2003): 129–42.

Lamloum, Olfa. "L'indéfectible soutien français à l'exclusion de l'islamisme tunisien." In *La Tunisie de Ben Ali: la société contre le régime*, edited by Olfa Lamloum and Bernard Ravenel, 103–22. Paris: L'Harmattan, 2002.

Lamloum, Olfa, and Bernard Ravenel. "La fiction pluraliste." *Confluences Méditerranée* 32 (1999–2000): 173–82.

Lamloum, Olfa, and Luiza Toscane. "Les femmes, alibi du pouvoir tunisien." *Le Monde diplomatique*, June 1998, 3.

Lamloum, Olfa and Luiza Toscane. "The Two Faces of the Tunisian Regime: Women's Rights, But Only for Some." *Le Monde diplomatique*, July 12, 1998. Accessed May 4, 2012. http://mondediplo.com/1998/07/12tunis.

Larif Béatrix, Asma. "Changement dans la symbolique du pouvoir en Tunisie." *Annuaire de l'Afrique du Nord* 28 (1989): 141–51.

Lawrence, Bruce B. *Defenders of God: The Fundamentalist Revolt against the Modern Age*. New York: Harper and Row, 1989.

Lewis, Aidan."Tracking Down the Ben Ali and Trabelsi Fortune." *BBC News Africa*, January 31, 2011. Accessed October 4, 2011. www.bbc.co.uk/news/world-africa-12302659.

Linz, Juan, and Alfred Stepan. *Problems of Democratic Transition and Consolidation: Southern Europe, South America, and Post-Communist Europe*. Baltimore, MD: The Johns Hopkins University Press, 1996.

Lipset, Seymour. "The Indispensability of Political Parties." *Journal of Democracy* 11.1 (2000): 48–55.

Lourimi, Ajmi. "Secularism is not the Role of the State." April 1, 2011. Accessed March 4, 2012. www.nahdha.info/arabe/News-file-article-sid-4570.html.

Luizard, Pierre-Jean. *Laïcités autoritaires en terre d'islam*. Paris: Fayard, 2008.

Lutterbeck, Derek. "After the Fall: Security Sector Reform in post-Ben Ali Tunisia." *Arab Reform Initiative* (September 2012): 1–29.

Lynch, Marc. *Voices of the New Arab Public. Iraq. Al-Jazeera, and Middle East Politics Today*. New York: Columbia University Press, 2006.

Lynch, Marc. "Where are the Democracy Promoters on Tunisia?" *Foreign Policy*, January 13, 2011. Accessed June 7, 2012. http://lynch.foreignpolicy.com/posts/2011/01/12/where_are_the_democracy_promoters_on_tunisia.

Lynch, Marc. "Tunisia and the New Arab Media Space." *Foreign Policy*, January 15, 2011. Accessed June 7, 2012. http://lynch.foreignpolicy.com/posts/2011/01/15/tunisia_and_the_new_arab_media_space.

Mabrouk, Mehdi. "A Revolution for Dignity and Freedom: Preliminary Observations on the Social and Cultural Background to the Tunisian Revolution." *The Journal of North African Studies* 16.4 (December 2011): 625–35.

Magharebia. "Ben Ali, Trabelsi Assets Found in 25 Countries." *Magharebia*, June 23, 2011. Accessed October 4, 2011. http://magharabia.com/en_GB/articles/awi/newsbriefs/general/2011/06/02.

Mair, Peter. "Populist Democracy *vs* Party Democracy." In *Democracies and the Populist Challenges*, edited by Yves Mény and Yves Surel, 81–98. Basingstoke: Palgrave Macmillan, 2002.

Mair, Peter. "Democracy Beyond Parties." Center for the Study of Democracy Working Paper Series 05/06. Berkeley, CA: University of California Irvine, 2005.

Marks, Monica. "Complementary Status for Tunisian Women." *Foreign Policy*, August 20, 2012. Accessed March 1, 2013. http://mideast.foreignpolicy.com/posts/2012/08/20/complementary_status_for_tunisian_women.

Marks, Monica, and Kareem Fahim. "Tunisia Moves to Contain Fallout After Opposition Figure is Assassinated." *The New York Times*, February 6, 2013. Accessed March 30, 2013. www.nytimes.com/2013/02/07/world/africa/chokri-belaid-tunisian-opposition-figure-is-killed.html?_r=0.

Martin, Florence. "Cinema and State." In *Film in the Middle East and North Africa: Creative Dissidence*, edited by Josef Gugler, 271–83. Austin, TX: University of Texas Press, 2011.

Marty, Martin E., and R. Scott Appleby, eds. *The Fundamentalism Project.* 5 vols. Chicago, IL: University of Chicago Press, 1991–5.

Marzouki, Ilhem. *Le mouvement des femmes en Tunisie au XXème siècle.* Tunis: Cérès Productions, 1993.

Marzouki, Moncef. *'Innahā al-thawratu yā Mawlaya* [It's Revolution, My Lord]. Tunis: Mediterranean Publisher, 2011.

Marzouki, Nadia. "From People to Citizens in Tunisia." *Middle East Report* 259 (Summer 2011): 16–19.

McCormick, Ty. "The Arc of Revolution: Egypt and Tunisia's Uphill Battle to Democracy." *Huffpostworld*, January 27, 2011. Accessed April 1, 2013. http://www.huffingtonpost.com/ty-mccormick/the-arc-of-revolution-egy_b_814748.html.

McElroy, Damien."Tunisia Orders Investigation into £5bn Fortune of Ben Ali." *The Telegraph*, January 19, 2011. Accessed April 26, 2011. www.telegraph.co.uk/news/worldnews/africaandindianocean/tunisia/8269734/Tunisia-orders-investigation-into-5bn-fortune-of-Ben-Ali.html.

Meijer, Roel. "Introduction." In *Global Salafism*, edited by Roel Mejer, 1–32. London: Hurst & Co., 2009.

Melki, Wiem. "Washington Institute for Near East Policy Releases Recording of Rachid Ghannouchi." *Tunisia Live*, December 22, 2011. Accessed May 3, 2012. http://www.tunisia-live.net/2011/12/22/washington-institute-for-near-east-policy-releases-recording-of-rachid-ghannouchi.

Merone, Fabio, and Francesco Cavatorta. "Salafist *Mouvance* and Sheikh-ism in the Tunisian Transition." Center for International Studies, Working Paper No. 7 (2012): 1–17. Accessed January 1, 2013. http://doras.dcu.ie/17570/1/1207.pdf

Miladi, Noureddine. "Tunisia: A Media Led Revolution?" *Al-Jazeera*, January 17, 2011. Accessed April 3, 2013. www.aljazeera.com/indepth/opinion/2011/01/2011116142317498666.html.

Mirak-Weissbach, Muriel. *Madmen at the Helm: Pathology and Politics in the Arab Spring.* Reading: Ithaca Press, 2012.

Mitchell, Jonathan. "Tunisia's Islamist Victory Good for Women, Says Female Figurehead." *The Telegraph*, November 1, 2011.

Mockli, Daniel, and Victor Mauer, eds. *European-American Relations and the Middle East.* London and New York: Routledge, 2011.

Moore, Clement Henry. "Tunisia and Bourguibisme: Twenty Years of Crisis." *Third World Quarterly* 10.1 (1988): 176–90.

Moore, Clement Henry. *Tunisia Since Independence.* Berkeley, CA: University of California Press, 1965.

Mubila, Maurice, and Mohamed-Safouane Ben Aissa. *The Middle of the Pyramid: Dynamics of the Middle Class in Africa*, Chief Economist Complex Market Brief. Tunis: African Development Bank, 2011.

Mulvey, Laura. "Moving Bodies: Interview with Moufida Tlatli." *Sight and Sound* 5.3 (1995): 18–21.

Murphy, Emma. "Women in Tunisia: A Survey of Achievements and Challenges." *The Journal of North African Studies* 1.2 (1996): 138–56.

Murphy, Emma C. *Economic and Political Change in Tunisia: From Bourguiba to Ben Ali.* London: Macmillan, 1999.

Murphy, Emma C. "The Foreign Policy of Tunisia." In *The Foreign Policies of Middle Eastern States*, edited by Raymond Hinnebusch and Anoushiravan Ehteshami, 235–56. Boulder, CO: Lynne Rienner, 2002.

Murphy, Emma. "Women in Tunisia: Between State Feminism and Economic Reform." In *Women and Globalization in the Arab Middle East*, edited by D. E. Abdella and P. Posusney, 169–93. Boulder, CO: Lynne Rienner, 2003.

Murphy, Emma."The Tunisian Mise à Niveau Programme and the Political Economy of Reform." *New Political Economy* 11.4 (2006): 519–40.

Myers, Steven Lee. "Tumult of Arab Spring Prompts Worries in Washington." *The New York Times*, September 17, 2011.

Nairn, Tom. "Nations Versus Imperial Unions in a Time of Globalization, 1707–2007." *Arena Journal 28* (2007): *33–44.*

Najar, Ridha and Fethi Houidi. *Presse, Radio et Télévision en Tunisie.* Tunis: Maison Tunisienne de l'Édition, 1983.

Nazemroaya, Mahdi Darius. "Dictatorship, Neo-liberalism and IMF's Diktats: The Tunisian People's Uprising." Accessed July 14, 2011. http://realisticbird.wordpress.com/2011/01/20/dictatorship-neo-liberalism-and-imfs-diktats-the-tunisian-peoples-uprising.

Noiriel, Gérard. "Histoire, mémoire, engagement civique." *Hommes et migrations* 1247 (2004): 17–26.

Norton, Augustus Richard, and Ashraf El-Sherif. "North Africa's Epochal Year of Freedom." *Current History* 110.736 (2011): 201–3.

Nouschi, André. *La France et le monde arabe depuis 1962: mythes et réalités d'une ambition.* Paris: Vuibert, 1994.

Nuland, Victoria. "Daily Press Briefing." February 6, 2013. Accessed May 27, 2013. http://www.state.gov/r/pa/prs/dpb/2013/02/203838.htm.

Obama, Barack. "State of the Union Address." January 25, 2011. Accessed March 24, 2012. http://www.whitehouse.gov/state-of-the-union-2011.

Office of the High Commissioner for Human Rights. "Universal Periodic Review of Tunisia." June 4, 2008. Accessed May 23, 2012. www.ohchr.org/EN/HRBodies/UPR/Pages/tnsession1.aspx.

O'Neill, Jim. "Building Better Global Economic BRICs." Global Economics Paper 66. London and New York: Goldman Sachs, 2001.

O'Neill, Nick. "How Facebook Kept The Tunisian Revolution Alive." *All Facebook*, January 24, 2011. Accessed January 4, 2012. http://allfacebook.com/how-facebook-kept-the-tunisian-revolution-alive_b30229.

Owen, Roger. *The Rise and Fall of Presidents for Life*. Cambridge, MA: Harvard University Press, 2012.

Panetta, Leon. "Remarks by Secretary of Defense Leon Panetta en Route to Tunisia." News transcript, US Department of Defense, July 29, 2012. Accessed May 2, 2013. http://www.defense.gov/transcripts/transcript.aspx?transcriptid=5090.

Paul, Jim. "States of Emergency in Tunisia and Morocco." *MERIP Reports* 127 (1984): 3–6.

Peisner, David. "Inside Tunisia's Hip-Hop Revolution." *Spin*, August 24, 2011. Accessed April 25, 2012. www.spin.com/articles/inside-tunisias-hip-hop-revolution.

Perkins, Kenneth J. *A History of Modern Tunisia*. New York: Cambridge University Press, 2004.

Perraud, Antoine. "Al Jazeera a donné le la. Les autres télés satellitaires ont suivi." *Mediapart*, January 18, 2011. Accessed May 30, 2012. www.mediapart.fr/journal/culture-idees/180111/al-jazeera-donne-le-la-les-autres-teles-satellitaires-ont-suivi.

Pickard, Duncan. "Challenges to Legitimate Governance in Post-Revolutionary Tunisia." *The Journal of North African Studies* 16.4 (December 2011): 637–52.

Pickard, Duncan. "The Current Status of Constitution Making in Tunisia." *Carnegie Endowment Commentary*, April 19, 2012. Accessed March 27, 2013. http://carnegieendowment.org/2012/04/19/current-status-of-constitution-making-in-tunisia.

Pilant, James. "Did the International Monetary Fund Push Tunisia into Revolution? YES." Pilant's Business Ethics Blog, September 10, 2010. Accessed July 20, 2011. http://pilantsbusinessethics.com/2011/01/29/did-the-international-monetary-fund-push-tunisia-into-revolution.

Piot, Olivier. *La révolution tunisienne. Dix jours qui ébranlèrent le monde arabe*. Paris: Les Petits Matins, 2011.

Poirier, Robert A., and Stephen Wright. "The Political Economy of Tourism in Tunisia." *The Journal of Modern African Studies* 31.1 (1993): 149–62.

Powel, Brieg Tomos. "The Stability Syndrome: US and EU Democracy Promotion in Tunisia." *The Journal of North African Studies* 14.1 (2009): 57–73.

Powel, Brieg, and Larbi Sadiki. *Europe and Tunisia: Democratisation Via Association*. New York: Routledge, 2010.

Prince, Rob. "The World Bank/IMF's Strange Fruit: Uprising in Tunisia: Part One." *Colorado Progressive Jewish News*, August 7, 2011. Accessed September 15, 2011. http://robertjprince.wordpress.com/2011/08/07/the-world-bankimfs-strange-fruit-civil-war-in-algeria-uprising-in-tunisia.

Przeworski, Adam. "Some Problems in the Study of the Transition to Democracy." In *Transitions from Authoritarian Rule: Comparative Perspectives*, edited by Guillermo O'Donnell, Philippe C. Schmitter, and Laurence Whitehead, 47–63. Baltimore, MD: The Johns Hopkins University Press, 1986.

Przeworski, Adam. *Democracy and Development: Political Institutions and Well-Being in the World, 1950–1990.* New York: Cambridge University Press, 2000.

Radio Monte Carlo. Interview with Constituent Assembly member Souad Abderrahim. Accessed May 12, 2013. www.youtube.com/watch?v=nxOAMHKIRAA.

Ramadan, Tariq. *L'islam et le réveil arabe.* Paris: Presses du Châtelet, 2011.

Rancière, Jacques. "The Politics of Literature." *SubStance* 33.1 (2004): 10–24.

Richter, Carola. "The Effects of Islamist Media on the Mainstream Press in Egypt." In *Arab Media. Power and Weakness*, edited by Kai Hafez, 46–65. New York: Continuum, 2008.

Ridgwell, Henry. "Fears Grow of Islamic Extremism in Tunisia." *Voice of America*, February 18, 2013. Accessed May 1, 2013. www.voanews.com/content/fears-grow-of-islamic-extremism-in-tunisia/1606060.html.

Ridgwell, Henry. "Opposition Leader's Murder Tests Tunisia's Judiciary." *Voice of America*, February 22, 2013. Accessed May 1, 2013. www.voanews.com/content/opposition-leader-murder-tests-tunisia-judiciary/1609011.html.

Ridley, Yvonne. "Tonight we are all Tunisians." *Foreign Policy Journal*, January 15, 2011. Accessed March 30, 2012. http://www.foreignpolicyjournal.com/2011/01/15/tonight-we-are-all-tunisians.

Rinnawi, Khalil, *Instant Nationalism: McArabism, Al-Jazeera, and Transnational Media in the Arab World.* Lanham, MD: University Press of America, 2006.

Rivers, Dan, and Laura Smith-Spark. "Jebali Vows to Press on with Plans for Caretaker Government in Tunisia." *CNN*, February 9, 2013. Accessed 30 March 2013. http://edition.cnn.com/2013/02/08/world/africa/tunisia-unrest.

Rivlin, Benjamin. "The Tunisian Nationalist Movement: Four Decades of Evolution." *Middle East Journal* 6.2 (1952): 168.

Roberts, Hugh. "Algeria's Ruinous Impasse and the Honourable Way Out." *International Affairs* 71.2 (1995): 247–67.

Rogin, Josh. "Washington Prepares to Ramp up Military Cooperation with Tunisia." *Foreign Policy*, July 30, 2012. Accessed March 1, 2013. http://thecable.foreignpolicy.com/posts/2012/07/30/washington_prepares_to_ramp_up_military_cooperation_with_tunisia.

Roy, Olivier. "Sur la politique arabe de la France." *Monde arabe Maghreb-Machrek* 132 (1991): 15–20.

Roy, Olivier. *The Failure of Political Islam.* Cambridge, MA: Harvard University Press, 1994.

Roy, Olivier. "Révolution post-islamiste." *Le Monde*, February 12, 2011. Accessed March 27, 2013. www.lemonde.fr/idees/article/2011/02/12/revolution-post-islamiste_1478858_3232.html.

Ruoff, Jeffrey. "The Gulf War, the Iraq War, and Nouri Bouzid's Cinema of Defeat: *It's Scheherazade We're Killing* (1993) and *Making of*." *South Central Review* 28.1 (2011): 18–35.

Sadiki, Larbi. "Bin Ali's Tunisia: Democracy by Non-Democratic Means." *British Journal of Middle Eastern Studies* 29.1 (2002): 57–78.

Sadiki, Larbi. "The Search for Citizenship in Ben Ali's Tunisia: Democracy versus Unity." *Political Studies* 50 (2002), 497–513.

Sadiki, Larbi. "Tunisia: Women's Rights and the New Constitution." *Al-Jazeera*, September 21, 2012. Accessed February 13, 2013. www.aljazeera.com/indepth/opinion/2012/09/2012918102423227362.html.

Sadri, Mahmoud, and Ahmad. Sadri, eds. *Reason, Freedom and Democracy in Islam, Essential Writings of Abdolkarim Soroush.* Oxford: Oxford University Press, 2000.

Saïdi, Raouf. "La pauvreté en Tunisie: présentation critique." In *La Tunisie de Ben Ali: la société contre le régime*, edited by Olfa Lamloum and Bernard Ravenel, 11–35. Paris: L'Harmattan, 2002.

Saleh, Heba. "Tunisia Arrests Four over Belaid's Murder." *Financial Times*, February 26, 2013. Accessed March 30, 2013. www.ft.com/cms/s/0/270106ae-8023-11e2-96ba-00144feabdc0.html - axzz2OpcJegRj.

Samti, Farah. "Tunisian Democratic Women Address Post-Revolution Access to Abortion Services." *Tunisia Live*, November 10, 2012. Accessed January 27, 2013. www.tunisia-live.net/2012/11/10/tunisian-democratic-women-address-post-revolution-access-to-abo rtion-services.

Sartori, Giovanni. *Parties and Party Systems: A Framework for Analysis.* Cambridge: Cambridge University Press, 1976.

Schattschneider, E. *Party Government.* New York: Rinehart, 1942.

Schedler, Andreas. *Electoral Authoritarianism: The Dynamics of Unfree Competition.* Boulder, CO: Lynne Rienner, 2006.

Schenker, David. "Arab Spring or Islamist Winter?" *World Affairs Journal*, January/February 2012. Accessed March 27, 2013. www.worldaffairsjournal.org/article/arab-spring-or-islamist-winter-0.

Schmitt, Eric. "US Weighs Base for Spy Drones in North Africa." *The New York Times*, January 28, 2013.

Schraeder, Peter J., and Hamadi Redissi. "Ben Ali's Fall." *Journal of Democracy* 22.3 (2011): 5–19.

Schumpeter, Joseph. *Capitalism, Socialism and Democracy.* New York: Harper and Row, 1942.

Scott, Joan Wallach. *The Politics of the Veil.* Princeton, NJ: Princeton University Press, 2007.

Sdiri, Wafa. "Portrait de Ali Larayedh, futur ministre de l'intérieur dans le gouvernement de Jebali." *Tunisie Numérique*, December 20, 2011.

Seddon, David. "Winter of Discontent: Economic Crisis in Tunisia and Morocco." *MERIP Reports* 127 (1984): 7–16.

Seib, Phillip. *The Al Jazeera Effect: How the New Global Media Are Reshaping World Politic.* Washington, DC: Potomac Books Inc., 2008.

Sfeir, Antoine. *Tunisie. Terre de Paradoxes.* Paris: L'Archipel, 2006.

Sghaier, Lamia Chaffai. "Le projet Publinet en Tunisie." Paper presented at the Séminaire Régionale de l'UIT pour États Arabes, Tunis, March 22–4, 1999.

Shakespeare, William. *Hamlet.* Edited by Susanne L. Wofford. Boston, MA: Bedford Books, 1994.

Shaw, Martin. "The Global Democratic Revolution: A New Stage." *Open Democracy*, March 7, 2011. Accessed May 12, 2011. www.opendemocracy.net/martin-shaw/global-demo cratic-revolution-new-stage.

Snoussi, Thouraya. *La télévision tunisienne dans les années 1990: Problématique entre monopole politique et les exigences de l'internationalisation.* Tunis: Public Press, 2007.

Somin, Ilya. "The Tea Party Movement and Popular Constitutionalism." *Northwestern University Law Review Colloquy* 105 (December 2011), 300–16.

Sraïeb, Noureddine. *Le mouvement littéraire et intellectuel en Tunisie.* Tunis: Alif, 1998.

Stampini, Marco, and Audrey Verdier-Chouchane. *Labour Market Dynamics in Tunisia: The*

Issue of Youth Unemployment, African Development Bank Group Working Paper No. 123. Tunis: African Development Bank, 2011.

Stapley, Kathryn. "Mizwid: An Urban Music with Rural Roots." *Journal of Ethnic and Migration Studies* 32.2 (2006): 243–65.

Storm, Lise. "An Elemental Definition of Democracy and its Advantages for Comparing Political Regime Types." *Democratization* 15.2 (2008): 215–29.

Storm, Lise. *Party Politics and Prospects for Democracy in North Africa*. Boulder, CO: Lynne Rienner, 2013.

Tamimi, Azzam. *Rachid Ghannouchi: A Democrat within Islamism*. New York: Oxford University Press, 2001.

Taylor, Charles. *A Secular Age*. Cambridge, MA: The Belknap Press, Harvard University Press, 2007.

Tchaicha, Jane D., and Khedija Arfaoui. "Tunisian Women in the Twenty-first Century: Past Achievements and Present Uncertainties in the Wake of the Jasmine Revolution." *The Journal of North African Studies* 17.2 (2012): 215–38.

Tessler, Mark. "Tunisia at the Crossroads." *Current History* 84 (May 1985): 217–23.

Tessler, Mark. "Tunisia's New Beginning." *Current History* 89 (April 1990): 169–84.

The Economist. "Ali Baba Gone, But What About the 40 Thieves?" *The Economist*, January 20, 2011. Accessed October 7, 2011. www.economist.com/node/17959620?story_id=17959620.

The Guardian. "US Embassy Cables: Tunisia – a US Foreign Policy Conundrum." *The Guardian*, December 17, 2010. Accessed March 14, 2012. www.guardian.co.uk/world/us-embassy-cables-documents/217138.

The Guardian. "US Embassy Cables: Finding a successor to Ben Ali in Tunisia," *The Guardian*, January 17, 2011. Accessed July 10, 2012. www.guardian.co.uk/world/us-embassy-cables-documents/49401.

The New York Times, "An Assassination in Tunisia." *The New York Times*, February 8, 2013. Accessed March 14, 2013. www.nytimes.com/2013/02/09/opinion/the-assassination-of-chokri-belaid-in-tunisia.html?_r=0.

The Wall Street Journal. "Turmoil in Tunisia." *The Wall Street Journal*, March 4, 2013. Accessed May 1, 2013. http://online.wsj.com/article/SB10001424127887323951904578288211023996472.html.

Thornton, Bruce. "The Arab Winter Approaches." *Defining Ideas*, November 2011. Accessed March 27, 2013. www.hoover.org/publications/defining-ideas/article/100526.

Tobia, P. J. "Tunisian Leader Comes to Washington, Preaches Moderate Political Islam." *PBS Newshour*, December 2, 2011. Accessed June 12, 2012. www.pbs.org/newshour/rundown/2011/12/tunisian-leader-comes-to-washington-preaches-moderate-political-islam.html

Toensing, Chris. "Tunisian Leaders Reflect Upon Revolt." *MERIP Report* 258 (2011): 30–2.

Topal, Semiha. "Everybody Wants Secularism—But Which One? Contesting Definitions of Secularism in Contemporary Turkey." *International Journal of Politics, Culture, and Society* 25.1–3 (2011): 1–14.

Toumi, Mohsen. *La Tunisie de Bourguiba à Ben Ali*. Paris: PUF, 1989.

Treutenaere, Michel. "La coopération culturelle, scientifique et technique entre la Tunisie et la France: évolution et perspectives." *Annuaire de l'Afrique du Nord* 20 (1982): 489–507.

Tufte, Thomas, and Florencia Enghel. *Youth Engaging with the world. Media, Communication and Social Change*. Gothenburg: The International Clearinghouse on Children, Youth and Media, Nordicom, 2009.

"Tunisia: Hillary Clinton's Unwelcome Visit." *Global Voices*, March 19, 2011. Accessed May 27, 2012. http://globalvoicesonline.org/2011/03/19/tunisia-hillary-clintons-unwelcome-visit.

"Tunisian Defense Minister Washes his Hands of the Ennahda Government" (in Arabic). www.middle-east-online.com, March 6, 2013.

"Tunisie: l'armée devrait se concentrer sur la menace islamiste, selon un ministre sortant." *Reuters*, March 6, 2013.

20 minutes.fr with *Reuters*. "Tunisie: l'armée devrait se concentrer sur la menace islamiste, selon un ministre sortant." March 6, 2013. Accessed May 4, 2013. www.20minutes.fr/ledirect/1113369/tunisie-armee-devrait-concentrer-menace-islamiste-selon-ministre-sortant.

Union Européenne. *Mission d'observation électorale: rapport final. Élections législatives Algérie 2012*. Brussels: Union Européenne, 2012.

Union Européenne. *Mission d'observation électorale en Tunisie 2011. Élection de l'Assemblée Nationale Constituante*. Tunis: Union Européenne, 2011.

Union Générale Tunisienne du Travail. "Vers un renouveau syndical: diagnostic quantitatif de l'U.G.T.T. par ses cadres." November 2006. Accessed March 21, 2012. http://library.fes.de/pdf-files/bueros/tunesien/04797.pdf.

United Nations. *Tunisia: National Report on Millennium Development Goals*. Geneva: IMF, 2004.

United Nations Department for Social and Economic Affairs, "Realizing the Millennium Development Goals through Socially Inclusive Macroeconomic Policies." Accessed June 3, 2012. www.un.org/en/development/desa/policy/capacity/output_studies/roa87_study_tun.pdf.

United Nations Development Programme/Arabic Fund for Economic and Social Development. *Arab Human Development Report 2003: Building a Knowledge Society*. New York: UNDP, 2003.

UN Working Group on Tunisian Women. "News Release, Tunisia: UN Expert Group Calls on New Government to Protect and Strengthen Achievements on Equality and Women's Human Rights." Geneva: August 21, 2012.

US Department of State. "US Support for Democratic Transitions in Egypt, Libya, Tunisia." Special Briefing by Ambassador William Taylor, Department of State, November 3, 2011. Accessed March 1, 2012. http://london.usembassy.gov/midest110.html.

US Department of State. "Patterns of Global Terrorism." April 29, 2004. Accessed March 1, 2012. www.state.gov/j/ct/rls/crt/2003/c12153.htm.

Valbjørn, Morten, and André Bank. "Examining the 'Post' in Post-democratization – The Future of Middle Eastern Political Rule through Lenses of the Past." *Middle East Critique* 19.3 (2010): 303–19.

Valluy, Jérôme. "Quelles sont les origines du ministère de l'identité nationale et de l'immigration?" *Cultures & Conflits* 69 (2008): 7–18.

Wagner, Ben. "Push-button-autocracy in Tunisia: Analysing the Role of the Internet Infrastructure, Institutions and International Markets in Creating a Tunisian Censorship Regime." *Telecommunication Policy* 36 (2012): 484–92.

Waltz, Susan. "Islamist Appeal in Tunisia." *Middle East Journal* 40 (1986): 651–70.

Waltz, Susan. "Another View of Feminine Networks: Tunisian Women and the

Development of Political Efficacy." *International Journal of Middle East Studies* 22 (1990): 21–36.

Waltz, Susan. *Human Rights and Reform: Changing the Face of North African Politics.* Berkeley, CA: University of California Press, 1995.

Whitaker, Brian. "Tunisia is Leading the Way on Women's Rights in the Middle East." *The Guardian,* September 10, 2011. Accessed March 27, 2013. http://www.guardian.co.uk/commentisfree/2011/sep/10/tunisia-un-human-rights-women.

White, Gregory. *A Comparative Political Economy Of Tunisia And Morocco: On The Outside Of Europe Looking In.* New York: State University of New York Press, 2001.

Wikileaks. "Corruption in Tunisia: What's Yours is Mine." Classified cable from Ambassador Robert F. Godec to Secretary of State Washington DC, Reference ID 08TUNIS679, EO 12958, June 23, 2008. Accessed October 27, 2011. www.wikileaks.ch/cable/2008/06/08TUNIS679.html.

Wiktorowicz, Quintan. "Anatomy of the Salafi Movement." *Studies in Conflict and Terrorism* 29 (2006): 207–39.

Wiktorowicz, Quintan. "Introduction: Islamic Activism and Social Movement Theory." In *Islamic Activism: A Social Movement Theory Approach,* edited by Quintan Wiktorowicz, 1–33. Indianapolis, IN: Indiana University Press, 2004.

Wilkinson, Bruce. "Tunisia: Security Environment to 2010." Masters thesis, Naval Postgraduate School, 1999.

Wittes, Tamara Cofman. "Learning to Live With the Islamist Winter." *Foreign Policy,* July 19, 2012. Accessed March 27, 2013. www.foreignpolicy.com/articles/2012/07/19/learning_to_live_with_the_islamist_winter?page=0,0.

Wood, Pia Christina. "French Foreign Policy and Tunisia: Do Human Rights Matter?" *Middle East Policy* 9.2 (2002): 92–110.

Wood, Pia Christina. "Chirac's 'New Arab Policy' and Middle East Challenges: The Arab-Israeli Conflict, Iraq and Iran." *Middle East Journal* 52.4 (1998): 563–80.

World Bank. "Economic Developments and Prospects: Job Creation in an Era of High Growth." Accessed October 3, 2011. http://web.worldbank.org/WBSITE/EXTERNAL/COUNTRIES/MENAEXT/0,,contentMDK:21483969~pagePK:146736~piPK:226340~theSitePK:256299,00.html.

World Bank. "Implementation Completion and Results Report IBRD 80750. On a Loan in the Amount of US$250 Million and EUR 168.3 Million to the Republic of Tunisia for a Governance and Opportunity Development Policy Loan." Washington, DC: World Bank, 2012.

World Bank. "International Bank for Reconstruction and Development Country Partnership Strategy for the Republic of Tunisia for the period FY10-13." Washington, DC: World Bank, 2009.

World Bank. "Memorandum of the President of the International Bank for Reconstruction and Development to the Executive Directors on a Country Assistance Strategy of the World Bank Group for the Republic of Tunisia." Report No. 20161-TN. Washington, DC: World Bank, 2000.

World Bank. "Memorandum of the President of the International Bank for Reconstruction and Development to the Executive Directors on a Country Assistance Strategy for the Republic of Tunisia." Report No. 28791-TUN. Washington, DC: World Bank, 2004.

World Bank. "Republic of Tunisia: Social and Structural Review 2000." Washington, DC: World Bank, 2000.

World Bank. "The Road Not Travelled: Educational Reform in the Middle East and Africa." MENA Development Report. Washington, DC: World Bank, 2008.

Wright, Claudia. "Tunisia: Next Friend to Fall?" *Foreign Policy* 46 (1982): 120–37.

Yousfi, Héla, "Les luttes sociales en Tunisie: malédiction ou opportunité révolution naire?" Nawaat, February 19, 2013. Accessed March 7, 2013. http://nawaat.org/portail/2013/02/19/les-luttes-sociales-en-tunisie-malediction-ou-opportunite-revolution naire.

Yousfi, Héla. "Ce syndicat qui incarne l'opposition tunisienne." *Le Monde Diplomatique,* 704 (2012): 17.

Zartman, I. William. "Introduction: Rewriting the Future of the Maghreb." In *Economic Crisis and Political Change in North Africa,* edited by Azzedine Layachi, 1–5. London: Praeger, 1998.

Zeghidi, Salah. "UGTT: à quand le véritable renouveau?" *Alternative Citoyennes* 1, April 20, 2001. Accessed May 12, 2012. www.alternatives-citoyennes.sgdg.org/num1/actu-syndi calisme-w.html.

Zeghidi, Salah. "L'UGTT, pôle central de la contestation sociale et politique." In *Tunisie: mouvements sociaux et modernité,* edited by Mohammed Ben Romdhane, 13–61. Dakar: CODESRIA, 1997.

Zemni, Sami, Brecht De Smet, and Koenraad Bogaert. "Luxemburg on Tahrir Square. Reading the Arab Revolutions with Rosa Luxemburg's *The Mass Strike.*" *Antipode* (2012). Accessed May 1, 2013. http://onlinelibrary.wiley.com/doi/10.1111/j.1467-8330.2012.01014.x/abstract, doi: 10.1111/j.1467-8330.2012.01014.x.

Zghal, Abdelkader. "Le retour du sacré et la nouvelle demande idéologique des jeunes scolarisés: le cas de Tunisie." *Annuaire de l'Afrique du Nord* 18 (1979): 41–64.

Zghal, Riadh. "Nouvelles orientations du syndicalisme tunisien." *Monde Arabe, Maghreb-Machrek* 162 (1998): 6–17.

Zlitni, Sami, and Zeineb Touati. "Social Networks and Women's Mobilization in Tunisia." *Journal of International Women's Studies* 3.5 (2012): 46–58.

List of Contributors

Francesco Cavatorta is Professeur Agrégé at the Department of Political Science, Université Laval, Québec. His research focuses on processes of democratization and authoritarian resilience in the Arab world, particularly North Africa. He has authored and co-authored articles for *Government and Opposition, Parliamentary Affairs, Mediterranean Politics, Journal of Modern African Studies, Journal of North African Studies, British Journal of Middle Eastern Studies, Middle East Policy*, and *Democratization*, among others. He is the author of *The International Dimension of the Failed Algerian Transition* (2009) and co-author of *Civil Society and Democratisation in the Arab World* (2010). In addition, he is the co-editor of *Civil Society in Syria and Iran* (2012).

Nouri Gana is Associate Professor of Comparative Literature & Near Eastern Languages and Cultures at the University of California, Los Angeles. He has published numerous articles and chapters on the literatures and cultures of the Arab world and its diasporas in such scholarly venues as *Comparative Literature Studies, PMLA, Public Culture*, and *Social Text.* He also contributed op-eds to such magazines and international newspapers as *The Guardian, El Pais, The Electronic Intifada, Jadaliyya*, and *CounterPunch.* He is the author of *Signifying Loss: Toward a Poetics of Narrative Mourning* (2011), and the editor of *The Edinburgh Companion to the Arab Novel in English* (Edinburgh University Press, 2013). He is currently completing a book manuscript on the cultural politics of melancholia in the Arab world and another on the history of cultural dissent in colonial and postcolonial Tunisia.

Rikke Hostrup Haugbølle is a doctoral fellow at the Department of Cross-Cultural and Regional Studies, University of Copenhagen. Her research project analyses the role of Islam and media reforms in Tunisia from 1987 to 2011. She has carried out field research in Tunisia since 1996 and lived for extended periods in Tunis, Hammamet, Douz, and Jerba. She has published peer-reviewed articles on Islam, media, and politics in Tunisia in *The Journal of North African Studies, The British Journal of Middle Eastern Studies*, and *The Middle East Report*, and has contributed chapters to a number of edited books. She is an external consultant for the Danish Ministry of Foreign Affairs, and has assisted various NGOs and research institutes with analyses of the transition process in

Tunisia. From 2004 to 2009, she was junior lecturer at the Centre for Middle East Studies, University of Southern Denmark.

Tarek Kahlaoui is Assistant Professor of history and art history at Rutgers. He received his Ph.D. from the University of Pennsylvania in 2008. His dissertation was titled "The Depiction of the Mediterranean in Islamic Cartography" (eleventh–sixteenth centuries). He teaches courses on Islamic history and civilizations, Islamic art and architecture, and contemporary visual culture in the Middle East. He comments regularly in Arabic and English on Middle Eastern politics in various news outlets (in Tunisia, the Middle East, and abroad). He was active in the student movement in Tunisia in the 1990s as well as in the cyberdissident movement before the revolution. He became a member of the political bureau of Congress for the Republic (CPR), one of the parties of the governing coalition in Tunisia. While on leave from Rutgers, Kahlaoui now serves as the General Director of the Tunisian Center for Strategic Studies, a think tank linked to the Tunisian presidency.

Amy Aisen Kallander is Assistant Professor of Middle East history and associated faculty with Women's and Gender Studies at Syracuse University. Her first book *Women, Gender, and the Palace Households in Ottoman Tunisia* is a social history of women and the family that governed Tunisia in the eighteenth and nineteenth centuries. Her writing on modern Tunisia has appeared in *Middle East Report Online* and *Arab Media & Society*.

Monica Marks is a Rhodes Scholar and doctoral student at Oxford University. She currently lives in Tunisia, where her research focuses on Islamism, youth politics, and security reform. She writes frequently about Tunisia for both academic and popular audiences. Her analytical work on Tunisia has appeared in *Mediterranean Politics*, *Foreign Policy*, and Carnegie Endowment's bilingual Arabic-English language blog, *Sada*. From December 2012 to March 2013, she was lead Tunisia researcher for the Institute for Integrated Transitions (IFIT), a Barcelona-based NGO for which she wrote a report analyzing the flows of international technical expertise to key sectors of Tunisia's transition. This report was published online in April 2013. She has also moonlighted as a freelance journalist for *The New York Times* in Tunisia.

Nadia Marzouki is a Research Fellow in the Mediterranean Program at the European University Institute, Florence, Italy. She received her Ph.D. in political science from Sciences-Po, Paris, in 2008. She was a postdoctoral fellow at the Council on Middle Eastern Studies, Yale University (2008–10), and a visiting scholar at the University of California at Berkeley (2004–5) and at Princeton University (2005–6). Her work examines public controversies about Islam in

Europe and the United States, and about Evangelical Christianity and religious freedom in North Africa. She is the author of *L'Islam, une religion américaine?* (2013) and co-editor (with Olivier Roy) of *Religious Conversions in the Mediterranean World* (2013).

Fabio Merone is research assistant on the project titled "From over-estimation to under-estimation: the trajectory of Political Islam in five MENA countries," Gerda Henkel Foundation. He is based in Tunis and his research focuses on Islamist parties and movements. He has authored and co-authored articles for *Middle East Policy*, *Democratization* and *Middle East Law and Governance*, among others. He also authored a volume in Italian on the Tunisian revolution.

Emma C. Murphy is professor of political economy at the School of Government and International Affairs, Durham University, UK. She is also a Fellow of the Royal Society of Arts and Humanities and an Academician of the Academy of Social Sciences. She has published widely on the Arab-Israeli conflict, political and economic transitions in the Arab world, the evolving role of new information and communications technologies in the Middle East, and the relationship between political economy and culture. Her research interest in Tunisia began in the early 1990s and she has written on a range of Tunisian issues including women's status, foreign policy, political reform processes, and industrial upgrading programs. Her best-known work on the country is *Economic and Political Change in Tunisia: From Bourguiba to Ben Ali* (1999). She was an international election observer in the October 2011 elections and is now researching the implications of Islamist transition for Tunisian women's rights.

Kenneth Perkins earned his M.A. and Ph.D. in Near Eastern Studies from Princeton University and is Emeritus Professor of History at the University of South Carolina, having served on its faculty from 1974 until his retirement in 2008. He is the author of *Qaids, Captains, and Colons: French Military Administration in the Colonial Maghrib, 1844–1934* (1981); *Port Sudan: The Evolution of a Colonial City* (1993); *The Maghrib in Question*, coeditor (1997); and *A History of Modern Tunisia* (2004); second edition in 2013. His scholarly articles include "The Transformation of Bizerte, 1881–1913: The Razing of a Traditional Tunisian Community and the Raising of a Modern French Naval Base," in *Revue d'Histoire Maghrébine*. He contributed a chapter on modern North Africa to the *New Cambridge History of Islam* (2010) and another specifically on Tunisia to Cambridge University Press's forthcoming *History of the Maghrib*.

Lotfi Ben Rejeb has taught American history and literature at the University of Tunis. He is currently an associate professor of US history at the University of Ottawa. He is working on a book on American nationalism. Among his latest articles are "'The General Belief of the World': Barbary as Genre and Discourse in Mediterranean History," in *European Review of History / Revue Européenne d'Histoire* and "Controverse sur la nomination d'un consul américain à Tunis en 1815," in *Revue d'Histoire Maghrébine.*

Lise Storm holds a Ph.D. in Middle East Politics from the Institute of Arab and Islamic Studies at the University of Exeter, where she is currently employed as a senior lecturer in Middle East Politics. Her work focuses on parties, party system institutionalization, and democratization in the Middle East and North Africa, particularly in the Maghreb. She is the author of *Democratization in Morocco* (2007) and *Party Politics and the Prospects for Democracy in North Africa* (2013). She has also authored several articles published in journals such as *Democratization, Electoral Studies, Mediterranean Politics, International Affairs,* and *Middle East Policy.*

Sami Zemni is Professor of Political and Social Sciences at Ghent University, Belgium, where he heads the Middle East and North Africa Research Group. He currently holds the Francqui Research Chair to carry out research on the Arab revolutions in general and the Tunisian revolution in particular. His area of expertise is politics within the Middle East and North Africa with a special focus on political Islam in Tunisia, Morocco, and Egypt. He has also written on issues of migration, integration, racism, and Islamophobia. His latest publications include *The Dynamics of Sunni-Shia Relationships Doctrine, Transnationalism, Intellectuals and the Media,* co-edited with Brigitte Maréchal (2013); "Moroccan Post-Islamism: Emerging Trend or Chimera?," in *Post-Islamism,* edited by Asef Bayat (2013) and "Urban Renewal and Social Development in Morocco in an Age of Neoliberal Government," in *Review of African Political Economy.*

Index